Covenant and Salvation

Also by Michael S. Horton

Covenant and Eschatology: The Divine Drama
Lord and Servant: A Covenant Christology

Covenant and Salvation:
Union with Christ

Michael S. Horton

Westminster John Knox Press
LOUISVILLE • LONDON

© 2007 Michael S. Horton

Scripture quotations from the New Revised Standard Version of the Bible are copyright © 1989 by the Division of Christian Education of the National Council of the Churches of Christ in the U.S.A. and are used by permission.

Scripture quotations marked RSV are from the Revised Standard Version of the Bible and are copyright © 1946, 1952, 1971, and 1973 by the Division of Christian Education of the National Council of the Churches of Christ in the U.S.A. and are used by permission.

Scripture quotations marked NIV are from *The Holy Bible, New International Version.* Copyright © 1973, 1978, 1984 International Bible Society. Used by permission of Zondervan Bible Publishers.

Scripture quotations marked NKJV are from the New King James Version. Copyright © 1979, 1980, 1982, Thomas Nelson Inc., Publishers. Used by permission.

Book design by Sharon Adams
Cover design by Eric Walljasper/Teri Vinson

First edition
Published by Westminster John Knox Press
Louisville, Kentucky

This book is printed on acid-free paper that meets the American National Standards Institute Z39.48 standard. ∞

PRINTED IN THE UNITED STATES OF AMERICA

07 08 09 10 11 12 13 14 15 16 — 10 9 8 7 6 5 4 3 2 1

Library of Congress Cataloging-in-Publication Data

Horton, Michael Scott.
    Covenant and salvation : union with Christ / Michael S. Horton.
       p. cm.
    Includes index.
    ISBN 978-0-664-23163-7 (alk. paper)
    1. Salvation—Christianity.   2. Covenant theology.   3. Mystical union.   I. Title.
    BT751.3.H67   2007
    234—dc22   2007003369

*To my brother Larry, who introduced me to Paul's Letter to the Romans,
and my partners at the White Horse Inn, who continually remind
me how urgently we need to read it again.*

Contents

Acknowledgments

I owe a debt of gratitude to many people in writing this volume, but especially the following. First to my teaching assistant, Brannan Ellis, and to colleagues at Westminster Seminary, California (R. S. Clark, David VanDrunen, and Kim Riddlebarger), and elsewhere (J. Todd Billings and Alan Spence) who gave invaluable input on the draft. Second, to WJK, especially Don McKim and Dan Braden. Most important, of course, has been the encouragement, analysis, and indulgences of my wife, Lisa.

Abbreviations

CD   Karl Barth. *Church Dogmatics*. Edited by G. W. Bromiley and
            T. F. Torrance. Translated by G. T. Thomson. 5 vols. in 14.
            Edinburgh: T&T Clark, 1936–77.
CO   John Calvin. *Calvini opera*. 59 vols. In CR, vols. 29–87.
            Brunsvigae (Braunschweig): Schwetschke, 1863–1900.
CR   Corpus reformatorum. Edited by C. G. Bretschneider, H. E. Bind-
            seil, et al. 101 vols. Halis Saxonum (Hall): Schwetschke; et al.,
            1834–1963. Reprinted, New York: Johnson, 1964.
Institutes John Calvin. *Institutes of the Christian Religion*. Edited by
            J. T. McNeill. Translated by F. L. Battles. 2 vols. Philadelphia:
            Westminster, 1960.
KD   Karl Barth. *Kirchliche Dogmatik*. 5 vols. in 14. Zollikon, Zurich:
            Evangelischer Verlag, 1932–70.
KJV   King James Version. 1611.
LW   Martin Luther. *Luther's Works*. Edited by J. Pelikan and
            H. T. Lehmann. 55 vols. St. Louis: Concordia; Philadelphia:
            Fortress, 1955–86.
LXX   Septuagint version of the Old Testament in Greek
NASB   *New American Standard Bible*. 1960, 1995.
NJKV   *New King James Version*. 1982.
NRSV   New Revised Standard Version. 1989.
NPP   New Perspective(s) on Paul
PG   Patrologia graeca [= Patrologiae cursus completus: Series graeca].
            Edited by J.-P. Migne. 162 vols. Paris: J.-P. Migne, 1857–66.
RO   Radical Orthodoxy
RSV   Revised Standard Version. 1946, 1952.
Sent.   Peter Lombard. *Libri quatuor sententiarum* (*Four Books of
            Sentences*). *Ca. 1150.* http://www.franciscan-archive.org/
            lombardus/index.html.
ST   Thomas Aquinas. *Summa theologiae*. 1265–74. Blackfriars edition.
            New York: McGraw Hill, 1964. www.newadvent.org/summa/.
WA   Weimarer Ausgabe. The definitive German edition of *Luthers
            Werke*. 127 vols. Weimar: Hermann Böhlau, 1883–.

Chapter One

Covenant and Salvation

As the third "act" of a four-part drama, *Covenant and Salvation* takes up the cluster of topics usually treated in dogmatics under the heading of soteriology. Like the first two volumes in this series, this work is not a systematic theology per se, but an exploration of the traditional loci or topics in the light of the covenantal motif. Among other results, this yields (so I have argued) an unfolding eschatological and historical drama. Since the first volume, *Covenant and Eschatology*, I have pointed to the promise of covenant theology for integrating themes that are often set in opposition. In no other section of dogmatics is that more apparent perhaps than in soteriology: the doctrine of salvation.

Much of this book is concerned with the doctrine of justification and relating it to other themes comprehended under the general topic of union with Christ. Regarded by confessional Protestantism as, in the words of Reformed scholastic J. H. Alsted, "the article of a standing or falling church,"[1] justification as a forensic declaration based on the imputation of Christ's righteousness is often either marginalized by or rejected in favor of other motifs. These other motifs

---

1. J. H. Alsted, *Theologia scholastica didactica* (Hanover, 1618), 211, cited in A. E. McGrath, *Iustitia Dei* (Cambridge: Cambridge University Press, 1986), 2:193n3.

include ontological participation and mystical union, various forms of transfor-mationalism (whether more individualistic or cultural), and a growing tendency to subsume soteriology under ecclesiology. I hope to demonstrate that the clas-sic Reformation formulation is not only still exegetically and theologically ten-able, but that a covenantal interpretation also enables us to see the forensic and the effective, the legal and the relational, the individual and the corporate dimen-sions of justification and union.

Part 1, therefore, offers the most direct and sustained treatment of the partic-ular type of covenant theology that I have drawn upon or assumed throughout this series. With recent debates over Pauline theology especially in view, I argue that despite the revived interest in the covenantal motif, the tendency to subsume quite different trajectories and nuances under a single type of covenant has led to a reductionistic understanding of Paul's doctrine of justification. Distinguishing covenants of law (suzerainty treaties) and covenants of promise (royal grants), this section offers a covenantal account of justification that engages recent biblical scholarship. From there, I relate justification to participation or union with Christ in part 2. Interacting with alternative schemes (especially Radical Orthodoxy) along the way, these chapters highlight the promise that covenantal thinking offers for our interpretation of familiar (and perhaps not so familiar) doctrines.

WHY A *COVENANTAL* ACCOUNT
OF JUSTIFICATION AND UNION?

Do we really need a "covenantal" view of union with Christ and its related doc-trines of election, justification, adoption, regeneration, sanctification, and glori-fication? N. T. Wright introduces his programmatic *The Climax of the Covenant: Christ and the Law in Pauline Theology* by explaining, "The overall title reflects my growing conviction that covenant theology is one of the main clues, usually neglected, for understanding Paul."[2] I agree, and let me suggest a few reasons why this focus is so important.

First, this covenantal matrix focuses our attention more on concrete questions of God's action and human response in history than on abstract speculations. There is, of course, a lot of talk these days about narrative theology, but the his-tory of God's covenantal purposes gives greater specificity to the biblical plot. Furthermore, it is not only a story but also a drama, with a script (canon), a God who is not only the playwright (Father), the plot (Son), and director (Spirit) but has the headlining part as well.[3]

2. N. T. Wright, *The Climax of the Covenant: Christ and the Law in Pauline Theology* (Edinburgh: T&T Clark, 1991), xi, 1.
3. Working on parallel lines in this respect is Kevin J. Vanhoozer's *The Drama of Doctrine: A Canonical Approach* (Louisville, KY: Westminster John Knox, 2006). Although we began our projects independently, we were surprised to learn how much overlap there was in the nature of our propos-als. This may be due in part to our shared Westminster training, especially its biblical-theological emphasis, but as these volumes have progressed, I have increasingly drawn on Vanhoozer's applica-tions of this model to topics such as effectual calling, as readers will notice in chap. 11.

At the same time, in the very nature of a covenant, this drama also includes human performers and even casts the nonhuman creation in supporting roles. (It is intriguing how often rocks, trees, rainbows, and wild animals, for example, are recruited for this drama.) "If one wishes to read the entire Torah as a covenant text," Jon Levenson suggests, "history begins at the beginning, the creation of the world and the story of primordial humanity (Genesis 1–11)."[4] Israel's "identity is not cosmic and primordial, but historical in a sense not so distant from that in which modern people use that term. . . . Covenant discloses the meaning of history."[5] Yet because it is drama of the Trinity, covenant not only discloses the meaning of history but also is the site of vertical irruptions (i.e., eschatology), which alter the course of history itself. Already, then, we recognize that a covenantal approach discourages metaphysical speculation. Covenantal history is not an allegory for more ostensibly basic eternal truths, but is itself constitutive of reality. Covenant is not something added to a metaphysics and ontology derived from some other source, but generates a worldview of its own. Covenant is not simply a theme, but an ontological paradigm in its own right. I will be defining and defending that claim in this volume.

Second, it is valuable to expose the covenantal architecture again at this point in order to highlight the unity of elements that are often otherwise left free-floating, in search of a central dogma to synthesize them, or are set in antithesis. The first volume staked the claim and the second tested it in relation to the doctrine of God, creation, and Christology. In this volume, I will argue that the categories of classic covenant theology unite individual and corporate, personal and cosmic, historical and eschatological, organic and federal, effective and forensic aspects of our union with Christ without confusing them or relativizing them by trying to find a higher synthesis. The word "salvation" is frequently given to reductionism. For some, it means cosmic victory; for others, new awareness or empowerment—a new way of being-in the world. Others understand salvation as "a personal relationship with Jesus," with an experience of being born again as the decisive focus, while there appears to be a growing reaction against this emphasis in the direction of salvation as ecclesial incorporation and transformation of social structures. A covenantal soteriology, I will argue, can help us overcome some of the false alternatives on offer.

To generalize, the New Perspective(s) on Paul (NPP) in its current phase at least began with the attempt to rescue Judaism from Paul and increasingly moved in the direction of trying to rescue Paul from Luther. As we will see, the New Finnish interpretation tries to rescue Luther from Lutheranism just as some Reformed theologians have sought to distance Calvin from Calvinism.[6] The

---

4. Ibid., 40.
5. Ibid., 41.
6. See, for example, T. F. Torrance's influential paradigm of "onto-relational participation," which he thinks subverts scholastic accounts of Christ's person and work, whether medieval, Reformation, post-Reformation, or modern: *The Mediation of Christ* (Exeter: Paternoster, 1983), 57–58. James B. Torrance has led the way in contrasting Calvin and the Calvinists along similar lines. See, for example,

"Calvin against the Calvinists" thesis seems to have run its course and is in the process of succumbing to its demise at least among specialists,[7] and I will interact directly with the New Finnish school in chapter 8. In my view, however, the caricatures of confessional Protestantism persist outside their field of historical specialization because of their polemical value in relation to the Reformation tradition and their ecumenical value in relation to other traditions. Whether in trying to salvage Jesus from Paul, Paul from the Reformers, or the Reformers from their "scholastic" heirs, the primary motive for each of these moves seems to be a reaction against a forensic/judicial ontology that is ostensibly opposed to a relational one.

Radical Orthodoxy (RO) enters the lists against "forensicism" and "extrinsicism," which it believes is the product of a decadent late medieval scholasticism. To be sure, these movements are quite different. RO is, for the most part, a philosophical theology advancing the interests of a particular metaphysics of participation (theurgic Neoplatonism), while the NPP obviously oriented to the field of biblical studies, and the New Finnish Perspective is more of a work of ecumenical and historical theology. Yet these "schools" share a set of common assumptions and aims, at least when it comes to the central topics of justification and union. In their view, confessional Protestantism (1) misunderstands Paul and/or the Reformers; (2) reduces the cosmic, eschatological, metaphysical, ontological, and ecclesiological dimensions of redemption to the forensic justification of individuals through the imputation of an external righteousness; (3) makes justification rather than union with/participation in Christ the center of the gospel, again reducing justification itself to a legal rather than eschatological concept; and consequently (4) too sharply distinguishes faith and works, law and gospel, and the work of Christ for us (*extra nos*) from the person of Christ in us (*in nobis*).

While each of these schools has developed independently of each other, there is evidence of growing appreciation between various representatives. In a charac-

---

"The Concept of Federal Theology," in *Calvinus Sacrae Scripturae Professor*, ed. William H. Neuser (Grand Rapids: Eerdmans, 1994); idem, "Covenant or Contract," *Scottish Journal of Theology* 23/1 (February 1970): esp. 53; cf. Basil Hall, "Calvin against the Calvinists," in *John Calvin*, ed. G. E. Duffield, Courtenay Studies in Reformation Theology (Appleford: Sutton Gourtenay, 1966); Holmes Rolston III, "Responsible Man in Reformed Theology: Calvin vs. The Westminster Confession," *Scottish Journal of Theology* 23/2 (May 1970): esp. 129; R. T. Kendall, *Calvin and English Calvinism* (Oxford: Oxford University Press, 1979); B. A. Armstrong, *Calvinism and the Amyraut Heresy: Protestant Scholasticism and Humanism in Seventeenth-Century France* (Madison: University of Wisconsin Press, 1969); Charles Bell, *Calvin and Scottish Theology: The Doctrine of Assurance* (Edinburgh: Handsel, 1985).

7. Rooted in the methodological approach of Heiko Oberman, David Steinmetz, and others, Richard Muller is joined by a growing number of historical theologians who have decisively refuted the Torrance school on the relation between Calvin and Calvinism. See, for example, Richard Muller, *After Calvin* (New York: Oxford University Press, 2004), which summarizes a lot of his research on this relationship; cf. Carl Trueman and R. S. Clark, eds., *Protestant Scholasticism: Essays in Reassessment* (Carlisle: Paternoster, 1998); Paul Helm, *Calvin and the Calvinists* (Edinburgh: Banner of Truth Trust, 1982); W. J. Van Asselt and E. Dekker, eds., *Reformation and Scholasticism: An Ecumenical Enterprise* (Grand Rapids: Baker Academic); J. Beeke, *Assurance of Faith: Calvin, English Puritanism and the Dutch Second Reformation* (New York: Peter Lang, 1991); L. D. Bierma, "Federal Theology in the Sixteenth Century: Two Traditions?" in the *Westminster Theological Journal* 45 (1983): 304–21; "The Role of Covenant Theology in Early Reformed Orthodoxy," *The Sixteenth Century Journal* 21 (1990): 453–62.

teristic flourish, John Milbank says that forensic justification is "a reading of Paul that E. P. Sanders has forever destroyed."[8] From different angles, these schools converge to present a formidable challenge to Reformation theology. However, I am convinced that a reevaluation of covenant theology in the light of such impressive scholarship has tremendous potential to provoke constructive rather than reactionary proposals.

REINTEGRATING THE RHETORIC OF REDEMPTION

Another goal of this book is to demonstrate my claim in *Covenant and Eschatology* that this approach offers rich resources for reintegrating biblical studies and dogmatics as well as ethics. Many biblical scholars, reared in evangelical traditions suspicious of creeds and confessions, seem largely unaware of or interested in "church theology," as Francis Watson has pointed out.[9] N. T. Wright himself offers a similar identification of this phenomenon, even though one may discern some of these tendencies in his own work.[10] Paul is a biblical theologian, not a systematic one, Wright declares against those who might suggest that he could be cited for such things as confessions of faith and catechisms.[11] Such efforts to systematize fail to appreciate Paul's richly eschatological horizon, Wright assumes, even though his own aim is to show the systematic coherence of Paul's theology.

Modern systematic theology has encouraged the impression that exegesis is secondary to controlling ideas: "The Theology of—" (fill in the blank). However, modern biblical scholarship has frequently shown itself equally capable of offering a central dogma from which all exegesis is deduced. In the NPP, this thesis can be covenantal nomism, Israel's exile and restoration, or Gentile inclusion. So the question is not systematic theology versus mere exegesis, but a matter of evaluating different accounts of the coherent patterns that we find in Scripture.

Nearly a century ago, Geerhardus Vos helpfully pointed out, "Biblical theology draws a line of development. Systematic theology draws a circle."[12] Each is different and yet both are essential for the health, vitality, and soundness of the

8. John Milbank, *Being Reconciled: Ontology and Pardon* (London and New York: Routledge, 2003), 103. At the same time, Milbank concludes, "But Sanders fails to disprove Paul's antinomian bent (in a certain sense)," and faults Sanders for failing to affirm that participation in Christ "substitutes for the old covenant" and therefore involves "belonging to a new group," viz., the church (223n5).
9. For a similar analysis, see Francis Watson, *Text and Truth: Redefining Biblical Theology* (Grand Rapids: Eerdmans; Edinburgh: T&T Clark, 1997), 111.
10. N. T. Wright, *Climax of the Covenant*, 21: "The dislocation of biblical studies from theology, particularly in many North American institutions (where the majority of contemporary biblical studies takes place) has meant that Paul is often studied by people who are not trained either philosophically or theologically, and who indeed resent the idea that such training should be necessary. Many New Testament scholars use detailed exegesis as a way of escaping from heavy-handed and stultifying conservatism; any attempt to articulate an overarching Pauline theology looks to them like an attempt to reconstruct the sort of system from which they themselves are glad to be free."
11. Ibid., 263–64.
12. Geerhardus Vos, *Biblical Theology: Old and New Testaments* (Grand Rapids: Eerdmans, 159), 16.

church. In *Covenant and Eschatology*, I drew the analogy of a relief map and a street map.[13] Not only theory but also daily life would be greatly impoverished if we were forced to choose between a topographical survey of peaks and valleys or logical intersections. "The Bible is not a dogmatic handbook but a historical book full of dramatic interest," Vos reminds us. And yet, biblical theology "can counteract the anti-doctrinal tendency of the present time" by showing the inherently theological interest and coherence of Scripture.[14] In fact, Richard Gaffin Jr. adds, it is the covenantal motif that helps to organize Scripture into a plot that can be summarized in both biblical-theological and systematic-theological ways. "The Bible is, as it were, conscious of its own organism; it feels, what we cannot always say of ourselves, its own anatomy. The principle of successive *Berith* [covenant]-makings, as marking the introduction of new periods, plays a large role in this, and should be carefully heeded."[15] Paul himself can define the gospel in terms of the history of salvation, as in Romans 1:1–6, and in terms of the logical chain of individual participation in that history, as in 8:29–30. We do not find here any basis for a choice between the historical drama of redemption and the logical order of individual election, calling, justification, and glorification.

As I have argued since the first volume, subtitled *The Divine Drama,* covenant theology inherently generates a redemptive-historical hermeneutic charged with dynamism and dramatic interest. Although more focal in the fourth volume, the integration of ecclesiology and soteriology, the history of redemption (*historia salutis*) with the application of redemption in the life of believers (*ordo salutis*), will be elaborated to some degree here as well. If this were a traditional systematic theology, I would seek to integrate soteriology and ecclesiology in one volume. Since the final volume is devoted to ecclesiology, however, I will hope that these two works will be read together. I agree with those who think that reducing Paul's teaching to "the theology of justification"—or for that matter, "the theology of covenant"—distorts his message. Biblical scholarship no less than systematic theology can engage in central dogma deductivism. Rather, I have argued, Scripture is an unfolding divine drama, and even the covenantal motif is just that: a motif that provides the context or setting for the plot, although it is not itself the center. This pride of place is reserved for Christ. Nevertheless, his identity in the drama is constituted by the covenant of which he is the mediator.

It can hardly be denied that salvation has sometimes been reduced to the question of individual salvation, as if justification were a "timeless truth" of a transaction between Jesus and the believer that had little connection to history, eschatology, participation, and the church. In this context, the NPP, RO, and

13. Michael Horton, *Covenant and Eschatology* (Louisville, KY: Westminster John Knox, 2002), 241.
14. Geerhardus Vos, *Redemptive History and Biblical Interpretation: The Shorter Writings of Geerhardus Vos,* ed. Richard Gaffin Jr. (Phillipsburg, NJ: P&R Publishing, 1980), 62.
15. Richard Gaffin Jr., *Resurrection and Redemption: A Study in Paul's Soteriology* (Phillipsburg, NJ: P&R Publishing, 1978), 26.

similar voices offer both a bracing emancipation and attractive alternative. One can hardly deny the truth in E. P. Sanders's caution:

> As long as one studies Paul under the loci of systematic theology, relegating eschatology to the last place in one's discussion, understanding of Paul is hindered if not completely obscured. Further, as long as one takes the central theme in Paul's gospel to be "righteousness by faith alone," one misses the significance of the realism with which Paul thought of incorporation in the body of Christ, and consequently the heart of his theology.[16]

Yet it was precisely from classic covenant or "federal" theology that many Christians recognized the redemptive-historical and eschatological character of revelation long before the advent of the New Perspective.

Barth, Pannenberg, and Moltmann have all pointed to the Reformed scholastics in their attention to the eschatological shape of theology.[17] These theologians also note the emphasis of this tradition on the history of redemption due to the unfolding of successive covenants. In fact, Barth's criticism of this covenant theology of the Reformed scholastics was not that it reduced the *historia salutis* to "timeless truths," as Wright suggests, but the very opposite; namely, that it represented "a theological historicism." "Can we historicize the activity and revelation of God? The Federal theologians were the first really to try to do this in principle."[18] For these older theologians, as for Paul, the question is not whether to place justification in its covenantal, eschatological, and historical context. The real difference between classic covenant theology and its newer rivals is the actual content, not the field of horizon.

While there is no "central dogma" in the Reformation, the Reformers certainly were systematic.[19] Yet, as Bruce McCormack suggests, we must work the leaven of their doctrine of justification into the ontology that constantly threatens it.

> The current crisis has many sources, many of them less than theological (having to do with the ongoing impact upon the churches of our increasingly secularized culture). So even if the Protestant doctrine of justification were suddenly to be believed, taught and confessed on a churchwide basis, there is no guarantee that such a turn of events would save Protestantism. But this much seems clear: the absence of clarity about this doctrine and the inability of its would-be defenders to offer an adequate response to the challenges which are currently being brought against it are contributing mightily to the

16. E. P. Sanders, *Paul and Palestinian Judaism* (Philadelphia: Fortress, 1977), 434.

17. Jürgen Moltmann, *Theology of Hope*, trans. James W. Leitch (Minneapolis: Fortress, 1993), 69–70; Wolfhart Pannenberg, *Systematic Theology* (Grand Rapids: Eerdmans, 1998), 3:530. Karl Barth noted the importance of this federal theology in shaping even certain forms of Lutheran theology in "the earlier form of the 'redemption-history' school of Erlangen," especially with its attempt "to understand the work and Word of God attested in Holy Scripture dynamically and not statically, as an event and not as a system of objective and self-contained truths" (*Church Dogmatics*, trans. G. W. Bromiley [Edinburgh: T&T Clark, 1956], 4/1:57–66).

18. Karl Barth, *Church Dogmatics*, trans. G. W. Bromiley (Edinburgh: T&T Clark, 1956), 4/1:57–66.

19. Ibid., 81.

theological confusion which reigns in the churches of the Reformation and, in all likelihood, hastening the demise of Protestantism in the West.[20]

We need to go beyond the Reformation, but *through* it, "not doing an end-run around it—as do those who today give every sign of wanting a Protestantism without the Reformation." I will offer McCormack's conclusion as my own: "My hope in the meantime is that the Reformation will not be brought to a premature conclusion by those whose power to affect the outcome is equaled only by their ignorance of the unexploited potential of their own tradition."[21]

20. Ibid., 83.
21. Ibid., 117.

PART ONE
COVENANT
AND JUSTIFICATION

Chapter Two

Sinai and Zion

A Tale of Two Covenants

If covenant theology provides the matrix for integrating biblical and systematic theology, then surely its relevance can be no more obvious than in consideration of election and justification. Much of modern dogmatics and biblical studies has been defined in contrast with Judaism and the Old Testament background. To the extent that this has changed in the postwar decades, the covenantal frame of reference has gained greater appreciation.

At the same time, simply to endorse the importance of this theme or to advocate covenant theology does not necessarily specify its content. When N. T. Wright, for example, champions "covenant theology," he sharply distinguishes his account from sixteenth- and seventeenth-century versions.[1] Nevertheless, elsewhere Wright concedes, "Like many New Testament scholars, I am largely ignorant of the Pauline exegesis of all but a few of the fathers and reformers. The Middle Ages, and the seventeenth and eighteenth centuries, had plenty to say about Paul, but I have not read it."[2] Classic covenant theology has therefore been,

---

1. N. T. Wright, *What Saint Paul Really Said: Was Paul of Tarsus the Real Founder of Christianity?* (Grand Rapids: Eerdmans, 1997), 117.
2. N. T. Wright, *Paul: In Fresh Perspective* (Minneapolis: Fortress, 2006), 13. With this volume, Wright distances himself in a more general way from the New Perspective. He suggests that even the

in my view, too lightly dismissed without serious firsthand evaluation. My primary goal in part 1 is not to exonerate the tradition, but to interact with the NPP from within it. The burden of this chapter is to demonstrate that the basic lines of thought that underwrite the distinction between law and gospel and the specific types of covenants advocated in confessional Reformed theology can be sustained on exegetical grounds.

Central to my thesis over the next several chapters is that while many contemporary Protestants treat "covenant" more or less univocally, Reformed theology properly recognizes the crucial differences between different types of covenants that we find in Scripture—specifically, law-covenants (suzerainty treaties) and promise-covenants (royal grants). I have traced the broad outline of these distinct covenant types in *Lord and Servant*, as elsewhere.[3] Yet since it lies at the heart of the particular type of covenant theology I am advocating throughout this project, further development of this distinction is required. This chapter will therefore provide the big picture, filling in the details in the following chapters.

A TALE OF TWO COVENANTS

Research over the last fifty years has highlighted with increasing clarity the distinction between two types of covenants in the biblical traditions. While there is still considerable debate over the precise relation of these covenants to each other, there is surprising consensus with respect to their distinct existence and the defining content of each. Ironically, just at the moment when so much Protestant biblical scholarship is challenging a sharp distinction between covenants of law and covenants of promise, Ancient Near Eastern scholars from Jewish and Roman Catholic traditions have demonstrated the accuracy of that seminal distinction.[4]

As Moshe Weinfeld pointed out in his important 1970 essay, Israel's history is determined by a covenantal tradition in the form of "royal grant" on one hand and the "suzerainty treaty" on the other, both well-attested in Ancient Near Eastern diplomacy.[5] The suzerainty treaty (or covenantal formulary) is akin to a contract between a greater and lesser ruler, or suzerain and vassal. Included in such ancient

---

NPP has been too interested in a theology of salvation rather than in the ostensibly Pauline interest in transforming society under the lordship of Christ.

3. Michael Horton, *Lord and Servant: A Covenant Christology* (Louisville, KY: Westminster John Knox, 2005); idem, *God of Promise: Introducing Covenant Theology* (Grand Rapids: Baker, 2006), esp. 23–110.

4. The account that I offer here, drawing on contemporary (non-Reformed) scholarship, is in its main thrust (i.e., the distinction between covenants of law and promise, as well as different "administrations" of the covenant of grace) already delineated at length in Francis Turretin's *Institutes of Elenctic Theology*, ed. J. T. Dennison Jr., trans. G. M. Giger, vol. 2 (Phillipsburg, NJ: P&R Publishing, 1994), Twelfth Topic, esp. QQ. 4, 6, 7.

5. Moshe Weinfeld, "The Covenant of Grant in the Old Testament and the Ancient Near East," *Journal of the American Oriental Society* 90 (1970): 185–86; cf. Suzanne Boorer, *The Promise of the Land as an Oath* (Berlin: W. de Gruyter, 1992), for a more recent and extended treatment.

Hittite formularies were the following features: (1) preamble (identifying the suzerain who imposes the treaty), (2) a historical prologue (justifying the suzerain's claims over the vassal's realm), (3) stipulations (commands), and (4) sanctions (curses for violation, blessings for obedience). Such treaties typically involved public ceremonies in which the new relationship was ratified and the treaty tablets were then deposited in the religious shrines of both parties, over which their respective deities witnessed in judgment.

However, the royal grant was a gift bestowed by the suzerain upon a vassal, usually in view of past performance on the suzerain's behalf—not unlike the peerages bestowed by monarchs in more recent times. Royal grants were "an outright gift by a king to a subject."[6]

Covenant of Law

The influences of these two forms of international diplomacy are easily discerned in both the form and content of the biblical covenants. Those who left Egypt were, according to Numbers 11:4, a "mixed multitude" (cf. Exod. 12:38 KJV), bound not by blood but by corporate election and covenant. G. E. Mendenhall notes that in response to God's deliverance, the "Israelites" "obligate themselves to obey the stipulations of the Decalogue." "Precise parallels to the statement are to be found in the Amarna letters," he adds.[7] The solemn ceremony putting the covenant into effect is twofold: "One ceremony is the sprinkling of blood upon altar and people, another is the banquet in the presence of Yahweh." Furthermore, "the tradition of the deposit of the law in the Ark of the Covenant is certainly connected with the covenant customs of pre-Mosaic times."[8] Given the equation of gossip or untrusting speech or conduct with breach of the covenant stipulations in the Hittite treaty, "the traditions of the 'murmurings' in the wilderness is also a motif which receives new meaning in the light of the covenant."[9]

The covenant at Sinai certainly bears the marks of a suzerainty treaty. In fact, the exact form is followed in Exodus 19 and 20 as well as in Deuteronomy 5: Yahweh identifies himself as the suzerain (preamble), with a brief historical prologue citing his deliverance of the people from Egypt, followed by the Ten Commandments (stipulations), with clear warnings (sanctions) about violating the treaty to which they have sworn their allegiance. The covenant of Joshua 24 follows this pattern as well.

---

6. Delbert R. Hillers, *Covenant: The History of a Biblical Idea* (Baltimore: Johns Hopkins University Press, 1969), 105. "A typical brief example runs as follows: 'From this day forward Niqmaddu son of Ammistamru king of Ugarit has taken the house of Pabeya [. . .] which is in Ullami, and given it to Nuriyana and to his descendants forever. Let no one take it from the hand of Nuriyana or his descendants forever. Seal of the king.'"

7. G. E. Mendenhall, *Law and Covenant in Israel and the Ancient Near East* (Pittsburgh: The Biblical Colloquium, 1955), 37–38.

8. Ibid., 38.

9. Ibid., 39.

This does not mean, borrowing on the marital analogy sometimes employed, that Israel was conceived by means of a mere contract. After all, God had chosen Abraham and promised the land of Canaan to his descendants apart from the patriarch's own efforts (a point to which we will return below). Further, God had delivered the children of promise from Egypt unilaterally, out of sheer commitment to his oath to Abraham and in merciful answer to the cry of the slaves for liberation. Even when the Israelites enter the land, they are to recognize that they are "a people holy to the LORD your God; the LORD your God has chosen you out of all the peoples on earth to be his people, his treasured possession" (Deut. 7:6). Thus, God's gracious initiative is asserted, adding,

> It was not because you were more numerous than any other people that the LORD set his heart on you and chose you—for you were the fewest of all peoples. It was because the LORD loved you and kept the oath that he swore to your ancestors, that the LORD has brought you out with a mighty hand, and redeemed you from the house of slavery, from the hand of Pharaoh king of Egypt. (vv. 7–8)

Yet while God's election and deliverance were entirely dependent on God's grace, the nation that now swears its oath at Sinai assumes responsibility for the stipulations and sanctions should it fail to keep the covenant. The God who has elected and delivered by grace now holds the nation responsible for keeping his commandments, warning that those who fail will be cut off (vv. 9–11).

E. P. Sanders's well-known formula, "Get in by grace, stay in by obedience," and the term he coins for this type of arrangement, "covenantal nomism," appear entirely justified by the form and content of this suzerainty treaty.[10] Yahweh's relationship with Israel is marital: it is simultaneously legal and deeply personal, yet divorce is always a real possibility in the case of adulterous breach.

Since Israel's calling occurs on this side of the fall, it is not only the result of God's goodness and love, but of his mercy and grace. Not only is God's election of Israel undeserved; it is the opposite of what is deserved. Yet as in humanity's original vocation, Israel is chosen in order to fulfill a vocation, and its status as God's covenant servant in God's land is dependent on Israel's own faithfulness. At Sinai, Moses recited the words of the law he had received; the people "answered with one voice, and said, 'All the words that the LORD has spoken we will do.'" Writing down the words, he set up an altar (the vassal's archive) with twelve pillars corresponding to the twelve tribes. After the people took the oath, "All [this] we will do, and we will be obedient," Moses dashed the blood on the people "and said, 'See the blood of the covenant that the LORD has made with you in accordance with all these words'" (Exod. 24:3–8).

The character of this covenant could not be more vividly portrayed: Israel had made the oath, and it was sealed by Moses' act of dashing the blood on the peo-

---

10. E. P. Sanders, *Paul and Palestinian Judaism* (Minneapolis: Fortress, 1977); for "getting in by grace, staying in by obedience," see 93, 178, 371, and for his definition of "covenantal nomism," see 75, 543–56.

ple, with the ominous warning that this act implied. *The Sinai covenant itself, then, is a law-covenant.* The land is *given* to Israel, but for the purpose of fulfilling its covenantal vocation. Remaining in the land is therefore conditional on Israel's personal performance of the stipulations that the people swore at Sinai.

This did not mean that individual Israelites themselves were defined in their relationship to God by law alone rather than by promise, but that the *national* covenant that Israel made with God was an oath made by the people as a nation, accepting responsibility for their side of the agreement. The conditional language is evident throughout the Torah: "If you do this, you will live; if you fail to do this, you will die" (Lev. 18:5; Deut. 4:1; 5:33; 6:24–25; 8:1; 30:15–18; Neh. 9:29; Ezek. 18:19; 20:11–21; etc.). The form and content are those of a suzerainty covenant and are evident also in the covenant between God and Adam (Gen. 2:16–17). Like Adam, Israel had a mission to undertake, a task to perform, a destiny to realize not only for itself but also for the whole world, and this vocation was Israel's to either keep or lose.

Covenant of Promise

The Decalogue and Joshua 24 fit this suzerainty pattern, but as Mendenhall observes, "It can readily be seen that the covenant with Abraham (and Noah) is of completely different form."

> Both in the narrative of Gen. 15 and 17, and in the later references to this covenant, it is clearly stated or implied that it is Yahweh Himself who swears to certain promises to be carried out in the future. It is not often enough seen that no obligations are imposed upon Abraham. Circumcision is not originally an obligation, but a sign of the covenant, like the rainbow in Gen. 9. It serves to identify the recipient(s) of the covenant, as well as to give a concrete indication that a covenant exists. It is for the protection of the promisee, perhaps, like the mark on Cain of Gen. 4. The covenant of Moses, on the other hand is almost the exact opposite. It imposes specific obligations upon the tribes or clans without binding Yahweh to specific obligations, though it goes without saying that the covenant relationship itself presupposed the protection and support of Yahweh to Israel.[11]

The promise maker in Genesis 15 is Yahweh, not Abram: "I am your shield; your reward shall be very great. . . . This man [Eliezer of Damascus] shall not be your heir; no one but your very own issue shall be your heir. . . . Look toward heaven and count the stars, if you are able to count them. . . . So shall your descendants be." Abraham believes and is justified then and there (vv. 1–6). In between all of these ellipses is a countertestimony on Abram's part, but Yahweh keeps responding with sheer promise, and finally in response to the patriarch's continuing doubts, Yahweh confirms the promise with a sign. This episode stands in sharp contrast to the Promethean boast of a different united federation at the tower of

---

11. Mendenhall, *Law and Covenant,* 36.

Babel: "We shall make a name for ourselves!" (11:4). However, Yahweh gives Abram ("father") a new name (Abraham, "father of many," 17:5), and this becomes paradigmatic for the covenant of promise to the end of the age (35:10; Isa. 45:4; 62:6; Rev. 2:17).

To understand the sign of this covenant, we must understand something of its Ancient Near Eastern background. There are various rituals associated with the making of covenants. However, a suzerainty treaty was typically sealed by a public ceremony in which the vassal (lesser king) passed through the halves of animals, testifying to the fact that the same curse-sanctions would be imposed by the suzerain on the vassal in the case of breach.[12]

That the national covenant (made at Sinai) conforms to this conditional sort of suzerainty treaty is evident enough in the fact that Moses sprinkles the blood on the oath-takers, ratifying the "words of this covenant" ("All that the LORD has spoken we will do"). It is also clear from the subsequent history of the covenant, as the prophets pronounce the curses for violation. Yahweh announces,

> And those who transgressed my covenant and did not keep the terms of the covenant that *they made* before me, I will make like the calf when they cut it in two and passed between its parts; the officials of Judah, the officials of Jerusalem, the eunuchs, the priests, and all the people of the land who passed between the parts of the calf shall be handed over to their enemies and to those who seek their lives. (Jer. 34:18–20, emphasis added)

"From this ceremony is derived the Hebrew idiom for making a treaty, *karat berit*, 'to cut a treaty.'" Homer uses the same idiom: *horkia tamnein*, "to cut oaths."[13] Dennis J. McCarthy, S.J., points out that "to cut a covenant" is used as early as the 1400s BCE in Aramaic and Phoenecian as well as Hebrew records.[14]

Something is askew in this picture, however, when we come to the covenant established and "cut" in Genesis 15, where we find Abram asleep, receiving a vision of a flaming torch walking through pieces of animals. Here, however, *God alone walks through the severed halves*, assuming on his own head the curses of the covenant should it fail to come to pass. Thus, the unilateral promise is signified and sealed in a unilateral treaty ceremony. In the Sinai covenant, the covenant mediator splashes blood upon the oath-taking Israelites, but in this covenant, of which God himself is the mediator, Abraham is merely a beneficiary, along with his heirs. Instead of the covenant servant, God has walked alone through the bloody pieces. Abraham is declared then and there "justified" and "father of many nations," even though everything he sees would seem to suggest otherwise. In both the word and sacrament of this covenant, Yahweh is the promise maker, assuming the burden of fulfilling its conditions in history.

12. Hillers, *Covenant,* 40–41.

13. Ibid., 41.

14. Dennis J. McCarthy, S.J., *Treaty and Covenant: A Study in the Ancient Oriental Documents and in the Old Testament* (Rome: Biblical Institute Press, 1963), 52–55.

The Noachian covenant too was a one-sided promise on God's part, with no conditions attached (Gen. 9). This pattern can be seen also in God's promise to David and his heirs. In the period of the monarchy, Yahweh was the *witness* in the anointing of the king.[15] Now, however, "the tradition of the covenant with Abraham became the pattern of a covenant between Yahweh and David, whereby *Yahweh promised* to maintain the Davidic line on the throne (II Sam 23:5)." No matter what David and his descendants do or fail to do vis-à-vis the Sinaitic covenant, God will unilaterally and unconditionally preserve an heir on his throne. "Yahweh bound Himself, exactly as in the Abrahamic and Noachite covenant, and therefore Israel could not escape responsibility to the king. The covenant with Abraham was the 'prophecy' and that with David the 'fulfillment.'" In fact, "the Mosaic legal tradition could hardly have been any more attractive to Solomon than it was to Paul."[16]

Only with the eighth-century prophets does the Mosaic covenant return to the foreground, along with the correspondences to the Hittite treaties. It is "back to the federation." The rediscovery of the "Book of the Law" led to "a thorough housecleaning."

> The king [Josiah] together with the people entered into covenant (before the Lord: i.e. with Yahweh as witness, not as a *party* to the covenant) to keep the commandments of the Lord. . . . It brought home to Josiah and the religious leadership that they had been living in a fool's paradise in their assumption that Yahweh had irrevocably committed Himself to preserve the nation in the Davidic-Abrahamic covenant. Moses was rediscovered after having been dormant for nearly three and a half centuries.[17]

They were astonished to realize that the covenant "provided for curses as well as blessings (II Kings 22:13)."[18] In other words, the returning exiles were astonished to learn that the national covenant was conditioned on their obedience rather than being an unconditional grant.

The point is this: *The deepest distinction in Scripture is not between the Old and New Testaments, but between the covenants of law and the covenants of promise that run throughout both.* The two covenant traditions are distinguished both in form and content. There is a covenant of law (the prelapsarian covenant with humanity in Adam as well as the Sinai covenant), according to which each and every person swears to personally fulfill the stipulations. There is also a covenant of promise (including the promise made to Adam and Eve after the fall, to Abraham and

---

15. See Mendenhall, *Law and Covenant*, 45.

16. Ibid., 46. Although Mendenhall perhaps speculates beyond the evidence on this point, it does remind us that while the two covenants were not intrinsically opposed (one pertained to the status of the nation, the other to the Davidic heir on the throne), they were not the same and tension could and did result between them in Israel's history. The love of the law is the goal of both covenants (Ps. 119 is consistent with Jer. 31); the difference is whether such love of the law and obedience to it function as a conditional basis or as the goal.

17. Ibid., 47.

18. Ibid., 48.

Sarah, Noah, David, and the new covenant), according to which God swears to bring redemption through the promised heir (seed). These two covenant traditions are united by many bonds, yet always remain distinguished. As we will see, they come into sharp contrast only when the question is raised as to the justification of the ungodly.

Evaluating the Differences in the Covenant Types

One of the things that I have found intriguing in researching this topic is the extent to which biblical scholars from religious traditions other than Protestantism (for instance, Jewish and Roman Catholic) have not only demonstrated the distinction between covenant types, but also offer an interpretation of the biblical traditions that is in many respects identical to that of classical covenant theology. Steven L. McKenzie sheds further light on the obvious differences between the Sinaitic and Davidic covenants in terms of their conditional versus promissory character. In 2 Samuel 7 the pure divine condescension (promissory covenant) is underscored (esp. v. 5, with the emphatic "you"). David wants to build a house for God, but the Davidic covenant is a unilateral promise from God to build a house for David. The narrative makes Yahweh appear stern and unwilling to receive his servant's well-meant zeal, but the rationale is clear. God knows what David is like, and he knows what his heirs will be like as well. The Abrahamic covenant will not be realized in history if it is in any way dependent on the zeal of his sinful people. If the promise is going to become a reality, it is Yahweh himself who will have to make it happen. "It is this promise of an eternal royal line that essentially constitutes the covenant with David," McKenzie notes.[19]

As soon as David's own son arrives on the scene, the vassal is unworthy, and yet the treaty is unaffected (1 Kgs. 11:33). Israel had, for all intents and purposes, so violated the treaty that Yahweh's continued presence could only be explained as "for the sake of my servant David" (2 Kgs. 8:19; 19:34; 20:6)—which, penultimately, means the same thing as "for the sake of the fathers/Abraham" and ultimately in retrospect (i.e., looking back from the New Testament), "for the sake of Christ," the promised seed of Abraham and David (Rom. 1:3; Gal. 3:16). This highlights the significance of the genealogy in Matthew (1:1–17) and the angelic announcement to Mary that "God will give him the throne of his father David" (Luke 1:32 NIV).

In Mendenhall's words, "The harmonization of the two covenant traditions meant that great emphasis had to be placed upon the divine forgiveness, and this becomes the foundation of the New Covenant predicted by Jeremiah."

> The New Covenant of Christianity obviously continued the tradition of the Abrahamic-Davidic covenant with its emphasis upon the Messiah, Son of

19. Steven L. McKenzie, *Covenant* (St. Louis: Chalice Press, 2000), 66. For the seminal Davidic covenant passages, see 2 Sam. 7; 23:5; 1 Kgs. 8:15–26; 9:1–9; 15:4–5; 2 Kgs. 8:19; 1 Chron. 17; 22:10–13; 28:7–10; 2 Chron. 6:4–17; 7:12–22; 21:7; Pss. 89; 132; Isa. 55:3; Jer. 33:14–26.

David. Paul uses the covenant of Abraham to show the temporary validity of the Mosaic covenant, but in spite of this, the basic structure of New Testament religion is actually, as the early church constantly maintained, the continuation of Mosaic religion.[20]

The nuance here is key: the New Testament views itself in continuity with Moses and Israel insofar as they serve the promise (through type and shadow, as well as through individual faith in God's oath), though on the basis of the Abrahamic/new, rather than the Mosaic/old covenant itself.

Therefore, Moses too can be regarded as a paradigmatic person of faith along with Abraham (Heb. 11:23–28). Stirkingly, however, there is no reference to the Sinai (Mosaic) covenant itself in that passage. Rather, Moses "considered abuse suffered for the Christ to be greater wealth than the treasures of Egypt, for he was looking ahead to the reward. By faith he left Egypt. . . . By faith he kept the Passover and the sprinkling of blood, so that the destroyer of the firstborn would not touch the firstborn of Israel" (vv. 26–28). As Abraham by faith looked beyond the promise of an earthly land to a heavenly one, Moses apprehended Christ by faith even through the shadows of the law.

Relating Sinai and Zion

Some biblical scholars recognize a sharp contrast between the law-covenant and promise-covenant types, even correlating the former with Sinai and the latter with Abraham, David, and the new covenant, only to conclude finally that the only way to handle the contrast is to assimilate gospel to law. I will refer to two examples here: Jon D. Levenson and Pope Benedict XVI.

Jon Levenson has offered a fascinating treatment of these two traditions from the perspective of Judaism. He first draws the obvious contrasts between Sinai and the Abrahamic/Davidic/new covenants. At Sinai, which is treated as a historical event to be taken at face value, "YHWH and Israel conclude a bilateral relationship: he will grant them a special status, one shared by none of his other people, if only they will obey him. This they agree to do, sending their assent up the mountain to God by way of the mediator of this new relationship, Moses."[21] The promise is given in Exodus 19:6: "You shall be to me a kingdom of priests and a holy nation" (RSV), which is "a reward for loyalty in covenant" dependent on Israel's oath, "All that Yahweh has spoken we will do!" (v. 8 RSV).[22] With the Ten Commandments in Exodus 20, "Awareness of divine grace sets the stage for the stipulations."[23] Then there is the covenant of Joshua 24.

20. Mendenhall, *Law and Covenant*, 49.
21. Jon D. Levenson, *Sinai and Zion: An Entry into the Jewish Bible* (San Francisco: HarperSan Francisco, 1985), 24–25. Levenson offers a sound argument for Exod. 19:3b–8 being part of a source earlier than the Deuteronomic, reflecting "a relatively early phase in the religion of Israel" (25).
22. Ibid., 31.
23. Ibid., 33.

> In v 27, the large rock assumes the role of the gods as witness to the covenant, "for it has heard all the words YHWH has spoken to us." The only hint in Joshua 24 of curses and blessings, the last item in the covenant formulary, occurs in v 20. YHWH has brought Israel success up to now, but if she abandons him and serves another suzerain, he will in turn reverse himself and annihilate Israel.[24]

However, the contrast between Sinai and Abraham cannot be allowed to stand: the latter must be assimilated into the former, according to Judaism. He therefore gives priority to law even over history, by adopting the priority of the suzerainty-treaty form over all others.

> Terms like "salvation history" (*Heilsgeschichte*) thus conveniently obscure essential differences. Moreover, when one understands covenant in its Near Eastern context, it becomes clear that it is not law, but the recitation of history, which is subordinate. . . . *The covenant without stipulations, the Abrahamic covenant of Genesis 15 and 17, is only a preparation for the Sinaitic covenant, into which it is absorbed.* (emphasis added)[25]

If Levenson accurately represents the views of early Judaism, then this interpretation (especially the last sentence) underscores the accuracy of the New Testament charge that we find especially in Paul; namely, that Judaism—and the "Judaizing" party within the church—had assimilated the Abrahamic covenant of promise to the Sinai law-covenant (see especially Gal. 3:15–18). Gospel had been absorbed into law. This is where Judaism and the New Testament part ways in their interpretation of the Hebrew Scriptures, as Levenson points out below.

To be sure, law and promise are not opposed in any abstract manner. In fact, the new covenant (along Abrahamic-Davidic lines) included God's unilateral promise to write his law in his people and on their hearts rather than merely on stone tablets (Jer. 31:33). The point is whether the *principle of inheritance* in question with any specific covenant is *law* (based on the personal performance of the servant), as in a suzerainty treaty, or *promise*, as in a royal grant. To be sure, even a royal grant is based on the personal performance of someone, yet as the story unfolds it becomes increasingly clear that it is the greater heir of Abraham and Sarah—the promised son greater than Isaac—through whom worldwide blessing and redemption will come. As for Abraham himself, he must simply take his place as first among equals in receiving his inheritance through faith alone. Thus, in the mystery of redemption, the patriarch is his descendant's heir. On the basis of the exploits performed by the coming heir, Abraham and Sarah and all others united by faith in the promise receive their "peerage" as an everlasting inheritance from generation to generation.

If one confuses the principle by which the national promises of land, temple, and kingdom are upheld (the people's obedience) with the principle by which the

---

24. Ibid., 34. It is worth noting that, with Dennis McCarthy, G. E. Mendenhall, and Delbert Hillers, among others, Levenson regards this material as pre-Penteteuchal and "quite early," in fact (35).
25. Ibid., 45.

heavenly reality to which these types pointed was inherited (sheer promise, by virtue of the obedience of the covenant head), then salvation (whether corporate or individual) comes through "the works of the law" (Sinai) rather than through "the faith of Abraham." In Christian preaching, this confusion often occurs when passages emphasizing the conditions of temporal blessing in the land are expounded, either literally or allegorically, as directly applicable to the question of personal salvation and right standing before God. By properly distinguishing these covenant types, we can better recognize in specific instances how corporate blessing was promised on the basis of Israel's obedience to the law, but individual salvation was always by grace alone.

Levenson recognizes that Israel's national covenant was a suzerainty treaty: "We have seen that the relationship of Israel to her God was conceived in the covenant theology along the lines of a contract between states and that one stipulation of such a contract was the requirement to love the lord in covenant."[26] Although in principle a covenant of law, this relationship between Yahweh and Israel was not "legalistic." (Legalism is the attempt to secure the eternal inheritance by one's own obedience.) Compared to marriage by the prophets (especially in Hosea, but also, for example, in Mal. 2:14), the national law-covenant was conditional: spiritual adultery could break the treaty. Love and law cannot be set in antithesis, since the law summarized the meaning of love in concrete relationships, as Levenson emphasizes.[27] He adds, "The romance of God and Israel is tempered by lawfulness and animated by eros, love purified in law, law impelled by love."[28]

However, even Levenson recognizes the different key that is sounded in the prophets when they speak of a "new covenant."

> In Hos 2:20, YHWH makes a new covenant, not one between himself and Israel, but between Israel and the beasts and birds and creeping things. In other words, God assumes the Mosaic office of covenant mediator, in order to extend the peace and security of the covenant relationship beyond the confines of the divine-human dialogue. Now even nature will participate. All threats, whether from nature or from war, will vanish. Lurking behind these great promises are the blessings of the covenant formulary. *But we hear nothing of the curses, for the vision is one of redemption through covenant, and the assumption seems to be that, where God mediates and thus guarantees covenant, the stipulations will be fulfilled as a matter of course.* (emphasis added)[29]

"In Hos 2:16–25 [14–23E], the making of a covenant moves beyond the limits of the juridical function in which it originated and becomes the stuff and substance of a vision of cosmic renewal."[30] However, Levenson is quick to add, "redemption is not 'liberation' from law; that would be, in Hosea's eyes, relapse into licentiousness.

26. Ibid., 75.
27. Ibid., 77.
28. Ibid., 78.
29. Ibid.
30. Ibid., 79.

Rather, redemption involves the gracious offer to Israel to reenter the legal/erotic relationship and the renewed willingness of Israel to do so."[31]

What is so striking in such observations is that in spite of recognizing the distinct character of the new covenant as an unconditional promise guaranteed by God, Levenson nevertheless concludes that it is, at the end of the day, simply a renewal of the Sinaitic covenant—a fresh start for regaining the inheritance by law. Regardless of whether Israel "got in by grace," the exile reveals that Israel is at least in some sense "out," and the only way of getting back in is by rededication to the law-covenant of Sinai. The goal of the various covenant renewals after the exile, says Levenson, "is to induce Israel to step into the position of the generation of Sinai, in other words, to actualize the past so that this new generation will become the Israel of the classic covenant relationship (cf. Deut 30:19–20)."[32] In fact, Levenson's thesis can be summarized in his statement: "There is, therefore, no voice more central to Judaism than the voice heard on Mount Sinai."[33]

Even where, in the Psalms (esp. Ps. 97) and the prophets, the emphasis shifts from Sinai (the earthly mountain) to Zion (the heavenly and everlasting sanctuary), "Sinai has not so much been forgotten as absorbed."[34] As "a pledge of divine support for a human dynasty," which is "something almost unthinkable in the case of Sinai," the Davidic covenant belongs to Zion rather than to Sinai, Levenson observes.[35] He even acknowledges, with other scholars I have cited, that "the Davidic covenant does not follow, even loosely, the formulary characteristic of the suzerainty treaty upon which so many of the texts dealing with the Sinaitic covenant are modeled."[36] However, Levenson immediately states that the directives of Sinai are understood as implied. "There is no text in the Hebrew Bible that holds that the Davidic replaces the Sinaitic. But within the national covenant lies another, restricted to one family, the royal house of David."[37]

So on one hand, Levenson affirms a clear distinction between the Sinaitic and Davidic covenants. The latter establishes an everlasting dynasty of Davidic heirs. "Their moral record is in no way essential to the validity of the covenant." And Levenson goes on, appealing to Moshe Weinfeld, to elaborate the differences between the suzerainty treaty and the "covenant of grant," noting the parallel, both in form and content, between the Davidic covenant and the unilateral covenant that God made with Noah and Abraham, concluding, "This Davidic covenant, then, is distinct in kind from the Sinaitic."[38]

So profoundly distinct is each covenant that it practically generates different ontological frames of reference. The contingencies of history to which morality

31. Ibid.
32. Ibid., 81.
33. Ibid., 86.
34. Ibid., 91.
35. Ibid., 92.
36. Ibid., 99.
37. Ibid.
38. Ibid., 100.

belongs no longer determine the outcome of the Davidic dynasty, which instead is secured in heaven.

> The dynamics of Sinai, which are the dynamics of the treaty, metamorphose history into morality, or in rabbinic language, *haggadah* into *halakhah*, lore into law. In the case of the Davidic covenant, history and morality are no longer the focus, for any claim God might make peculiarly upon the house of David has already been satisfied by its founder. Rather, the Davidic covenant, a covenant of grant, looks beyond the vicissitudes of history, since they cease to be critical. This covenant fixes attention to that which is constant beneath—or perhaps I should say, above—the flux of history. . . . And since the focus is upon the constancy of God rather than the changeability of man, it brings to light what is secure and inviolable, whereas the Sinaitic texts tend to emphasize the precariousness of life and the consequent need for a continuously reinvigorated obedience.[39]

Hence "for the sake of David," even bad kings rule (1 Kgs. 15:4; 2 Kgs. 8:19). The everlasting promise trumps the moral conduct of its heirs. "Jerusalem and . . . especially Mount Zion are a sign that beneath and beyond the pain and chaos of the realm we call history, there is another realm, upheld by the indefectible promise of God. Dynasty and Temple, the house of David and house of God, function within the order of history, but are rooted in that other order of things."[40]

In the prophets (see Isa. 29:1–8; Jer. 7:1–15), the earthly Zion is violable, the heavenly one inviolable.[41] "The Temple exists and functions in the spiritual universe by his grace alone."[42] Jeremiah (ch. 7) faults those who "have taken the cosmos out of the cosmic mountain," turning it "into a matter of mere real estate. They do not long in joy and awe for the mountain."

> Why should they? They are standing on it. The edifice on Mount Zion does not correspond to the gate of heaven; it *is* the gate of heaven. In other words, they have lost the sense of the delicacy of relationship between the higher and lower Jerusalem, and have assumed that the latter always reflects the former perfectly.[43]

On one hand, Levenson points out the prophets' criticism of collapsing the earthly and heavenly Jerusalem, Sinai and Zion, yet on the other hand he too finally seems to assimilate the former to the latter.

With this background from Levenson, Paul's contrast in Galatians 4 between "two covenants" (law and promise) in terms of two mountains (earthly Jerusalem, now corresponding to Sinai; heavenly Jerusalem, corresponding to Zion) and two mothers (Hagar and Sarah respectively) is all the more significant. So too is the contrast drawn by Hebrews between the "old covenant" and the "better covenant,"

39. Ibid., 101.
40. Ibid.
41. Ibid., 165.
42. Ibid., 166.
43. Ibid., 169.

whose mediator is God himself, heavenly, and inviolable: Zion rather than Sinai (esp. 12:18–29).

So how can Judaism go on affirming the inviolability of the national covenant in the face of exile, not to mention the destruction of the temple in 70 CE? Levenson says that this could only be maintained—in the absence of land, temple, and kingdom—by redefining the whole faith of Israel.

> Even in modern Israel, the Judaism practiced is not that of the Hebrew Bible, but the continuation of its rabbinic successor, which fashioned a tradition that could deal with a world without a Temple, Jewish sovereignty, or, increasingly, a homeland. . . . Prayer, for example, is seen as the replacement for the sacrifices. . . . Just as prayer replaces sacrifice, so does the synagogue succeed the Temple, the rabbi inherits the authority of the priests, and the family table replaces the altar. "Rabbi Hochanan and Rabbi Eleazar both used to say," reads the Talmud, "'So long as the Temple stood, the altar made atonement for Israel. Now a man's table makes atonement for him.'"[44]

The question for a Jewish person then becomes what it was already in Psalms 15 and 24: "How does one climb that mountain? What must one do to move from profane space to sacred space, from this world to the world-to-come? The question is a large one in rabbinic theology."[45] Even in Second Temple Judaism, therefore, the question, "How can I be saved?" is provoked not by the introspective conscience of a modern individualism, but by a sense of urgency in the face of history (exile) and a growing sense of an imminent and final judgment of the individual beyond the exile (eschatology).

Levenson is even able to use the contrasting categories, "Mosaic/Sinaitic and the Davidic/Zionistic orientations," to the point of recognizing, "In fact, the Davidic theology is the origin of Jewish messianism and the christology of the church."[46] Of course, this is just where Judaism and Christianity part company. The Sinai legacy, according to Levenson, rather than being the "schoolmaster" to lead us to Christ, is integrated into the Zion tradition in that the messiah will come with "Israel's observance of the stipulations of Sinai."[47]

This is a good place to remind ourselves that in the covenant theology of the Reformed tradition, these two covenants and "mountains" meet in Christ, who as the covenantal *head* fulfills the Sinaitic law (already anticipated in the Adamic covenant) and as the covenant *mediator* dispenses the fruit of his labors to his heirs in a covenant of grace.[48] Rather than set aside the law-covenant, he fulfills it (positively) and bears its curses (negatively), so that the inheritance can legitimately (legally) be conferred on the terms of grace alone (i.e., royal grant).

---

44. Ibid., 180–81.
45. Ibid., 183.
46. Ibid., 194.
47. Ibid., 209.
48. For a representative summary of this very position among the seventeenth-century federal theologians, see Herman Witsius, *Economy of the Covenants* (Escondido, CA: den Dulk Christian Foundation, 1990), bk. 2, chap. 2.

Even Levenson recognizes that there are interpretive difficulties with the traditional view of Judaism that he has defended: that the kingdom will come as a result of Israel's obedience, especially in light of "the unexpected dimension of the advent of the new king," as in Isaiah 9:6–7.

> One does not sense in these oracles that the messianic reign comes as something deserved, as a divine response to human righteousness. On the contrary, the prophets who deliver messianic promises are the same prophets who savage Israel for her wickedness. Seybold's observation about the covenantal context of the Davidic promise is equally weak, for as we saw in Part 2, the Sinaitic and Davidic covenants, at least as the latter appears in 2 Samuel 7 and Psalm 89, are of radically different types. The former is a *treaty*; the latter is a *grant*. Since covenant was not a unitary concept in ancient Israel, the use of the term should not be taken to indicate an integrative movement.[49]

In contrast to Sinai, the Davidic covenant "is an alliance between YHWH and David, not with Israel per se."[50] (The close relationship between Abraham and David, as representing promise-covenants, is also affirmed by Paul's point in Galatians 3:16, that God made the promise to Abraham's *seed*, meaning Christ, not to *seeds*, meaning individual Israelites.) With great insight, though at variance with the NPP, Levenson notes, "If the Davidic covenant never displaced the Sinaitic in the Hebrew Bible, it did, in a sense, in the New Testament."[51]

I would only add that in the New Testament, Sinai is fulfilled, not displaced. It is rendered obsolete not because it was wrong, but because it was always a temporary regime and reached its goal despite Israel's failures. In fact, precisely because Israel's representative servant has kept his Father's word, even in this deeper (legal, not just typological) sense, the law-covenant has been fulfilled.

To be sure, there are many different interpretations of the relation between these two covenant traditions. David Noel Freedman, for example, sees the land grant and suzerainty treaty in more of a dialectic (rather than former subsumed under latter).[52] Nevertheless, all of these scholars of the Hebrew Bible affirm a distinction. So too does Pope Benedict XVI, drawing on many of the same sources.

Pope Benedict rightly emphasizes the unity of the two testaments: law and gospel do not correspond to Old and New Testaments in any sort of Marcionite opposition.[53] "This very word 'testament' is, in a way, an attempt to utter the 'essence of Christianity,' in a single, summary, expression—which is itself drawn from this fundamental source," the Last Supper. "The old Latin version says

---

49. Levenson, *Sinai and Zion*, 210.
50. Ibid.
51. Ibid., 216.
52. David Noel Freedman, "Divine Commitment and Human Obligation," *Interpretation* 18 (1964): 419–31.
53. Joseph Cardinal Ratzinger, *Many Religions—One Covenant: Israel, the Church and the World* (San Francisco: Ignatius Press, 1999), 36–47.

testamentum, but Jerome opted for *foedus* or *pactum.*"[54] He even notes that there is no single definition of *berit* [covenant]; the meaning "can only be gathered from the particular biblical contexts."[55]

With respect to what we are calling the covenant of grace, Pope Benedict points out the significance of the word choice employed by the translators of the Hebrew Bible into Greek (LXX), translating *berit* with the word *diathēkē.*

> Evidently, their theological insight into the text led them to the view that the biblical content was not that of a *syn-thēkē*—a reciprocal agreement— but a *dia-thēkē:* it is not a case of two wills agreeing together but of *one* will establishing an ordinance. Exegetical scholarship is convinced, as far as I can see, that the men of the Septuagint were correct in understanding the biblical text in this way. In the Bible, what we call "covenant" is not a symmetrical relationship between two partners who make a contractual agreement involving reciprocal obligations and penalties: this idea of partnership among equals cannot be reconciled with a biblical concept of God. According to the latter, man is in no position to create a relationship with God, let alone give him anything and receive something in return; it is quite out of the question that man should bind God to obligations in return for undertakings on his own part.[56]

He elaborates the implications of this definition:

> If there is to be a relationship between God and man, it can only come about through God's free ordinance, in which his sovereignty remains intact. The relationship is therefore completely asymmetrical, because God, for the creature, is and remains the "wholly Other." The "covenant" is not a two-sided contract but a gift, a creative act of God's love. . . . Although the covenant is patterned on Hittite and Assyrian contracts between states, in which the lord imposes his law on his vassal, God's covenant with Israel is far more: here God, the King, receives nothing from man; but in giving him his law, he gives him the path of life.[57]

Yet just at this point, he recognizes, "This raises a question." "Formally, the Old Testament type of covenant corresponds strictly to the genre of the vassal contract with its asymmetrical structure." "If it is to be seen no longer in terms of a contract between states but in the image of bridal love (as in the Prophets, most movingly in Ezekiel 16), if the contractual act is presented as a love story between God and the Chosen People, what happens to the inherent asymmetry?"[58] The New Testament "sees the covenant made with Abraham as the real, fundamental, and abiding covenant; according to Paul, the covenant made with

54. Ibid., 48.
55. Ibid.
56. Ibid., 50–51.
57. Ibid.
58. Ibid.

Moses was interposed (Rom 5:20) 430 years after the Abrahamic covenant (Gal 3:17); it could not abrogate the covenant with Abraham but constituted only an intermediary stage in God's providential plan."[59]

On one hand, Pope Benedict's exegesis leads him to conclude that "Paul distinguishes very sharply between two kinds of covenant that we find in the Old Testament": "a covenant that consists of legal prescriptions and the covenant that is essentially a promise, the gift of friendship, bestowed without conditions." In fact, "*Whereas the covenant imposing obligations is patterned on the vassal contract, the covenant of promise has the royal grant as its model.* To that extent Paul, with his contrast between the covenant with Abraham and the covenant with Moses, has rightly interpreted the biblical text" (emphasis added).[60] On the other hand, he concludes, "The covenant with Moses is incorporated into the covenant with Abraham, and the Law becomes a mediator of promise."[61]

So while recognizing the obvious contrasts between the Abrahamic-Davidic-new covenants on one side and the Sinaitic covenant on the other, Levenson and Pope Benedict both resist simply letting the difference stand. The former assimilates the promise to the law, while the latter assimilates the law to the promise. In both cases the result, however, is to lose the radical differences between these two principles for covenantal inheritance. Conditionality becomes relativized by unconditionality and vice versa in the direction of a single historical covenant. "The one Covenant," says Pope Benedict, "is realized in the plurality of covenants."[62] The new covenant that is ratified at the Last Supper "is *the prolongation of the Sinai covenant, which is not abrogated, but renewed*" (emphasis added).[63] This would seem not only to subvert the point of Jeremiah 31:31–32, that the new covenant "will *not* be like" the Sinai treaty, which Israel broke, but also the careful distinctions that the writer otherwise followed earlier. It likewise fails to appreciate the asymmetry between the "blood of the covenant" dashed on the Israelites at Sinai in confirmation of their oath ("All this we will do") and Jesus' inauguration of the new covenant in *his* blood (as if to say, "All this I will do").

Pope Benedict, however, seems reluctant to simply leave the matter at a synthesis between law and gospel. Only a couple of pages later, he writes, "The conditional covenant, which depended on man's faithful observance of the Law, is replaced by the unconditional covenant in which God binds himself irrevocably. We are unmistakably here in the same conceptual milieu as we found earlier in 2 Corinthians, with its contrast between two covenants."[64] He even appears to contradict his earlier statement that the new covenant inaugurated in the Upper Room is a renewal of the Sinaitic covenant when he adds,

59. Ibid., 55.
60. Ibid., 56–57.
61. Ibid.
62. Ibid.
63. Ibid., 62.
64. Ibid., 64.

The Old Covenant is conditional: since it depends on the keeping of the Law, that is, on man's behavior; it can be broken and has been broken. Since its essential content is the Law, it is expressed in the formulation, "If you do all this . . ." This "if" draws man's changeable will into the very essence of the covenant itself and thus makes it a provisional covenant. By contrast, the covenant sealed in the Last Supper, in its inner essence, seems "new" in the sense of the prophetic promise: it is not a contract with conditions but the gift of friendship, irrevocably bestowed. Instead of law we have grace.[65]

Remarkably, Pope Benedict even acknowledges the proximity of this interpretation to the Reformation perspective:

The rediscovery of Pauline theology at the Reformation laid special emphasis on this point: not works, but faith; not man's achievement, but the free bestowal of God's goodness. It emphatically underlined, therefore, that what was involved was not a "covenant" but a "testament," a pure decision and act on God's part. This is the context in which we must understand the teaching that it is God alone who does everything. (All the *solus* terms—*solus Deus, solus Christus*—must be understood in this context.)[66]

It is therefore when he returns, like Levenson, to the original distinction between the two types of covenants in the Old Testament that the author recovers the connection of the new covenant with Abraham rather than Sinai.

With regard to the Sinai covenant, we must again draw a distinction. It is strictly limited to the people of Israel; it gives this nation a legal and cultic order (the two are inseparable) that as such cannot simply be extended to all nations. Since the juridical order is constitutive of the Sinai covenant, the law's "if"; is part of its essence. To that extent, it is conditional, that is, temporal; within God's providential rule it is a stage that has its own allocated period of time. Paul set this forth very clearly, and no Christian can revoke it; history itself confirms this view.[67]

Yet it is when the question of Israel's current status is in view that the pope lays stress on the continuity of the new covenant with Sinai: law simply becomes a form of gospel—in fact, "the Law itself is the concrete form of grace. For to know God's will is grace."[68] Like Levenson, Pope Benedict recognizes the contrast between God's ceremonial passing through the halves in Genesis 15 and the

65. Ibid., 66.
66. Ibid., 67. However, the Reformers (certainly the covenant theology that arose in the Reformed tradition) did not contrast *covenant* and *testament*, as the writer suggests, but recognized that the specific type of *berit* that the Abrahamic-Davidic-new covenant exemplified was a promised inheritance (testament) rather than a mutual contract, and so could only be served by the Greek *diathēkē* rather than *synthēkē*. On this point, see Geerhardus Vos, "Hebrews: The Epistle of the Diathēkē," *Princeton Theological Review* 13 (1915): 587–632 and 14 (1916): 1–61, included in Richard B. Gaffin Jr., ed., *Redemptive History and Biblical Interpretation: The Shorter Writings of Geerhardus Vos* (Phillipsburg, NJ: P&R Publishing, 1980), 161–233.
67. Ibid., 67–68.
68. Ibid., 68–71.

conditionality of Sinai pact, yet also like Levenson, he conflates them within a higher synthesis.[69]

My purpose in engaging with these two conversation partners is twofold. The first is to point out that the distinction between law and gospel is grounded in the history of the covenants—that is, in biblical theology—rather than being an imposition of dogmatic categories. Given the fact that Jewish and Roman Catholic scholars recognize simply on exegetical grounds a distinction between covenants of law and promise—and even Pope Benedict concedes that this lends a certain degree of credibility to the Reformation's chief theses, it is all the more remarkable that so many Protestant biblical scholars today dismiss such a distinction as the imposition of Reformation polemics. The second reason for appealing to these interpreters is to point out how, despite such overwhelming exegetical considerations, the contrast is not ultimately allowed to stand when it comes to theological determinations.

The target of both goals is the view represented by Walter Brueggemann, for example, when he rejects the attempt to distinguish conditional and unconditional aspects as an intrusion of the Pelagian debate. Rather, we should treat "covenant" as a univocal concept. "Thus I suggest that E. P. Sanders's term covenantal nomism is about right, because it subsumes law (*nomos*) under the rubric of covenant. By inference, I suggest that grace must also be subsumed under covenant."[70] This question lies at the heart of the debates over justification. Is the promissory covenant subsumed under (or absorbed into) the covenant of law, resulting in a covenantal nomism? Or are these two covenants always distinguished and, on the point of justification, to be treated in fact as antithetical means of inheriting eternal life?

NEW TESTAMENT INTERPRETATIONS OF THE OLD COVENANT

It would seem that we are on better exegetical ground to hold, with Levenson, that the definitive break with Sinai in favor of Zion occurs with the Christian proclamation. The various covenant renewal movements of Second Temple Judaism were united in their belief that the new covenant (i.e., the messianic kingdom) would be a rehabilitation of the old covenant as a result of a renewed commitment to the law.

By contrast, as Hillers describes, "Early Christians, even those of Jewish descent, did not look on themselves either as an unbroken continuation of the old Israel or as a group attempting to return to an ancient pattern of faith, like the Essenes. Instead, they stood over against the days 'of old' as men living in the 'last days.'" Part of this "newness," says Hebrews 1, is that the new covenant coalesces

---

69. Ibid., 73.
70. Walter Brueggemann, *Theology of the Old Testament* (Minneapolis: Fortress, 1997), 419.

around a person—a Son, a "better covenant," one "enacted on better promises."[71]
The writer says of Jeremiah's prophecy, "In speaking of a new covenant, he treats
the first as obsolete. And what is becoming obsolete and growing old is ready to
vanish away" (Heb. 8:13 RSV; cf. 9:11–23).

In fact, Hebrews 10:28–29 outright contrasts this older covenantal understanding (Sinai) with the new.[72] Just as the blessings of being in Christ are greater
than being in Moses, the curses are greater. To forfeit the earthly rest is tragic, but
far greater still is the tragedy of giving up the heavenly rest by failing to believe
the promise (4:1–11). While Moses was faithful in God's house, "Jesus is worthy
of more glory than Moses, just as the builder of a house has more honor than the
house itself" (3:3). Moses was faithful as a servant, but Jesus as Son. In fact, the
"house" itself, identified thus far as *God's* house, is here referred to as "*his*
[Christ's] house" (v. 6). With thorough knowledge of the temple cult, this writer
advances the figural hermeneutic with great detail yet impressive, sweeping vis-
tas. The priesthood of Christ is eternal, that of the Levites temporal (chap. 7); he
is a better mediator of a better covenant with better promises (chap. 8); his sacrifice once and for all takes away sin forever, instead of repeated offerings; he has
entered the heavenly sanctuary not made by human hands—the true temple, not
the earthly copy, to bring his "blood of the eternal covenant" and to intercede on
our behalf (chaps. 9–10). In the writer's view, the old covenant *itself* did not have
adequate provisions for transgression, but could only point believers typologi-
cally to the new covenant, in which they participated by faith.

It is not Paul who introduces a law-promise, Sinai-Abraham, Moses-Christ
contrast. Following the prophets, Jesus enacts in his teaching and actions the
redefinition of the people of God around himself rather than Moses. Peter is
brought around on the point when the "clean/unclean" distinction is dramatically dissolved for him in a dream. It was Jeremiah who said that the new covenant
"will not be like the covenant" at Sinai (Jer. 31:31–32). Thus, the contrast
between the Sinai covenant of law and the Abrahamic/new covenant of promise
is drawn not merely by the Protestant Reformers, nor even merely by Paul, but
also by the Hebrew prophets and Jesus. By justifying the wicked by faith apart
from works of the law, God will be able finally to realize the promise made to
Abraham and heralded by the prophets (Isa. 9; 49; 60; 66; Jer. 4:2; Ezek. 39),
that in him and his Seed all the nations of the earth will be blessed.

Instead of forcing a choice between the gospel as a message of how we are saved
(soteriology) versus a message of inclusion of the Gentiles (ecclesiology), this perspective reminds us that the redefinition of Israel and its boundaries is itself
dependent on the justification of the ungodly by faith alone apart from works.
In the following chapters, I will be referring to Jesus' ministry in an effort to show
that for all of the differences in emphasis and redemptive-historical context (nar-

71. Hillers, *Covenant*, 179.
72. Ibid., 182.

rating the unfolding of the kingdom in Jesus' ministry more than interpretation
of its significance), Jesus and Paul—or for that matter, the Gospels and Epistles,
are telling this same tale of two covenants.

If Paul is not the founder of Christianity, he does nevertheless elucidate the
contrast between Sinai and Zion, law and gospel, that Jesus' ministry and exaltation provoked. In 2 Corinthians 3, we find what seems to be a gloss on Jeremiah 31, contrasting the old covenant (Sinai) written on tables of stone, which
kills and condemns, and the new covenant written on human hearts by the Spirit,
which gives life and justification. The former is fading—a veiled glory, such as
Moses exhibited—while the latter is a direct sight of God's glory in the face of
Christ. After comparing the Abrahamic promise to a last will and testament in
Galatians, Paul says,

> Now the promises were made to Abraham and to his seed; it does not say,
> "And to seeds," as of many; but it says, "And to your seed," that is, to one
> person, who is Christ. My point is this: the law, which came four hundred
> thirty years later, does not annul a covenant previously ratified by God, so
> as to nullify the promise. For if the inheritance comes from the law, it no
> longer comes from the promise; but God granted it to Abraham through
> the promise. (Gal. 3:16–18 NRSV mg.).

Thus, for Paul there are two ways of inheriting the divine estate: law and promise.
Each excludes or nullifies the other when the question arises as to how one obtains
the eternal inheritance of the heavenly Jerusalem. "Now this is an allegory: these
women are two covenants," of "law" and "promise" respectively, standing for "the
present Jerusalem, . . . in slavery with her children," and "the Jerusalem above;
she is free, and she is our mother" (4:21–27).

Consequently, that which stands in the way of the unification of all of God's
elect—Jew and Gentile, in one body, which is of such concern in Paul's mission—
is not simply the ceremonial laws defining ethnic boundaries, but the law-
covenant as such. It is not that the moral laws of the Old Testament are to be set
aside, but that with respect to *the method for obtaining the inheritance,* law is to
be strictly opposed to the principle of faith in the promise that God has done
everything already in Christ. In fact, that has always been so.

> Just as Abraham "believed God, and it was reckoned to him as righteous-
> ness," so, you see, those who believe are the descendants of Abraham. And
> the scripture, foreseeing that God would justify the Gentiles by faith,
> declared the gospel beforehand to Abraham, saying, "All the Gentiles shall
> be blessed in you." For this reason, those who believe are blessed with Abra-
> ham who believed. (3:6–9)

In the New Testament in addition to Paul and the writer to the Hebrews, Peter
exhibits this tendency to read the old covenant story and the new covenant story
as part of one story of promise and fulfillment, type and antitype, shadow and

reality, and not only in terms of the law-promise antithesis. In fact, it is the same Peter who at first accepted the Gentile mission only begrudgingly who now recognizes the wideness in God's mercy, hanging over his readers a welcome sign designating them as God's elect. Peter addressed the Jerusalem Council with these words:

> My brothers, you know that in the early days God made a choice among you, that I should be the one through whom the Gentiles would hear the message of the good news and become believers. And God, who knows the human heart, testified to them by giving them the Holy Spirit, just as he did to us; and in cleansing their hearts by faith he has made no distinction between them and us. Now therefore why are you putting God to the test by placing on the neck of the disciples a yoke that neither our ancestors nor we have been able to bear? On the contrary, we believe that we will be saved through the grace of the Lord Jesus, just as they will. (Acts 15:7–11)

It is converts among the Jewish Diaspora who are addressed by Peter as those "who have been chosen and destined by God the Father and sanctified by the Spirit to be obedient to Jesus Christ and to be sprinkled with his blood" (1 Pet. 1:2). The allusion to Moses' liturgical act of sprinkling the people with the blood of the Sinai covenant is obvious, although in this case it is the greater blood of a greater mediator and a greater covenant. Believers are sprinkled with his blood not to ratify their words, "All this we will do," but in order to ratify his words to the Father that we find in his prayer: "I have accomplished everything that you gave me to do. . . . And for their sakes I sanctify myself, so that they also may be sanctified in truth" (John 17:4, 19 NRSV alt.).

These believers, Peter goes on to relate, are "living stones" being "built into a spiritual house, to be a holy priesthood, to offer spiritual sacrifices acceptable to God through Jesus Christ."

> But you are a chosen race, a royal priesthood, a holy nation, God's own people, in order that you may proclaim the mighty acts of him who called you out of darkness into his marvelous light. Once you were not a people, but now you are God's people; once you had not received mercy, but now you have received mercy. (1 Pet. 2:5, 9–10)

Thus, it is in Christ and by his Spirit that the prophecy of a new covenant is fulfilled, a covenant that "will not be like the covenant that I made with their ancestors" at Sinai (Jer. 31:32).

Only through this covenant of promise and royal grant is it possible for Israel, now (like the Gentiles) "dead in trespasses and sins," to be raised again to life as a new people, not only resuscitated but also reborn as part of the new creation. Furthermore, it is only in such a "new and living way" that the promise of universal blessing given to Abraham be realized through his Seed. And it was the confession of the earliest church that this is precisely what had occurred in the life, death, resurrection, and ascension of Christ, who was in fact the mediator and the firstfruits of this long-expected world to come.

GOOD NEWS AND THE REIGN OF GOD

"Gospel," Wright complains, means "*ordo salutis*" for many today, "a description of how people get saved." He does not have a problem with those things being true. "I simply wouldn't use the word 'gospel' to denote those things," since it is, properly, "*the return of Israel from exile*" (emphasis original).[73]

In my view, Wright does have a point: for many (especially evangelicals, but also for those in other Christian traditions), "the gospel" refers to the morphology of conversion or how one becomes a Christian. I would agree with him that this is not the gospel, and so would the Protestant Reformers: nothing that happens within us is the gospel, but is rather the gospel's effect. The good news is a public announcement of the climax of the covenant, but *which* covenant? Furthermore, can the good news be restricted to "the return of Israel from exile"? Does this marginalize equally important elements in the prophets: forgiveness of sins, a new heart, eternal life, all of which were both issues of individual salvation and the fulfillment of God's promise to restore Israel?

According to Wright, the gospel, then, is the true story "about a human life, death and resurrection through which the living God becomes king of the world. . . . It is not, then, a system of how people get saved. The announcement of the gospel results in people being saved—Paul says as much a few verses later. But 'the gospel' itself, strictly speaking, is *the narrative proclamation of King Jesus*" (emphasis added).[74]

Yet this appears to be a terrific half-truth. If the gospel is not "how people get saved," it is certainly the news of how *God has saved* people. To be sure, the gospel is announced in Scripture within the context of a great drama, both cosmic and historical in scope, according to which the Creator reasserts his covenantal rights over his creation by "great deeds of righteousness" which evoke a "new song" from the redeemed creation (Ps. 98). If the gospel necessarily includes the announcement of the justification of the ungodly at its core, it also cannot be reduced to a personal transaction between God and the individual believer. The gospel is, properly speaking, the declaration of the historical events surrounding the life, death, and resurrection of Jesus Christ, not our own autobiography, much less personal psychology. The *extra nos* that is so much a part of the Reformation's emphasis challenges Wright's tendency to lump together Pietism with confessional Lutheran and Reformed theologies.

However, if the relevance of the announcement "Israel's exile is over!" is not obvious to Gentiles, then the declaration "God is King" is similarly, by itself, ambiguous in its force, for Jew and Gentile alike. Under the banner "Yahweh is King," the enemies of God were driven out of the land of Canaan, anticipating the last judgment that will sweep unfaithful Israelites as well as Gentiles into the stream of divine wrath a position tenaciously maintained, in fact, by restorationist

73. Wright, *What Saint Paul Really Said,* 36, 43.
74. Ibid., 45.

groups in the Second Temple era. "God is King!" also meant doom for Israel if the people failed to keep the covenant. In the prophets, too, we recognize the two-edged sword of this announcement of Yahweh's universal lordship in judgment: "Alas for you who desire the day of the LORD! Why do you want the day of the LORD?" Exile at the hands of the nations is nothing compared to Yahweh's judgment. "It is darkness, not light; as if someone fled from a lion, and was met by a bear; or went into the house and rested a hand against the wall, and was bitten by a snake. Is not the day of the LORD darkness, not light, and gloom with no brightness in it?" (Amos 5:18–20). The image of "King Jesus" in the Olivet Discourse or in the Apocalypse, for example, is far from unambiguously good news for those who cry for the rocks to fall on them.

Rather than *constituting* the gospel, the announcement that God is King is itself *qualified by* the gospel in order to be good news. Apart from the revelation of God's justification of the ungodly, the news of God's kingship may legitimately evoke fear or despair. It is significant that in the sermons that we find in Acts, the recurring focus is on Christ as the fulfillment of the promises for the forgiveness of sins and eternal life. These statements are more explicit in the early proclamation of the gospel than the announcement "God is King."

The sermons in Acts can be basically summarized as the announcement that, although Jesus was recently crucified outside the city gate in Jerusalem, he has been raised from the dead in fulfillment of the prophets. The only appropriate response is, "Repent, and be baptized every one of you in the name of Jesus Christ so that your sins may be forgiven; and you will receive the gift of the Holy Spirit" (Acts 2:14–38). "There is salvation in no one else" (4:12). "God exalted him [Jesus] at his right hand as Leader and Savior that he might give repentance to Israel and forgiveness of sins" (5:31). We meet the Ethiopian eunuch, reading about the Suffering Servant in Isaiah 53, which Philip explained as "the good news about Jesus" (8:32–35). "All the prophets testify about him that everyone who believes in him receives forgiveness of sins through his name," says Peter (10:43).

Like the other apostolic sermons, Paul recounts the history of Israel with Christ as its fulfillment, announcing, "Let it be known to you therefore, my brothers, that through this man forgiveness of sins is proclaimed to you; by this Jesus everyone who believes is set free from all those sins from which you could not be freed by the law of Moses" (13:38–39). These examples should suffice to make the point that the earliest Christian preaching centered chiefly on the announcement of the forgiveness of sins. It is this Jesus who absolves us from all guilt who is Lord of all: that is the good news of the kingdom. In the Epistles, the good news is that righteousness "will be reckoned [imputed] to us who believe in him who raised Jesus our Lord from the dead, who was handed over to death for our trespasses and was raised for our justification" (Rom. 4:24–25). The gospel proclaims Christ's resurrection from the dead "Jesus, who rescues us from the wrath that is coming" (1 Thess. 1:10).

The gospel is an announcement or proclamation, but according to Wright it is a proclamation essentially of law: "The proclamation is an authoritative summons to obedience—in Paul's case, to what he calls 'the obedience of faith.'"[75] Here Wright would seem to affirm a close connection between the gospel and individual salvation, but only to affirm that it is a call to fulfill conditions rather than to rest in conditions fulfilled.

As a corollary to his understanding of justification (*historia salutis*, not *ordo salutis*), Wright's doctrine of the atonement, reflecting the influence of Ernst Käsemann, J. Christiaan Beker, and others, is more in line with *Christus Victor* (cosmic conquest) than with forensic models. The cross chiefly represents Christ's victory over the powers.[76] He does speak of the announcement of that victory including the fact that "Jesus has offered God the obedience and faithfulness which should have characterized Israel but did not."[77] Yet there is no imputation of Christ's obedience and faithfulness to believers. In the place of imputation is Christ's representative conquest over the powers of evil. "According to [Gal.] 4:1–11, the message of the Pauline gospel is this: the true God has sent his Son, in fulfillment of the prophecies of scripture, to redeem his people from their bondage to false gods, the 'elements of the world' (4:3, 9)."[78]

First of all, given the comparatively greater number of references in Galatians to being redeemed from bondage to the law and its curse, these two references to "elements of the world" should (especially in the light of the argument in Rom. 1–3) be taken simply as a reference to the universal law of creation. Second, there is good exegetical reason to regard *stoicheia* as referring not to demonic spirits (false gods), but to basic rules and regulations of this age (cf. Col. 2:8, 20–23). In other words, they refer to the moral law inscribed on the conscience of every person, Jew and Gentile alike (Rom. 1–2).

Aside from that point, however, Wright takes what is important but somewhat secondary and not only makes it central but assimilates everything else into it. "My proposal has been that 'the gospel' is not, for Paul, a message about 'how one gets saved,' in an individual and ahistorical sense. It is a fourfold announcement about Jesus" that includes his victory over "the powers of evil, including sin and death"; the dawn of the new age in fulfillment of the prophets; Jesus as representative Messiah and therefore Lord over all.[79] There is no mention in Wright's definition of *individuals* being reconciled to God, forgiven, called, and renewed

75. Ibid. Paul's reference to "the obedience of faith" I take to be equivalent to embracing the gospel, not to faithfulness. In Gal. 5:7, Paul asks, "Who prevented you from obeying the truth?" which in the context refers to believing the gospel Paul had delivered. Likewise, in 2 Thess. 3:14, Paul warns the church, "Take note of those who do not obey what we say in this letter," although the entire epistle is doctrinal in nature. The only other Pauline passage in which the phrase appears is Rom. 1:5: "Through whom [Christ] we have received grace and apostleship to bring about the obedience of faith among all the Gentiles for the sake of his name." This is clearly not obedience in general, but the specific kind of obedience that paradoxically refuses to give place to our obedience, since Paul also regards faith itself as a gift of God (Eph. 2:8).

76. Ibid., 47.
77. Ibid., 54.
78. Ibid., 59.
79. Ibid., 60.

as part of a wider cosmic renewal. By contrast, I am defending a covenant theology that refuses to choose between these two horizons.

Precisely by electing, calling, justifying, sanctifying, and glorifying particular people, the triune God is drawing mere individuals in their subjectivity into a historical drama of cosmic proportions. As individuals are called, justified, and renewed, they become part of the new creation, not only a renewed Israel but also a redeemed humanity. This can also be stated in a converse fashion: The cosmic, eschatological, and redemptive-historical horizon of "these last days" (the *historia salutis*) is the source of the justification and of the blessings of union with Christ that characterize individual salvation (the *ordo salutis*).

What makes this announcement that God is King evangelical is the fact that *this* suzerain became the servant of the covenant, fulfilling the stipulations of the covenant, obedience to which he required as suzerain and we owed as servant. He carried out this vocation even to the point of bearing the curse for us on the cross, imputing his righteousness to us and thereby providing the forensic basis for the inward and outward renewal of all things. Only because *this one* was, by virtue of his resurrection, proclaimed Lord and King, does God's reign mean for us salvation from the "curse of the law," which includes redemption from the tyranny of sin, death, Satan, and evil powers. The opening question and answer of the Heidelberg Catechism, for example, confesses Christ as the one who "has fully paid for all my sins with his precious blood and has set me free from the tyranny of the devil."[80] All that is intended in the theme of Christus Victor ("God is King") is entailed by the good news of forgiveness and justification that gives it specificity. Even the disarming of the powers and their public humiliation are predicated on the fact that God "forgave us all our trespasses, erasing the record that stood against us with its legal demands. He set this aside, nailing it to the cross" (Col. 2:13–14). Renewal of the entire cosmos is rooted in atoning sacrifice, justification, and adoption that reach their climax in the "revealing of the children of God" (Rom. 8:19). Even salvation from the exile of death itself is merely the consequence of a more basic liberation, precisely because death is not a natural threat but a covenantal sanction. "The sting of death is sin, and the power of sin is the law. But thanks be to God, who gives us the victory through our Lord Jesus Christ" (1 Cor. 15:56).

---

80. The Heidelberg Catechism in *Ecumenical Creeds and Reformed Confessions* (Grand Rapids: CRC Publications, 1988), Lord's Day 1, Q. 1.

Chapter Three

Covenantal Nomism in Palestinian Judaism

Getting In and Staying In

Having proposed the main outline of the covenant theology that will be elaborated throughout this volume, I will begin a sustained conversation with the New Perspective(s) on Paul (hereafter NPP), which has also stressed the importance of the covenantal motif. Not without precedents, the NPP was nevertheless "officially" launched in the 1970s with the appearance of E. P. Sanders's *Paul and Palestinian Judaism* (1977). Sanders extended the complaint that Paul had been read through the lens of the Reformation: the Pharisees of Jesus' day were treated as if they were medieval cardinals, caps and all, proclaiming a rigid legalistic system of works-righteousness. As noted in the previous chapter, Sanders defines the religion of Second Temple (first-century) Judaism as "covenantal nomism" (from *nomos*, law), according to which one gets in by grace, but remains in by obedience.

As I mentioned in passing in the last chapter, I accept Sanders's slogan and, once the heavy typecasting is qualified, even his category of covenantal nomism seems like a good way of describing the sort of covenant theology that united the otherwise quite disparate Second Temple groups.[1] In fact, I will argue that it was

---

1. Some scholars have suggested that Sanders's method (finding "patterns of religion") imposes conclusions more than systematizing them. Early on, this criticism was lodged, for example, by

just such a religious pattern that provoked the clashes in the Jerusalem community and elsewhere (esp. the Galatian church). Covenantal nomism is also a generally appropriate way of describing the Sinai covenant, on the basis of which the national status of Israel in the land was established.

Problems arise, however, when the covenants of law and promise are synthesized under one type: *covenantal nomism*. In short, in this chapter I argue that Sanders's own detailed study of Second Temple sources, while helpfully challenging twentieth-century caricatures, nevertheless reinforces the parallels between a "covenantal nomism" characteristic of medieval Christian theology and that of early Judaism. Cautioning us against hasty generalizations of Judaism as a form of works-righteousness without grace, he is refuting a position that he himself identifies as that of nineteenth- and twentieth-century (mostly German) scholarship (esp. F. Weber, Schrenk, Thackeray, and Bultmann), although it is repeatedly asserted or assumed that these scholars represented the views of the Reformers.[2] The NPP proponents warn against reading the debates between Augustine and Pelagius or Rome and the Reformers into Second Temple Judaism, although these writers themselves often engage in anachronism with respect to the Reformation. If we can readily grant that the covenantal nomism of Paul's day was not "Pelagian," then it should also be recognized that Bultmann's neo-Kantian and existentialist recasting of Lutheran categories was not actually Lutheran, at least as that tradition has defined itself confessionally.

Furthermore, apart from polemical flourishes, the Reformers routinely recognized that in both Judaism and Rome there was the affirmation of grace and a provision for atonement and forgiveness. In fact, much of what Sanders says about Judaism, they would have recognized in their own context. The difference is that where Sanders, Judaism, and Rome thought that grace was necessary, the Reformers thought it was the sole sufficient basis of salvation. Does it really matter whether exegetes and theologians in the sixteenth century exaggerated this connection? It does to the extent that the NPP thesis depends on the argument that the Reformation read Paul as if he were Luther and Judaism as if it were Rome

---

Anthony J. Saldarini, in his review of *Paul and Palestinian Judaism* in *Journal of Biblical Literature* 98:2 (June 1979), 299–303.

> Sanders recognizes that rabbinic literature is not systematic, but he contends that a unified thrust and point of view underlie it (pp. 69–70, 180). Though individual sayings may contradict each other, when they are marshaled in order and their meaning is taken in context, a generally coherent viewpoint prevails. (See his treatment of sayings concerned with the weighing of good and evil on pp. 133–41). Though this method has been used often and Sanders uses it well, I am deeply uncertain of the results it produces." These sayings belong to scores of different genres, over centuries, with distinct histories representing different types of Judaism (302). His method hampers him as much in his attempt to get at what Paul meant (302).

2. E. P. Sanders, *Paul and Palestinian Judaism* (Minneapolis: Fortress, 1977), 6–7; cf. F. Weber, *System der altsynagogalen palästinischen Theologie aus Targum, Midrasch und Talmud*, ed. Franz Delitzsch and Georg Schnedermann (1880); revised as *Jüdische Theologie auf Grund des Talmud und verwandter Schriften* (Leipzig: Dörffling & Franke, 1897; repr., Hildesheim: Olms, 1975).

and therefore misread both. While there are other planks in the NPP platform to be evaluated in chapters 4 and 5, I will focus here on the foundational claim that Second Temple Judaism (covenantal nomism) was essentially a religion of grace.

WAS SECOND TEMPLE JUDAISM "LEGALISTIC"?

Following G. F. Moore and C. G. Montefiore, Sanders objects to the caricature of Judaism as works-righteousness chiefly on the basis that forgiveness and repentance were present all along in the Jewish understanding of covenant. The "nomism" is qualified by the adjective "covenantal," which Sanders systematically treats as equivalent to "gracious." This conflation of distinct covenant types into a single "pattern of religion" of gracious law is a fundamental presupposition of Sanders's thesis (and the NPP generally).

Despite their sharp dismissal of the charge of legalism, Sanders (following Montefiore) nevertheless allows that such a misunderstanding "appears to rest on solid evidence."

> The view that weighing fulfilments and transgressions constitutes Rabbinic (or Pharisaic or Jewish) soteriology can apparently be supported by actual texts concerning weighing. In support of the doctrine of the treasury of merits which can (or cannot) be transferred at the judgment, it is possible to cite passages containing the phrase *zekut 'abot*, "merit of the fathers."[3]

Explaining election, the rabbis, he says (with ample citations), "wished to explain that it was not 'odd of God to choose the Jews.'" On this question, the rabbis offered varying answers, but on Sanders's own analysis, it cannot be claimed that there was a general consensus that election was independent of human merit.[4] This would seem to call into question the position that Israel even "got in" by grace, according to the rabbinical interpretation. Sanders's theological presuppositions are reflected in his own defense of this strategy when he suggests that an unconditional election such as Paul seems to have taught would never be able to escape the charge of arbitrariness. Election must somehow be based on an analytic judgment concerning the deserts of those chosen.[5]

Regardless of whether "getting in" (election) was based on unconditional grace, all of the sources are agreed that the covenantal status is dependent on continuing obedience.[6] After providing numerous citations affirming the strict conditionality, Sanders qualifies the position: "The intention to obey is the condition of remaining in the covenant. . . . Thus the 'on condition that' passages are not

---

3. Ibid., 58.
4. Ibid., 88.
5. Ibid., 97–98.
6. As will become clearer as my argument unfolds, I can affirm that Israel's status is conditioned upon obedience in terms of the national covenant (Sinai), while distinguishing this covenant from the Abrahamic.

so narrowly legalistic as they might at first appear."[7] This however is a theological verdict, as much as the Reformation's interpretation. The Protestant Reformers did not charge medieval Rome with being "narrowly legalistic," but with including the merit of anyone other than Christ as the ground or anything other than faith as the instrument of justification. Medieval theology also qualified meritorious obedience with the category of "the *intention* to obey"—otherwise known as implicit faith (*fides implicita*). Medieval theology also recognized a "treasury of merit" that could be transferred from the saints to believers upon fulfillment of certain conditions (especially penance). Sanders devotes numerous pages to the *zekut 'abot* (merit of the fathers) and repentance (virtually indistinguishable from the medieval formulation of penance in principle) as means of atoning for transgressions.[8]

The attempt to exonerate Judaism from works-righteousness does not succeed, from a Reformation perspective, simply by showing that it is not Pelagian, since medieval theology was clearly not Pelagian either. The question, which is finally theological as well as historical, is whether one gets in and stays in by grace alone or by one's own obedience—even if the latter is assisted by grace. Nevertheless, says Sanders, "The Rabbis did not have the Pauline/Lutheran problem of 'works-righteousness,' and so felt no embarrassment at saying that the exodus was earned; yet that it was earned is certainly not a Rabbinical doctrine. It is only an explanatory device."[9] Regardless of whether rabbinic tradition would have endorsed such a distinction between a doctrine and an explanatory device, the point, affirmed even by Sanders, is that the tradition did teach that the exodus was in some sense earned.

Again Sanders's own theological assumptions are as apparent as those he critiques when he argues,

> The Rabbis could not, *because of the biblical evidence that God rewards fulfilment of commandments*, give up the idea of reward for merit; nor could they accept the *capriciousness* on God's part that the doctrine of election *apart from just cause* seems to imply. . . . In attempting to give a rationale for the election, the Rabbis appealed to the free grace of God and sometimes to the concept of merit. [emphasis added][10]

Therefore, despite the fact that he was trained by Gamaliel II, Paul misunderstood both the Hebrew Bible and Second Temple Judaism, and therefore his view of election "apart from just cause" Sanders judges (again, as a theological verdict) to be arbitrary and capricious. Merit of some sort *must* be the only way of justifying God's election and exodus-liberation of Israel (in spite of such passages as Deut. 7:7–8). Does this not reflect a tendency similar to that of Sanders's neme-

---

7. Sanders, *Paul and Palestinian Judaism*, 94.
8. Ibid., esp. 97–176.
9. Ibid., 100. The basis for Sanders's distinction between a "doctrine" and an "explanatory device" is not immediately apparent.
10. Ibid., 101, 106.

ses when he complained that recent "Lutheran" interpretation "permits, as [Jacob] Neusner has said, the writing of theology as if it were history"?[11]

Sanders accepts at face value the rabbinical consensus that reward and punishment operate on a principle of merit in some sense.[12] In fact, "the theory operative in such passages is that of 'measure for measure.'"[13] Once more we see that Sanders's exegesis is as theologically motivated as any other: "It was the biblical view, and one that remained influential in Judaism, that God's justice is meted out within this life."[14] Furthermore, this judgment of rewards and punishment was conceived along the lines of a "weighing of merits"—in other words, as to whether good deeds outweighed transgressions.[15] However, this does not constitute "works-righteousness," because the judgment is mixed with grace. "It is gratifying to be able to quote Finkelstein in support of this view: 'Sometimes [Akiba] asserted God's mercy to be such that a single meritorious act will win a man admission to the future world.'"[16] Thus, "mercy" is equivalent to lowering the bar of justice and is not a free gift granted to those who deserve the very opposite.

One might reasonably ask how election and justification could depend on the "weighing of merits," conditioned upon one's personal obedience to the law's demands, without concluding that salvation is earned. Sanders assumes that grace is sufficiently affirmed when, because of God's mercy, one's repentance or at least one's intention to obey is sometimes allowed to weigh more heavily than it otherwise might on its own terms. Mercy and merit are held in balance, he says.

> But if there is a "doctrine" of salvation in Rabbinic religion, it is election and repentance. Sayings about fulfilling one law and being given a share in the world to come are balanced by sayings indicating that damnation is the consequence of one's transgressions. The truth is that these three groups of sayings—damnation for one transgression, salvation for one fulfilment and judgment according to the majority of deeds—have a common ground and purpose. . . . Each type of saying is an effective way of urging people to obey the commandments as best they can and of insisting upon the importance of doing so.[17]

The position that Sanders has thus far described is remarkably similar to the position of the late medieval nominalism in which Luther was schooled and

---

11. Ibid., 57.

12. Ibid., 116–18; see esp. the citations on 118.

13. Ibid., 119.

14. Ibid., 125. This is not the place to explore the preexilic understanding of the "afterlife" or the nature of the "age to come" in Second Temple literature. However, Sanders's assumption is a matter of debate. For example, see Jon Levenson's recent work *Resurrection and the Restoration of Israel: The Ultimate Victory of the God of Life* (New Haven, CT: Yale University Press, 2006).

15. Ibid., 130, 132.

16. Ibid., 138–39. Once more, references such as Akiba's to winning "admission to the future world" would seem at least to qualify Sanders's (as well as Dunn's and Wright's) dismissal of individual salvation (How can I be saved?) in Judaism.

17. Ibid.

which he strenuously rejected, with its slogan *facientibus quod in se est Deus non denigat gratiam* (God will not deny his grace to those who do what lies within them). According to this theology, no one deserves salvation in any strict sense, but God has decreed a covenant according to which those who do their best (assisted by grace) will attain final justification as if they had merited it. God will accept their imperfect righteousness as meritorious in a *congruent* (satisfactory) rather than *condign* (strict) sense.[18] It was against just such covenantal nomism that Luther thundered in Thesis 16 of his Heidelberg Disputation: "The person who believes that he can obtain grace by doing what is in him adds sin to sin so that he becomes doubly guilty," adding the insult of both God's majestic holiness and grace to the injury of one's own failure to recognize such attempts to satisfy God's law as sinful self-justification.[19]

Indeed, "getting in by grace and staying in by obedience" admirably summarizes the covenantal nomism of the medieval system as it evolved especially in nominalism and become officially sanctioned at Trent. Baptism, the first justification, was by grace alone (an infusion of grace that wiped away original sin and filled the passive recipient with a transformed *habitus*), followed by various sacramental resources for cooperating grace, which (hopefully) would lead to final justification in the life to come.[20] In addition to a view of election that parallels Semi-Pelagianism, along with the concepts of a "treasury of merit" (*zekut 'abot*), penance (repentance) atoning for transgression, and the "weighing of merits," according to some of Sanders's sources at least, there is something rather close to the medieval concept of purgatory.[21] Paul F. M. Zahl's comment is exactly right: "E. P. Sanders mistakes the 'semi-Pelagianism' of Second Temple Judaism for 'Pelagianism' and thus misunderstands Luther's critique of the Roman Catholic Church as well as Luther's grasp of Paul."[22]

The *good* news, according to Sanders and his sources, is that "no matter how numerous a man's transgressions, God has provided for their forgiveness, as long as he indicates his intention to remain in the covenant by repenting and doing other appropriate acts of atonement."[23] Regardless of one's own theological verdict, this was the position that the Reformers recognized in the late medieval theology that they rejected. Repentance is defined in terms similar to the traditional Roman Catholic doctrine of penance as well: "But both repentance and the Day of Atonement together atone for one half. And chastisements atone for half. . . . However, if one has profaned the name of God and repents, his repentance cannot make the case pending, neither can the Day of Atonement effect atonement,

18. Anyone familiar with the notion of congruent merit in late medieval theology will recognize striking similarities with Sanders's quotes on ibid., 176.

19. See Gerhard O. Forde, *On Being a Theologian of the Cross: Reflections on Luther's Heidelberg Disputation, 1518* (Grand Rapids: Eerdmans, 1997), 59.

20. For a contemporary statement of this position, see *Catechism of the Catholic Church* (Libreria Editrice Vaticana; distributed by Liguori, MO: Liguori Publications, 1994), 363–73, 481–89.

21. Sanders, *Paul and Palestinian Judaism*, 142.

22. Paul F. M. Zahl, "Mistakes of the New Perspective on Paul," *Themelios* 27, no. 1 (2001): 7.

23. Ibid., 157.

nor can sufferings cleanse him of guilt."[24] "The Rabbinic theory is that a sacrifice commanded in the law can be 'fulfilled' by substituting something else commanded in the law."[25] Such calculative speculation is also replete in medieval (especially later medieval) scholasticism. "'What is appropriate'" in such repentance "may include the bringing of a sacrifice, making restitution and other obvious acts of contrition."[26] Yet this is precisely the system, in broad lines at least, that Rome had in place for dealing with sins. Repentance, says Sanders, "is a 'status-maintaining' or 'status-restoring' attitude which indicates that one intends to remain in the covenant. . . . Without it, the mercy of God is of no avail."[27] In perhaps a slip of the pen, Sanders adds, "Their *legalism* falls within a larger context of gracious election and assured salvation" (emphasis added).[28] Whatever "gracious" and "assured" mean in this context, they are qualified by the "legalism."

While no doubt important differences do exist, the logic is precisely that of medieval Rome, when Sanders summarizes:

> If God is just and if man sins, it is not possible that no payment will be exacted for transgression. Sacrifices may atone, or even a ransom paid in money, but suffering is more effective and atones for more serious sins, because it is costlier. Thus the righteous are punished on earth for their sins in order to enjoy uninterrupted bliss hereafter.[29]

"A similar view," says Sanders, "is represented by R. Meir: if two men suffer from the same disease and only one survives, it is because he repented."[30]

Sanders can only see the specter of Luther (and Paul!) hanging over criticism of such views.

> To the mind sensitized to the question by centuries of Lutheranism, even repentance may appear as a legalistic performance to earn God's mercy. The Rabbis can in fact state the matter in such a way as to make man's initiative in repenting the absolute condition of God's mercy. That is, it will sometimes appear in an individual passage as if the imperative "repent" precedes the indicative "and God will be merciful." . . . In a sense, this impression is true. Repentance was considered to be the condition on the basis of which God forgives. . . . What is wrong with the view that repentance in Rabbinic religion is a work which earns "mercy" is that it leaves out of account the fundamental basis of that religion, namely, God's election of Israel. . . . This view, it is clear, is based on an understanding of the grace of God.[31]

However, Sanders himself has demonstrated that at least a lot of his rabbinical sources thought that election was based on merits of some sort. Further, whenever

24. Ibid., 158–59.
25. Ibid., 164.
26. Ibid., 177.
27. Ibid., 178.
28. Ibid., 181.
29. Ibid., 170.
30. Ibid., 176.
31. Ibid., 177.

he meets (and quotes) statements that reinforce this idea, he appeals to election (which he has already shown to be based on merits of some kind), sacrifices, and repentance (which are really human attempts to "make up" for transgressions).

In summation, Sanders affirms a point he has been attempting in other ways to refute: "That the Rabbis believed obedience to be meritorious and to be rewarded by God is not in question." And, he says, the term is not unjustly translated as "merit" (*zekut*: prepositional [*bizekut*] = "on account of"; substantive [*zikut*] = merit).[32] Although Sanders himself is ambiguous about whether this translation is adequate, he offers an entire page of quotes referring to merit as a legitimate belief in Palestinian Judaism.[33]

Consistent with the account in my previous chapter, Sanders notes that, according to the midrash, God gave some things to Israel conditionally (such as the land and temple) and others unconditionally (such as Torah). Some rabbinic sources, however, insist that land, temple, and kingdom were unconditionally granted to Israel and could not be lost through disobedience.[34]

I argue that in one crucial sense, both views have some biblical warrant. At the typological level, Israel's role as witness to the coming messianic kingdom could be lost (hence, the exile), although the greater reality to which these shadows pointed was in fact fulfilled in history with Jesus Christ. The Sinai covenant provides the basis for the one, while the Abrahamic covenant is the basis for the other. "After the exile, however, these prophetic elements receded from Israel's religion," noted Herman Bavinck a century ago, "a process that steered it in a one-sided, nomistic direction."[35] We can find similar explanations in Jewish sources as well, as for instance in Michael Wyschogrod's analysis. In the Second Temple period, it was thought that repentance more than makes up for sins. "The repentant sinner thus emerges with a large accumulation of merit, especially if his sins were particularly weighty and numerous. . . . With the destruction of the Temple, sacrifice was no longer possible, and the emphasis therefore shifted to repentance."[36]

PAUL AND COVENANTAL NOMISM

Where does all of this leave us with respect to Paul, then? "Paul's 'pattern of religion,'" Sanders judges, "cannot be described as 'covenantal nomism,' and therefore Paul presents an essentially different type of religiousness from any found in Palestinian Jewish literature." However, the fissure is not where we ordinarily think that it is (as grace versus works).[37]

32. Ibid., 183.
33. Ibid., 185, 189.
34. Ibid., 94–95.
35. Herman Bavinck, *Reformed Dogmatics,* ed. John Bolt, trans. John Vriend, vol. 3 (Grand Rapids: Baker Academic, 2006), 495.
36. Michael Wyschogrod, *Abraham's Promise: Judaism and Jewish-Christian Relations,* ed. R. Kendall Soulen (Grand Rapids: Eerdmans, 2004), 70.
37. Sanders, *Paul and Palestinian Judaism,* 543.

Here, however, there is also a major shift; for to be righteous in Jewish literature means to obey the Torah and to repent of transgression, but in Paul it means to be saved by Christ. Most succinctly, righteousness in Judaism is a term which implies the maintenance of status among the group of the elect; in Paul it is a transfer term. In Judaism, that is, commitment to the covenant puts one "in," while obedience (righteousness) subsequently keeps one in. In Paul's usage, "be made righteous" ("be justified") is a term indicating getting in, not staying in the body of the saved. Thus when Paul says that one cannot be made righteous by works of the law, he means that one cannot, by works of law, "transfer to the body of the saved."[38]

Therefore, the misunderstanding of Judaism is finally due not to the Reformers but to Paul's shift from ecclesiology to soteriology, we might say.

When Judaism said that one is righteous who obeys the law, the meaning is that one thereby stays in the covenant. The debate about righteousness by faith or by works of law thus turns out to result from the different usage of the "righteous" word-group. The difference in usage can be seen in part by noting the agreement on the point that correct behaviour is the condition of staying "in." In most of Judaism the principal term for one who behaves correctly is "righteous" . . . , while Paul never uses the term to refer to continuing correct behaviour. He refers rather to remaining "blameless," "innocent," "steadfast," "sound," "guiltless," and the like . . . , but never to being righteous, when speaking of the correct behaviour that keeps one "in."[39]

Paul's radically different understanding of works and faith, law and promise, are exhibited in his treatment of justification, Sanders points out. Though in the Hebrew literature God is said to "declare righteous" (*yiṣdaq*), it is never said that he can declare the *wicked* righteous—in fact, quite the opposite. However, not only does Paul claim that God justifies the wicked; he typically focuses on the verb *dikaioō*, to justify (and its passive forms), while the Hebrew Scriptures typically speak of "righteousness" as an adjective describing those who are actually, inherently righteous (the righteous, *ṣaddîqîm*).[40] "One is 'justified' from transgressions or from sin (I Cor. 6.9–11; Rom. 6.7); that is, one *transfers* from not being saved to being saved. This forces the righteousness terminology out of its customary meaning, and the shift helps show the distinctiveness of Paul's thought."[41]

38. Ibid., 544. This point represents a significant difference of interpretation among NPP scholars. As we will see, N. T. Wright does not think that justification is a transfer term that answers the question as to how one gets in, but rather a definitional term that identifies *who* is "in."
39. Ibid.
40. Once again, according to federal theology, including its interpretation both of the Old Testament and of Paul, there is no discrepancy between these two sources. It is true that God cannot acquit and accept the wicked at the expense of justice. However, in Paul's teaching the law is fulfilled representatively and its fulfillment is imputed, so that God's judgment of Christ is his judgment of all who trust in him.
41. Sanders, *Paul and Palestinian Judaism*, 544–45. However, the only places where it is said that the guilty cannot be justified is in the context of human judgments (Exod. 23:7; Deut. 25:1; Prov. 17:15; 24:24; Isa. 5:23), and specifically in reference to the covenant code of Sinai or as an elaboration of it. Abraham was certainly both guilty and justified through faith (Gen. 15:6). David confessed

Further, says Sanders, there is no real equivalent concern for repentance in Paul that is evident in Jewish literature, especially Qumran. "Repentance is not part of his scheme, not because he is pessimistic [as in *4 Ezra*], but because he has a different scheme."[42] According to Pauline teaching, then, repentance cannot usher in the new age. The new covenant cannot be a renewal of the old covenant; rather, one must be transferred out of "this age" (which includes the law-covenant and the old covenant worship) into "the age to come" (that is, into Christ under the dominion of the Spirit). For Paul, it is pure transfer: from the power of sin to the lordship of Christ.[43]

In agreement with this point, I would only add that this is also the teaching of the New Testament more generally (viz., Matt. 3:11–12 and parallels; John 3:3; throughout Hebrews; 1 Pet. 2:9; etc.), which itself rests on the Old Testament witness to the new covenant. Addressing the synagogue in Antioch, Paul proclaimed, "Let it be known to you therefore, my brothers, that through this man [Jesus] forgiveness of sins is proclaimed to you; by this Jesus everyone who believes is set free *from all those sins from which you could not be freed by the law of Moses*" (Acts 13:38–39).

Paul and Judaism differ on the nature of sin and therefore also on the nature of death, Sanders recognizes. "The Rabbinic statements have to do with death as *atoning for transgression*, not death to a *power* so that one may live to another power" (emphasis original).[44]

> It perhaps goes without saying that the formulation of being among the saved is different. There is, to be sure, an important similarity: *both Judaism and Paul take full account of the individual and the group*. In Judaism God's covenant is with Israel, but this in no way removes the individual's personal relation with God. He must be pious before God, remain right with God, and thus retain his membership in the group of the saved. In Paul one comes to be among the saved by the act of faith which results in participating *in Christ*. (emphasis original)[45]

Notice here that Sanders, more than Dunn and Wright (as my next chapter explores), does not demand a false choice between the group and the individual. Furthermore, his claim that in Judaism the individual's continuing relationship with God is conditioned on one's own piety and obedience—in contrast to Paul's

---

his guilt and was forgiven ("For your name's sake, O LORD, pardon my guilt, for it is great," Ps. 25:11; cf. Ps. 51). Even the Sinai covenant, as Sanders insists, provided for forgiveness (although, I would add, only provisionally as an act of faith in the reality to which the sacrifices pointed). Paul is no less concerned than the Pentateuch to uphold God's justice. Whatever the radical differences with Second Temple Judaism (and his agitators), Paul was affirming the law in his doctrine of justification. Unlike simply acquitting a criminal (as the passages above reprove), justification forgives guilt and imputes the covenantal obedience of Christ, so that God is "just and justifier" of everyone who believes (Rom. 3:26 KJV).

42. Ibid., 546.
43. Ibid., 547.
44. Ibid.
45. Ibid.

emphasis on "the act of faith which results in participating *in Christ*," is more accurate in my view than the attempts of Dunn and Wright (engaged in the next chapter) to bring Paul into closer proximity to Second Temple sources.

There is no parallel in Judaism for the participation language "in Christ," much less, "Christ in you" ("Israel in you"?), Sanders observes. "Here the nature of the group identity is different. The body of Christ is not analogous to Israel, and being in Christ is not formally the same as being in the covenant between God and Israel."[46] Yet this verdict of discontinuity rests on Sanders's failure to distinguish the Abrahamic and Sinaitic covenants. Paul does in fact believe that the new covenant people of God are Israel, because Christ is the true Israel in whom all of God's promises are fulfilled. Nevertheless, when the issue is the relation between covenantal nomism (Sinai) and the new covenant, I agree with Sanders's contrast: "Conversion" equals repentance and a return to the law for Qumran, but participation in the body of Christ for Paul.[47] Remarkably, at least on these points Sanders's interpretation of Paul parallels classic Reformation theology: "Thus in all these essential points—the meaning of 'righteousness,' the role of repentance, the nature of sin, the nature of the saved 'group' and, most important, the necessity of transferring from the damned to the saved—Paul's thought can be sharply distinguished from anything to be found in Palestinian Judaism. . . . Despite agreements, there is a fundamental difference."[48]

Therefore, as we suspected above, Sanders is motivated by his own theological discomfort with Paul's soteriology (especially election), since ". . . the basis for Paul's polemic against the law, and consequently against doing the law, was his exclusivist soteriology."

> Since salvation is only by Christ, the following of *any* other path is wrong. . . . What is wrong with it is not that it implies petty obedience and minimization of important matters, nor that it results in the tabulation of merit points before God, but *that it is not worth anything in comparison with being in Christ*. . . . Doing the law, in short, is wrong only because it is not faith. . . . What is wrong with Judaism is not that Jews seek to save themselves and become self-righteous about it, but that their seeking is not directed toward the right goal.[49]

Paul does not simply tinker with the Jewish system, although his own alternative system is unthinkable without it:

> The law is good, even *doing* the law is good, but salvation is only by Christ; therefore the entire system represented by the law is worthless for salvation. *It is the change of "entire systems" which makes it unnecessary for him to speak about repentance or the grace of God shown in the giving of the covenant.* These

---

46. Ibid.
47. Ibid., 548.
48. Ibid.
49. Ibid., 550.

fade into the background because of the surpassing glory of the new dispensation (II Cor. 3.9ff). (emphasis in original)[50]

Although his analysis enriches our understanding of Judaism and Paul, challenging certain stereotypes, his own theological assumptions and conclusions seem to lead Sanders to think that Paul was fighting a straw opponent. More fundamentally, it leads him to reject Paul's formulation of the gospel, although in my view, with respect to the contrasting paradigms, he understands Paul better than many in the NPP circle:

> Paul himself often formulated his critique of Judaism (or Judaizing) as having to do with the *means* of attaining righteousness, "by faith and not by works of the law," and this formulation has been held to be accurate: Paul agreed on the *goal*, righteousness, but saw that it should be received by grace through faith, not achieved by works. But this formulation, though it is Paul's own, actually misstates the fundamental point of disagreement. Just as what is wrong with the law is that it is not Christ, so what is wrong with the "righteousness based on the law" (Phil. 3.9) is that it is not *the* righteousness from God which depends on faith, which is received when one is "found in Christ," shares his suffering and is placed among those who will share in his resurrection.

It is not simply that Paul thinks that the righteousness Judaism pursues can only be attained in Christ, but that Christ himself *is* that righteousness.

> That is, "righteousness" itself is a different righteousness. . . . Thus Paul does not differ only on the means. Means and end correspond. The *real* righteousness is being saved by Christ, and it comes only through faith. This implies, again, that it is not the activity of doing the law which is wrong as an activity. Rather, such a means leads to the wrong end (righteousness based on the law); and the end itself is wrong, since it is not salvation in Christ. . . . *Paul in fact explicitly denies that the Jewish covenant can be effective for salvation, thus consciously denying the basis of Judaism.* Circumcision without complete obedience is worthless or worse (Rom. 2.25–3.3; Gal. 3.10). More important, *the covenantal promises to Abraham do not apply to his descendants, but to Christians* (Rom. 4.13–25; Gal. 3.15–29). (emphasis in original)[51]

So Paul's message represents a basic critique of the fundamentals of Judaism: "election, the covenant and the law; and it is because these are wrong that the means appropriate to 'righteousness according to the law' (Torah observance and repentance) are held to be wrong or are not mentioned." Sanders famously concludes, "In short, *this is what Paul finds wrong with Judaism: it is not Christianity.*"[52]

As a result, Paul replaces "covenantal nomism" with a "participationist eschatology," although Sanders judges that "there seems to be no reason for thinking

50. Ibid., 551–52.
51. Ibid., 551.
52. Ibid., 552.

one is superior to another." At the end of the day, the dispute does not really matter. In a sweeping generalization of the whole history of Christian interpretation, Sanders concludes:

> Paul's view could hardly be maintained, and it was not maintained. Christianity rapidly became a new covenantal nomism, but Paulinism is not thereby proved inferior or superior. In saying that participationist eschatology is different from covenantal nomism, I mean only to say that it is different, not that the difference is instructive for seeing the error of Judaism's way.[53]

While acknowledging differences in how Judaism and medieval Rome practiced this, the polemics of the NPP in its various permutations appears to have reconciled Judaism and Christianity on this point only by surrendering the latter to synergism.

There is no "view from nowhere," even for biblical scholars, and the vista from which the NPP assays the horizon of Paul and Palestinian Judaism is well defined as covenantal nomism. It is a synergistic perspective that, for all of the important differences, unites Judaism, the medieval theology codified at Trent, and includes myriad Protestant attempts in the modern era all the way to the present moment.

ONE COVENANT OR TWO?

Comparisons between early Judaism and medieval Rome break down, of course, the deeper one goes into the rationale. Surely no one thinks that the rabbis taught an elaborate theory of infused habits, for example. However, the logic that gives rise to a covenantal nomism in both cases seems remarkably similar. Regardless of what this should be called, it is a type of religion that is conditional and synergistic rather than unconditional and a unilateral gift of grace. Finally, the choice between these two will come down, one hopes at least, to basic theological convictions about what the Scriptures teach. Normative theological assumptions about election, grace, justification, merit, and repentance are at work in all of the Pauline research programs, from the Reformation to the present.

While Sanders provides a useful description of Second Temple Judaism as covenantal nomism, the further question is whether the Hebrew Bible itself justifies the reduction of covenant theology to a single "pattern of religion." If the narrative I offered in the last chapter is accurate, we can account for the obvious elements of grace and forgiveness in the Old Testament (as old covenant expressions of the covenant of grace) and the equally obvious elements of command and conditional acceptance (as expressions of the covenant of law).

Reading the Old Testament canonically (in the light of the New Testament interpretation), we can affirm that both the Abrahamic covenant of grace and the law-covenant of Sinai point forward to Christ. His person and work are unconditionally

53. Ibid.

promised in the one, while the latter was a temporary, conditional, and typological covenant that was intended to become obsolete with his advent. As the seed
of Abraham, Christ fulfills the promise in his unique person; as the second Adam
and true Israel, he fulfills the law on our behalf.

In this way, we neither *deny* one or the other nor *assimilate* one to the other
but acknowledge them as *two different covenants* running parallel to each other
through the Scriptures. Accordingly, God's patience in the midst of Israel's violation of the Sinai pact and his promises for a future restoration are founded on
his unconditional oath to Abraham, Isaac, and Jacob. Sanders notes that the rabbis thought differently, relying on the merit of the patriarchs, as well as one's own
obedience, for suspending God's judgment.[54] Yet Sanders repeats what seems to
me to be an artificial distinction deriving from his theological presuppositions:
"Being righteous in the sense of obeying the law to the best of one's ability and
repenting and atoning for transgression *preserves* one's place in the covenant (it is
the opposite of rebelling), but it does not *earn* it."[55] Such distinctions have been
offered throughout the history of Roman Catholic–Protestant dialogue; the question is whether, even after all caricatures are deconstructed, they are sufficient to
vindicate synergism in any form on the basis of biblical exegesis.[56] Whether one's
own inherent righteousness (covenant faithfulness) *preserves* one's status before
God or *earns* it matters very little for the person asking, "How can I be saved?"
And we have seen that even with respect to "getting in," Sanders's own sources
are at least ambiguous.

To embrace covenantal nomism as an appropriate system for the national
covenant of Israel is, I have argued, properly to interpret the old covenant history. However, to embrace it as an appropriate system for answering the question
as to how an individual is rightly related to God remains, as it has always been,
a confusion of Abraham with Moses, which Paul relates as a confusion of Sarah
with Hagar, freedom with bondage, Sinai with Zion, and law with gospel. To put
it differently, it is appropriate to treat the earthly promises (land, temple, kingdom) as conditioned upon the covenant people's personal obedience to the law,
but fatal in Paul's view to treat the heavenly promises (the new creation, Christ,
and his everlasting Davidic reign) as conditioned on the obedience of anyone
other than Christ himself.

---

54. Cited ibid., 196. One source, commenting on Lev. 26:42 (where the order is Jacob, Isaac,
Abraham), glosses, "Why are the fathers named in reverse order? Because if the deeds (Heb. Singular, *ma'aseh*) of Abraham are not sufficient, the deeds of Isaac are [are]; and if the deeds of Isaac are not
sufficient, the deeds of Jacob [are]. [The deeds of] any one of them are sufficient that [God] will suspend [punishment] for the world on his account (*begino*)."

55. Ibid., 205.

56. Sanders's tendency to "waffle" on the question of legalism is apparent once more in the following statement concerning *4 Ezra*: "[O]ne sees how Judaism works when it actually does become
a religion of individual-self-righteousness. In IV Ezra, in short, we see an instance in which covenantal nomism has collapsed. All that is left is legalistic perfectionism" (409). Repeatedly, Sanders's thesis (no legalism!) is more sweeping than his own evidence seems to allow (not *merely* legalism). In any
case "legalism" is a pejorative term that is always a theological charge. Therefore, its stability for referring to the views of others in simply descriptive rather than normative terms is questionable.

In Hillers's words, the conflation of distinct covenants into a single type "is not the case of six blind men and the elephant, but of a group of learned paleontologists creating different monsters from the fossils of six separate species."[57] It is certainly wrong to characterize Judaism as mere legalism, much less the Old Testament as a religion of works-righteousness, but it is just as wrong from a Christian perspective to characterize synergism (covenantal nomism) as a legitimate description of the covenant of grace when it is as obvious from the Hebrew narratives as it is from their New Testament interpretation that the Abrahamic inheritance comes by grace apart from works, by promise apart from law.

Far different from such covenantal nomism is the expectation that comes from the new covenant, in fulfillment of the royal promises of the Abrahamic and Davidic covenants:

> But you have not come to a mountain that can be touched, a blazing fire, and darkness, and gloom, and a tempest, and the sound of a trumpet, and a voice whose words made the hearers beg that not another word be spoken to them. (For they could not endure the order that was given, "If even an animal touches the mountain, it shall be stoned to death." Indeed, so terrifying was the sight that Moses said, "I tremble with fear.") But you have come to Mount Zion and to the city of the living God, the heavenly Jerusalem, and to innumerable angels in festal gathering, and to the assembly of the firstborn who are enrolled in heaven, and to God the judge of all, and to the spirits of the righteous made perfect, and to Jesus, the mediator of a new covenant, and to the sprinkled blood that speaks a better word than the blood of Abel. (Heb. 12:18–24)

And because of this, the nations stream not to Sinai or the earthly Jerusalem but to the Zion coming down from heaven. They come from Jerusalem, Judea, Samaria, and the uttermost parts of the earth for their dramatic role in the new creation, in the great and unceasing parade of the vassals, now adopted children, before their Suzerain-Father in the everlasting Sabbath day.

SUMMARIZING THUS FAR

While the medieval system is surely not simply a repristination of Second Temple Judaism, both exhibit something like the covenantal nomism that Sanders describes. *No matter how covenantal nomism is adjusted to make allowances for failures, it is the nomistic principle of justification that provoked the sharp polemics not only of the Reformers, but Paul as well.*

The Reformers challenged this entire nomistic paradigm by insisting that one gets in and stays in by grace *alone*. Election, justification, and all of the blessings ordinarily considered under the locus of soteriology are found "in Christ," not

57. Delbert R. Hillers, *Covenant: The History of a Biblical Idea* (Baltimore: Johns Hopkins University Press, 1969), 7.

in believers themselves, in the community (whether the nation of Israel or the church), or in the law. Paul's contrast between "the righteousness that is by the law" and "the righteousness that is by faith" (Rom. 10:5–6 NIV; passim) is that of the Reformers as well. Thus they felt warranted in saying of their critics what Paul had said of his "kindred according to the flesh" (9:3): "being ignorant of the righteousness that comes from God, and seeking to establish their own, they have not submitted to God's righteousness. For Christ is the end of the law so that there may be righteousness for everyone who believes" (10:3–4).

Although the Reformers' responses to the exegesis of their critics reveal that they too were acquainted with the argument that "works of the law" refers merely to the ceremonial and dietary laws, according to the Reformers' reading of Paul and the rest of the New Testament, it was the *principle* of law that was, in the matter of justification, the antithesis of the principle of grace and faith; *doing* the law contrasted with "*believing* what you *heard*" (Gal. 3:2; Rom. 10:17). Of course, making that argument from Paul requires greater elaboration, so we turn to this crucial topic next.

Chapter Four

Paul's Polemic against the "Works of the Law"

Beyond False Choices

More like a symposium than a school, the NPP defies easy generalizations. Yet concerning the central thesis of Sanders's revolutionary work, N. T. Wright concludes, "I do not myself believe . . . a refutation can or will be offered; serious modifications are required, but I regard his basic point as established."[1] James D. G. Dunn concludes, "The Judaism of what Sanders christened as 'covenantal nomism' can now be seen to preach good Protestant doctrine: that grace is always prior; that human effort is ever the response to divine initiative; that good works are the fruit and not the root of salvation."[2]

I have argued thus far, however, that Sanders's own analysis of the Second Temple material makes Dunn's verdict untenable. From the perspective of Judaism, of course, it does not matter whether one is preaching "good Protestant

1. N. T. Wright, *What Saint Paul Really Said: Was Paul of Tarsus the Real Founder of Christianity?* (Grand Rapids: Eerdmans, 1997), 20.

2. James D. G. Dunn, "The Justice of God: A Renewed Perspective on Justification by Faith," *Journal of Theological Studies* 43 (1992): 7. Dunn's description of "good Protestant doctrine" is indistinguishable from traditional Roman Catholic teaching. Certainly for Rome, grace precedes all merit. The critical difference between covenantal nomism of any stripe and Reformation soteriology is the simple yet radical qualifier: *sola*, as in *sola gratia, solo Christo, sola fide*.

doctrine," and in my view the attempt to conflate these different theological paradigms does not advance our understanding of either.

Of course, the foil for the NPP is Luther's "tortured subjectivity," read through the lens of Schweitzer and interpreted along the lines of Bultmann's existentialist hermeneutic. William Wrede's *Paul* basically made the apostle out to be an antinomian, the antithesis of Jesus.[3] However, ever since Schweitzer the move has been to reduce the importance of justification in Paul's teaching.[4] And the NPP has adopted the thesis of Krister Stendahl that Luther's own psychological and spiritual struggles distorted Protestant interpretation of the apostle, as if the Reformer's experience was basically Paul's. After all, Paul regarded his preconversion life as "blameless," while Luther was, by his own admission, riddled with sin and doubt. Luther's individualistic concern, it is suggested, bequeathed the Protestant obsession with individual salvation over cosmic victory and ecclesial incorporation.

However, I argue that another reading of both figures is possible. In Philippians 3, the "righteousness" that Paul calls "blameless" he also calls "dung." Putting words in his mouth, one could say that Luther too considered himself, "as to the righteousness of my monastic vows, blameless." In fact, it is well-attested by Luther and others who knew him that he was an unusually zealous, scrupulous monk who wore himself out, along with his unfortunate confessors, with spiritual exercises. In both cases, the cross of Christ (*solus Christus*) provides a new reality by which "righteousness" is judged and in retrospect found wanting.

Can the Reformation really be explained in terms of Luther's tortured subjectivity—the personal obsession with how one can find a gracious God?[5] Or were the Reformers onto something when they thought that they had discovered not only in Paul but in the total canonical Scriptures the revolutionary insight that had been corrupted by centuries of misunderstanding?[6] To answer this question, I will begin with a broad outline of the argument and then engage the specific exegetical arguments. Challenging the NPP claim to have transcended false antitheses, the next few chapters defends a covenant theology that is more successful at integrating the following relationships often given to reductionism: (1) individual and community, (2) badges of membership and works-righteousness, and (3) law and

3. William Wrede, *Paul* (Lexington, MA: America Library Association Committee on Reprinting, 1962).
4. Albert Schweitzer, *The Mysticism of Paul the Apostle*, trans. William Montgomery (New York: Seabury, 1968).
5. See Krister Stendahl's important article, "The Apostle Paul and the Introspective Conscience of the West," *Harvard Theological Review* 56 (1963): 199–215; reprinted in *Paul among Jews and Gentiles* (London: SCM, 1977), 78–96.
6. Moisés Silva astutely points out that Thomas Aquinas, in his commentary on Gal. 3, affirmed that "Paul was opposing those who 'trust in the works of the Law and believe that they are made just by them,' and that 'to be of the works of the Law is to trust in them and place one's hope in them'" ("Faith versus Works of Law in Galatians," in D. A. Carson et al., eds., *Justification and Variegated Nomism*, vol. 2, *The Paradoxes of Paul* (Grand Rapids: Baker Academic, 2004), 244, from Thomas Aquinas, *Commentary on Saint Paul's Epistle to the Galatians*, trans. F. R. Larcher, Aquinas Scripture Series 1 (Albany: Magi, 1966), 79. If such interpretations are provoked by an "introspective conscience," then the Reformers were hardly alone in suffering from it.

gospel. I deal with the first two in this chapter. In this chapter my thesis is that the target of Paul's polemics against "works of the law" is more sweeping than the NPP suggests.

INDIVIDUALISM VERSUS COMMUNITY, OR, SOTERIOLOGY VERSUS ECCLESIOLOGY

According to the NPP, "How can I be saved?" is the wrong question in the first place—at least if we want to understand Second Temple Judaism (for Sanders) or Paul (for Dunn and Wright). E. P. Sanders laid the groundwork for the NPP thesis that works of the law, at least in Palestinian Judaism, had to do with boundary markers rather than with the question about personal salvation. However, Sanders at least included the membership question under the rubric of "soteriology," recognizing that the question about whether one is "in" or "out" of the covenant is indeed "a 'soteriological' concern."[7] In fact, Sanders is more balanced than some proponents when he suggests that "both Judaism and Paul take full account of the individual and the group."[8] We have already seen many of his Second Temple references to how individuals can be saved through the weighing of merits, acts of atonement, and personal obedience. God's final judgment is of individuals, not simply of groups.

Nevertheless, Sanders writes that in the Tannaitic sources, "The query, 'What can I do to be saved?' is one which is not prominent in the literature."[9] Despite his affirmation of individual as well as corporate dimensions being included in early Jewish soteriology, Sanders here sets the stage for the subsequent NPP antithesis between the two. Emphasizing continuity with Judaism more than discontinuity, the NPP has increasingly marginalized soteriology (*ordo salutis*) in favor of ecclesiology (*historia salutis*).

That Protestants have sometimes abstracted the question of personal salvation from its corporate (ecclesial) and cosmic (eschatological) dimensions is obvious enough. However, by definition, covenant theology of any variety is inherently communal. It resists being restricted to "me and my personal relationship with God" or to the question, "How can I be saved?" Not a single Reformed confession or catechism fails to relate the question of how we are saved to the question of who or what constitutes the covenant community.[10]

At the same time, Reformed theology resists the opposite reduction to the question of covenant membership. After all, while the focus of the Old Testament is certainly on God's purposes for the world *through Israel* collectively, the covenantal and

7. Ibid.
8. E. P. Sanders, *Paul and Palestinian Judaism* (Minneapolis: Fortress, 1977), 547.
9. Ibid., 75.
10. Comparing and contrasting various ecclesiologies will be postponed until my fourth and final volume in this series. It will suffice to say that Reformation churches exhibit a markedly different ecclesiology than the more individualistic approach often taken in Protestant evangelicalism.

corporate emphasis evident in the New Testament as well is not threatened by the question that NPP proponents often suggest it does not ask: "How can I be saved?" It is not by withdrawing into the sphere of inner subjectivity that this question arises, but within the context of both the exile and the apocalyptic arrival of the King and his kingdom that this question of personal salvation becomes acute.

Apocalyptic and the Quest for a Gracious God

As we saw above in Sanders's summary, individual Israelites could be "cut off" or exiled from the people of God (the "staying in" part of the covenantal nomism). Surely it would not be too great of an anachronism to suggest that in such circumstances as the exile, which first-century Jews believed themselves to still be experiencing, individual Jews had reason to question their own status as individuals in the covenant community. If the average person did not feel this question as acutely, it certainly would have been on the mind of the "publicans and sinners" who sat on the precipice, if not in the *tōhû wābōhû* (cf. Gen. 1:2), of such exclusion, and it was precisely to such that the gospel was announced.

Especially in the apocalyptic movements, "belonging" to the covenant kingdom cannot be assumed, since the Messiah comes to separate and does "not come to bring peace but a sword," even dividing households in Israel (Matt. 10:34–39). This is the message of John the Baptist when he challenges their presumption of being heirs of Abraham. Thus, individuals are baptized into the new covenant community, while the "chaff" will be thrown into the fire (3:9–12). One might say that the Deuteronomistic community (national, theocratic Israel) is being called away from Sinai to become part of the universal Abrahamic community through faith alone in Christ alone. The more primordial promissory covenant has now reached its telos with Christ's priestly ministry.

The Jewish sources themselves do not simply assimilate the question of individual salvation into that of corporate, covenantal membership. As Roland Deines concludes, "In this, the Pharisaic movement stands for the tradition of the Deuteronomistic view of history: obedience to the revealed will of God brings salvation and blessing; disobedience, on the other hand, leads to exile and loss of the land."[11] This is why strict laws beyond those in Torah constitute necessary extensions of Torah. Furthermore, *each* Israelite must make a personal commitment to Torah—especially given the pull toward capitulation to the pagan powers.[12] *Every individual*, in every aspect of one's daily life, must conform to Torah in order for the nation to be saved.[13]

If this is so, the relevance of Paul's argument in Galatians 3:15 that the Abrahamic covenant pertains to a seed (Christ), and is not based on the personal ful-

---

11. Roland Deines, "The Pharisees between 'Judaisms' and 'Common Judaism,'" in D. A. Carson et al., eds., *Justification and Variegated Nomism*, vol. 1, *The Complexities of Second Temple Judaism* (Tübingen: Mohr Siebeck/Grand Rapids: Baker Academic, 2001), 495.

12. Ibid., 497.

13. Ibid.

fillment of the Israelites themselves (seeds), is yet again demonstrated. National-ism and individualism thus combined in Pharisaic piety. The "nationalist" side of Pharasaic Judaism expressed itself in the Zealots, notes Deines.[14] "In this system the Messiah was subordinated to the Torah."[15] While Sanders prefers to think in terms of a "Common Judaism," reducing the Pharisees to a relatively unimpor-tant group, Deines concludes that Phariseeism was "the fundamental and most influential religious movement within Palestinian Judaism between 150 B.C. and A.D. 70."[16]

When it is asserted that "not all of Abraham's children are his true descen-dants" (Rom. 9:7), the question becomes especially acute: If the true descendants are defined by their being "in Christ," how does one come to be "in Christ" in the first place?

The question of individual salvation is therefore crucial to the gospel. The very name "Jesus" exhibits this interest ("for he will save his people from their sins," Matt. 1:21). In fact, the problem of individual salvation gains intensity with Jesus' emphasis on the eschatological message of judgment. "Do not presume to say to yourselves, 'We have Abraham as our ancestor,'" John the Baptist warns. "For I tell you, God is able from these stones to raise up children to Abraham. Even now the ax is lying at the root of the trees; *every tree* therefore that does not bear good fruit is cut down and thrown into the fire" (3:9–10, emphasis added). Jesus continues and intensifies this apocalyptic message: "Those who want to save their life will lose it" (16:25).

The wealthy young man, who by his own account was steeped in Second Tem-ple Judaism ("All this I have done since my youth"), nevertheless asked the ques-tion about personal salvation: "Teacher, what good deed must I do to have eternal life?" (19:16). Jesus presses him on what "good deed" means and shows him why he has not kept the law from his youth, as he had claimed. In one sense, of course, he had probably kept the law—at least, according to the NPP definition (and, I argue, according to the Mosaic code as the regulation for the nation). As a pious leader, he had been circumcised and offered an annual sacrifice, in addition to observing the ritual days, washings, dietary laws, and other ethnic markers. On what basis then could Jesus drive this inquirer to despair of entering the kingdom simply because he was unwilling to sell everything he owned and give it to the poor (vv. 17–22)? Does the law prescribe such radical demands?

To answer this question, we must recognize that Jesus is not just another law-giver or prophet, but is inaugurating the kingdom in his very person. Just as the law that God gave Adam in paradise had an eschatological aim, so too the goal of the Sinai law is "a kingdom of priests," in which each person in one's rela-tionships with God and neighbor fulfills not simply the letter but also the spirit of the law from the heart.

---

14. Ibid., 499.
15. Ibid., 500.
16. Ibid., 503.

Jesus was not simply engaging in hyperbole in order to point up the young man's hypocrisy; he was also revealing the eschatological kingdom in its deepest character. Contrary to the popular perception, Moses cannot be distinguished from Jesus in terms of law versus love. However different this new era of redemptive history (viz., suspension of the theocracy and its holy wars against the enemies of Yahweh in the land) and however different from rabbinic interpretation it may be, Jesus' famous summary of the law as love is simply a repetition of Deuteronomy 6:5 (cf. 10:12; 30:6). It is with the prophets and with Jesus, not Paul, that we are introduced to this recurring theme that righteousness consists not simply of outward actions but also of purity of heart. Law defines love, and love is the animating soul of the law. Just as one may be outwardly circumcised and ethnically descended from Abraham without being circumcised in heart and a child of promise in truth, one could be designated a "keeper of the law" in terms of obvious violations yet completely fail to love God with all one's heart, soul, mind, and strength and one's neighbor as oneself. Yet, Jesus says, the *whole law* rests on this (Matt. 22:40).

Therefore, in the Sermon on the Mount, Jesus challenges the rabbinic interpretation of the law: hatred toward a neighbor is tantamount to murder, and entertaining lustful thoughts to adultery (5:21–30). Divorce, except on grounds of adultery, is out of the question (vv. 31–33); love must be extended to enemies and not just to friends (vv. 38–47). The demand is, "Be perfect, therefore, as your heavenly Father is perfect" (v. 48). With such rigorous definitions of covenant faithfulness in mind, the Westminster Confession defines sin as "any transgression of the law of God *or any lack of conformity thereto*," and the Book of Common Prayer offers the confession of sin not only as "what I have done," but also as "what I have left undone." It is one thing to refrain outwardly from violation and quite another to positively fulfill the law's intention.

Returning to the story of the wealthy young man, we note that Jesus takes the opportunity to warn the disciples of the difficulty of wealthy people being saved. Yet the climax of Jesus' point comes in 19:25–26: "When the disciples heard this, they were greatly astounded and said, 'Then who can be saved?' But Jesus looked at them and said, 'For mortals it is impossible, but for God all things are possible.'" It is not only difficult for rich people to be saved, but impossible; in fact, *it is impossible for anyone to be saved*—at least according to the law.

Jesus presses the argument not to absurdity but to the point of crisis: his interlocutor was not faulted for asking how he might be saved. Rather, his problem was that he thought that he had obeyed the law yet needed merely to supplement his lifelong fidelity with the one work that he might have left undone. Yet *he* is undone by Jesus' stripping away of his pretense. At the end of it all, no one can be saved, not even the disciples—"but with God all things are possible." "Then Peter said in reply, 'Look, we have left everything and followed you. What then will we have?" (v. 27). This is hardly the first or last time that Peter has missed Jesus' point. While Jesus promises Peter and the disciples blessing in the kingdom, he cautions, "But many who are first will be last, and the last will be first" (v. 30).

When one focuses on the potential of human beings for righteousness and salvation, the situation is precarious, even impossible. The kingdom upsets the way things are usually done, and to the extent that Jesus preaches the kingdom, he heightens the sense of personal emergency in his hearers. Jesus speaks of only a few being saved, for example (Luke 13:23–24). There is also his famous parable of the Pharisee and the tax collector, which Jesus told "to some who trusted in themselves that they were righteous and regarded others with contempt" (18:9). Clearly, it is self-righteousness—the presumption of self-justification, and not an ethnic superiority, at issue in this description of the Pharisee. Interestingly, the Pharisee's prayer, enumerating his exemplary moral character, includes a pretentious thanksgiving to God for his righteousness, which the NPP might cite as an example of grace in Second Temple Judaism. By contrast, the tax collector, "standing far off, would not even look up to heaven, but was beating his breast and saying, 'God, be merciful to me, a sinner!'" Jesus' verdict is clear: "I tell you, this man went down to his home justified rather than the other; for all who exalt themselves will be humbled, but all who humble themselves will be exalted" (vv. 13–14).

Even in John's ministry, the insiders were on the verge of becoming outsiders, and in his Olivet discourse (Matt. 25), Jesus uses the most dramatic language to speak of a separation of sheep and goats, with the angels collecting the elect at the end of the age. The "goats" are not only unbelieving Gentiles, but also those who claim to have done great works in his name. All of this eschatological, apocalyptic talk, far from being antithetical to the question of individual salvation, provokes it. It is no wonder, then, that the goal of Jesus' work and witness is "so that you may be saved" (John 5:34).

The sermons in Acts integrate the cosmic and the individual dimensions. There we find examples of the question "How can I be saved?" (for example, 2:37–41). In his report to the Jerusalem church, Peter explains, "God gave them [the Gentiles] the same gift that he gave us when we believed in the Lord Jesus Christ" (11:17).

By recapitulating the narrative of redemption (*historia salutis*), Paul also brought the question of salvation to the point of the individuals (*ordo salutis*) to whom he was preaching in the synagogue, proclaiming the forgiveness for sins that could not be forgiven under the law (13:38–39). On the next Sabbath "almost the whole city gathered to hear the word of the Lord," and many Gentiles "were glad and praised the word of the Lord; and as many as had been destined for eternal life became believers" (vv. 44, 48). When the jailer asked Paul and Silas, "What must I do to be saved?" (16:30), they were not met with a blank stare, as if this could only be a Gentile (or perhaps a Protestant) question. "They answered, 'Believe on the Lord Jesus, and you will be saved, you and your household'" (v. 31).

Throughout Acts are abundant examples of individuals responding in faith and being saved even as they are incorporated visibly into Christ's body through baptism. In both the preaching and the responses, the redemptive-historical horizon and personal salvation, communal identity and individual faith—all are woven into a single bolt of fabric. The Epistles exhibit this complementary concern as well (Rom. 5:9; 8:24; 9:27; 11:26; 1 Cor. 1:18; 7:16; 9:22; 1 Tim. 2:4; 2 Tim. 1:9; Titus 3:5; Heb. 7:25; James 5:20; 1 Pet. 3:20; Jude 23), even to the point of summarizing an earlier creedal formula: "The saying is sure and worthy of full acceptance, that Christ Jesus came into the world to save sinners—of whom I am the foremost" (1 Tim. 1:15). Paul can even speak, in what is incontrovertibly an autobiographical, first-person narrative, about his having died to the law and been crucified with Christ, so that he, now raised with Christ, lives to God. "And the life I now live in the flesh I live by faith in the Son of God, who loved me and gave himself for me. I do not nullify the grace of God; for if justification comes through the law, then Christ died for nothing" (Gal. 2:18–21).[17] If there was a radical concern for whether one is "in" or "out" that motivated individual Jews to separate from the compromised Jerusalem *cultus* and *polis* in order to belong to the true torah-community, then surely the apocalyptic sensibility would be heightened with the announcement that the Messiah had arrived. Becoming a disciple of Jesus (in the Gospels) and being incorporated into Christ (in the Epistles) is the way that individuals understand themselves to be the true children of Abraham.

There are further problems with the sharp contrast between communal identity and the question of personal salvation. As Heikki Räisänen points out, this thesis itself is unraveling, especially with the appearance of M. A. Elliott's *The Survivors of Israel: A Reconsideration of Pre-Christian Judaism* (Grand Rapids: Eerdmans, 2000). Citing additional examples of new studies of pre-Christian Jewish literature, he notes that they demonstrate (in Elliott's words) "'a highly individualistic and conditional view of covenant' (p. 639)." "Thus the work deprives the New Perspective School of its basis in Judaism and so makes its proposed revolution in Pauline studies abortive."[18]

Even if Räisänen overstates Elliott's achievement, our approach is able to give place to the NPP emphasis on a national election theology and its corollary covenantal nomism, without confusing this law-covenant with the covenant of grace that unites the Old and New Testaments. In fact, it is my contention that it was just such a confusion that gave rise to the erroneous views of Paul's opponents.

"Covenantal" versus "Soteriological"?

According to Wright, justification is not "how one gets saved" language but "covenant" language, which already points up the sharp antithesis between soteriology and covenant that even Sanders rejected. "First it is *covenant* language," adds Wright, "not in the sense of that word made famous through some sixteenth- and seventeenth-century discussions, but in the first-century Jewish sense."[19] It

---

17. This passage may lend further credibility to the classic interpretation of Rom. 7 as Paul's own personal experience in the Christian life.

18. Heikki Räisänen, *Paul and the Law*, 2nd ed. (Philadelphia: Fortress, 1986), 147.

19. Wright, *What Saint Paul Really Said*, 117. Again, the antipathy toward historical and systematic theology fuels reductionism here as elsewhere. "Covenant," as "made famous through some

is simply assumed that authentic covenant theology is "first-century Jewish" (i.e., covenantal nomism), as defined by the NPP. The gospel is "the return of Israel from exile" rather than "a description of how people get saved."[20]

While Wright's work has enriched our understanding of the significance of "the return of Israel from exile," it is not for him merely a theme or an implication of the gospel, it simply *is* the gospel. Consequently, despite his criticism of reductionistic formulas, it becomes a central dogma to which all else is subservient. I have already challenged the claim that the return of Israel from exile is the principal claim in the preaching that we find in Acts. Yet beyond the fact that no explicit mention is even made of this motif in these sermons, does it seem obvious from the typical *reactions* of those who received the message that this would have been the most significant reason for conversion, baptism, and possible persecution? It is even more implausible that Gentiles would have recognized the immediate relevance of the gospel as such an announcement and be prepared to surrender their own lives for the claim that Israel's exile is over.

Just as the Gentile mission would hardly have made sense if the gospel were simply the announcement of Israel's return from exile, the Jewish mission would not have had any better success with the good news reduced to the imperative to relax the entrance requirements. "No more dietary laws or circumcision!" does not equate to "Israel has returned from exile!" What of all those places where Paul explicitly articulates the gospel in terms of Christ's propitiatory death and justifying resurrection (such as Rom. 3:25; 4:25; 5:6–11, 16–21; 8:34; 1 Cor. 2:2; 15:1–5; Gal. 1:4; 3:1; 1 Thess. 1:10; 5:9–10)? Whereas Wright regards the story of the nation of Israel (i.e., the Sinai covenant) as the plot and the universal human story as the subplot, Paul appears to think in the reverse terms (Rom. 1–3; 5; and 1 Cor. 15 in particular). It is not the case that the whole world is in Israel, but that even Israel is "in Adam": this is what exposes human sin as such a deeper tragedy even than the fall itself. Though entrusted with the promise, Israel can no longer stand for the world, much less against it, but must stand with the world and in the world, hearing and receiving the announcement that is good news for everyone.

Reformed theology shares the important eschatological-apocalyptic dimension that proponents of the NPP want to highlight—it is what made the old federal theology the seedbed of the discipline of biblical theology.[21] God is working

---

sixteenth- and seventeenth-century discussions," may not get everything right (there were significant differences among Reformed theologians themselves). Nevertheless, they gave rigorous exegetical attention to *berit* and *diathēkē* and wove them into a biblical-theological and systematic-theological pattern with great sophistication. With one bold stroke, Wright sweeps away this remarkably fruitful period of reflection without so much as a footnote. As I noted in the introduction, Wright himself acknowledges that he has not read these theologians, which may explain why so many of his indictments devolve into caricature.

20. Ibid., 43.

21. See, for example, Geerhardus Vos's comments on the inherently eschatological orientation of both the covenants of works and grace in "The Doctrine of the Covenant in Reformed Theology," in Richard B. Gaffin Jr., ed., *Redemptive History and Biblical Interpretation: The Shorter Writings of Geerhardus Vos* (Phillipsburg, NJ: P&R Publishing, 1980), 243.

in history to bring about a redeemed community, not just saved individuals. However, the passages do not allow such a sweeping elimination of the *ordo salutis*. Wright notes that "the Israel-Adam link, which simply focuses the meaning of the covenant, seems to have been woven so thoroughly into Jewish thought and writing that it emerges in one form or another practically everywhere we look."[22] Reformed (federal) theology has also consistently defended this position against those who denied the connection between the Adamic and Sinaitic covenants. However, where it distinguished this type of covenant (law) from the covenant of grace, Wright simply speaks of "the covenant."

The NPP opposes itself to the individualist and existentialist interpretations of Bultmann, as if there were no third alternative—and as if these views accurately reflected those of the Reformers and Protestant confessions. However, as Mark Seifrid observes, Paul's polemic against "works of the law" is as far from Bultmann's "decisionism" as it is from any reduction to ethnic tribalism. Rather, Paul rejected justification by the works of the law "because they represented a false claim to righteousness."[23] Seifrid points out the irony of criticizing the "Lutheran" view as allegedly motivated by introspective guilt while arguing that Paul was motivated by the concern to curb Israel's ethnic hubris. "To shift from speaking of the burden of personal guilt to that of the nation," Seifrid responds, "represents no real movement away from psychologism."[24] In Paul's allegory in Galatians 4, Paul "declares that the earthly Jerusalem 'is enslaved with her children,' not because of Roman occupation (of which his converts already would have been aware), but because of its failure to believe the gospel (Gal. 4:25)."[25]

Soteriology versus Ecclesiology?

In spite of their important differences, the covenantal nomism of Judaism, Trent, and some recent Protestant biblical scholars and theologians not only relates but subordinates soteriology to ecclesiology. For Judaism, ethnic solidarity is primary; for traditional Roman Catholic theology, what is most important is that one belongs to the body whose visible head is in Rome; for Protestant nomism, it is that one belongs to the covenant community. While we should resist the tendency in some Protestant theologies to dissociate personal salvation from ecclesiology, Sanders is basically right to suggest that Paul's use of *dikaioō* is transitive rather than qualitative, although (as I will argue) it is first of all forensic. It does not describe an actual state of affairs *in* the believer *or* the community, but a declaration of righteousness pronounced upon those who are in themselves sinful.

22. N. T. Wright, *The New Testament and the People of God* (Minneapolis: Fortress, 1992), 266.
23. Mark A. Seifrid, *Christ, Our Righteousness. Paul's Theology of Justification* (Downers Grove, IL: InterVarsity Press, 2000), 21.
24. Ibid., 22.
25. Ibid.

That Paul's agitators reacted so strongly against this message points up its radical discontinuity with at least their version of covenantal nomism. It is not clear to me on what basis those who follow in Sanders's wake can find sufficient evidence in Paul to reconcile the apostle's understanding with that of Second Temple Judaism. On this point Dunn and Wright are not only at odds with Reformation exegesis, but also with the interpretations of Paul found in Judaism even as interpreted by Sanders.

From a covenantal perspective of any stripe, the question of "getting in and staying in" is not really all that different from the question "How can I be saved?" Ephesians 1:1–13, for example, defines the people of God (ecclesiology) in terms not of the national election of Israel and the conditions of Sinai, but on the basis of God's unconditional election of Jews and Gentiles "in [Christ] before the foundation of the world," who are redeemed by Christ and sealed with Christ for the day of redemption.

The gospel is not *merely* about how one is made right with God, we are told, yet at the end of the day NPP proponents do not seem to allow that it might even *include* that concern. If some interpretations reduce everything to the individual experience of salvation, Dunn, Wright, and others seem so suspicious of this question (which is, after all, explicitly raised in the New Testament) that qualifications such as "not merely" end up meaning "not at all."

As noted above, the NPP is eager to underscore the covenantal framework of Jewish and Christian theology. However, as we have also seen, there are different covenant theologies at work. If we accept a monocovenantalism, we will reduce the history of Israel to some form of covenantal nomism, with "covenant" modifying "nomism" in an ostensibly more gracious direction. Yet, I have argued, this severely limits the hermeneutical space within which to integrate not only the striking nuances of Paul's arguments, but also the Old Testament's own witness to these two covenants, yielding reductionism on all sides.

All participants in this debate recognize that there are formal, syntactical differences between commands (imperatives) and promises (indicatives) as distinct illocutionary stances. Further, most recognize that Paul sometimes sets these in antithesis. However, according to Dunn, for example, "wherever Paul poses the antithesis in his writings (explicitly or implicitly), he does so within the context of and as part of what amounts to a redefinition of the people of God."[26] In other words, the implications are always ecclesiological, not soteriological. But is it not rather the case that in the vast majority of circumstances, even where the redefinition of the people of God is involved, it is the consequence of rather than the substitute for the question of how to obtain the Abrahamic inheritance?

So while the question of individual status is not prominent in the national covenant, it certainly is in the new covenant. The question, "How can I be saved?" is at the heart of Paul's theology, when he answers, appealing to Abraham and

26. Ibid., 99.

David as examples, that it is by faith in Christ alone, apart from works (Rom. 4:6)—indeed, *apart from human decision or effort in any sense* (Rom. 9:16). It is by hearing the promise, not by doing the commands, that one is right with God and *therefore* a member of the justified community.

The choice of ecclesiology over soteriology as the horizon of Paul's thought is exegetically grounded in the NPP definition of "the works of the law" as referring specifically to the boundary markers that distinguish Jews from Gentiles. Is this a revolutionary paradigm for redefining justification or evidence of further reductionism?

BADGES OF MEMBERSHIP VERSUS WORKS-RIGHTEOUSNESS

In the Reformed version of covenant theology, the issue of boundary markers (ecclesiology) is clearly addressed and included in the sweep of Paul's concern about the question of justification (soteriology). For the NPP, however, the latter is lost in the former.

Building on the ground-breaking works of Wrede and Stendahl, the NPP argues that the main question addressed in Paul's theology in general and his doctrine of justification in particular is the inclusion of the Gentiles in God's plan.[27] Often at this point we meet objections to "abstract" doctrines of justification, as if Protestant exegesis had missed the larger redemptive-historical context of Paul's mission to the Gentiles. A further challenge to the Reformation interpretation of justification is the contrast often drawn by the NPP between Hebrew and Hellenistic approaches to "righteousness."

"Righteousness" in the Hebrew Scriptures and Paul

As Sanders pointed out, part of the problem begins with the fact that "justify" and "righteousness"—different words in English—are used to translate what are in fact cognate terms in Greek (*dikaioō* and *dikaiosynē*).[28] However, in light of the new eschatological reality that the new covenant has inaugurated, Sanders is correct to recognize in Paul a different (I would say more fully realized) eschatological perspective on righteousness. In fact, I would urge that to whatever extent Paul must certainly have been out of step with Second Temple Judaism (inasmuch as it conflated the Abrahamic and Sinaitic covenants), his scheme is consistent with the new covenant anticipated by the prophets. While the Sinai covenant and its laws—the whole law, not only the boundary markers—define the community of the just and therefore exclude the unrighteous, Paul announces

27. For a review of this trajectory, see James D. G. Dunn, "Paul and Justification by Faith," in Richard N. Longenecker, ed., *The Road from Damascus: The Impact of Paul's Conversion on His Life, Thought, and Ministry* (Grand Rapids: Eerdmans, 1997), 86.

28. Sanders, *Paul and Palestinian Judaism*, 44–47.

as a present reality that could only be anticipated by the prophets: namely, that God has at last justified *the ungodly.*

On the other hand, James D. G. Dunn tries to reconcile Paul with Second Temple Judaism by setting both against an ostensibly Hellenistic concept of jurisprudence—a trail that was blazed by Albrecht Ritschl.[29] Dunn explains:

> For in the typical Greek worldview, "righteousness" is an idea or ideal against which the individual and individual action can be measured. Our contemporary English usage reflects this ancient mind-set when it continues to use such expressions as "Justice must be satisfied." In contrast, however, "righteousness" in Hebrew thought is actually a more relational concept—that is, "righteousness" in Hebrew thinking has to do with the meeting of obligations that are laid on an individual by the relationship of which he or she is part.[30]

Yet does this contrast between Hebrew and Hellenistic concepts of justice square with Sanders's own analysis of the rabbinic emphasis on the weighing of merits? His entire discussion of the speculations concerning how one can atone for specific sins and how much obedience is required is as rigorously juridical as anything that we find in the medieval system, much less in Protestant theology.

Modern dogmatics and biblical theology have tended to contrast law and love, the legal and the relational, at least since Ritschl. However ironic it may seem, this is an intrusion of modern Protestant ethics on the Hebrew Scriptures and Judaism. Paul knows nothing of this contrast before or after his conversion. Love, in fact, *is* the fulfillment of the law—and in this he was not only following the teaching of Jesus but also of the Old Testament. For him the real antithesis that he recognized after the Damascus road encounter was not between law and love but between law and gospel, the principle of works and the principle of grace alone with respect to justification and the inheritance of all of the benefits promised to Abraham and his heirs. As we have seen, Dunn simply sees "legal" in antithesis to "covenant." Part of the problem is that "covenant" is always a code word for covenantal nomism and, more specifically, ethnic distinctiveness. Therefore, any theological distinctiveness of specific covenants is lost.

Dunn recognizes the challenge that the NPP faces on this point:

> The more we stress the continuity between Paul's teaching on justification and Paul's Jewish heritage, the more pressing becomes the question: Why, then, is Paul's teaching formulated in such a polemical manner, as in Gal 2:16 and Rom 3:20? . . . In a word, the primary answer seems to be that Paul was reacting not so much against Jewish legalism as against Jewish *restrictiveness.*[31]

---

29. Albrecht Ritschl, *The Christian Doctrine of Justification and Reconciliation* (Edinburgh: T&T Clark, 1900).

30. Dunn, "Paul and Justification by Faith," 88; cf. Gerhard von Rad, *Old Testament Theology,* trans. D. M. G. Stalker (San Francisco: HarperSanFrancisco, 1962), 1:370–76.

31. Dunn, "Paul and Justification by Faith," 90.

To make this case, Dunn emphasizes that the context for his sharp contrasts between works and faith is his announcement that the gospel has come to all and for all, Gentiles as well as Jews. For example, he cites Romans 10:4: "Christ is the end of the law as a means to righteousness for all who believe." Thus, the "for all who believe" is meant to qualify Paul's reference to "the law as a means to righteousness."[32]

But does this lead to reductionism? Isn't Paul's argument reversed here? It seems that Paul is saying that by denying that the law is a means for righteousness, he is not only opening the door to Gentiles, but also to Jews who have in fact barred themselves from a right relationship with God, despite—or rather, precisely because of, their tenacious grasp of Torah-righteousness. After all, in the first three chapters of Romans, Paul's charge is not simply that the Jews are being exclusivistic in their concern for legal purity, but that they *have not obeyed* the law—despite the fact that they *do keep* the ceremonial and dietary laws. Paul faults them not for failing to include Gentiles, but for failing to keep the law to which their circumcision holds them accountable. In my view, Dunn is not wrong in what he includes here but in what he excludes when he writes, "For in [Rom.] 3:27–30, the polemical antithesis between the 'law of works' and the 'law of faith' (3:27) is elaborated by the antithesis between 'God of the Jews only' and 'God also of the Gentiles' (3:29)."[33] However, both in Romans 3 and chapter 10, the reverse appears to be the case: the Jew-Gentile antithesis is resolved by the gospel of free justification.

In his programmatic monograph, Wright carefully emphasized that Paul is arguing for "justification by *belief*, i.e., covenant membership demarcated by that which is believed." He recognizes that this amounts to "my redefinition of what 'justification' thus actually *means*."[34] He adds, "It is perhaps important to say that, while I disagree with Dunn's exegesis of this particular passage, I am in substantial agreement with his general thesis about 'works of law' in Paul."[35] He correctly sees that Galatians 3 "should be seen as an extended discussion of Genesis 15."[36] However, the "two covenants" distinguished in Galatians 4 are reduced to a single covenant— "the renewed covenant" of Sinai. As a consequence, the principial use of *nomos* (law as the covenantal basis) is folded into the narrative or redemptive-historical use.

A further problem especially in Dunn and Wright's exegesis is the fact that Paul had never imposed the distinctive laws on the Gentiles. Seifrid queries, "When they had not had the 'works of the law' [as defined by Dunn] imposed on them in the first place, how could their justification be a liberation from them or from the laws?" Rather, the Galatian Christians, according to Paul's gospel, are liberated "from 'the elemental forces of the world' (Gal 4:3, 9) to which their own religious law that was functionally analogous to the Jewish law belonged."

---

32. Ibid.
33. Ibid., 91.
34. N. T. Wright, *The Climax of the Covenant: Christ and the Law in Pauline Theology* (Edinburgh: T&T Clark, 1991), 2–3.
35. Ibid., 138 n. 10.
36. Ibid., 140.

Further, the cry of relief in Rom 8:2 (cf. Gal 5:1, 13) is not evoked by liberation from Israel's covenant distinctives but from the desperate situation into which the law forces human beings: faced with the *Sollen* of the law ("Thou shalt not covet"), fleshly human beings inevitably fall into the dilemma of being willing but unable to keep the law or to do good and consequently into sin and death (Rom 7:7–25). The liberation is from condemnation for not having kept the law (8:1).[37]

How could Paul talk about fear and slavery in Romans 8:15 if the law itself had in fact provided for sufficient atonement?[38]

Dunn explicitly writes that the curse Paul has in mind here is "the curse *of a wrong understanding* of the law," not of the law itself (emphasis added).[39] But this not only fails to do justice to the Pauline gloss on Deuteronomy 27 (Gal. 3:10–14); it does not even match the language of Deuteronomy: "Cursed is the one who does not *do everything* contained in it" (Gal. 3:10, au. trans.; cf. Deut. 27:26). Weakening the severity of the law's stipulations and sanctions, this view tends toward a corollary weakening of Christ's accomplishment. Could Christ's having "redeemed us from the curse of the law" amounted to nothing more than a new understanding of the law? Furthermore, Paul does not say that Christ endured a wrong understanding of the law's curse, but the curse itself. Nor could this curse have been a sanction for violating the ethnic distinctives, since Paul's nomistic opponents not only kept but also insisted vehemently on the Gentile believers' keeping them.

The contrast falls unmistakably on *promises versus commands*, not on *some commands versus others*.

> For as many as are of the works of the law are under the curse; for it is written, "Cursed is everyone who does not *continue* in *all things which are written in the book of the law*, to *do* them." But that no one is justified by the law in the sight of God is evident, for "the just shall live by faith." Yet the law is not of faith, but "the man who does them shall live by them." Christ has redeemed us from the curse of the law, having become a curse for us. (Gal. 3:10–12 NKJV, emphasis added; cf. 3:2–3).

In fact, after elaborating these sharp antitheses in Galatians 2:1 through 5:12, the apostle turns to the ethical implications of life in the Spirit, interpreting "the works of the Spirit" not only in relation to certain boundary-marking laws but also in terms of "love, joy, peace, patience, kindness, generosity, faithfulness, gentleness, and self-control" (Gal. 5:22–23).

As Jesus summarized the whole law in terms of loving God and neighbor (Matt. 22:37–40), Paul thought of the law as a whole system revealing God's moral will and repeated Jesus' statement: "For the one who loves another has fulfilled the law"

---

37. Ibid., 73.
38. Ibid.
39. James D. G. Dunn, "Works of the Law," in *Jesus, Paul and the Law: Studies in Mark and Galatians* (Louisville, KY: Westminster/John Knox, 1990), 229.

(Rom. 13:8). Although the Sinai treaty included the moral law (summarized in the Decalogue), the latter transcends the former. The ceremonial and civil laws of the theocracy are abrogated along with the earthly kingdom that they served, but the law of love—the moral law, was founded in creation, not at Sinai. Paul, with other New Testament writers (indeed, with Jewish interpretation concerning the Noachian laws), recognized that the moral law was eternal and unchangeable. Originating before Sinai, in creation itself, this law of love remains an obligation of the new covenant community (Rom. 13:8–10; Gal. 5:14; cf. Heb. 8:10).[40] The fact that Paul speaks of the law in such broad terms cautions us against arbitrarily restricting his reference to ceremonial and dietary codes.

Not only does Paul speak of *law* broadly; he also refers to *works* as a general principle of debt, not simply to specific works as badges of covenantal identity: "Now to the one who works, the wages are not counted as grace but as debt" (Rom. 4:4 NKJV alt.). It is the *principle* of works-as-wages that Paul opposes to the principle of justification-as-gift. As Seyoon Kim points out, "It is a puzzle how [James] Dunn is able to see 'works' in Rom 9:11b refer to the Jewish covenant distinctives when it clearly refers to 'doing something good or bad' (*praxantōn ti agathon he phaulon*) in the foregoing clause (v. 11a), in contrast to God's election of grace."[41]

In Romans 4, it seems clear that it is not certain laws and works that Paul excludes, but works of any kind (which incur debt) in contrast to believing the gospel (v. 4). "But to one who *without works* trusts him who justifies the *ungodly*, such faith is reckoned as righteousness" (v. 5, emphasis added). Even if covenantal nomism has room for a weakened definition of grace (and law), it is only a perfecting (sanctifying grace) that believers must improve by their cooperation. However, Paul not only says that human works are not sufficient apart from grace and the Spirit, but that they cannot *even under these circumstances* contribute to God's declaration of righteousness: "But to him who does not work but believes on the one who justifies the ungodly, his faith is accounted for righteousness, just as David also describes the blessedness of the man to whom God imputes righteousness apart from works" (vv. 5–6 NKJV).

Paul therefore does not simply say that his strict obedience to the law is insufficient apart from grace or that those who seek to define the boundary markers in terms of circumcision and dietary laws are "under a curse." After all, surely the Jews he had in mind were circumcised and kept the dietary laws, or they would hardly have had any reason to question Paul's laxity in admitting Gentiles. Yet, "all who rely on the works of the law are under a curse; for it is written, 'Cursed is everyone who does not observe and obey *all* the things written in the book of the law'" (Gal. 3:10, emphasis added). The last words of Stephen's sermon make

---

40. On Jewish interpretation of the Noachian laws as equivalent to "natural law," see David Novak, *Covenantal Rights: A Study in Jewish Political Theory* (Princeton: Princeton University Press, 2000), esp. 36–77.

41. Seyoon Kim, *Paul and the New Perspective: Second Thoughts on the Origin of Paul's Gospel* (Grand Rapids: Eerdmans, 2002), 59.

the same point: "You are the ones that received the law as ordained by angels, and yet you have not kept it" (Acts 7:53), repeating Jesus' indictment in John 7:19.

In Philippians, the apostle draws two columns, assets and liabilities, and places his former life as "a Pharisee of Pharisees" in the latter:

> But what things were gain to me, these I have counted loss for Christ. But indeed I also count all things loss for the excellence of the knowledge of Christ Jesus my Lord . . . and count them as rubbish, that I may gain Christ and be found in him, not having my own righteousness, which is from the law, but that which is through faith in Christ, the righteousness which is from God by faith. (Phil. 3:5–9 NKJV)[42]

Consequently, those who seek to be justified by law are not children of Abraham (the father of faith). In fact, they are slaves, not sons, heirs of Hagar the slave rather than of Sarah the free woman. Or to change the metaphor, he says that the Jerusalem below is in bondage, while the Jerusalem above is free. There are two covenants, not one: a covenant of law (Sinai) and a covenant of promise (Abraham and his Seed) (Gal. 4:21–31).

All of this is consistent with the prophets, as we have already seen, especially in Jeremiah 31, where God reissues the unilateral promise that the new covenant "will not be like the covenant I made with their ancestors" at Sinai, "a covenant that they broke, though I was their husband, says the LORD" (v. 32 NRSV). Paul does not invent the gospel; he is simply reminding them that the covenant of promise (Abrahamic) cannot be annulled by the later covenant at Sinai (Gal. 3:15–18).

The fact that Saul of Tarsus was probably not terribly worried about his status before conversion yet considered himself a "chief of sinners" afterward reminds us that Second Temple Judaism cannot be our standard for judging what Paul meant. If Paul thought that the scribes had misinterpreted the Hebrew Scriptures, then he was in company with Jesus in thinking so. Not even the disciples understand the plot that is thickening around their master as they journey toward Jerusalem, and after the resurrection they are met with consternation by an angel who, like Jesus later in the same passage, gently upbraids them for not realizing all that the Scriptures had promised concerning Christ (Luke 24:6–7, 21–27, 44–49). It all began to make sense for the disciples, but in retrospect.

Similarly for Paul, the disorienting experience with the cursed one as in truth the exalted one made him read the whole history of Israel and indeed of humanity with Christ at the center. Paul now realizes that he himself is the cursed one, but that in Christ he can be found blameless, so now, going back to the requirements

---

42. Wright offers a different interpretation of this passage in *What Saint Paul Really Said*, 124: "[Paul] is saying, in effect: I, though possessing covenant membership according to the flesh, did not regard that covenant membership as something to exploit; I emptied myself, sharing the death of the Messiah; wherefore God has given me the membership that really counts, in which I too will share the glory of Christ. . . . That which he is refusing in the first half of Phil. 3:9 is not a moralistic or self-help righteousness, but the status of orthodox Jewish covenant membership."

of the whole law, he also realizes that he has not kept them as he (and others) thought he had. He too stands condemned "under the law," although he is circumcised and has always kept the dietary laws (Phil. 3:5–6). It is therefore clear that "the works of the law" cannot be restricted to these codes of ethnic distinction. To some extent it may even be that Paul's polemic is directed against his opponents' false assumption that "works of the law" simply meant boundary markers. Perhaps on this basis they had therefore convinced themselves that they were law-keepers, while in fact *circumcision and the dietary laws had only made them more deeply obligated to the whole law, which they had not actually kept.*

Even if the NPP were exactly right in its descriptions of Second Temple Judaism, our conclusions about what Paul taught concerning the law could not be determined on that basis. Whatever we may learn from Second Temple sources, Paul asserts that "the gospel that was proclaimed by me is not of human origin; for I did not receive it from a human source, nor was I taught it, but I received it through a revelation of Jesus Christ" (Gal. 1:11–12). If we prejudice continuity with early Judaism, we will undoubtedly fail to account for the sharp confrontations and polemics in Paul's Epistles.

Continuing Exile as the Narrative Plot

The continuing exile motif (particularly central for Wright) is questioned by some scholars.[43] However, it is possible to affirm the exile-restoration motif without making it a central dogma from which everything else is deduced. In Galatians 3, it is not just the Jews but all (*pasin*, both in Deut. 27:26 LXX and Gal. 3:10) who are "under the curse" because nobody keeps the law. However, one has to understand Deuteronomy 27, Wright insists:

> The blessing and curse are not merely "take-it-or-leave-it" options: Deuteronomy declares that Israel will in fact eventually make the wrong choice, and, as a result, suffer the curse of all curses, that is, exile (Deuteronomy 28.15–29.29). But that will not be the end of the story, or of the covenant. Deuteronomy 30 then holds out hope the other side of covenant failure, a hope of covenant renewal, of the regathering of the people after exile, of the circumcision of the heart, of the word being "near you, on your lips and in your heart" (30.1–14). In other words, Deuteronomy 27–30 is all about exile and restoration, *understood as* covenant judgment and covenant renewal.[44]

The problem is that Wright is working with a single covenant. Therefore, the subplot (the typological theocracy of the old covenant) becomes the main plot,

---

43. See for example Bruce W. Longenecker, *The Triumph of Abraham's God: The Transformation of Identity in Galatians* (Nashville: Abingdon, 1998), 137–39; cf. Douglas Moo, "Israel and the Law in Romans 5–11: Interaction with the New Perspective," in D. A. Carson et al., eds., *Justification and Variegated Nomism*, vol. 2, *The Paradoxes of Paul* (Grand Rapids: Baker Academic, 2004), 200–205.
44. Wright, *Climax of the Covenant*, 140.

which is Israel's exile and restoration. However, the prophets announce the covenant sanctions against Israel (exile) on the basis of the Sinai covenant, while they hold out hope for restoration for Israel *and* the nations on the basis of the Abrahamic and Davidic covenants as they come to fruition in the new covenant. Wright correctly points out that the ultimate failure of Israel to fulfill the Sinai covenant is already anticipated in Deuteronomy, but that covenant code itself did not offer the basis for any relief from its sanctions.

For Wright, as for Second Temple Judaism at least in this respect, salvation equals covenant renewal—that is, renewal of the Sinai treaty, while for the prophets and the New Testament, salvation is based on "better promises," namely, God's, which cannot be broken (Heb. 8:1–13). The career of that "better covenant" does not begin with Christ's advent, but was already promised to Adam and Eve after the fall and to Abraham—in both situations, referring to a redeemer-seed.

Despite the fact that Galatians 3:10 (appealing to Deut. 27:26) actually reads, "Cursed is *everyone* who does not observe and obey *all the things written in the book of the law*, Wright declares, "This is not a matter of counting up individual transgressions, or proving that each individual Israelite is in fact guilty of sin. It is a matter of the life of the nation as a whole."[45] However, the Sinai covenant was entered into by every Israelite (or at least every household). The oath ("All this we will do!") was not sworn by an abstract corporation, but by each and every Israelite as one people. Having said this, it can be readily conceded that the covenant made at Sinai chiefly concerned the status of the nation as a whole. Nevertheless, the blessings of the new covenant—in which believing Israelites shared by type and shadow under the old covenant—are of an entirely different order.

Once again, saying, "This is *more than* simply the plight of the sinner convicted by a holy law; *more*, too, than the plight of Israel caught in the trap of nationalism" (emphasis added) seems to amount to saying that it does not include that aspect.[46] Any interpretation that does not recognize the centrality of "the family of Abraham," says Wright, "is doomed to failure."[47] While this account makes sense of Israel's condemnation under the law, it does not account for the rest of the world. How can Gentiles be under the same law and the same curse as Israel (Rom. 1:18–3:20; 5:12–21)?

This problem of what appears to be God's failed promises (but is really Israel's failure) has been dealt with in Israel's Messiah.[48] Again, this helps us understand the argument of Romans 9–11, but Wright routinely appears to interpret this epistle as if it began with these chapters. Paul's eschatology is far more sweeping than the exile-restoration motif might suggest. "But," Wright counters, "it would be a complete mistake to think that Paul's actual point is a general and abstract one, a truth about salvation or justification which could be expressed in principle

45. Ibid., 142.
46. Ibid.
47. Ibid., 143.
48. Ibid.

without reference to the story of Israel," the sort of approach taken when "the writers of the Westminster Confession added scriptural footnotes to 'prove' their supposed general or timeless truths. *The whole question* at issue between Paul and his opponents is clearly: *to whom do the promises really belong*? Who are the children of Abraham?" (emphasis added).[49]

I will put Wright's polemic against the Westminster Confession to one side.[50] My material criticism is not that he is telling a story instead of contemplating a timeless truth, but that his story is not of sufficient breadth or depth to account for the scope of Paul's arguments. That the ecclesiological questions, "Who are the children of Abraham?" and "To whom do the promises really belong?" are important in Paul's argument cannot be doubted—but are they "the *whole question* at issue between Paul and his opponents"? It seems that Paul is at least also interested in the question, *How* can one inherit the estate: is it by works of law or by a unilateral gift? The *how* question (soteriology) necessarily leads to the *who* question (ecclesiology)—and vice versa. However, Wright's presupposition is the central dogma of the NPP: "I am assuming here a controversial point, that the δικαι-language is best rendered in terms of 'membership within the covenant.'"[51] Paul's polemics against "doing," Wright says, are "best taken in the sense of 'doing the things that mark Israel out.'"[52]

> Paul is not here speaking of those problems with which existentialist theologians have wrestled—"achievement," "accomplishment" and the like; nor yet with those traditional in Protestantism, "legalism" (or "nomism"), "self-righteousness," and so forth. Nor is he offering an abstract account of "how one gets saved."[53]

In fact, these lines of inquiry themselves are simply dismissed as "nonsense."[54]

For classic covenant theology, these contrasts can be explained by reference to "the things that mark Israel out" (i.e., ethnic distinctives) without marginalizing or doing away with the more basic point at the heart of the contrast: namely, that

49. Ibid., 144.
50. At this point, Wright fails to recognize the difference in purpose, method, and genre between confessions of faith and commentaries. Yet not even the confessions offer "timeless truths," but refer (especially in the Westminster Confession!) to the differences and continuities in the history of the covenant of grace. Imputing a Cartesian-rationalist epistemology to the Reformed scholastics is a classic example of historical anachronism. The covenant theology embodied in this confession was developed in the sixteenth century, and Descartes's principal philosophical works were being published at the same time as (and after) the Westminster Assembly. When Descartes's works did appear, they met a flurry of criticism from Reformed writers. For only one example of a biblical-theological treatment of these themes from classic covenant theology, see Herman Witsius, *The Economy of the Covenants between God and Man* (1677), trans. William Crookshank, 2 vols. (London: R. Baynes, 1822; repr., Phillipsburg, NJ: P&R Publishing, 1990). In fact, Witsius, like his mentor Gisbert Voetius, was an ardent opponent of Cartesian philosophy. Cf. R. Scott Clark, *Caspar Olevian and the Substance of the Covenant: The Double Benefit of Christ*, ed. David F. Wright, Rutherford Studies in Historical Theology (Edinburgh: Rutherford House, 2005). These examples are only representative of a large body of primary and secondary literature.
51. Wright, *The Climax of the Covenant*, 148.
52. Ibid., 150.
53. Ibid.
54. Ibid.

one method is a matter of *doing* what is *commanded*, while the other is a *resting* in what has been *done* by God in Christ. The ethnic markers are simply the tip of the iceberg of law: those who are circumcised are under a legal obligation to do everything the *whole* law requires.

Wright argues that in Galatians 3 Paul *modifies* the Jewish doctrine of election.[55] Our view is that there are *two* elections and two covenants in view (as Paul says in terms of the latter explicitly). They are not just two successive covenants that could be correlated with Old and New Testaments, but two covenants that coexist side by side, one earthly (typological yet inherently bound to this age) and the other heavenly (the realities of the age to come). The problem of Paul's agitators was that they were monocovenantalists (covenantal nomists) and had confused the blessings of Abraham with the Mosaic covenant described in Deuteronomy 27–30, failing to realize that in this way they were only under covenant curses rather than blessings. Additional evidence from Hebrews suggests that many Jewish Christians were turning back to the shadows of Sinai even though the "perfect" had arrived, and the writer appeals to the whole history of Israel to demonstrate that the same gospel was preached then as now (4:2), and that Abel, Enoch, Abraham, Moses, and other Israelite heroes obtained the same promise by faith alone (Heb. 11:1–39). They looked beyond the earthly Sinai and Jerusalem to the heavenly Zion, where Christ has entered as a forerunner for us (11:13–16; 12:18–29).

Wright even says, concerning Galatians 3:23–29, that "the temporary status of the Torah has given way to the permanent creation, in Christ, of a worldwide people characterized by faith." "This people is the single family promised to Abraham. We may compare Romans 8.3 f.: what the law could not do, being weak because of human sinfulness, God has done in Christ and by the Spirit."[56] But then he returns to the false dilemma that seems to result from his abiding commitment to Dunn's membership identity thesis: "It [my view] supports, for instance, the view (which seems to be gaining ground fast, though not without some opposition) that the real problem is not 'legalism' as usually conceived within traditional Protestant theology, but rather the question of whether one has to become a Jew in order to belong to the people of God."[57]

However, Paul's agitators accused Paul of antinomianism, not merely of weakening ethnic identity (Rom. 3:8; 5:20–6:1). Paul would have had every opportunity to clear up the misunderstanding by narrowing his polemics to membership identity, but instead he simply elaborates his broader thesis. Even in 2 Corinthians 3:18, according to Wright, "Torah and gospel are not the same, but nor are they here antithetical."[58]

---

55. Ibid., 171.
56. Ibid., 172.
57. Ibid., 173. On criticism of this point, see Bruce W. Longenecker, "Defining the Faithful Character of the Covenant Community: Galatians 2.15–21 and Beyond," in *Paul and the Mosaic Law: The Third Durham-Tübingen Research Symposium on Earliest Christianity and Judaism*, ed. James D. G. Dunn (Grand Rapids: Eerdmans, 2001), 88.
58. Ibid., 182.

It is worth observing Calvin's nuance in this connection. Far from being intrinsically opposed—law as an inherently, metaphysically antithetical category to grace, Paul asserts that "the 'law is the minister of death' (2 Cor 3:7) . . . *accidentally*, and from the corruption of our nature" (emphasis added).[59] In view of our treatment above of the various ways Paul refers to *torah/nomos*, the question to be raised throughout this section is whether the NPP in its own way mirrors the reductionistic tendencies of Bultmann and Betz. For the latter, law is in its very essence a minister of death; for the NPP, it is only the ethnic distinctives (although how boundary markers minister *death* is another question). Yet for classic covenant theology, the law as a total system ministers death only because of who *we* are in Adam, not because of what *it* is in God.

Although Wright refers in passing to Paul's mention in Philippians 3 of this status as "a gift," one wonders what the contrast might be in Wright's understanding of "gift" as opposed to "ethnic badge"? But does that really fit, especially since circumcision was certainly a gift as well as an obligation? In fact, in Wright's view (as Sanders's and Dunn's), first-century Judaism already was quite clear that one's "getting in" was based on grace. So if Paul and his opponents agree that it is "by grace," but disagree only on the matter of ethnic exclusivity, is the apostle beating the air? What are his opponents saying that would serve as a counterpoise to "gift"? Surely not an ethnic status that was, in fact, already a given.

Finally, justification for Wright (and, he argues, for Paul) refers to the last judgment, a judgment by works:

> It is strange, above all, that the first mention of justification in Romans is a mention of justification by works—apparently with Paul's approval (2:13: "It is not the hearers of the law who will be justified before God, but the doers of the law who will be justified"). The right way to understand this, I believe, is to see that Paul is talking about the final justification.[60]

Therefore, however much "getting in" (the first justification) may be determined by grace, "staying in" (the final justification) is by works.

If this is so, where does verse 25 fit in Paul's argument above ("circumcision indeed is of value if you obey the law")? In the first place, Paul's claim is not about ethnic markers but obedience. Circumcision not only inaugurates a life of obedience, but also signifies and seals to those who receive it the curse if they violate it. Paul is simply showing us how high the bar is set for justification by works: the law does not justify those who claim its patrimony by circumcision, but those who do everything contained in the law. As Michael Wyschogrod comments, rabbinic tradition (and Orthodox Judaism today) puts would-be Gentile converts to Judaism through a gauntlet for admission, since circumcision obligates a person

---

59. John Calvin, *Commentary on Genesis*, trans. John King (repr., Grand Rapids: Baker, 1996), 126–27; cf. his *The Second Epistle of Paul the Apostle to the Corinthians . . .* , ed. D. W. Torrance and T. F. Torrance (Grand Rapids: Eerdmans; Carlisle: Paternoster, 1996), 2 Cor. 3:12.

60. Calvin, *Commentary on Genesis*, 126.

to keep the whole law, while the nations will be judged according to the less rigorous universal law.[61]

Thus, Paul's comment in Romans 2:13 is part of an argument that reaches its apogee in 3:19–20, which even assumes that "the whole world" is "under the law": "Now we know that whatever the law says, it speaks to those who are under the law, so that every mouth may be silenced, and the whole world may be held accountable to God. For 'no human being will be justified in his sight' by deeds prescribed by the law, for through the law comes the knowledge of sin." Neither present nor future justification can come by our obedience to the law. Given human corruption, the law cannot accomplish anything except to expose sin as sin. Again, it is difficult to see how the ethnic distinctives alone could bring about the knowledge of sin for Jews, much less silence the whole world.

Romans 2:25 must be read together with Galatians 3:10 ("For all who rely on the works of the law are under a curse; for it is written, 'Cursed is everyone who does not observe and obey all the things written in the book of the law'") and 5:2–4:

> Listen! I, Paul, am telling you that if you let yourselves be circumcised, Christ will be of no benefit to you. Once again I testify to every man who lets himself be circumcised that he is obliged to obey the entire law. You who want to be justified by the law have cut yourselves off from Christ; you have fallen away from grace.

In fact, Galatians 5:11–13 puts it in the starkest terms: "But my friends, why am I still being persecuted if I am still preaching circumcision? In that case the offense of the cross has been removed. I wish those who unsettle you would castrate themselves!" Yet elsewhere Paul states that circumcision itself is indifferent (1 Cor. 7:19; Gal. 5:6) or perhaps even an advantage from a redemptive-historical standpoint (Rom. 3:1). Also indifferent is the matter of eating meat that had been sacrificed to idols (Rom. 14).

Boasting in the Law

What makes an indifferent matter otherwise is the status it is given not only as a boundary marker of exclusion (although it is certainly that), but the role that such an act plays in one's view of how to be justified before God. *The problem is not circumcision per se, but appealing to it as part of a covenant of law that simultaneously determines who is true covenant partner (ecclesiology) and how one is saved (soteriology).*

Nevertheless, Wright (like Dunn) regards Romans 2 as crucial for the argument. In fact, elsewhere Wright suggests, "Romans 2 is the joker in the pack."[62] "And the offence with which he charges 'the Jew' is, in this passage, clearly not

---

61. Michael Wyschogrod, *Abraham's Promise: Judaism and Jewish-Christian Relations*, ed. R. Kendall Soulen (Grand Rapids: Eerdmans, 2004), 188–201.
62. N. T. Wright, "Law in Romans 2," in Dunn, *Paul and the Mosaic Law,* 131.

'boasting' in the law," Wright claims, despite the grammatical sense of the words in verse 23: *hos en nomō kauchasai*. Nor is Paul targeting "the attempt to keep the law and so earn status, or 'righteousness,' or indeed anything else, through the law. The offence with which he charges 'the Jew' is *breaking* the law" (emphasis original).[63] Yet how have these Jews broken the laws that mark *ethnic* boundaries? Paul's charge is not that they have failed to be circumcised or to keep the dietary laws, but that they have failed to do everything that such identifying markers require. Furthermore, it seems arbitrary to suggest that in Romans 3:27, "This 'boasting' which is excluded is not the boasting of the successful moralist; it is the racial boast of the Jew, as in 2:17–24."[64] How could this "boasting" be anything other than that of the "successful moralist" if, as Wright himself acknowledges, Paul argues "that the lack of moral achievements vitiates the boast (2.23)"?[65]

It seems much simpler (and consistent) to assume that the covenantal framework of Galatians is basically the same as that of Romans. The Sinai covenant is restricted to the ethnic nation of Israel, while the Abrahamic covenant promised blessing for the nations. However, the Sinaitic and Abrahamic covenants not only differ in their ethnic boundaries but in the principle or basis of their respective inheritances: law and promise. The Abrahamic promise can only come to ethnic Jews, not to mention the Gentiles, because it is an unconditional divine oath rather than a law-covenant. The basis for their boasting is therefore not racism but a zeal for Torah that the Gentiles obviously do not share. Even if it is a zeal that is ignorant of God's gift of righteousness in Christ through faith alone (Rom. 10:1–4), it is not the same as a claim of ethnic superiority.

The NPP fails to account for the deeper and broader Pauline arguments by reducing them to this ethnic superiority: again, this is a question of ecclesiology rather than soteriology. This does not mean, however, that the NPP lacks soteriological assumptions and conclusions. At the end of the day, they remain within the exclusive ambit of covenantal nomism.

The emphasis on continuity with covenantal nomism, however, does not account for Paul's radical shift from persecutor of the church to apostle to the Gentiles, as Seyoon Kim has argued: "Only because Paul saw Christ's death and resurrection as God's redemptive act for our justification *sola gratia* and *sola fide*, could he so freely go to the Gentiles and proclaim the gospel of God's grace to them, while the Jewish Christians, failing to see the principle of *sola fide* so clearly as he, hesitated to do the same but rather criticized him for his law-free Gentile mission."[66] It is "beyond my comprehension," Kim adds, "that Dunn can sepa-

---

63. Ibid., 133.
64. Wright, *What Saint Paul Really Said*, 129.
65. Ibid., 139.
66. Kim, *Paul and the New Perspective*, 2–3. This repeats his argument in *The Origin of Paul's Gospel* (Tübingen: J. C. B. Mohr, 1981; Grand Rapids: Eerdmans, 1982), 310–11; cf. C. E. B. Cranfield, "'The Works of the Law' in the Epistle to the Romans," *Journal for the Study of the New Testament* 43 (1991): 89–101.

rate Paul's new commission from his new convictions about the gospel, when Paul's own comments in Galatians 1:13–17 keep them together." The emphasis in Galatians 1–2 is on the *gospel* and not just on the apostle's being sent to the Gentiles.[67] For Dunn, even the claim concerning Christ crucified as Israel's Messiah was well within the parameters of what a good first-century Jew could accept. But what about 1 Corinthians 1? Why does Paul say that the gospel is a stumbling block?[68] Romans 5–8 does not touch on the Jew-Gentile relation; it is simply the Adam-Christ relation, without Moses in the middle.[69]

Repeatedly, Kim notes, Dunn and Wright attempt to reinsert some validity to the forensic dimension, but then take it away with statements about the debate being about boundaries and not about how one is accepted before God.[70] In opposing the traditional Protestant exegesis of Philippians 3, "Dunn dutifully starts with a citation of his dogma: 'The need to attain one's own righteousness was no part of traditional Jewish teaching.' This dogma does not allow him to take 'my own righteousness' in verse 9 in its natural grammatical sense of Paul's personal righteousness, the righteousness that he attained through his faithful observance of the law."[71] If these are not Paul's "personal achievements," Kim wonders, then whose? "If they were not what he could claim as his personal achievement, what was the basis on which he could have *greater* 'confidence in the flesh' than his Jewish opponents (v. 4b)?"[72] If it was merely a national righteousness, he would have said "our righteousness."[73] We might add the same critique in relation to the NPP exegesis of Romans 7. The crux of Paul's gospel is not simply that it is good news for Gentiles, but that it is good news for Jews as well: God *justifies* the *wicked*. This is the scandal that provokes all of the other related debates. The issue of ethnicity is swept into this wake: We are all in this mess together in Adam, says Paul, and we get out of it together in Christ. Both the plight and the solution are deeper than Paul's antagonists imagined.

Paul's polemics against "the works of the law" cannot be reduced to merely that part of the law that highlights Jewish identity. One may continue to hold, with Räisänen (like Sanders), that Paul simply got Judaism wrong in this respect.[74] However, so far, the NPP has not successfully demonstrated that Paul

67. Kim, *Paul and the New Perspective*, 10–11.
68. Ibid., 15.
69. Ibid., 55.
70. Ibid., 66.
71. Ibid., 76.
72. Ibid.
73. Ibid., 77.
74. Räisänen, *Paul and the Law*; cf. his "Legalism and Salvation by the Law," in *Die paulinische Literatur und Theologie*, ed. S. Pedersen (Aarhus: Aros, 1980), 72–73: "For Paul, Judaism was legalism. . . . It should not have been possible to do away with the 'law as the way to salvation' for the simple reason that the law never was (or was conceived to be) that way. . . . Paul is wrong." But this claim flies in the face of the OT itself. The law was given with *sanctions*. It was not simply something to be followed to the best of one's ability, but a covenant to be fulfilled. Personally perform its stipulations, and you will live; fail, and you will die: that is the legal context of the specific

did not consider Judaism legalistic. On the other hand, Hans Dieter Betz goes to the opposite extreme: law and curse are basically equivalent ontologically.[75] However, Paul never says that one stands condemned for having kept, or for trying to keep, the works of the law; rather, all stand condemned for *not* having kept it.

It is not the law's essence to condemn, but rather to pronounce a just verdict upon those who have sworn, "All this we will do." That is why Calvin said, in the quote above, that the condemning function of the law is accidental to its being, due to human sin. The law would have justified if Adam had fulfilled the commission entrusted to him as humanity's covenant head. Dunn explicitly writes that the curse that Paul has in mind is "the curse of a wrong understanding of the law." However, Kim responds, "A mere correction of the Jews' 'wrong understanding of the law' can hardly be said to be redemption from the curse that the law pronounces upon their not 'abiding by all that has been written in the book of the law to do it' ([Gal. 3] v. 10b; Deut 27:26)."[76] Since Dunn designates this the "test case" for the New Perspective, there is little reason to expect the NPP to recover from refutation of its exegesis of this verse.[77]

It is true that Paul's polemics target ethnic restrictiveness, notes Bruce Longenecker. "On the other hand, there are other passages where Paul does seem to suggest that nomistic observance can be a form of legalism," even though obedience to the law itself cannot be characterized as "legalism." "So just a few verses after reworking the significance of the Shema in Rom 3:29–30, Paul gives an analogy concerning a worker who expected to be rewarded according to his labors, trusting in his own works rather than in God (4:4–5)."[78] Dunn and similar writers simply cannot exonerate Paul's targets from the charge of legalism here, or in Romans 9:11–12, 32; and 11:5–6, "where Paul contrasts the Jewish interest in 'works' with divine 'grace.'"[79] Yet it is not legalism per se against which Paul is striving, according to Longenecker. Everything apart from Christ can be viewed legalistically, or as a form of legalism, for Paul. "Even if, in their own minds, their own observance of the law is being carried out as a response to God's gracious election of Israel, in Paul's mind they are guilty of acting by their own efforts in order to gain their reward from God."[80] As we have seen, Sanders realized that this was Paul's point but concluded that he was wrong, on the basis of his own

---

regulations (Lev. 18:5; Deut. 4:1; 5:33; 6:24–25; 8:1; 30:15–18; Neh. 9:29; Ezek. 18:19; cf. 18:9, 21; 20:11, 13, 21). What Räisänen misses is the distinction between the national covenant (Sinai), according to which the status of the people in the land was determined by obedience and individual salvation according to promise (Abraham). In my view, the failure to distinguish these was precisely the heart of the confusion that Paul was compelled to address.

75. Hans Dieter Betz, *Galatians* (Minneapolis: Fortress, 1979), 145–46.

76. Kim, *Paul and the New Perspective*, 133, referring to Dunn, "Works of the Law," in *Jesus, Paul, and the Law*, 229.

77. Ibid., referring to Dunn, "Works of the Law," in *Jesus, Paul, and the Law*, 225.

78. Bruce W. Longenecker, "Contours of Covenant Theology in the Post-Conversion Paul," in Longenecker, *The Road from Damascus*, 140.

79. Ibid.

80. Ibid., 141.

theological conviction that synergism (i.e., covenantal nomism) is closer to the truth of the matter.

In order to appreciate more fully the depth and scope of Paul's definition of and polemics against the works of the law, it is necessary to examine the relationship of law and promise as distinct covenantal principles in his arguments. It is to that question that we now turn.

Chapter Five

Law and Gospel

Contrast or Continuity?

So far I have argued that we can transcend false choices between soteriology or ecclesiology, the *ordo salutis* or the *historia salutis*, and therefore "works of the law" understood as either badges of membership (ecclesiology) or a way of seeking reconciliation with God (soteriology). If reductionism abounds on these points, then it is positively rampant when we consider the relation of law and gospel. On one hand, there is a tendency to contrast law and gospel in a rather abstract way, as if the very idea of law implied bondage and death. On the other hand, continuity can be so stressed that the gospel simply becomes a relaxed version of the law. In my view, the approach of Hans Dieter Betz and Rudolf Bultmann represents the former tendency, while the NPP—partly in reaction against this abstraction—represents the latter.

No less than Lutheranism, the confessions and formative theologians in sixteenth- and seventeenth-century Reformed churches strongly affirmed the law-gospel distinction. However, as federal theology flourished, the Reformed drew this distinction into the ambit of the various historical covenants. So, for example, specific questions such as to what extent the theocracy was a republication of the covenant of creation (and therefore, strictly speaking, a covenant of works) or the way law functions in the Abrahamic as opposed to the Sinaitic covenants introduced more nuance. This covenantal approach was also more sensitive to the concrete contexts and circumstances of particular passages in determining the relation of law and gospel. Building on the previous arguments, this chapter will provide a covenantal account of this relation that gets us beyond some of the cul-de-sacs of abstract contrast or an equally one-sided continuity.

LAW AND GOSPEL: CONTRAST OR CONTINUITY?

Since we have already provided a basic narrative of the two covenant traditions, our focus will be Paul's relation to Judaism. Against the assumption of radical discontinuity (F. Weber, Bultmann, Hans Dieter Betz, et al.), the NPP proposes a radical continuity, albeit with a range of opinions about Paul's proximity to Judaism in comparison to Jesus. Dunn appeals to what he regards as the "consensus" that not only Paul but also the Gospels (especially Matthew and John) misrepresent to some extent the true convictions of the Pharisees.[1] In this section I suggest that once again false choices are resolved when we substitute a two-covenant paradigm for the single "pattern of religion" known as covenantal nomism.

In 1914 C. G. Montefiore distinguished rabbinic, apocalyptic, and Hellenistic Judaisms in the world of 50 CE.[2] Yet all schools were agreed: "For every *decent* Israelite there was a place in the future world" (emphasis added).[3] As an aside, it is difficult to imagine that this imperative would not have provoked anxiety about personal salvation. Nor is it obvious that "decent" is simply equivalent to being circumcised and keeping the dietary laws.

The important thing to notice, however, is that according to Montefiore repentance and forgiveness, central to rabbinic Judaism, are nowhere to be found in Paul.[4] From the Jewish perspective, then, Paul was overly concerned with sin and human helplessness to overcome it—the "introspective conscience" thesis that, ironically, Stendahl and the NPP criticize the "Lutheran" view for allegedly imposing on Paul. From the Jewish perspective, added Montefiore, neither the cross nor the new "birth from above" (John 3:3, 5–8) is necessary, since human beings "could receive salvation, and get the better of sin, (for God was always helping and forgiving) even without so strange and wonderful a device."[5] Therefore, Montefiore and Schoeps concluded that Paul misrepresented Judaism as a religion of works-righteousness. Once again we recognize that deciding what constitutes "works-righteousness" depends to a large extent on one's theological commitments concerning the human condition and the content of grace and the gospel. Be that as it may, Montefiore's (and Schoeps's) thesis made a deep impression on Sanders,

1. James D. G. Dunn, *Jesus, Paul, and the Law: Studies in Mark and Galatians* (Louisville, KY: Westminster/John Knox, 1990), 61.
2. C. G. Montefiore, *Judaism and St. Paul* (London: Max Goschen, 1914), 35.
3. Ibid., 44.
4. Ibid., 38.
5. Ibid., 78.

while Dunn and Wright attempt greater reconciliation between Paul and Judaism by distinguishing the former from the Reformation traditions of interpretation.

MONOCOVENANTALISM: GRACE-MODIFIED LAW

Dunn, like Sanders, argues that the Jewish covenantal understanding was basically grounded in grace. God's righteousness is his initiative in electing Israel and remaining faithful to it. It was not Israel's works, but God's grace, that provided the basis for security (Deut. 4). Unlike Sanders, however, Dunn argues that Paul was not departing from his heritage in his understanding of covenant and justification. The Damascus road encounter changed his mission (inclusion of Gentiles), but did not radically alter his theology.[6] Dunn says this view stands against the historical apologetic tradition, from Ignatius to the Reformation and ever since, which pits Christianity against Judaism. "So it needs to be said clearly: justification by faith is at heart a Jewish doctrine; dependence on divine grace remains a consistent emphasis throughout Jewish thought, at least up to the time of Paul . . . ; and there is no clear teaching in pre-Pauline Jewish literature that acceptance of God has to be earned (Sanders, *Paul and Palestinian Judaism*; Dunn, 'New Perspective on Paul')."[7]

Furthermore, Dunn, like the NPP generally, has room for only a single covenant. Since it must be primarily gracious, elements that seem to suggest a different kind of covenant (a conditional law-covenant) must be assimilated. I do not doubt that this approach generally fits Second Temple Judaism. In fact, the conflation of these two covenants (and therefore of law and gospel) is precisely the focus of the Pauline critique. Graham Stanton offers further support of this conclusion:

> As C. K. Barrett notes, "They probably took the view that the Abrahamic covenant had been redefined by the Sinaitic." Paul will have none of this. God's covenant with Abraham was based on faith; it was not set aside, supplemented, or reinterpreted by the law, given 430 years later. . . . In Paul's re-interpretation of the traditions concerning Abraham's two sons, those who belong to Christ trace their line of descent directly back to Abraham, by-passing completely Mount Sinai and the law.[8]

To see the new covenant about which Paul is speaking as a renewed Sinai covenant is to miss the most central point the apostle makes. In fact, it is to miss

---

6. James D. G. Dunn, "Paul and Justification by Faith," in Richard N. Longenecker, ed., *The Road from Damascus: The Impact of Paul's Conversion on His Life, Thought, and Ministry* (Grand Rapids: Eerdmans, 1997), 89.

7. Ibid.

8. Graham Stanton, "The Law of Moses and the Law of Christ: Galatians 3:1–6:2," in *Paul and the Mosaic Law: The Third Durham-Tübingen Research Symposium on Earliest Christianity and Judaism*, ed. James D. G. Dunn (Grand Rapids: Eerdmans, 2001), 108–9.

the explicit point in Jeremiah 31, where Yahweh pledges that the new covenant "will not be like the covenant that I made with their ancestors" at Sinai, which they broke (v. 32).

Wright suggests that although Paul's nemesis was not legalism, it was certainly a rigorism that he himself once held as a Shammaite rather than a more lenient Hillel Pharisee. "This is what it means to be 'zealous for God' or 'zealous for the traditions of the fathers' in first-century Judaism."[9] Illustrating the contrast, "The Gamaliel of Acts 5," says Wright, "would not have approved of the stoning of Stephen."[10] Sanders is right that we have misjudged Judaism as Pelagian, but his view of "Judaism" corresponds exclusively to the less rigorous Hillelite position expressed in the Mishnah.[11] Preconversion Paul (i.e., Saul) was interested neither in "a timeless system of salvation" (the view that Wright attributes to Protestant orthodoxy) or a system of "getting in or staying in" (Sanders). "He wanted God to redeem Israel."[12]

Although Wright differs on the details, he shares Sanders's basic paradigm, especially when it comes to the assumption that here we are dealing with one covenant—"the renewed covenant."[13] Monocovenantalism leads Wright to further reductionism: "In [Gal. 3] vv. 15–18, then, Paul is not merely contrasting 'law' and 'promise' as mutually incompatible types of religious systems."[14] Fine: not "merely," but is it *part* of what Paul is up to in this passage? "The Torah, if taken absolutely, would undercut the promise (v. 18) not so much because of the difference between 'works' and 'faith'. . . ."[15] According to Wright, Paul's point in this passage is that "Moses is not the mediator through whom this promised 'one seed' is brought into existence. He cannot be, since he (Moses) is the mediator of a revelation to Israel only, οἱ ἐκ νόμου."[16] So while he acknowledges different *mediators*, Wright does not recognize that this requires a different *covenant*, and any differences that might obtain he restricts to the question of membership (ecclesiology) rather than the basis of justification (soteriology). The circularity of the argument is apparent: As a Jew, Paul was not interested in "how to be saved" but in opening the covenant to Gentiles. Therefore, "works of the law" must refer to boundary markers, not to law-keeping in general. These assumptions control the exegesis of any and all specific passages.

9. N. T. Wright, *What Saint Paul Really Said: Was Paul of Tarsus the Real Founder of Christianity?* (Grand Rapids: Eerdmans, 1997), 27.

10. Ibid., 29.

11. Ibid., 32. Besides misjudging medieval theology as "Pelagian," the NPP does not even give Pelagius his due. After all, at least from what we know about his views in his commentary on Romans and the writings of his students, along with Augustine's (admittedly prejudiced) citations and the church's condemnations, Pelagianism at least held that baptism was a gift of grace, as were the provisions for repentance and satisfactions.

12. Ibid.

13. N. T. Wright, *Climax of the Covenant: Christ and the Law in Pauline Theology* (Edinburgh: T&T Clark, 1991), 156.

14. Ibid., 166.

15. Ibid.

16. Ibid., 169.

By contrast, I would argue that according to Paul (as well as Hebrews), there are more radical reasons why Moses cannot mediate the promised blessing to the world. It is not simply because the Sinai covenant is exclusively concerned with Israel, but also because Christ is the mediator of a better covenant, founded on better promises. Paul's target is the monocovenantalism (covenantal nomism) that, for all of their differences, Sanders, Dunn, and Wright seem largely to affirm. The single covenant may undergo ecclesiological redefinition (inclusion of Gentiles), thereby modifying its doctrine of election, but there are not two covenants with distinct foundations (law and promise).

By contrast, when we distinguish these covenants, the Abrahamic/new covenant promises are seen to be better not merely because they include Gentiles, but because they are unconditional, sworn by God himself, with a better ministry (conducted in the heavenly sanctuary), high priest, and sacrifices (in addition to Galatians, see Heb. esp. 7–10). As the prophets promised, something more radical has appeared with Christ than the renewal of the Sinai covenant and restoration of Israel, only this time ethnically diverse. John's Gospel expresses the decisiveness of the event that Paul elaborates: "From [Christ's] fullness we have all received, grace upon grace. The law indeed was given through Moses; grace and truth came through Jesus Christ" (John 1:16–17). Moses was a recipient of and witness to the eschatological gift, but Jesus—who is no less than God incarnate—is its mediator. Moses was a servant, but Jesus is the Son. In fact, Moses' own entrance into the typological land was forfeited by disobedience, even though he entered the heavenly Zion through faith in Christ (Heb. 11:23–29).

Even some scholars sympathetic to the NPP have challenged the one-sidedness of attempts at radical continuity. In Qumran, according to Hermann Lichtenberger, "Along with the Torah the 'hidden things' form the core of the divine direction whose observance gives life (CD 3, 15f)."[17] "The covenant at Sinai also defined the identity of the community."[18] Entrance into this remnant community (the covenant) is grounded in a voluntary obedience to Torah. "Living according to the Torah can be depicted as a perfect walk along the ways of God (1QS 2, 2)," with blessings and curses falling appropriately. "It offers a framework within the community in which they can lead their lives in a way that is pleasing to God and gives the promise of salvation."[19] Even those who sinned before Sinai are judged by Torah, since God the Lawgiver is also God the Creator (CD II, 17ff.).[20] There is the prayer that God will keep them from sins, "so that you may find joy at the end of the age by finding some portion of what we say to be true, this *being counted to you for righteousness* if you *do* what is true and good before God for the salvation *of yourself and of Israel*" (C 25–32, emphasis added).[21] Clearly, the question

---

17. Hermann Lichtenberger, "The Understanding of the Torah in the Judaism of Paul's Day," in Dunn, *Paul and the Mosaic Law*, 12.
18. Ibid.
19. Ibid., 13.
20. Ibid., 14.
21. Ibid., 16.

of how one can be saved is crucial in this perspective and the answer is just as explicit. Qumran was a community of covenant renewal—that is, a revival of the Mosaic economy—rather than a community that relied on "better promises" and "a better mediator." Although he repeats the familiar verdict that such Second Temple groups did not embrace a purely legalistic soteriology, Lichtenberger concludes from the sources, "The attainment of eternal life could certainly be attributed to a judgment on human deeds."[22]

Where Dunn thinks that Paul gradually came to his views in continuity rather than conflict with Judaism, Martin Hengel offers persuasive evidence that Galatians is Paul's first epistle, and therefore the doctrine of justification was central for him before any controversy between Antioch and Jerusalem. This challenges the idea first suggested by Schweitzer and the history-of-religions school that justification was a "subsidiary crater" in Paul that emerged in polemical conflict.[23] Hengel adds, "As a legacy from Jewish Pharisaism, a comparatively unthinking practical 'synergism' seems to have held sway, and this defined later piety in the church. . . . For contemporary Judaism the law in its varied forms was the epitome of salvation. It could be fundamentally equated with 'life.'"[24] But now for Paul, "The Risen Lord is now ζωή for believers (2 Cor. 4:11f., cf. 2:16). Being in or under the law is replaced by being ἐν Χριστῷ."[25] "So far as I can see," Hengel adds, "there were no basic changes in Paul's central message from the days of his conversion or from the beginning of his missionary work as an apostle."[26] In fact, his christological building blocks (Christ, Son of God, Lord) are all drawn from earlier elements of the Jesus tradition he had once opposed.[27] "We must reject as fully nonhistorical the ideas that Paul was influenced by Hellenistic syncretism, by the Mystery Religions, or by Gnosticism." The dating just does not allow it.[28]

Suspecting that much of the debate over the relation of law and gospel in Paul results from missing the forest for the trees, Graham Stanton has suggested that since Galatians was composed and heard as an oral text, "we need to attend to the 'sound map' of this letter."[29] "If we attend to the 'sound map' of these chapters, Paul's main point is crystal clear: πίστις and νόμος are at odds with one another."[30]

> The phrase, "the works of the law," is used five times within eleven verses (2:16 three times; 3:2, 5). The repetition of this phrase as part of a sharp antithesis was intended to make a strong impact on the initial hearers: the

22. Ibid., 22.
23. Martin Hengel, "The Attitude of Paul to the Law in the Unknown Years between Damascus and Antioch," in Dunn, *Paul and the Mosaic Law,* 25.
24. Ibid., 33.
25. Ibid.
26. Ibid., 34.
27. Ibid.
28. Ibid., 40–41.
29. Stanton, "The Law of Moses and the Law of Christ: Galatians 3:1–6:2," in Dunn, *Paul and the Mosaic Law,* 100.
30. Ibid., 100–101.

initial recipients could hardly have missed the contrast Paul was drawing between two different ways of establishing one's standing before God.... I am convinced that Paul is refuting the agitators' claim that one's standing before God was dependent on carrying out the requirements of the Mosaic law.[31]

Faith alone is necessary for getting in and staying in (3:5).[32]

Although in the end Räisänen judges Paul to be wrong, he seems justified in concluding, "I repeat what I have written in concession to those who criticize Sanders' position on Paul's view of 'works of the law': 'It may be too much to exclude all overtones of the idea of anthropocentric legalism.'"[33] "Sanders was right to stress God's grace and mercy in the system," writes Andrew Das, "but he stated matters too strongly when he denied that God commands strict obedience of the law."[34] In fact, as we have seen, Sanders himself goes back and forth on this point. "Further, Sanders fails to define the 'covenant.'" It is simply identified as the other side of the coin of "law" (torah), as in the Sinaitic covenant.[35] In the light of Galatians 3:15–17, Das concludes:

> If Sanders is right that covenant and law are two sides of the same coin in "covenantal nomism," then Paul's argument here would be troubling. First, Paul asserts that the law came 430 years after the promise and "covenant" (διαθήκη). Where obedience to the law, according to covenantal nomism, is grounded in the covenant relationship begun with Abraham, Paul sunders that relationship.... Paul disrupts the theology of Judaism and Jewish Christianity by severing the connection between the covenant and promises on one side and the Sinaitic legislation on the other.[36]

In the allegory in Galatians 4, "Paul therefore grants an association between the Mosaic law and an Abrahamic covenant. Unfortunately for the covenantal nomist, it is the wrong one, the covenant of slavery."[37]

The same point is made by J. Louis Martyn, although instead of two types of covenants he contrasts covenant (as inherently gracious) with law: "Separating covenant and Law in this radical manner, then, Paul is scarcely pursuing a line of thought that moves within the frame of reference properly identified as covenantal nomism. On the contrary, it explodes that frame of reference by a bill of divorce, the divorcing of covenant from Law."[38] Here, Martyn recognizes the sharp antithe-

31. Ibid., 103.
32. Ibid., 104.
33. Heikki Räisänen, "Faith, Works and Election in Romans 9," in Dunn, *Paul and the Mosaic Law*, 242, citing his own "Paul's Call Experience and His Later View of the Law," in *Jesus, Paul and Torah*, JSNTSup 43 (Sheffield: JSOT Press, 1992), 37 (cf. 46).
34. Andrew Das, *Paul, the Law, and the Covenant* (Peabody, MA: Hendrickson, 2001), 44.
35. Ibid., 71.
36. Ibid., 75.
37. Ibid., 76.
38. J. Louis Martyn, "Events in Galatia: Modified Covenantal Nomism versus God's Invasion of the Cosmos in the Singular Gospel," in *Thessalonians, Philippians, Galatians, Philemon*, ed. Jouette M. Bassler, vol. 1 of *Pauline Theology* (Minneapolis: Fortress, 1991), 171.

sis of law and gospel, but perpetuates the tendency to reduce "covenant" to a single type: in this case, exclusively gracious. The proper distinction is not between covenant and law, but between law-covenant and promise-covenant.

DISTINGUISHING LAW-AS-HISTORY
FROM LAW-AS-COVENANTAL PRINCIPLE

As Heikki Räisänen, Stephen Westerholm, and others have argued recently, *nomos* can be translated "principle" (as it has been in some translations).[39] This is precisely the nature of a covenant: a principle ordering the individual and community, the canon or constitution that makes a community what it is. If this is so, then Paul would seem to be working with more systematic-theological categories than we usually give him credit for. Particularly when he speaks of law and promise as representing "two covenants" in Galatians 4, can we not conclude that these are for Paul equivalent to the covenant of works (or law) and the covenant of grace?

Law as Covenantal Principle

The mere presence of law does not create a law-covenant, since the writing of the law upon hearts is part of what is promised in the covenant of grace. The question is how law functions: either as the principle or basis for punishment and reward (as in a law-covenant) or as a normative guide that is no longer able to condemn (as in a promise-covenant). Justification by the works of the law, for example, would represent the law not only as something to be followed but also as the basis or at least the means of attaining it. What makes something a law-covenant is how law functions in the economy.

Crucial for this chapter, then, is a distinction between law in the broader *redemptive-historical* sense (i.e., Old Testament promise and New Testament fulfillment) and law in the more precise, *technical* sense (in terms of principles), identifying the specific terms and bases of inheritance (i.e., law-covenant versus promise-covenant). The first accounts for continuity, while the latter underscores discontinuity. Bearing in mind these different senses in which "law" is meant in Paul and elsewhere in the New Testament enables us to avoid some of the exegetical reductionism that forces a choice between them.

Ever since the fall, the law can only condemn those who are under it, and to be "under the law" is to be under the terms of the law as the condition for receiving blessing and avoiding the curse-sanctions. Obedience to the law was, of course, a condition of "long life" in the land of Canaan, but it could not—and cannot—bring eschatological life (Gal. 3:21).

---

39. Stephen Westerholm, *Israel's Law and the Church's Faith: Paul and His Recent Interpreters* (Grand Rapids: Eerdmans, 1988), 147.

Yet Paul is hardly an innovator on this point. Deuteronomy itself moves from the command to the Israelites to circumcise their own hearts (10:16) to the promise that, given what God knows will happen in this unfolding drama, he will himself accomplish this since they cannot (30:6). Unlike the Second Temple literature we have reviewed, Deuteronomy—the archive of the Sinai covenant itself—displays a full awareness of the differences between these covenants and, we can even infer, the weakness of the law itself due to human sin.

The prophets not only approve of the Sinai covenant but also prosecute its claims. However, they too hold out hope in the future only on the basis of the new covenant, as the realization of the Abrahamic promise. Bad news is announced on the basis of Sinai and good news on the basis of Zion. Assimilating these two covenants, Paul's agitators expected good news from Sinai, and that was their crucial blunder. So here his opponents stood, on this side of the cross and resurrection, reswearing the Sinai oath, "All this we will do." Whatever Jesus adds to Judaism, he does not fundamentally alter their attempt (like other Second Temple groups) at renewing the Sinai covenant.

The Law as Covenantal History

Bringing these exegetical insights together for theological formulation, I suggest, requires exactly the sort of nuance that one finds in the Reformers, especially in Calvin, although he never formalized his practice into a theory. Like Paul, Calvin moves back and forth between what I have elsewhere identified as two hermeneutical gears: the redemptive-historical and the more technical sense of "law."[40] One moment, *the* law is equivalent to the Old Testament or, more narrowly, the old covenant (specifically identified with the Sinaitic economy), both of which evidence continuity redemptive-historically, that is, in terms of promise and fulfillment. The sacrifices are pointers to Christ. The righteousness *required* in the law is the same righteousness *given* in the new covenant. In these respects, there is perfect agreement between law (old covenant) and gospel (new covenant). Subsequent Reformed interpretation especially highlighted this redemptive-historical aspect in a covenant theology that is nothing like the "timeless principles of salvation" that Wright seems to attribute to this tradition.[41] What Wright seems to identify with timeless principles is what I have been calling the technical use of *nomos*. While it is hardly timeless, it does reflect God's unchanging moral character and is engraved on the human conscience in creation, as Jewish theology also well attests.[42]

---

40. See Michael Horton, "Calvin and the Law-Gospel Hermeneutic," *Pro ecclesia* 6 (1997): 27–42.

41. In fact, the debate between Cocceius and Voetius in the seventeenth century turned on the question of continuity. In the most spirited controversy within early federal theology, neither party was advocating "timeless principles" versus a redemptive-historical paradigm. For a good example of the typical approach of these writers, see Herman Witsius, *The Economy of the Covenants between God and Man* (1677), trans. William Crookshank, 2 vols. (London: R. Baynes, 1822; repr., Phillipsburg, NJ: P&R Publishing, 1990); for the unity and diversity of the covenant of grace in its OT and NT administrations in particular, see book 3, chaps. 2–3.

42. See chap. 4, n. 4.

However, there is also the redemptive-historical use of the law as the old covenant history leading to Christ. In this redemptive-historical sense, law and promise are entirely in agreement: Christ as the *telos* of the law in the sense of fulfillment. This became a major emphasis particularly in Calvin's responses to Anabaptist challenges to the unity of the covenant of grace in both Testaments. One might call this, anachronistically, his *historia salutis* (redemptive-historical) approach. By contrast, when the question was justification and the way a sinner can obtain salvation, law was regarded as a principle or method of salvation in antithesis to promise or gospel—a question of *ordo salutis*. Such gear-shifting, far from arbitrary, is simply a way of interpreting the same term (*nomos*) in different texts and different contexts.

When the laws are set before the people as a covenant to be personally fulfilled (Josh. 8:34), with attendant sanctions (Deut. 30:15–20), it is clear that we are dealing with law as command (the principle of law) and, specifically, the covenant mediated by Moses at Sinai. We encounter here not simply free-floating laws (*nomoi*), but stipulations that are part of a specific covenant canon.

However, "the Law" can also refer to a body of writings as a whole, especially the Pentateuch, which of course also includes the promise of the gospel apart from "law" (Pss. 19; 119). Similarly, when we read in the New Testament, "The law indeed was given through Moses; grace and truth came through Jesus Christ" (John 1:17), or that the law itself "made nothing perfect" (Heb. 7:19) but was "only a shadow of the good things to come" (10:1), it is obvious that although the law of Moses/Sinai (i.e., the old covenant) is in view, it is considered in its redemptive-historical (*historia salutis*) relation of promise and fulfillment. The old covenant is glorious, but the new covenant more radiant still. There is a continuum rather than a sharp antithesis. In this sense, the contrast is from bright to brighter, not with any inherent tension.

Yet when law/commandment and gospel/promise are strictly set in opposition, the issue in question is how one obtains the promise (*ordo salutis*). Commenting on Galatians 3:10–12, Calvin writes,

> The argument is drawn from the contradictory nature of the two schemes. . . . The law justifies him who fulfils all its precepts, while faith justifies those who are destitute of the merit of works and who rely on Christ alone. . . . The law evidently is not contrary to faith; otherwise, God would be unlike himself; but we must return to a principle already noticed, that Paul's language is modified by the present aspect of the case. The contradiction between the law and faith lies in the matter of justification. You will more easily unite fire and water, than reconcile these two statements, that men are justified by faith, and that they are justified by the law. "The law is not of faith"; that is, it has a method of justifying a man which is wholly at variance with faith.[43]

---

43. John Calvin, *Commentary on Galatians*, trans. John King (repr., Grand Rapids: Baker, 1996), on Gal. 3:10–12.

Paul can even switch hermeneutical gears in the same sentence, as in Romans 3:21–22, as we have seen above: the law and the prophets (Old Testament) testify to a justification apart from law (as covenantal principle). We have already seen an example of this in Deuteronomy itself, where the law-as-covenant commands what the law-as-Scripture says the people will not accomplish but will be freely given sometime in the future, when God circumcises their hearts. To use a crude analogy, the redemptive-historical sense of law and gospel is like a dimmer switch (darker to brighter by degrees), while the principial sense is more binary, like an off/on switch. The difference between the Old and New Testaments (i.e., "the law and the prophets") is quantitative, while the difference between a law-covenant and a promise-covenant as the means of our attaining the inheritance is qualitative and antithetical.

It may even be the case that such a hermeneutical distinction was already part of Paul's Jewish milieu, as in Judaism's familiar distinction between haggadah (story) and halakah (command). While the Sinai covenant transforms "history into morality, or in rabbinic language, haggadah into halakah, lore into law," notes Levenson, "In the case of the Davidic covenant, history and morality are no longer the focus, for any claim that God might make peculiarly upon the house of David has already been satisfied by its founder. Rather, the Davidic covenant, a covenant of grace, looks beyond the vicissitudes of history, since they cease to be critical." The Davidic covenant "fixes its attention" on "the constancy of God rather than the changeability of man, it brings to light what is secure and inviolable, whereas the Sinaitic texts tend to emphasize the precariousness of life and the consequent need for a continuously reinvigorated obedience."[44]

Not only Paul but also the writer to the Hebrews especially emphasizes the contrast between Sinai and Zion in terms of that which is earthly, temporary, anticipatory, and conditional on one hand and that which is heavenly, eternal, consummate, and unconditional on the other. This is because whereas the Sinai covenant was mediated through Moses in history, the covenant of grace is grounded in God's eternal decree—the covenant of redemption (Gal. 3:20).[45] The entire gospel is nothing other than the story of what God did in Jesus Christ. The gospel is always the announcement of this unfolding redemptive plot. As good *news*, it can only be told, not done, by us. Although law is still present even in the covenant of grace (as it was in the Davidic covenant, where God's unconditional promise does not void the potential for temporal discipline), it is not the covenantal principle for obtaining justification and life.

With respect to the principle of inheritance (law in the principial sense), Sinai and Zion are related by contrast rather than by continuum (Gal. 4; Heb. 13; etc.). Nevertheless, the story (*haggadah*) is never absorbed into law and morality; even the law (in the redemptive-historical sense), as the Old Testament, witnesses to

---

44. Jon Levenson, *Sinai and Zion: An Entry into the Jewish Bible* (San Francisco: HarperSanFrancisco, 1985), 101.

45. See S. M. Baugh's outstanding exegetical treatment of this connection in "Galatians 3:20 and the Covenant of Redemption," *Westminster Theological Journal* 66 (2004): 49–70.

the gospel. Identified with the typological service it renders in pointing forward to Christ, it is not only a story of death and condemnation, but also of life through him as the true Israel who fulfilled the law and bore its sanctions for us.

Identified with the principle of attaining the Abrahamic promise, however, law ends up recapitulating the story of Adam. Paul appeals to a principle of law (*ergon nomou*) and a redemptive-historical drama (*paidagōgos*, or as in Rom. 3:21, *martyroumenē hpo tou nomou kai tōn prophētōn*). Even with respect to the former sense, pace Bultmann and Betz, law and gospel (as principles of inheritance) are not inherently opposed. In fact, the comparison and contrast of the two Adams in Romans 5 requires fulfillment of the law as the condition for the eschatological blessing of those whom they represent. Thus, believers are justified by the works of the law, but by Christ's work rather than their own personal performance.

Law and gospel only become sharply opposed when the question is raised as to how we, being found covenant-breakers in Adam, are to be reconciled to God and to receive the everlasting blessing.

The Reference Range of *Nomos* in Paul

Since these categories at best can only illumine the background of Paul's usage, we are left with the context to determine in any given case what Paul means by law. It has been persuasively demonstrated that the apostle refers to "law" both in terms of the specific stipulations of the Sinai covenant (things that need "doing"), as the terms for covenantal blessing, and in terms of the history of Israel. In the first (principial) sense, Paul can only "see 'law' and 'gospel' as standing in contrast with each other."[46] Westerholm even employs the categories widely used by Reformation theology here: law in the broader and narrower sense.[47] There is the Law, which is the Pentateuch generally, and "the law which can be 'kept,' 'done,' 'fulfilled,' or 'transgressed'"—clearly 'the legal parts' of the Pentateuch."[48] "The Sinaitic legislation was accompanied by sanctions, and Paul includes these when he speaks of the 'law.' Thus the law promises life to those who perform its commands (Rom. 10:5; Gal. 3:12; cf. Rom. 2:13, 25; 7:10)."[49] So "under the law" means "bound by the demands of the Mosaic law code and subject to its sanctions."[50] It seems clear enough that for Paul law and promise are two different ways of securing this inheritance. "Of Paul's 119 uses of *nomos*," notes Douglas Moo, "none occurs in the plural," and the occurrence in the LXX citations by him account for this in part, though it also suggests that "Paul discusses the law as a single entity rather than as a series of commands."[51] Further, "*nomos*

---

46. Westerholm, *Israel's Law and the Church's Faith*, 106.
47. Ibid., 107–9.
48. Ibid., 109.
49. Ibid.
50. Ibid.
51. Douglas Moo, "'Law,' 'Works of the Law,' and Legalism in Paul," *Westminster Theological Journal* 45 (1983): 75.

appears to possess the root meaning 'something laid down, ordered, or assigned' and hence the system of customs or rules governing equitable and/or just distribution of things and duties. In a formal sense, then, the term can be used generally of an 'order,' 'system,' or even 'authority.'"[52] Law in this sense refers not simply to specific laws but to the whole system or covenant according to which both promise and threat depend on our personal performance of the stipulations.

According to Moo, Romans 7:21 is an instance of what I am calling law in a principial sense:

> I would maintain that Paul distinguishes promise and law *by definition* (see Gal 3:15–25 and Rom 4:14–16), so that the denial that justification can come through the law (e.g., Gal 3:11) is not a denial that those "under the law" could be justified. It *does* constitute a denial that man could ever be justified *by means of* the law (see Gal 2:21; 3:21).[53]

"In other words, Paul appears to criticize 'works of the law' not because they are *nomou* ('of the law') but because they are *erga* ('works')."[54] Human beings, "according to Paul, required redemption from 'the curse of the law' (Gal 3:13), not better teaching about the meaning and use of the law."[55]

It is striking how the prophets typically invoke the covenant sanctions for injustice, oppression, immorality, and idolatry. Notably absent are references to the failure to be circumcised or to observe the dietary laws. In fact, they routinely upbraid Israel for its confidence in the temple and the outward rites while their hearts remain uncircumcised. Paul's alleged pessimism is already expressed in Deuteronomy and in the prophets, as Israel's fall and exile are predicted and confirmed.[56] It is also found in *4 Ezra* (2 Esd.) 9:36: "We who have received the law must nevertheless perish on account of our sins."[57] It is into this void that Paul announces the justification of the ungodly apart from law.

It is difficult to see the logic in Paul's argument in Romans 1:18–3:20 apart from this interpretation. After all, everyone's mouth is stopped and held accountable precisely because (as is also taught in the Jewish doctrine of the Noachian laws) the moral core of the Sinai law is engraved on the conscience of every person.[58] Gentiles are thus, indirectly, under the law by virtue of the covenant of creation (also a law-covenant), just as the Jews are also under the law in a more fully delineated sense in the Sinai covenant.

52. Ibid., 77.
53. Ibid., 88.
54. Ibid., 100.
55. Ibid.
56. Whatever the dating of the final edition of Deuteronomy, I am assuming here that these later chapters are also preexilic.
57. Cited by Herman Bavinck, *Reformed Dogmatics*, ed. John Bolt, trans. John Vriend, vol. 3 (Grand Rapids: Baker Academic, 2006), 497; from F. Loofs, *Leitfaden zum Studium der Dogmengeschichte*, 4th ed. (Halle a. S.: M. Niemeyer, 1906), 59.
58. David Novak, *Covenantal Rights: A Study in Jewish Political Theory* (Princeton, NJ: Princeton University Press, 2000), 20–25. See also idem, *Jewish-Christian Dialogue: A Jewish Justification* (New York: Oxford University Press, 1989), esp. 27.

Westerholm's point is more specific, however, and more directly targets the NPP claim that in Paul's usage "law" or "the law" is something other than a body of commands: "But, as we have seen, 'law' in Paul most often means the Sinaitic legislation; and *it is not legitimate to apply what Paul says of the scriptures in general to the Sinaitic laws without further ado*" (emphasis original).[59] Therefore, Paul's argument is that "since the law requires 'doing,' it 'does not rest on faith.'"[60] It is not any particular law or set of laws, but *doing* as opposed to *believing*, that marks Paul's polemical contrast of law and gospel, works and faith.

> The law requires that its subjects comply with its commands. God's promise to Abraham, however, cannot be made conditional upon what humans do. Therefore, if adherence to the law is required of Abraham's descendants, "the promise is void" (Rom. 4:14). The same point is made in Gal. 3:18: "If the inheritance is by the law, it is no longer by promise."[61]

In Paul's view (see Phil. 3) it is possible to be righteous in a first-century-Jewish or even Sinaitic sort of way and yet remain unrighteous in relation to the real demands of the law, which reverberate in the consciences even of Gentiles as the law of our very being as covenant creatures.

Even if one could keep the Decalogue externally, this does not mean that the spirit of the law (unreserved love for God and neighbor) has been fulfilled. In fact, it is conceivable that the sense in which Paul regarded himself as "blameless" was that external conformity to the law that Jesus identified as "the righteousness of the scribes and Pharisees" that one must *surpass* in order to inherit the kingdom of God (Matt. 5:20). With the rich young man whom Jesus encountered, Paul could well have said, "I have kept all these; what do I still lack?" (19:20), yet both are found guilty of violating the whole law by failing to fulfill the deepest intentions of the law on any specific point. "I would not have known what it is to covet if the law had not said, 'You shall not covet.' But sin, seizing an opportunity in the commandment, produced in me all kinds of covetousness" (Rom. 7:7–8).

It is clear enough that Paul no less than Jesus made such statements within the context of Jewish exclusivism but as Westerholm notes, "in rejecting 'works of law,' Paul moves the discussion onto another level."[62] Crucially, and devastatingly for the NPP, Westerholm points out, "The 'works of the law' which do not justify are the demands of the law that are not met, not those observed for the wrong reasons by Jews."[63] One might add that if in Romans 2 the Jews are condemned

---

59. Westerholm, *Israel's Law and the Church's Faith*, 109. He adds on 111, "To repeat: according to Paul's most frequent usage of *nomos*, the term refers to the sum of specific divine requirements given to Israel through Moses. They are intended to be 'done' (*poiein, prassein*) or 'kept' (*phylassein, telein*), though the placing of concrete demands of course makes possible the 'transgression' (*parabasis*) of the law as well."
60. Ibid.
61. Ibid., 114.
62. Ibid., 117.
63. Ibid., 118.

for not fulfilling the works of the law, this can hardly fit circumcision and dietary laws, which they did in fact keep scrupulously.

> That Paul supports his rejection of the "works of the law" in Rom. 3:20, 28 by showing that Abraham was justified by faith, not works (4:1–5), is positively fatal to Dunn's proposal, as it was to that of Gaston. For the "works" by which Abraham could conceivably have been justified, and of which he might have boasted (4:2), were certainly not observances of the peculiarly Jewish parts of the Mosaic code. Paul is here demonstrating that the broad category of "works" cannot be a factor in salvation in order to exclude the subcategory, "works of law." Not particular works which set Jews apart, but works in general—anything "done" that might deserve a recompense (*misthos*, 4:4) or justify pride (*kauchēma*, v. 2)—are meant, and that in contrast with the "faith" of one who "does not work" but benefits by divine grace without any consideration of personal merit.[64]

Thus, Westerholm concludes, Luther's "contrast between 'law' and 'gospel,' though never explicit in the epistles, does not distort Paul's point."[65] If, however, "gospel" is synonymous with "promise"—and the Reformers in fact used these terms interchangeably—then we can go one step further and recognize that Luther's contrast (which Calvin and the Reformed tradition shared) is in fact explicitly found in Paul (Rom. 4:14–16; Gal. 3:18; cf. Heb. 4:1–9).

The interpretation I am arguing for on this point is also close to that of Richard Hays's conclusions concerning Romans 4. If, according to Paul, the gospel upholds the law, then in what sense? "His discussion of Abraham in chapter 4 seeks to show that the νόμος πίστεως [3:27] is consistent with the Law—now understood to mean, however, not the Mosaic covenant, but Scripture taken as a narrative whole. This is the hermeneutical transmutation that allows Paul to claim continuity between Law and gospel."[66] Hays adds:

> Either way, the Law, being associated with wrath and condemnation, is set in juxtaposition to faith and to the promise given to Abraham (4:13–17). The provocative rhetorical force of this move should not be overlooked. Against the common Jewish view that the Law is a secure foundation, a source of life and hope for the elect community, Paul highlights its negative functions, its power to curse and condemn.

In Romans Paul has chosen "to focus on its awesome capacity to pronounce judgment and to bring condemnation by demanding a righteousness that it has no power to produce (cf. 8:3–4)."[67]

Would this not suggest that Paul was actually refuting covenantal nomism just as it has been summarized by its sympathetic interpreters? "When Paul insists

64. Ibid., 119.
65. Ibid., 122.
66. Richard B. Hays, "Three Dramatic Roles: The Law in Romans 3–4," in Dunn, *Paul and the Mosaic Law*, 155.
67. Ibid., 157.

that through faith 'we uphold the Law' (3:31)"—and that the Law and Prophets testify to this gospel (3:21), "and then supports that claim by appealing to the story of Abraham, the 'Law' that is being upheld seems to be not only the Shema (3:30a) but also the Pentateuchal narrative, construed as a prefiguration of the gospel."[68] So concerning Romans 3:21, at least, Hays thinks—correctly, in my estimation—that J. A. Sanders is closer to the mark: Paul reads Torah in this place not as halakah, but as haggadah. And this is the basis for Paul's *narrative* unity of law and gospel, despite their *principial* antithesis as two distinct covenants with their own historical prologue and mediator (a covenant made exclusively between Yahweh and Israel) and basis (law rather than promise).

Paul is therefore not being contradictory, as Räisänen and others suggest, nor must we force a unity by recourse to covenantal nomism. Rather, Paul speaks of law in two distinct senses. The law as *haggadah*—the history of redemption—is simply the Old Testament anticipation of Christ. Elsewhere Hays writes, "Moses and the Law of Sinai are assigned a temporary supporting role, not the lead, in the drama of God's redemptive purpose. Thus, the Torah is neither superseded nor nullified but transformed into a witness to the gospel."[69] In another sense (law as the basis for salvation: this latter confusion evidenced by his antagonists), Paul could not be more emphatic on the antithesis between law and gospel. This, I would suggest, is the law as *halakah,* or the law as the principial means of securing the promise. And as Hays reminds us, "We see within Romans Paul's movement from one hermeneutical perspective to another." As commandment, the law could only condemn; as historical narrative (Old Testament Scripture), it leads to Christ and therefore to redemption apart from law.[70]

In one sense, of course, Paul does not think that law and gospel are opposed *even in the technical sense* (i.e., as the terms in a covenant that serve as the basis for blessing or curse). Christ is the end of the law both as redemptive-historical telos and as the termination of its condemning sentence because he offers to the Father, in the Spirit, that perfect internal and external conformity to the law in our place. Therefore, the law is not set aside but upheld—fulfilled. We are justified apart from our personal performance only because his fulfillment of the law-covenant counts as our own.

Thus, the distinction between two covenants within the Old Testament itself becomes the crucial prerequisite for integrating a host of passages that are otherwise so susceptible to false dilemmas. As M. G. Kline reminds us, "Paul found the difference between two of the Old Testament covenants to be so radical that he felt obliged to defend the thesis that the one did not annul the other (Gal 3:15ff)."[71] Moisés Silva adds, "We could hardly be accused of falling into speculation, for instance, if we should argue that the Judaizers insisted on the compatibility

---

68. Ibid., 158.
69. Richard B. Hays, *Echoes of Scripture in the Letters of Paul* (New Haven: Yale University Press, 1989), 157.
70. Hays, "Three Dramatic Roles: The Law in Romans 3–4," 164.
71. M. G. Kline, *By Oath Consigned* (Grand Rapids: Eerdmans, 1968), 22.

between the Abrahamic and Sinaitic covenants. This rather obvious point, however, has seldom affected our reading of Galatians 3 the way it ought to." Paul's critics were probably saying that he was basically annulling God's covenant with Israel, so in Galatians 3 "Paul is on the defensive." The agitators were raising "law keeping to a level that it was never intended to occupy."[72] So it is Paul's opponents who are setting law and promise in antithesis (law *over* promise, Sinai *over* Abraham, the nation *over* the nations) and when this occurs, Paul has no choice but to take up their challenge by emphasizing the opposite conclusion.

Restricting "works of the law" to ethnic distinctives is not a new exegetical proposal. In fact, the Reformers repeatedly encountered this view. Acknowledging that sometimes Paul has the ethnic markers in mind, Calvin nevertheless offers examples that confirm a wider intention. "Therefore no cavils of theirs can prevent us from holding to the exclusive expression ["apart from works"] as a general principle." In Romans 4:6 Paul contrasts debt and gift, not simply some works and other works, Calvin adds.[73] When Paul speaks of the wall of partition between Jews and Gentiles being torn down by the abolition of the law (Eph. 2:14–15; Col. 2:13–14), Calvin recognizes:

> There is no doubt that this statement concerns the ceremonies, for he speaks of them as a wall that divides the Jews from the Gentiles. Hence, I admit that the second group of expositors rightly criticizes the first. But the second group also still does not seem to explain the meaning of the apostle very well. For I am not at all happy about comparing the two passages in every detail. When Paul would assure the Ephesians of their adoption into the fellowship of Israel, he teaches that the hindrance which once held them back has now been removed. That was in the ceremonies. . . . Now who cannot see that a loftier mystery is referred to in the letter to the Colossians? The question there concerns the Mosaic observances, to which the false apostles were trying to drive the Christian people. But as in the letter to the Galatians he carries that discussion deeper—reverting, so to speak, to its starting point—so he does in this passage. For if you consider nothing else in the rites than the necessity of performing them, what is the point in calling them "the written bond against us" [Col 2:14]? Moreover, why lodge nearly the whole of our redemption in the fact that they are "blotted out"?[74]

After defending a similar point in relation to Philippians 3, Kim notes:

> To oppose this interpretation, Dunn dutifully starts with a citation of his dogma: "the need to attain one's own righteousness was no part of traditional Jewish teaching." This dogma does not allow him to take "my own righteousness" in verse 9 in its natural grammatical sense of Paul's personal

72. Moisés Silva, "Is the Law Against the Promises? The Significance of Galatians 3:21 for Covenant Continuity," in *Theonomy: A Reformed Critique*, ed. William S. Barker and W. Robert Godfrey (Phillipsburg, NJ: Presbyterian & Reformed, 1990), 153–54.
73. Calvin, *Institutes* 3.11.20 (1:750).
74. Calvin, *Institutes* 2.7.17.

righteousness, the righteousness that he attained through his faithful observance of the law.[75]

So these are not "personal achievements," Dunn insists. Then, Kim wonders, whose achievements? "If they were not what he could claim as his personal achievement, what was the basis on which he could have *greater* 'confidence in the flesh' than his Jewish opponents (v. 4b)?"[76] If it was merely a national righteousness, he would have said "our righteousness."[77]

The NPP challenges any qualitative distinction between law and gospel (much less a covenant of works and a covenant of grace). Even such a seminal architect of the new perspective as Dunn recognizes, "The more obvious line of reasoning is that Paul was so remembered [as Judaism's chief heretic] because he was in fact the one who brought the tension between law and gospel (already present in Jesus' own ministry—Mark 7:1–23//Matt. 15:1–20) to its sharpest and indeed antithetical expression."[78] However, as we have seen, he restricts this to the question of corporate identity ("a redefinition of the people of God") rather than the way one is justified.[79] In this way he defuses the very tension that he concedes as crucial to Paul's polemics.

Even Wright makes a distinction between commands and promises.[80] In fact, although he would not wish to be seen aiding and abetting a confessional dogmatic system, throughout *Climax of the Covenant* especially, Wright repeatedly strengthens the exegetical case for the Mosaic theocracy as a law-covenant distinguished from the Abrahamic promise-covenant.[81] Just at this point, however, Wright introduces us again to a false choice: "In [Gal. 3] vv. 15–18, then, Paul is not merely contrasting 'law' and 'promise' as mutually incompatible types of religious systems."[82] Once more, "not *merely*" really seems to mean "not at all." It is not clear who he has in mind as asserting "merely," but the dominant view of the Reformed covenant theology was never that the old covenant was a republication of the covenant of works *simpliciter*, but that it contained a works-principle (the Sinai covenant) alongside the promise-principle of the Abrahamic covenant.[83]

75. Seyoon Kim, *Paul and the New Perspective: Second Thoughts on the Origin of Paul's Gospel* (Grand Rapids: Eerdmans, 2002), 76.

76. Ibid.

77. Ibid., 77; cf. Reginald Fuller, "Here We Stand," in *By Faith Alone: Essays on Justification in Honor of Gerhard O. Forde*, ed. Joseph A. Burgess and Marc Kolden (Grand Rapids: Eerdmans, 2004), 89.

78. Dunn, "Paul and Justification by Faith," 93.

79. Ibid., 95.

80. Wright, *Climax of the Covenant*, 23.

81. Ibid., 146: For example, Paul's point, then, is that Israel as a nation has failed to keep Torah and is thus as a nation under its curse, so that Torah can hardly be the means of returning after exile and retaining membership and becoming a blessing to the world. This can only happen (Gal. 3:10–14) when Israel becomes "the means of blessing the world in accordance with the promise to Abraham"; cf. 197.

82. Ibid., 166.

83. This view is articulated, for example, by Herman Witsius, throughout his work *The Economy of the Covenants*, and by federal theologians from the early period (e.g., Olevianus) all the way up to Charles Hodge and Louis Berkhof.

M. G. Kline has offered an insightful summary of this point.[84] He concentrates on "the cryptic parenthesis that appears in Rom 5:13–14, following the anacoluthon at the end of v. 12."[85]

> Classical covenantalism recognizes that the old Mosaic order (at its foundational level—that is, as a program of individual salvation in Christ) was in continuity with previous and subsequent administrations of the overarching covenant of grace. But it also sees and takes at face value the massive Biblical evidence for a peculiar discontinuity present in the old covenant in the form of a principle of meritorious works, operating not as a way of eternal salvation but as the principle governing Israel's retention of its provisional, typological inheritance.[86]

Therefore, Kline adds, "Paul does repeatedly oppose a Judaistic misinterpretation of the law, but their error was not the assertion that there was a works principle operating in the old covenant. Rather, it was the application of that principle to eternal salvation instead of to the typological level of national Israel's history."[87] Those who regard "covenant" as a univocal concept that is always gracious in principle have to somehow reduce, relativize, or explain away the obvious biblical references to the works-principle, treating them as merely hypothetical. Yet, Kline concludes:

> The law's principle of works was not just something hypothetical. It was actually applied—and with a vengeance. It was the judicial principle that governed the corporate life of Israel as recipient of the national election and controlled Israel's tenure in the typological kingdom of Canaan. Termination of that typological order and Israel's loss of the national election in the divine execution of the covenant curse in the Babylonian exile and again in A.D. 70, exactly as threatened in the Torah treaty, emphatically contradict the notion that the law's stipulations and sanctions were mere hypothetical formulations. . . . On the classic covenantal understanding, the law that came 430 years later did not annul the promise (Gal 3:17)—not because the old covenant did not really introduce an operative works principle, but because works and faith were operating on two different levels in the Mosaic economy.[88]

We have a concrete historical example of what happens when the sanctions of the law-covenant governing the *temporary* theocracy are actually carried out, so why would anyone think that the *everlasting* blessing promised to Abraham might be fulfilled on similar terms?

On election in Galatians 3, Wright says that Paul *modifies* the Jewish doctrine of covenant.[89] However, the New Testament does not treat Jesus as modifying a

---

84. Meredith G. Kline, "Gospel until the Law: Rom 5:13–14 and the Old Covenant," *Journal of the Evangelical Theological Society* 34/4 (December 1991): 433–46.
85. Ibid., 433.
86. Ibid., 434.
87. Ibid., 434 n. 5.
88. Ibid., 435.
89. Ibid., 171.

Jewish doctrine of election, covenant, and justification, but as the one in whom all of the elect (Jew and Gentile) were chosen before creation, and the one by whom the law-covenant is fulfilled so that justification can be obtained in a covenant of grace. As the writer to the Hebrews asserts, the Sinai covenant is "obsolete" (Heb. 8:13). Though thoroughly violated by the national servant, it has been fulfilled by the true Israel, to whom its ceremonies, institutions, and ethnic distinctives merely pointed. Partly because he adheres exclusively to a redemptive-historical meaning of law, Wright can conclude (interpreting 2 Cor. 3:18), "Torah and gospel are not the same, but nor are they here antithetical."[90]

Working within the narrow confines of the NPP presuppositions, with a univocal view of "covenant," "law," and "works of the law," Wright's conclusions on this question are far less nuanced than those of the Reformers and classic covenant theology, as well as those of many contemporary Pauline scholars.[91] In his disputes with Anabaptists, Calvin underscored the unity of the covenant of grace and therefore the redemptive-historical continuity of promise and fulfillment. However, he stands squarely with Luther when the question is how one is made right with God (law versus gospel as the principle for obtaining the inheritance): "Removing, then, mention of law, and laying aside all consideration of works, we should, when justification is being discussed, embrace God's mercy alone, turn our attention from ourselves, and look only to Christ. . . . If consciences wish to attain any certainty in this matter, they ought to give no place to the law."[92]

In spite of his polemics against any principial antithesis between law and gospel, Wright concedes, "The Lutheran wants to maintain the sharp antithesis between law and gospel; so does Paul, but within the context of a single plan of God, and with no suggestion that the Torah itself is a bad thing."[93] Further, "the Lutheran view is not without its merit; it simply needs setting in a wider context," namely, seeing the relation as "contained within the sense of climax, of 'goal.' When I reach my goal I stop traveling; not because my journey was a silly idea but because it was a good idea now fully worked out."[94] Since there are no citations, and neither Luther nor the other Reformers ever said that the law was a silly idea, it is once again unclear whom Wright has in mind as holding this view. At least with respect to the covenant theology that emerged within the

---

90. Ibid., 182.

91. Even Luther displayed remarkably different attitudes toward the law depending on the exegetical context and his own disputes with both Rome and Protestant antinomians. Despite a few examples of rhetorical overstatement, Luther's *How Christians Should Regard Moses* indicates continuities as well as discontinuities between Moses and Christ (in *LW,* 35:161–74). He is even more affirmative in his revised edition of his *Preface to the Old Testament* (in *LW,* 35:235–51). On Melanchthon's dispute with Agricola, see Timothy Wengert, *Law and Gospel: Philip Melanchthon's Debate with John Agricola of Eisleben over Poenitentia* (Grand Rapids: Baker, 1997). I still think that Calvin was more nuanced, however, in formulating a hermeneutical approach to these questions in his commentaries and in his brief but illuminating summary of continuities and discontinuities in the *Institutes* (3.17).

92. Calvin, *Institutes* 3.19.2.

93. Wright, *The Climax of the Covenant,* 241.

94. Ibid., 244.

Reformed tradition, the "wider context" is indeed provided for talking about the law in its redemptive-historical sense as the climax of the covenant without downplaying or eliminating talk of the law as a principle of inheritance opposed to gospel.

Neither Paul nor the Reformers thought that the law was itself the problem, as Bultmann, Betz, and others have (i.e., the law simply equals "curse").[95] But as Seyoon Kim keenly observes, "Deuteronomy 27:26 condemns not those who try to keep the law faithfully, but on the contrary, those who do not do that!"[96] Similarly, as we have seen above, Jesus, Stephen, and Paul do not criticize their hearers for being keepers of the law, but for being lawbreakers. Neither as a covenant of life nor as the Old Testament is the law itself considered silly, much less bad. It is because of our ethical condition as a fallen race and individuals that places us in an adversarial relationship to the law, resulting in death and condemnation.

In addition to Wright, Scott Hafemann suggests that Paul's problem is not with the law but with the law *without the Spirit*.[97] But as Räisänen observes, "Was not the absence of the Spirit in the law or the inability of the law to change the hearts of Israel an inherent weakness of the law itself (cf. Gal. 3:21)?"[98] At least that seems to be Paul's argument, says Räisänen, although he judges that it is the result of the apostle's misunderstanding of Judaism as a religion of "works-righteousness."[99]

More important, Hafemann's contention weakens both the gravity of the situation "under the law" and the blessings realized in the new covenant. The problem is the same: working with a single covenant that simply requires modification (in this case, the law *with the Spirit*), Hafemann does not recognize the principial antithesis between law and gospel. While the Abrahamic covenant is purely promissory, the Sinaitic is certainly represented as conditioning Israel's national status by the works of the law (viz., Lev. 18:5; Deut. 4:1; 5:33; 6:24–25; 8:1; 30:15–18; Neh. 9:29; Ezek. 18:19; cf. 18:9, 21; 20:11, 13, 21). As Westerholm comments, "If Paul is wrong in considering the law a path to salvation, it is an error he shares with Leviticus, Deuteronomy, and Ezekiel."[100] Furthermore, if the law requires compliance with all of its stipulations, then *even with the Spirit*, believers remain under its curse. If we fail to locate Paul's treatment of law within the total order of any particular covenant, we miss critical nuances by an abstract principle of law-plus-the Spirit. As the prophets announced (as in Jer. 31), the new covenant, in contrast to the Sinaitic, includes the gift of the Spirit on the premise that sins are forgiven and the transgressors are justified apart from their own covenant faithfulness.

95. Hans Dieter Betz, *Galatians* (Minneapolis: Fortress, 1979), 145–46.
96. Kim, *Paul and the New Perspective*, 130.
97. Scott Hafemann, *Paul, Moses, and the History of Israel* (Tübingen: Mohr-Siebeck, 1995), 438–51.
98. Räisänen, "Faith, Works and Election in Romans 9," 158 n. 112.
99. Ibid.
100. Westerholm, *Israel's Law and the Church's Faith*, 147.

SUMMARY

If the major condition that Paul's gospel addresses is ethnic rather than ethical and ecclesiological rather than soteriological, it makes little sense that he would spend his first three chapters of Romans (and chap. 5) developing the argument that all people—Jew and Gentile alike—are in Adam, under judgment according to the principle or covenant of works. This is why law—*any* imperative—cannot bring life. Justification and new life depend on a divine indicative and not just any such indicative, but God's deed in Christ as offered in the covenant of grace.

Interestingly, Michael Wyschogrod sees from a contemporary Jewish perspective the way in which Christology changes everything for Paul and gives rise to his classic emphasis on justification and the law-gospel contrast. In Judaism, says Wyschogrod, merit is still a live category, and it is hoped that human beings will come to deserve their redemption. If not, however, "only God justifies and he justifies far more on the basis of mercy than on the basis of rewards earned by good deeds."

> This being so, how could Paul have so misunderstood things? Part of the answer is his fixation on Jesus. The Jesus event so absorbed his theological attention that nothing could be permitted to compete with Jesus including the Torah, which had the deep loyalty of most Jews. Reverence for the Torah was so great that, in the mind of Paul, it was a threat to the proper appreciation of Jesus.[101]

Whatever it was that Paul learned on the Damascus road itself, the event of Christ does not merely provide a supplement to his inherited faith but initiates a paradigm shift that makes all things new.

---

101. Ibid., 232.

Chapter Six

Covenant and Imputation
Justification of the Ungodly

Understanding what Paul meant by justification depends on whether we can come to terms with his anthropology (universal human depravity)[1] and therefore his compelling interest in, as Peter Stuhlmacher puts it, "whether Jews and Gentiles will or will not survive before God's throne of judgment."[2] The gospel is not simply that Jesus was crucified and raised, or that these events demonstrate his lordship, but that he "was crucified for our sins and was raised for our justification" (Rom. 4:25, au. trans.). One of the clearest summaries of the evangelical doctrine of justification is found in chapter 13 of the Westminster Confession:

> Those whom God effectually calls, he also freely justifies: not by infusing righteousness into them, but by pardoning their sins and by accounting and accepting their persons as righteous; not for anything wrought in them or done by them, but for Christ's sake alone; not by imputing faith itself, the act of believing, or any other evangelical obedience to them as their righteousness; but by imputing the obedience and satisfaction of Christ unto

---

1. See Timo Laato, *Paul and Judaism: An Anthropological Approach* (Atlanta: Scholars Press, 1995).
2. Peter Stuhlmacher, *Revisiting Paul's Doctrine of Justification: A Challenge to the New Perspective* (Downers Grove, IL: InterVarsity Press, 2001), 43.

them, they receiving and resting on him and his righteousness by faith; which faith they have not of themselves, it is the gift of God. Faith, thus receiving and resting on Christ and his righteousness, is the sole instrument of justification; yet is it not alone in the person justified, but is ever accompanied with all other saving graces, and is no dead faith, but works by love.

The justified may fall into grave sin and "fall under God's Fatherly displeasure," but they "can never fall from the state of justification."[3]

The Heidelberg Catechism also emphasizes that this divine verdict has Christ's righteousness, not ours, as its basis, so that through faith alone we who "have grievously sinned against all the commandments of God and have not kept any one of them" are nevertheless regarded as though we had never sinned and had perfectly kept the commands. Not even the gift of faith itself can be considered the ground of justification, but simply the empty hand that receives it. This teaching cannot be used to justify moral carelessness, however, "for it is impossible for those who are engrafted into Christ by true faith not to bring forth the fruit of gratitude."[4] Similar summaries can be found, of course, in the Lutheran Book of Concord, the Anglican Thirty-Nine Articles, and the London/Philadelphia (Baptist) Confession.

However, on the basis of the contrasts that we have already encountered in the last five chapters, the NPP suggests two more false choices that touch most directly on the doctrine of justification: imputation (*ordo salutis*) versus God's covenantal faithfulness (*historia salutis*) and, on this basis, an additional choice between a forensic and an effective or transformative view of salvation more broadly.

"THE RIGHTEOUSNESS OF GOD" AND COVENANT THEOLOGY

Assuming a false antithesis between biblical and systematic theology, the *historia salutis* and the *ordo salutis*, ecclesiology and soteriology, NPP advocates conclude that justification is chiefly about God's own vindication of divine faithfulness to the covenant.

God's Righteousness

"For a reader of the Septuagint," says Wright, "'the righteousness of God' would have one obvious meaning: God's own faithfulness to his promises, to the covenant."[5] Wright does not deny that righteousness is a forensic term, and he

3. The Westminster Confession of Faith, chap. XIII, in *The Book of Confessions* (Louisville, KY: General Assembly of the PC[USA], 1991).
4. The Heidelberg Catechism, Q. 60–64, in *The Book of Confessions* (PC[USA], 1991).
5. N. T. Wright, *What Saint Paul Really Said: Was Paul of Tarsus the Real Founder of Christianity?* (Grand Rapids: Eerdmans, 1997), 96.

even places it within the wider context of the covenantal trial, just as one finds it in classic covenant theology.

> "Righteousness" is a forensic term, that is, taken from the law court. . . . Applied to the judge, it means (as is clear from the Old Testament) that the judge must try the case according to the law; that he must be impartial; that he must punish sin as it deserves; and that he must support and uphold those who are defenceless and who have no-one but him to plead their cause. . . . For the plaintiff and the defendant, however, to be "righteous" has none of these connotations. They, after all, are not trying the case. Nor, less obvious to us because of the moral overtones the word "righteous" now has in our own language, does the word mean that they are, before the case starts, morally upright and so deserving to have the verdict go their way. No; for the plaintiff or defendant to be "righteous" in the biblical sense *within the law-court setting* is for them to have that status *as a result of the decision of the court.*[6]

However, he adds, this decision of the court cannot involve an imputation of righteousness to the defendant:

> If we use the language of the law court, it makes no sense whatever to say that the judge imputes, imparts, bequeaths, conveys or otherwise transfers his righteousness to either the plaintiff or the defendant. . . . To imagine the defendant somehow receiving the judge's righteousness is simply a category mistake. That is not how the language works.[7]

God's people will be "justified." "*But the righteousness they have will not be God's own righteousness.* That makes no sense at all. God's own righteousness is his covenant faithfulness" (emphasis original).[8] God cannot credit his faithfulness to someone else.

Yet again Wright is refuting a position that confessional Lutheran and Reformed traditions do not hold. None of the Reformers taught that *God's righteousness* is imputed, although the one who fulfilled the terms of the law-covenant as the human servant is also the divine Lord. A third party, a representative, is left out of the courtroom in Wright's description. There is only a judge/plaintiff (God) and the defendant (Israel). However, Christ is both, and this complicates the picture.

In fact, the mature Reformation doctrine of justification was articulated against both Rome's understanding of justification as an infused quality of righteousness and Andreas Osiander's notion of the believer's participation in God's essential righteousness. The Reformers and their heirs labored the point that it is Christ's successful fulfillment of the trial of the covenantal representative that is imputed or credited to all who believe. His meritorious achievement, not God's own essential righteousness, is imputed. In Christ as the Lord-Servant, God's faithfulness to the covenant and human faithfulness to the covenant finally and

6. Ibid., 97–98.
7. Ibid., 98.
8. Ibid., 99.

fully converge. Yet it is the covenantal obedience that he has "worked out" in his earthly trial that serves as the content of imputation. This is what keeps justification from being abstract or a legal fiction, since the justified do in fact possess "in Christ" the status of those who have perfectly fulfilled all righteousness.

To build on Paul's banking analogy, for one to have not only one's debts cancelled but also a full account by a transfer of funds from someone else renders that wealth no more a fiction than if it were the fruit of one's own labors. As Paul looks over his ledger in Philippians 3, he places all of his own righteousness in the liabilities column and all of Christ's righteousness in his assets column. Wright's account so far does not seem to allow for an inheritance to actually be given to anyone in particular. Justification may be forensic (that is, judicial), but there can be no transfer of assets, if you will, from a faithful representative to the ungodly.

The concept of merit is not unique to medieval theology, as we have seen in Sanders's own treatment of this prominent theme in Jewish sources. If so much of the Second Temple literature affirms the "merit of the fathers" being credited to Israelite transgressors, would it be inimical (perhaps even Hellenistic) to suggest the same in relation to the merit of Christ? That is not even yet to issue a verdict as to what Paul is teaching; it simply recognizes that the notion of imputing acts of obedience from one representative person or group of people to others is not foreign to Jewish thinking. Furthermore, we have seen that Wright himself emphasizes the point that sin is swept into one heap and laid upon Christ, so there is at least a concept of *negative* imputation implicit in his view. If guilt can be imputed from one person to another, why not righteousness? The sin of Adam was imputed to the human race as a covenantal entity in solidarity because it was imputed to each member (Rom. 5:12). This notion of imputing the sin of one person to each Israelite—and thus to the nation generally—is found elsewhere, as in Achan's theft (Josh. 7:10–26). Imputation (either of guilt or righteousness) pertains to the whole (ecclesiology), because it pertains to the parts (soteriology).

If justification is not a matter of imputing righteousness, can one know now who will be vindicated at the last? Yes, say the Jews of Paul's day: by the "works of the law," says Wright, understood of course as the ethnic distinctives.[9] So in interpreting "the righteousness of God," "The basic distinction here is between those who see 'the righteousness of God' as referring to God's own righteousness [either a possessive or subjective genitive], and those who see it as referring to a status of righteousness which humans have before God [either a genitive of origin or objective genitive]."[10] Taking the former view, Wright paraphrases Romans 1:17 to read, "The gospel, he says, reveals or unveils God's own righteousness, his covenant faithfulness, which operates through the faithfulness of Jesus Christ for the benefit of all those who in turn are faithful ('from faith to faith')."[11]

9. Ibid.
10. Ibid., 100.
11. Ibid., 109.

Again we are faced with a false choice, as if Paul could never refer both to the righteousness of God (i.e., his essential righteousness and covenantal faithfulness) and the righteousness that God gives through the obedience of Jesus Christ.[12] Yet the dialectical play between these two seems to lie at the heart of Paul's argument especially in Romans 1–3: the righteousness that God *is* (as revealed in the law) condemns everyone, Jew and Gentile alike. "But now, apart from law, the righteousness of/from God has been disclosed, and is attested by the law and the prophets, the righteousness of God through faith in Jesus Christ for all who believe" (3:21). Does it make sense to say that *God's* covenant faithfulness is disclosed through *our faith* in Christ? Or does it make more sense to say that, rather than revealing the righteousness that God *is* (i.e., his essential righteousness that judges), the gospel reveals the judgment of righteousness (i.e., verdict of justification) that God gives on the basis of Christ's obedience, received through faith? The revelation of God's righteousness that is revealed by the law, "so that every mouth may be silenced, and the whole world may be held accountable to God" (3:19), is different from the revelation of God's righteousness that is revealed in the gospel "apart from law," through faith in Christ (v. 21). The law reveals that God is just (and therefore must condemn all transgressors), but the gospel reveals that God is just and justifier (v. 26).

Our Righteousness

Just as there is apparently only one legitimately eschatological interpretation of justification, there is only one legitimately covenantal interpretation, according to Wright: "When this [justification] is cashed out in terms of the underlying covenantal theme, it means that they are declared, in the present, to be what they will be seen to be in the future, namely the true people of God. Present justification declares, on the basis of faith, what future justification will affirm publicly (according to 2:14–16 and 8:9–11) *on the basis of the entire life*" (emphasis added).[13]

However, it is difficult to conceive of a more serious breach of Paul's evangelical logic than to suggest that the eschatological verdict of justification depends on "the entire life" of the believer rather than Christ's. According to Wright, faith

---

12. Related to this debate over the righteousness of God is the question as to whether "faith in Christ" should also be given the subjective genitive construction (as "the faith of Christ"). This does not seem to make sense of the ordinary way Paul describes the relation of faith and justification, however. For example, Paul speaks of "the righteousness of God through faith in Jesus Christ for all who believe" (Rom. 3:22), the last clause repeating the same idea as the middle (*dia pisteōs Iēsou Christou*) and in verse 25 adds that his propitiatory death is "to be received by faith" (RSV). This debate is beyond our scope here, but for a defense of the subjective genitive construction, see Bruce W. Longenecker, "Contours of Covenant Theology in the Post-Conversion Paul," in *The Road from Damascus: The Impact of Paul's Conversion on His Life, Thought, and Ministry*, ed. Richard N. Longenecker (Grand Rapids: Eerdmans, 1997), 133, cf. Richard Hays, *The Faith of Jesus Christ. An Investigation of the Narrative Substructure of Galatians 3:1–4:11* (Chico, CA: Scholars Press, 1983); "Justification," in *The Anchor Bible Dictionary*, ed. D. N. Freedman et al. (New York: Doubleday, 1992), 268–90.

13. Wright, *What Saint Paul Really Said*, 129.

is not how one gets in (since this would be a question about individual salvation) but "is the badge of the sin-forgiven family." "The emphasis of the chapter [Rom. 4] is therefore that covenant membership is defined, not by circumcision (4:9–12), nor by race, but by faith."[14] However, this faith is now also redefined as faithfulness—our own covenantal obedience, which is the basis for the final justification. Crucially absent from his list is "nor by works," even though in this passage Paul explicitly says that this justification comes to the one (notice the individual-personal reference) "who without works trusts him who justifies the ungodly" (v. 5). Paul's contrast is between working and trusting, not between circumcision and our Spirit-led obedience. Basically, Wright's claim is tantamount to saying that we are justified by some works (our covenant faithfulness), but not by others (ethnic purity). This is not because he is employing a covenantal understanding, but because the particular version he presupposes is something like covenantal nomism.

Vindication according to Jewish Apocalyptic

It is perhaps worth noting that not even J. Christiaan Beker, who seems to have decisively shaped Wright's emphasis on the eschatological, cosmic, and redemptive-historical dimension over against the interest in the *ordo salutis* and individual salvation, is as one-sided. Although Beker's efforts to highlight the apocalyptic character of Pauline soteriology often reflect the false antithesis we have already pointed to above (*historia salutis* and cosmic redemption versus *ordo salutis* and individual salvation), his insights can serve to correct one-sided emphases on the latter. Beker maintains that "Jewish apocalyptic forms the basis of Paul's thought."[15] In fact, "the coherence of the gospel actually consists of the apocalyptic interpretation of the death and resurrection of Christ." While there is an antithesis between Moses and Christ, Sinai and Zion, there is continuity between Abraham and Christ.[16] Beker's observations fit well with the account I have offered for the continuity and discontinuity, based on the two covenants. He further notes that "in Adam" versus "in Christ" has no parallel with Abraham and Christ.[17] In Galatians, "Paul must safeguard the *solus Christus* and the *sola fide* of his gospel against the Judaizing synthesis of law and gospel."[18]

As I have argued in treating the atonement doctrine in *Lord and Servant*, reductionism begets reductionism, and we have often seen the work of Christ and justification reduced to a commercial transaction that ignores the wider biblical-theological horizon. However, the trend ever since Wrede and Schweitzer has

---

14. Ibid.
15. J. Christiaan Beker, *The Triumph of God: The Essence of Paul's Thought*, trans. Loren T. Stuckenbruck (Minneapolis: Fortress, 1990), 19.
16. Ibid., 52.
17. Ibid.
18. Ibid., 53.

been to move in the opposite direction of an "eschatological" (read "mystical") understanding in contrast to an older "legalistic" model.[19] According to Schweitzer, law and eschatology are essentially at odds, since law concerns that which is stable (horizontal), while eschatology is a suspension of time by an interruption of eternity with its own "immediate and absolute" events.[20] Ever since Kant (and especially Ritschl), modern theology has sought substitutes for a "legalistic" interpretation of atonement and justification—whether ethical, organic, mystical, existential, or eschatological. Adding *covenantal* to that genealogy of substitution, however, seriously misunderstands the inherently legal and objective character of that divine-human relationship.

However, even apart from the viability of the hypothesis itself (which, given the redemptive-historical conditioning of the law itself, seems implausible), this understanding of Paul's "mysticism" is far from the way Paul actually talks about God's covenantal dealings in history, particularly at the cross (Col. 2:11–15). The victory of Christ over the forces that oppose God and his kingdom is accomplished through the cross precisely because there and only there can the forgiveness and true circumcision promised in the new covenant (Jer. 31) and the inheritance promised to Abraham (Gen. 15) be found. It achieves this cosmic victory precisely because it cancels "the record that stood against us with its legal demands" (Col. 2:14).

In this passage (Col. 2) we find a classic example of the integral relationship between the redemptive-historical (*historia salutis*) and the individual (*ordo salutis*); the accomplishment of redemption in history and its application to individual people who are "dead in trespasses" and sins (v. 13). In addition, we see the simultaneous affirmation of the legal and the transformative dimensions of redemption. Here as elsewhere, the law is not set aside, rejected, ignored, or disparaged, but fulfilled precisely through the eschatological triumph of Christ at the cross. That curse removed, every treasure of the inheritance is poured out: the new birth, sanctification, the resurrection of the body, and the life of a creation not only renewed but also brought beyond the status of creation into the consummation won for us by that triumph. The lesson to be learned from this, I suggest, is that when we recognize the fundamentally legal character of sin and salvation, we get cosmic victory, the restoration of Israel and the nations, sanctification, and ecclesiology in the bargain. Without it, each of these other aspects of redemption becomes suspended in midair.

---

19. Michael S. Horton, *Lord and Servant: A Covenant Christology* (Louisville, KY: Westminster John Knox Press, 2005), chap. 7. In addition, as Stephen Westerholm points out in *Israel's Law and the Church's Faith: Paul and His Recent Interpreters* (Grand Rapids: Eerdmans, 1988), 26, "Ernst Käsemann, among others, also considered apocalyptic to be the 'mother' of early Christian theology" (cf., e.g., Käsemann, *New Testament Questions of Today*, trans. W. J. Montague [London: SCM, 1969], 236–37). Albert Schweitzer, *The Mysticism of Paul the Apostle*, trans. W. Montgomery (London: Black, 1931), 192, says, "In effect, Paul took the opposite course to the one ultimately chosen by Judaism: he sacrificed the Law to eschatology; Judaism abandoned eschatology and retained the law."

20. Schweitzer, *Mysticism*, 189.

Justification and Covenant Faithfulness:
Integrating Apocalyptic (Christus Victor) and Forensic Motifs

How then are we to respond to the argument that God's righteousness, given the concept's Old Testament background, cannot be imputed or distributed to another, but is always the property of the judge in issuing the verdict?

Although I will take issue with some aspects of his account below, Mark Seifrid has prosecuted a persuasive case (especially in the light of such texts as Pss. 72 and 98) against treating "covenant faithfulness" as a synonym for "the righteousness of God." God's righteous acts are judgment as well as mercy and pertain to the whole earth as well as Israel.[21] "'Justification' is viewed [in Jer. 22:3] as a definite action, the rectification of the weak in a particular dispute. . . . 'Righteousness' therefore cannot be reduced to the idea of a 'proper relation,' as often has been done in recent interpretation."[22] Justification is not merely God's decision to overlook faults and reestablish friendship, but to "right" that which has been wronged.[23] In his extended lexical discussion of the broader uses of "righteousness" than "covenant faithfulness," Seifrid makes a good case for his conclusion that the NPP "comes remarkably close to Ritschl's idealistic conception, and ignores Cremer's insight into the implicit involvement of punitive action in God's 'ruling and judging,' not to mention the instances in which God's righteousness is associated with retribution."[24]

The bottom line is that equating righteousness with God's covenant faithfulness or Israel's covenant status is inadequate. "The associations from the Psalms and Isaiah which Paul evokes by speaking of the 'revelation of God's righteousness' (Rom 1:17) belong to creational thought."[25] It is God's ruling and judging, not necessarily just saving (see Ps. 98 above) that are in view here, and the compass of this action is the whole earth, not just Israel. Justification is not just a matter of saving or of covenant faithfulness, but of God's retributive justice.[26]

This seems to get at the heart of contemporary problems with juridical language about the atonement (propitiation and sacrifice) as well as justification, at least since Ritschl. As George Lindbeck has recently argued, there is an inseparable

---

21. Mark A. Seifrid, *Christ, Our Righteousness: Paul's Theology of Justification* (Downers Grove, IL: InterVarsity, 2000), 39–41.

22. Ibid., 41.

23. Mark A. Seifrid, "Righteousness Language in the Hebrew Scriptures and Early Judaism," in *Justification and Variegated Nomism*, vol. 1, *The Complexities of Second Temple Judaism*, ed. D. A. Carson, Peter T. O'Brien, Mark A. Seifrid (Tübingen: Mohr Siebeck; Grand Rapids: Baker Academic, 2001), 417: Identifying legal definitions of "righteousness" with hellenization, Ritschl eliminated any juridical (especially retributive) aspect of atonement and justification. Hermann Cremer, however, argued that in the Old Testament, "the punishment of the wicked represented an essential element of the salvation of the righteous." "In other words, while Ritschl (along the lines of Grotius) insisted that God acts as rector and not iudex in his saving acts, Cremer insisted that in biblical thought the roles of 'ruling and judging' belong together, and that the Scriptures regularly speak of concrete acts of divine judgment."

24. Ibid., 425.

25. Ibid., 441.

26. Ibid., 441–42.

connection between atonement theories and one's doctrine of justification.[27] If we have trouble with juridical themes in the one, we will encounter the same difficulties in the other.

In Psalm 143:1–3, Seifrid points out, "the psalmist petitions God to contend *for* him against his enemies, while at the same time asking that God might not enter into contention *with* him. Should God press his own claims, the petitioner himself would be undone. God's saving righteousness stands in juxtaposition to his retributive justice, without immediate explanation."[28] In addition to the context of such passages, Seifrid provides a helpful treatment of the lexical distinctions between righteousness (*ṣĕdāqâ*) as a noun or verb and as an adjective.[29]

Given these reflections on the Old Testament understanding of righteousness, how does Paul employ the term? In using the phrase "the righteousness of God" in Romans 1, says Seifrid, "Paul speaks here not of an attribute of God, but an act of God" and "in speaking of 'God's righteousness' Paul has in view God's role as 'ruler and judge,' who will savingly bring about 'justice and righteousness' for the world which he has made."[30] All of this comes together in the resurrection, where God is vindicated, sinners are vindicated, and the Servant is vindicated along with all those identified with him. "Salvation comes through destruction, justification through condemnation."[31] "The simultaneous justification of God and the sinner," Seifrid reminds us, "drives Paul's argument in 1:18–3:26."[32] This seems clear enough from 3:26: "It was to prove at the present time that he himself is righteous and that he justifies the one who has faith in Jesus." At the same time, Seifrid wisely reminds us of the important difference between "law court" in the biblical sense and in our own. In the former, God himself is a party to the dispute and not just an impartial judge. "For Paul, the justification of human beings takes place only through God's triumph and their defeat."[33]

Thus we cannot reduce this covenantal dispute to the legal sphere. The courtroom and battlefield, forensic justification and *Christus Victor*, converge in the covenant lawsuit, with Isaiah 59 serving as a prime example. Paul does not lose any of the *Christus Victor* element in his gloss on this passage in Ephesians 6:10–17, yet, as in Isaiah 59, the warfare theme is grounded in the forensic character of justification. Only by putting on Christ's righteousness as a breastplate, with the belt of truth fastened around one's waist, with shoes making "you ready to proclaim the gospel of peace," along with "the shield of faith, with which you will be able to quench all the flaming arrows of the evil one," and "the helmet of salvation, and the sword of the Spirit, which is the word of God"—only thus can

27. George Lindbeck, "Justification and Atonement: An Ecumenical Trajectory," in *By Faith Alone: Essays on Justification in Honor of Gerhard O. Forde*, ed. Joseph A. Burgess and Marc Kolden (Grand Rapids: Eerdmans, 2004), 205.

28. Seifrid, *Christ, Our Righteousness*, 42.

29. Ibid., 44.

30. Ibid., 46.

31. Ibid., 47.

32. Ibid., 48.

33. Ibid., 59.

one stand firm against Satan in the divine courtroom. We may also discern echoes of Zechariah 3 here, with the vision of Joshua the high priest dressed in filthy clothes, accused by Satan as prosecutor, and "the angel of the LORD" as the defense attorney who secures a new wardrobe. This vision is "an omen of things to come: I am going to bring my servant the Branch, . . . and I will remove the guilt of this land in a single day" (Zech. 3:1–9).

It is not that justification eliminates the divine judgment, but that it ensures that the believer passes through that judgment with Christ to the other side, from the cross to the resurrection. God does in fact condemn the guilty in baptism with Christ, but precisely because of their identification with him, they are "circumcised" by the "cutting off" of the old self while Christ himself fully undergoes the "cutting off" in death, suffering the divine wrath that is inseparable from the righteousness of God in the Old Testament as well as the New. Believers are thereby justified in the sight of the very law that required their condemnation—but how, if they do not possess the righteousness of God in him?

The question is not the imputation or infusion of a divine "substance" or "quality," but the declaration that those who have not by their own covenant faithfulness attained the required righteousness are nevertheless regarded as if they have because they are credited with someone else's righteous deeds. To change the metaphor (yet still keeping with Pauline language), as deep in debt as the covenant-breaker certainly is, he or she is through faith alone heir of the entire estate that properly belongs to Christ. This is hardly a legal fiction, since the estate is truly transferred; the righteousness is fulfilled by the mediator of the covenant.

With this wider understanding of the righteousness of God, we are in a better position to grasp Paul's point in Romans 2:

> You say, "We know that God's judgment on those who do such things [worship idols and practice sexual immorality] is in accordance with the truth." . . . Do you imagine, whoever you are, that . . . you will escape the judgment of God? . . . But by your hard and impenitent heart you are storing up wrath for yourself on the day of wrath, when God's righteous judgment will be revealed. For he will repay according to each one's deeds. . . . All who have sinned apart from the law will also perish apart from the law, and all who have sinned under the law will be judged by the law. (vv. 2, 3, 5–6, 12)

It is only then that we read, "For it is not the hearers of the law who will be justified" (v. 13). The gospel is an announcement to be heard and received with joy; the law is a command to do something. God cannot justly justify those who merely hear and receive the law, but he can justly justify those who merely hear and receive the gospel. If anyone insists on being justified by the law, he or she should at least be prepared to do everything that it commands, which, Paul argues, none of us—including Jews—has ever done. Righteousness cannot therefore be restricted to God's covenantal faithfulness, since Paul says that it is according to this very righteousness that everyone, Jew and Gentile, stands condemned (3:19–20). Only with this broader understanding of righteousness can we discern the rest of Paul's argument:

But now, apart from law, the righteousness of God has been disclosed, and
is attested by the law and the prophets, the righteousness of God through
faith in Jesus Christ for all who believe. For there is no distinction, since all
have sinned and fall short of the glory of God [not simply failed to keep the
ceremonial laws]; they are now justified by his grace as a gift, through the
redemption that is in Christ Jesus, whom God put forward as a propitiation
by his blood, effective through faith. . . . For we hold that a person is justified by faith apart from works prescribed by the law. (3:21–25a [alt via
NKJV], 28)

Would it make sense to speak of *God's* covenantal faithfulness as a righteousness
"apart from law," especially since the law is the expression of that righteousness?
Furthermore, why would this "righteousness of God" be said to come "through
faith in Jesus Christ" rather than "through the faithfulness of Christ/God" if
righteousness is exclusively understood as God's own covenant faithfulness?

It is no wonder that Luther's much-debated breakthrough was connected with
his exegesis of this transition from the righteousness *of* God that condemns and
the righteousness *from* God that justifies through faith. That is the sweeping and
marvelous contrast that gets lost if we reduce works of the law to boundary markers and justification to God's covenant faithfulness (much less to our own). The
righteousness by which God justifies is the same righteousness by which God
condemns, and in both cases the standard of judgment is the law. The difference
is whether one remains "under the law" (and thus under a curse) or "in Christ"
(and thus under grace), as "those to whom God reckons righteousness apart from
works" (Rom. 4:6). What makes all the difference is whether one is legally incorporated into a promise-covenant or a law-covenant. What is transferred to the
believer, therefore, is not the inherent person of God or Christ, but the record of
a perfectly acceptable life that has been lived, offered up, received, and raised
again for us. It is a verdict declared because of Christ's faithfulness to the covenant,
which is the middle term that is left out of Wright's syllogism. While it is far from
nomistic, such a representational view of justification is surely, from beginning
to end, *covenantal*.

Bruce W. Longenecker thinks that, in Paul's view, Christians participate in
Jesus' covenant fidelity simply by faith. "This is why Paul says in [Gal.] 2:16b: 'We
believed in Christ Jesus, in order that his covenant faithfulness might be effective
for us'"—as also in 3:22. "Paul's 'faith' language in these verses is fundamentally a
language of participation."[34] So justification (i.e., covenant membership) is based
for Paul now not on the law but on Jesus' covenant faithfulness, which he receives
by faith. His faithfulness is "rubbish"; "only Christ's faithfulness [is] . . . the mark
of his covenant membership before God."[35] It becomes clear that while covenantal nomism demands a choice between the forensic and the participatory, a genuinely covenantal theology is conceivable on other grounds.

---

34. Longenecker, "Contours of Covenant Theology in the Post-Conversion Paul," 135.
35. Ibid. See also Gal. 3:13–14; 4:4–5; and Rom. 15:8–9 in this light.

Elsewhere, Longenecker makes the important point that "if covenant theology is simply a matter of defining the membership of God's people, then the adjective 'covenant' does not do justice to the depths of Paul's theological worldview.... At its heart, in fact, covenant theology is first and foremost about divine presence—both in relation to Israel as God's people, and ultimately in relation to the world as God's creation."[36] Justification can only be understood within the realization that Paul's framework is covenant theology, Longenecker affirms.[37] "Righteousness" is grounded in "covenant" in that it is not one's own obedience that counts, but Christ's.[38] For Paul (in Phil. 3), "blamelessness in nomistic righteousness is discounted as dung."[39]

Paul's criticism therefore appears to be far more sweeping than the NPP allows. The problem with "the righteousness that is by law" is not *only* that it separates Jews and Gentiles, but also that such righteousness (though, of course, not the law itself) is actually a *deficit* before God. "To be in Christ is to have *his* (and only his) faithfulness as the mark of one's own covenant fidelity."[40] Referring specifically to Galatians 2, Longenecker's conclusion could extend to the whole of Paul's teaching: "If in this passage Paul's presentation is indebted to a theology of covenant relationship, it is a theology that has severed itself from the 'givens' of covenant theology typical of most forms of Early Judaism, where the will and grace of God are inseparable from νόμος.... Consequently, Paul redraws the boundaries of the covenant, resulting in a redefinition of the term 'sinners' in Gal. 2:17."[41] Only if the "covenant theology" we adopt is able to account for the two covenants that Paul explicitly contrasts (as does Jeremiah), will it be able to elucidate rather than obscure the apostle's central teaching on justification.

Finally, even advocates of the NPP concede the individual as well as corporate character of salvation and justification in particular as we find it in the New Testament. Even concerning Second Temple Judaism, Sanders observes that while God will not forsake his covenant with Israel, "individuals may, however, be excluded from Israel if they sin in such a way as to spurn the covenant itself."[42]

In Acts 22:17, Ananias tells the newly converted Paul to call on Jesus' name for the forgiveness of sins, not first of all as "lord over the powers," "redeemer from the exile," or "sender to the Gentiles," but for Paul's own forgiveness of sins. Numerous passages in Acts underscore the point that the query "How can I be saved?" though not the whole story, is integral to it (Matt. 14:30; 19:25; 27:42; Luke 7:50; 13:23; John 5:34; Acts 11:14, and esp. 16:30, in addition to the

---

36. Bruce W. Longenecker, "Defining the Faithful Character of the Covenant Community: Galatians 2.15–21 and Beyond," in *Paul and the Mosaic Law: The Third Durham-Tübingen Research Symposium on Earliest Christianity and Judaism*, ed. James D. G. Dunn (Grand Rapids: Eerdmans, 2001), 76.
37. Ibid., 78.
38. Ibid., 81.
39. Ibid., 83.
40. Ibid.
41. Ibid., 84.
42. E. P. Sanders, *Paul and Palestinian Judaism* (Minneapolis: Fortress, 1977), 370–71.

Pauline corpus, such as Rom. 5:9; 8:24; 1 Cor. 1:18; 9:22; 1 Tim. 1:15; 2:4; 2 Tim. 1:9; Titus 3:5, and elsewhere, such as Heb. 7:25; James 5:20; 1 Pet. 3:20; Jude 23).

Rounding out my defense of a covenantal account of justification, the discussion transitions from interaction with the NPP to additional exegetical critiques and, finally, to an analysis of and response to the contemporary dislocation of the doctrine even within more confessional circles. If justification is forensic— that is, a legal verdict pronounced upon those who are in themselves ungodly on the basis of Christ's righteousness—then how is this righteousness communicated to us?

IMPUTED RIGHTEOUSNESS?

Criticisms of imputation are not restricted to representatives of the NPP. In spite of his critique of Wright and the NPP, Mark Seifrid remains unconvinced that the language of "imputation" is necessary, sharing the suspicion that the *historia salutis* is sacrificed to the *ordo salutis* by traditional Protestant confessions and dogmatics. We do not need the additional category of imputation to maintain the doctrine of justification, he argues. Justification is simply the forgiveness of sins. "Likewise, the further distinction which some Protestants made between the imputation of Christ's active righteousness (in fulfilling the law) and his passive obedience (in dying on the cross) is unnecessary and misleading."[43] We only need the "passive obedience" of Christ—the sacrifice on the cross, not the imputation of an "active obedience."

> His "passive obedience" was the fulfilment of the law which condemned us! In Christ and in hope, the triumph over sin and death is ours here and now. Yet it is not ours: we possess it only in faith. In this way, and only in this way, the grace of God and the demand for obedience meet. In reducing "justification" to a present possession of "Christ's imputed righteousness," Protestant divines inadvertently bruised the nerve which runs between justification and obedience. It is not so much *wrong* to use the expression "the imputed righteousness of Christ" as it is *deficient*.[44]

However, the Reformed interpretation cannot be reductive or deficient if it actually says *more* than Seifrid allows.[45] More critically, the question arises, how does forgiveness by itself establish rectitude? It is not *forgiveness* (negation of guilt) that withstands the last judgment, but *righteousness* (positive standing). Without the latter, the goal of the covenant as well as its conditions are unfulfilled.

---

43. Seifrid, *Christ, Our Righteousness*, 175.
44. Ibid.
45. In an intriguing remark, Herman Bavinck judges, "The rationalistic school is rooted basically in Piscator's teaching, according to which the righteousness we need is accomplished not by the active but solely by the passive obedience of Christ!" (*Reformed Dogmatics*, ed. John Bolt, trans. John Vriend, vol. 3 [Grand Rapids: Baker Academic, 2006], 531).

Seifrid concludes, "Justification" cannot be "reduced to an event which takes place for the individual at the beginning of the Christian life" within "an 'order of salvation' (*ordo salutis*)."[46] Yet it would appear that Paul places it in an *ordo salutis* in Romans 8:30. "Here, however, we find a sequence of divine acts rather than operations within the individual," Seifrid replies. "Paul's 'order of salvation' retains a call to faith and hope lacking in the usual Protestant schemes, because it proceeds from God and his work. For Paul, God's justifying work *extra nos* in Christ determines all that we are and shall be."[47] Yet, as with Wright, Seifrid misunderstands the Reformation position, in this case confusing the doctrine of imputation with an internal operation within the believer, the sort of "infused" righteousness that the Lutheran and Reformed confessions explicitly rejected in their definition of justification.

A second and more troubling problem is that by referring justification only to Christ's passive righteousness (the cross), Seifrid fails to account for how justification establishes us as righteous rather than simply as forgiven.

A final objection is his opposition between divine acts and internal operations. It is unclear to me why "a sequence of divine acts" should be contrasted with "operations within the individual." Does Seifrid mean that God only acts *for* but never *within* people? Is the new birth, as a divine act, *extra nos* along with justification? And can we conceive of sanctification apart from "operations within the individual"? Ironically, Seifrid simultaneously leaves justification bereft of its positive ground (Christ's active obedience imputed) while putting in question the transforming work of Christ in us: a hyperforensicism without imputation.

Seifrid judges that Wright misses the mark when "he regards justification as an analytical judgment of God deriving from regeneration. God declares the state of affairs which he sees, namely precisely who (by the work of the Spirit) are 'the true people of God,' who will be vindicated at the Last Day." "One wonders why Wright proposes that such persons must be granted the forgiveness of sins. In any event, 'faith' plays a secondary role in Wright's view. It is not an act of obedience of the sinner before God, but a badge of 'membership' in the covenant community."[48] Nevertheless, in Seifrid's account, there is forgiveness without righteousness. Justification is a forensic decree, not an infusion of grace, he argues. "Justification is a matter of death and life, wrath and vindication," and in Christ as the God-Man both are executed.[49] Yet without Christ's positive fulfillment of the law as the ground and imputation as the means by which this declaration takes place, we are left with a forgiveness that falls short of the justifying verdict. *Forgiveness* has its legal basis, but *justification* indeed becomes a legal fiction.

Other objections to imputation than those offered by the NPP include those of Robert Gundry. He begins by highlighting the texts that refer to imputation of righteousness explicitly (Rom. 4:3, 6, 9, 11, 22–24; Gal. 3:6). ("Counting as"

46. Seifrid, *Christ, Our Righteousness*, 176.
47. Ibid., 177.
48. Ibid., 176 n. 13.
49. Ibid., 184.

or "being counted as," *logizomai eis*, is also found in Rom. 2:26; 9:8; and 2 Cor. 12:6; as well as Acts 19:27 and James 2:23). "But none of these texts says that Christ's righteousness was counted," writes Gundry, "so that righteousness comes into view not as what is counted but as what God counts faith to be."[50]

Gundry's position inevitably makes faith rather than Christ the ground of justification. Furthermore, the notion of one person's righteousness being imputed to another is already present, as we have seen, in Second Temple Judaism (the "merit of the fathers"). Herman Lichtenberger refers to a prayer in the rabbinical sources that God will keep petitioners from sin "so that you may find joy at the end of the age . . . , this being *counted to you for righteousness* if you do what is true and good before God for the salvation of yourself and of Israel" (CD 25–32).[51] It is also found in 4QPseudo-Jubilees[a] (=4Q225) 2 I: "And Abraham believed God, and righteousness was counted for him." In the LXX, various acts are "credited as righteousness": Phineas's zeal (Ps. 106:31 [105:31 LXX]); also in the pseudepigraphic literature: the killing of the Shechemites by two of Jacob's sons (*Jubilees* 30:17), Jacob's obedience to his mother (35:2), or more generally, doing "what is upright and good before him" (4QMMT 117 (=4Q398 frg. 7 II, 4; and frg. 2 II, 7). However, Gundry concludes, "In none of these cases does an instrumental interpretation make good contextual sense."[52]

He notes that in these cases, the "counting" follows what is there. "But in Romans 2:26 a Gentile law-keeper's uncircumcision will be counted as circumcision even though it is not. . . . And in 2 Samuel 19:19 Shimei asks David not to count him guilty even though he is in fact guilty." But what God counts is faith, not Christ's righteousness, Gundry argues.[53] To be sure, "Paul rejects the Jewish tradition that God counted Abraham's faith as righteousness because it was a work (a good one, of course)."[54] Yet if faith is the ground of justification rather than the instrument, one wonders how that Jewish interpretation could be faulted. Gundry clearly states that "the righteousness that comes 'from' (*ek*) faith (Rom 9:30; 10:6) and from God 'through' (*dia*) faith and 'on the basis of' (*epi*) faith (Phil 3:9) is the faith that God counts as righteousness. Paul's language is supple: faith is the *origin*, the means, and the *basis* of righteousness in that God counts it as righteousness" (emphasis added).[55]

However, I would argue that Paul is in fact more supple than Gundry's account suggests. Foremost, *epi* has a much broader lexical range than Gundry

---

50. Robert Gundry, "The Nonimputation of Christ's Righteousness," in *Justification: What's at Stake in the Current Debates*, ed. Mark Husbands and Daniel J. Treier (Downers Grove, IL: InterVarsity Press, 2004), 18.
51. Hermann Lichtenberger, "The Understanding of the Torah in the Judaism of Paul's Day," in Dunn, *Paul and the Mosaic Law*, 16.
52. Ibid., 20–21.
53. Ibid., 22.
54. Ibid. Gundry notes the following survey of the Jewish literature: J. A. Ziesler, *The Meaning of Righteousness in Paul: A Linguistic and Theological Inquiry* (Cambridge: Cambridge University Press, 1972), 43, 103–4, 109, 123, 125–26, 175, 182–83.
55. Ibid., 25.

allows.[56] While in technical theological jargon, the basis (or formal cause) of something is distinguished from the means (or instrumental cause), *epi* and *dia* both are used with greater range and flexibility in Scripture, as their English equivalents are in common use. In numerous places, in fact, *epi* appears as a basis ("on account of/because of"), a marker of basis for a state of being, an action, or a result.[57] In other words, *epi* (on account of) is interchangeable with *dia* (through). In the light of various challenges to the Reformation understanding of justification from Protestant as well as Roman Catholic quarters, the terminology became more refined: justification by grace, through faith, because of Christ. However, it would be anachronistic to impose the more refined distinctions of scholasticism on the New Testament. In his exegesis of Galatians, even Luther can say that we are justified "for the sake of our faith in Christ or for the sake of Christ," as if the two phrases are interchangeable.[58] It all depends on what one is contrasting: faith and works, or faith as an inherently worthy basis versus passive instrument. In Gundry's formulation, however, one would say that we are justified by faith, through faith, on the basis of faith. Beyond the question of imputation, this exegesis represents a remarkable position in the history of exegesis and doctrine.

Rejecting the imputation of Adam's sin, since the people's sinning (before the law) was "not after the likeness of Adam's transgression," Gundry denies imputation in relation to justification.[59] Yet this verse (Rom. 5:14) seems to make the opposite point, that even though they did not commit the *same* sin, they were still sinners in Adam. Further, Gundry speaks of "the failure of Paul, despite his extensive discussion of law and writing that Christ was 'born under the law' (Gal 4:4), ever to make a point of Christ's keeping the law perfectly on our behalf (not even his sinlessness in 2 Cor 5:21 being put in relation to law-keeping)."[60] Yet what other import might the phrase "born under the law" have served? And how else would a Jew have understood sinlessness other than "in relation to law-keeping"? And why does Paul contrast Adam's one act of disobedience and Christ's one act of obedience? Does this not suggest that Christ's obedience, rather than our faith, is imputed?

> To be sure, *dikaiōma*, translated "act of righteousness" in Romans 5:18 and "righteous requirement" in Romans 8:4 (also in Rom 1:32), may be collective in Romans 8:4 for all the requirements of the law. But that collective meaning is unsure, even unlikely, for Paul writes in Galatians 5:14 that "the whole law is fulfilled in one command, 'You shall love your neighbor as yourself.'"[61]

56. According to Frederick William Danker, rev. and ed., *A Greek-English Lexicon of the New Testament and Other Early Christian Literature*, 3rd ed. (BDAG) (Chicago: University of Chicago Press, 2000), 363–67, there are no fewer than eighteen possible renderings.

57. Ibid., esp. 366.

58. Martin Luther's 1535 Galatians commentary, in *Luther's Works*, ed. J. Pelikan, vol. 26 (St. Louis: Concordia, 1963), 233.

59. Gundry, "The Nonimputation of Christ's Righteousness," 28.

60. Ibid., 32.

61. Ibid., 34.

Yet even such an interpretation of Galatians 5:14 seems strained. Paul was merely summarizing the law: "the whole law" (i.e., all the requirements of the law collectively comprehended). Surely loving one's neighbor does not consist in one act. And in the context of his running polemic in Galatians, would it not be legitimate to assume here that Paul is simply repeating the claim in 3:10 that to offend at one point (failing to love God and neighbor perfectly) is to be "under the curse" of the law?

Gundry does not reject the forensic character of justification altogether, however. "The resurrection of Christ demonstrates God's acceptance of that death as the basis of this declaration (Rom 4:25)."[62] As with Seifrid's interpretation, Christ's life (active obedience) does not seem to have any significance for us other than to ensure a blameless sacrifice. In my view, this is at least in part the consequence of failing to treat justification in a sufficiently covenantal light. However, where Seifrid clearly affirms that Christ's death is the basis for justification (i.e., forgiveness), Gundry's argument is more ambiguous. Although he says that Christ's death is "the basis of this declaration," his main thesis seems to be that *faith* is its basis.

Gundry refuses to set the covenantal against the legal, "for in the biblical world covenants were legally binding treaties."[63] Nevertheless, it is at best unclear as to whether this legal verdict is based on human effort. Although he has argued that faith is not a work, he says, "The righteousness of faith is *the moral accomplishment* that God counts faith to be even though it is not *intrinsically* such an accomplishment" (emphasis added).[64] Christ's "obediently righteous act of propitiation made it right for God to count faith as righteousness."[65]

It is worth noting in passing that this view has a theological history. Hugo Grotius and the Remonstrant (Arminian) party argued a similar position, which is targeted in chapter 13 of the Westminster Confession when it states that believers are justified "not by imputing faith itself, the act of believing, or any other evangelical obedience to them as their righteousness; but by imputing the obedience and satisfaction of Christ unto them, they receiving and resting on him and his righteousness by faith; which faith they have not of themselves, it is the gift of God."[66] In fact, it is possible to recognize parallels between Gundry's conclusion and the covenant (or better, contractual) theology of late medieval nominalism, according to which justification is granted on the basis of one's imperfect obedience. No one merits final justification according to strict merit (*de condigno*), but only according to God's gracious decision to accept it as if it were meritorious (*de congruo*). My intention is not to dismiss the work of biblical scholars through "guilt by association," but to point out that the alternatives to Reformation theology on this matter are not simply fresh exegetical feats. Like the conclusions of the Refor-

62. Ibid., 35.
63. Ibid.
64. Ibid., 36.
65. Ibid., 39.
66. The Westminster Confession of Faith, chap. 13, in *The Book of Confessions* (PC[USA], 1991).

mation confessions, those of biblical scholars today also belong to traditions, acknowledged or not.

Aside from historical parallels, is Gundry's position exegetically plausible? D. A. Carson responds, first by offering a salutary reminder that systematic and biblical (or exegetical) theology represent different fields of discourse that should serve each other's ends, but often speak past each other, failing to take each other's fields and research into account.[67]

Carson widens his defense of imputation beyond the criticisms of Gundry, to encompass the NPP. Ernst Käsemann, "mediated through E. P. Sanders and others, has convinced many that 'justification' has primarily to do with God's covenantal faithfulness. In the further step taken by N. T. Wright, if people are 'justified' they are declared to belong to God's covenantal community," so that (a) justification is no longer "an entry-point of the believer's experience with God, but is now bound up with the believer's ongoing status with respect to the covenant community; and (b) justification is no longer immediately tied to justice/righteousness."[68]

"In Jewish exegesis," Carson points out, "Genesis 15:6 was not quoted to prove that Abraham was justified by faith and not by works," but rather as meritorious obedience (Rabbi Shemaiah, 50 BCE; *Mekilta* 35b and 40b, on Exod. 14:15). "What this means, for our purposes, is that Paul, who certainly knew of these traditions, was explicitly interpreting Genesis 15:6 in a way quite different from that found in his own tradition, and he was convinced that this new way was the correct way to understand the text."[69]

More specifically, Carson draws our attention to the parallelism in Romans 4:5–6:

| 4:5 | God | justifies | the ungodly |
| 4:6 | God | credits righteousness | apart from works |

"In other words, 'justifies' is parallel to 'credits righteousness'; or, to put the matter in nominal terms, justification is parallel to the imputation of righteousness."[70] And it has to be an "alien" righteousness, since "God justifies *the ungodly* (Rom 4:5); he credits righteousness *apart from works* (Rom 4:6)."[71]

In response to Gundry's argument, Carson reasons, "If God has counted or imputed our faith to us as righteousness, then, once he has so counted or imputed it, does he then count or impute the righteousness to us, a kind of second imputation?"[72] In Philippians 3 it clearly is not an inherent righteousness.[73]

67. Donald Carson, "The Vindication of Imputation," in Husbands and Treier, *Justification: What's at Stake in the Current Debates*, 49.
68. Ibid., 50.
69. Ibid., 56,
70. Ibid., 61.
71. Ibid.
72. Ibid., 64.
73. Ibid., 69.

In 2 Corinthians 5:19–21, we are told that God made Christ who had no sin to be sin for us, so that *in him* we might become the *righteousness* of God. It is because of God that we are in Christ Jesus, who has become for us *righteousness* (and other things: 1 Cor 1:30). Passage after passage in Paul runs down the same track.[74]

Faith—even if is faith in Christ—is not the same as having a righteousness that is "not of my own." Faith, not Christ, becomes the basis for the transfer from unrighteous to righteous.[75]

There is a broader challenge to the Reformation view of justification within Protestant circles today than the NPP. I have in mind the false antithesis between forensic or legal categories and ontological and moral ones. On this score the NPP frequently points up the judicial character and context of God's "covenantal righteousness." Therefore, Milbank's declaration that the forensic notion of justification is "a reading of Paul that E. P. Sanders has forever destroyed"[76] is an overstatement not only of Sanders's achievement but also his intention.

It is true that Sanders is more sympathetic to Schweitzer's view that mystical participation replaces the covenant concept in Paul, since "covenant" is equivalent to covenantal nomism for Sanders. However, in our summary of Sanders's arguments and sources, we have seen that Palestinian Judaism was every bit as forensic as anything that developed either in the medieval penitential system or in the Reformation. "In the *qal*," notes Sanders, "the verb [*ṣādaq*] usually means 'to be cleared in court' and is not really distinguishable from the use of the *zākāh* root to mean 'innocent.'"[77] "It may also mean to make something correct, as in the phrase 'make the scales just.' The *hif'il*, 'to justify,' also has a forensic connotation. When the passage in Ex. 23.7 says 'I will not justify the wicked,' it is clearly understood to mean 'hold innocent.'"[78]

The suspicion of legal or forensic fields of discourse by some within the NPP is somewhat ironic especially given the fact that *covenant* and *nomism* are both intrinsically legal terms. Dunn writes, "But Abraham believed in confident hope: that was the character of his faith—*not dependent or qualified by any legal enactment, but dependent solely on God.* This was trust in the Creator God which Adam had failed to exercise. Abraham gave the glory to God which humankind had refused to give ([Rom.] 1:21). . . . This, then, is what Paul meant by justification by faith alone" (emphasis added).[79] Yet this assumes that "legal" is an inherently bad category and somehow is the antithesis of "covenant." Needless to say, such an antithesis is certainly difficult to reconcile with a position defined as *covenantal nomism.*

74. Ibid., 72.
75. Ibid.
76. John Milbank, *Being Reconciled: Ontology and Pardon* (London and New York: Routledge, 2003), 103.
77. Sanders, *Paul and Palestinian Judaism*, 198.
78. Ibid., 199.
79. James D. G. Dunn, *The Theology of Paul* (Edinburgh: T&T Clark, 1998), 378–79.

Since the promise to Abraham was a covenant, complete with ratification cere-monies, the patriarch's faith was indeed dependent on a legal enactment. It is "legal" not only because of its forensic character but also because it will only be realized in history by the personal obedience of the one who will "fulfill all righteousness" (Matt. 3:15; 5:18; Luke 24:44; John 17:4). Further, Paul distinguishes between *two covenants*, not between *covenant* and *law*. The entire argument of Galatians 3–4 rests on the legal basis for inheriting the Abrahamic promise: it is a covenant "rat-ified by God," just as was the Sinai covenant 430 years later (Gal. 3:17).

A last will and testament is just as legal in its basis as a suzerainty treaty. In his high-priestly prayer, Jesus anticipates his victorious resurrection and ascension as the meritorious reward for his obedience:

> I glorified you on earth by finishing the work that you gave me to do. So now, Father, glorify me in your own presence with the glory that I had in your presence before the world existed. . . . And for their sakes I sanctify myself, so that they also may be sanctified in truth. (John 17:4–5, 19)

Justification is therefore in its deepest sense dependent and qualified by law: it is the covenant verdict pronounced on Christ and his coheirs on the basis of his merits. Therefore, in an important sense, we are justified by the works of the law—that is, by Christ's representative work in his active and passive obedience, in his justification-resurrection, and in his ascension-exaltation.

Also, while I would agree that the law, far from being set aside, exercises its full judicial role in these proceedings (both in condemnation and justification), it would seem foreign to Paul's arguments to suggest with Wright that the Torah itself, *when helped by the Spirit*, becomes the source of life and "the required δικαίωμα to God's people."[80] To be sure, the "circumcision not made with hands" is part of the promise of the new covenant in Jeremiah 31. Yet as in other rival accounts, jus-tification itself takes on the character of moral transformation, according to Wright. Is Paul's good news really that now that we have the Spirit, we can have life by the law? Or is this closer to the view that he is rejecting in Galatians 3:2–5?

Only when Wright has defined justification as regeneration and sanctification is the *ordo salutis* finally given its due: "When God by his Spirit works to bring life to a person (Romans 8.9–11), the desire and purpose of the Torah is thereby being fulfilled."[81] When the question of how an individual is saved is finally admitted into the discussion, the answer is essentially Rome's answer to the Reformers: *by cooperating with the Spirit in such a way as to produce the covenant faithfulness required by the moral law.* "The righteousness of the law" in Romans 8:4 speaks "first, of a decree which is itself just, and second, of a decree which announces, justly, that certain people are in the right, i.e. a justifying decree."[82]

---

80. N. T. Wright, *Climax of the Covenant: Christ and the Law in Pauline Theology* (Edinburgh: T&T Clark, 1991), 209.
81. Ibid.
82. Ibid., 211.

The Reformation doctrine says as much as well: the law declares us righteous, since Christ's righteousness is credited to us. However, in Wright's view, the law declares us righteous *because there is an inherent righteousness* of some sort upon which a righteous verdict may be favorably rendered.

We know, of course, that Augustine and the Reformers were accused of breeding license by their doctrine of grace, but could the Paul reconstructed by any version of covenantal nomism old or new ever be accused of preaching antinomianism? Ethnic inclusion, perhaps, but license? Yet Paul was in fact accused of preaching the latter: "And why not say (as some people slander us by saying that we say), 'Let us do evil so that good may come'?" (Rom. 3:8). "What then are we to say? Should we continue in sin in order that grace may abound?" (6:1). One test of whether we have properly understood Paul, then, is the plausibility of the antinomian charge. Of course, Paul refutes it (as Augustine and the Reformers did), but that it was a charge seems to point up that he had a lot more in mind than ethnic boundaries.

The upshot of the analysis thus far is that covenantal nomism past and present, whether in Judaism or Christianity, Roman Catholic or Protestant, conflates law and gospel so that the former is not really legal and the latter is not really evangelical. Part of the problem is that covenant is always a code word for covenantal nomism and, more specifically, ethnic distinctiveness, engendering a circular argument. Repeatedly, Kim notes, Dunn and Wright attempt to reinsert some validity to the forensic dimension, but then take it away with statements about the debate being about boundaries and not acceptance before God.[83]

Wright helpfully refuses to pit juristic against participationist views.[84] However, he argues that the declaration of righteousness is "merely one aspect" of justification, and one that is subservient to the membership thesis: "This I take to be the real meaning of the classic Pauline statements of justification: God declares that those who believe the gospel are his covenant people."[85] While I would agree that the law gives life in one sense—namely, in pronouncing its vindication of Jesus in the resurrection, this is true for us only by covenantal participation in Christ. Justification is indeed a final judgment on "the entirety of a life lived," as Wright suggests, but a judgment on Christ's life lived rather than on the believer's. "For through the law I died to the law, so that I might live to God. I have been crucified with Christ; and it is no longer I who live, but it is Christ who lives in me. . . . I do not nullify the grace of God; for if justification comes through the law, then Christ died for nothing" (Gal. 2:19–21). Thus, far from being set aside, the law is fulfilled, agreeing with the gospel in the pronouncement of the justification of the wicked.

83. Seyoon Kim, *Paul and the New Perspective: Second Thoughts on the Origin of Paul's Gospel* (Grand Rapids: Eerdmans, 2002), 66.
84. Ibid., 213.
85. Ibid., 214.

THEOLOGICAL PRESUPPOSITIONS AND EXEGESIS
REGARDING JUSTIFICATION

In the opening chapter I briefly discussed the sibling rivalry between biblical and systematic theology, and the arguments we have encountered thus far in opposition to the traditional Protestant account of justification reveal that theological convictions and exegetical conclusions belong to the hermeneutical spiral. Schweitzer judged, "But those who subsequently made [Paul's] doctrine of justification by faith the centre of Christian belief, have had the tragic experience of finding that they were dealing with a conception of redemption, from which no ethic could logically be derived."[86] Yet this conclusion, which swept the apostle into its critique, completely misses the quite natural transition in Paul's logic even in Galatians, where, as in his other Epistles, ethics is informed by rather than in antithesis to the ethical imperatives. The gospel of free justification gives rise to a spontaneous embrace of the very law that once condemned us. This spontaneous life Paul calls "life in the Spirit," yielding "the fruit of the Spirit" (Gal. 5:16–26). When we were "in Adam," that law yielded death and condemnation; "in Christ," the law approves us—hence, Calvin's view that the so-called third use (guiding believers in the way of gratitude) is, for the Christian, "the principal use" of the law.[87] Reformation theology, as we will see, has certainly derived an ethic from justification—as well as from the rest of the *ordo*, as evidenced by the division of the Heidelberg Catechism into guilt, grace, and *gratitude*. Every Lutheran and Reformed catechism includes an application of the Ten Commandments to the Christian life. In fact, the first question-and-answer of the Heidelberg Catechism underscores the point that by paying the price for our redemption and sending the Spirit, "my only comfort in life and in death is that I am not my own, but belong, both in body and soul, not to myself, but to my faithful Savior Jesus Christ." Justification is not only a promise; it is also a claim upon my total life.

Proponents of covenantal nomism have from time immemorial insisted that a gospel of free grace—*sola gratia, solo Christo, sola fide*—can only lead logically to license. Sanders, we have seen, assumes that an unconditional election is arbitrary: there must be *something* in the chosen that explains the gift. To be sure, "getting in" depends on obedience, but this does not constitute "works-righteousness," since there are things that we can do to make up for our mistakes. These theological presuppositions guide Sanders's verdicts on Second Temple Judaism and Paul.

"If Christians could only get this [doctrine of justification] right," says Wright, "they would find that not only would they be believing the gospel, they would be practicing it; and that is the best basis for proclaiming it."[88] Thus, the gospel

---

86. Schweitzer, *Mysticism*, 225.
87. John Calvin, *Institutes* 2.7.12 (1:360).
88. Wright, *What Saint Paul Really Said*, 159.

is something to be done after all, not simply an astonishing and disruptive announcement of what has already been achieved once and for all on our behalf.[89] Faith and holiness belong together, Wright properly insists, but the only way to keep them together, he seems to suggest, is to conflate them. "Indeed, very often the word 'faith' itself could properly be translated as 'faithfulness,' which makes the point just as well."[90]

Gundry appeals to Mark Seifrid's far-from-novel charge that "in reducing 'justification' to a present possession of 'Christ's imputed righteousness,' Protestant divines inadvertently bruised the nerve which runs between justification and obedience." He appeals also to Wesley's criticism on the same ground: it leads to antinomianism.[91] This follows a well-worn path of criticism, illustrated in Albert Schweitzer's charge that "there is no road from it [forensic justification] to ethics."[92] Gundry sees his treatment as going "a long way toward satisfying the legitimate concerns not only of Roman Catholics but also of pietists in the Lutheran tradition, in the Anabaptist and Baptist tradition, in the Keswick movement, in the Holiness movement and in Pentecostalism."[93] Once again we see that exegetical conclusions can never be entirely innocent of the working assumptions of one's ecclesial and systematic-theological framework.

At the same time, this should not lead us to a fatalism with respect to our theological and confessional location. As we have seen, even some of the principal advocates of the NPP recognize that justification is a forensic declaration. Despite the Vulgate's use of *iustificare* (to make righteous), a number of Roman Catholic New Testament scholars have pointed out that *dikaioō* has to do with a legal vindication.[94] The lexical definition of "justification" is "to be cleared in court,"[95] which, as Sanders has said above even in relation to the Old Testament (*ṣādaq* and cognates), can be amply attested. That significant consensus can be reached on this point even among those who stand in some critical relation to the Reformation interpretation demonstrates that we are quite far from witnessing the destruction of a forensic definition of justification.

Moving through the so-called *ordo salutis*, following the "golden chain" of election, calling, justification, and glorification that we find in Romans 8:30, I

---

89. Even where Paul speaks of "obeying" the gospel, what he has in mind is believing: "But not all have obeyed the good news; for Isaiah says, 'Lord, who has *believed* our message?' So faith comes from what is heard, and what is heard comes through the word of Christ" (Rom. 10:16–17, emphasis added).

90. Wright, *What Saint Paul Really Said*, 160.

91. Gundry, "The Nonimputation of Christ's Righteousness," 44, citing Seifrid, *Christ, Our Righteousness*, 175.

92. Schweitzer, *Mysticism*, 225.

93. Gundry, "The Nonimputation of Christ's Righteousness," 44–45.

94. See for instance Joseph Fitzmeyer, "The Letter to the Romans," and "The Letter to the Galatians," in *The Jerome Biblical Commentary*, ed. Raymond S. Brown, S.S.; Joseph A. Fitzmyer, S.J.; and Roland E. Murphy, O.Carm. (Englewood Cliffs, NJ: Prentice-Hall, 1968), esp. 241–44 and 303–15 respectively.

95. See Danker, BDAG, 246–50.

will elaborate a covenantal ontology that gives rise to a restored economy of grace, and response that finally surrenders to doxology:

> What then are we to say about these things? If God is for us, who is against us? He who did not withhold his own Son, but gave him up for all of us, will he not with him also give us everything else? Who will bring any charge against God's elect? It is God who justifies. Who is to condemn? It is Christ Jesus, who died, yes, who was raised, who is at the right hand of God, who indeed intercedes for us. Who will separate us from the love of Christ? (Rom. 8:31–35)

PART TWO
COVENANT
AND PARTICIPATION

Chapter Seven

Mystical Union
in Reformed Soteriology

Since Albert Schweitzer, the thesis has repeatedly been advanced, refuted, and then advanced again that justification is a "subsidiary crater" in Paul, while the real central dogma is mystical union. Reginald Fuller notes, "Attempts have been made to pinpoint some other center or focus for Pauline theology, such as 'being in Christ' (Schweitzer) or salvation history (Johannes Munck)." However, "Romans, the most systematic exposition of Paul's thought, clearly makes justification the center." Not only in Paul but also in the pre-Pauline creedal hymns we find this affirmation (2 Tim. 1:9 and Titus 3:4–5).[1] This does not mean, of course, that justification functions as a central dogma from which the entire system may be logically deduced. Nevertheless, it is the forensic basis of union with Christ and is therefore the source of our calling, sanctification, and glorification.

---

1. Reginald Fuller, "Here We Stand," in *By Faith Alone: Essays on Justification in Honor of Gerhard O. Forde,* ed. Joseph A. Burgess and Mark Kolden (Grand Rapids: Eerdmans, 2004), 91. Especially in light of my earlier criticism of the "central dogma" thesis, I point out that to discern a central emphasis on the basis of Paul's explicit arguments is different from starting with an abstract proposition or thesis and requiring the data to be subsumed under it or deduced from it. I have argued that the NPP is actually closer to modern dogmatics at this point than are pre-Enlightenment systems.

Forcing a choice between forensic and participationist soteriologies, the basic outlines of Schweitzer's thesis reappear in myriad calls to give priority to union with Christ over justification. Not only has this thesis been applied to Paul; it has also been argued that Luther (according to the New Finnish school) and Calvin (according to T. F. Torrance and others) were chiefly interested not in justification as a forensic declaration so much as with mystical union as an ontic participation in the Trinity's being.[2]

Sanders has correctly pointed out the contrast between covenantal nomism and Paul's "participationist eschatology."[3] However, because of his restrictive view of the reference range for the noun *covenant*, he failed to see the complementary—indeed, inextricable—relationship between the themes of covenant and participation. Whether these themes in fact can be harmonized will depend to a large extent on which covenant theology and which account of participation we adopt. In classic covenant theology, the solidarity of the body with its head is simultaneously legal and relational, judicial and familial. In such a union, there can be no facile oppositions between law and love, the courtroom and the family room, a verdict of righteousness *extra nos* and an organic, living, and growing relationship in which the justified grow up into Christ.

This chapter begins by summarizing the way in which Reformed theology has traditionally approached the *unio mystica* by way of its covenant theology. Next, I will more directly explore Calvin's treatment of the character of this union, representative of Reformed treatments to the present. Finally, I will offer my own analysis with the goal of discerning the purchase of a Trinitarian, covenantal, and forensic-communicative ontology outlined in this chapter and the next.

TRINITY AND COVENANT: *PACTUM SALUTIS*

Paul's *ordo* in Romans 8:30–31 explicitly connects God's eternal decree to its execution in time: "Those whom he predestined he also called; those whom he called he also justified; those whom he justified he also glorified." Just as God sees nothing in the elect that could ground his electing favor and no preparation that could welcome his advent, he declares the ungodly to be righteous only on the basis of Christ's saving mediation. Furthermore, we never leave the theme of justification when we go on to talk about regeneration, sanctification, and glorification; we are always returning to our justification in Christ as the source. In the wake of justification we discover Christ's victory over the powers, the hope of creation's

---

2. See, for example, T. F. Torrance, "Justification: Its Radical Nature and Place in Reformed Doctrine and Life," *Scottish Journal of Theology* 13 (1960): 223–46; cf. chap. 1 n. 6 for more sources.

3. Anthony J. Saldarini, review of *Paul and Palestinian Judaism*, by E. P. Sanders, in *Journal of Biblical Literature* 98, no. 2 (June 1979): 299–303: "Sanders concludes (cf. chap. 4 and the final conclusion) that Judaism taught covenantal nomism and Paul participationist eschatology (A. Schweitzer)" (299).

complete renewal, new birth, the church, and other benefits of participation that could not be ours on any other basis.

The theme of union with Christ brings together the temporal tenses of our salvation—past, present, and future, as well as the objective and subjective, historical and existential, corporate and individual, forensic and transformative, and a unilateral gift that establishes a reciprocal relationship of faithful speaking and answering within the covenant as the nucleus of cosmic renewal. Although each element of the so-called *ordo salutis* must be allowed its own distinct role in what William Perkins called "a golden chain" of Romans 8:30, the chain itself is greater than the sum of its parts.[4]

Thus far, our attention has been directed toward the covenants that we find in the history of revelation, generally grouped under the covenant of law (Adamic and Sinaitic) and the covenant of grace (Abrahamic-Davidic-new). However, behind all of these covenants lies the "eternal purpose in election" to which Paul repeatedly refers (Rom. 8:28; 9:11; Eph. 1:4–5, 11; 3:11; 2 Tim. 1:9). The story behind all of these stories is the *pactum salutis* (covenant of redemption or counsel of peace) between the persons of the Trinity for the salvation of the elect. Unlike the covenants sworn by the people on earth ("All this we will do"), this covenant serves as the "unchangeable oath" (Heb. 6:17–20) that guarantees redemption even "before the foundation of the world" (Eph. 1:4–11). "Here the basis of all covenants was found in the eternal counsel of God," writes Bavinck, "in a covenant between the very persons of the Trinity, the *pactum salutis* (counsel of peace)."[5]

The Trinitarian Structure

In all three *loci*—election, justification, and calling, we recognize the marvelous symmetry of love between the Father, the Son, and the Spirit, yet not in a circle of exclusion but in an ecstatic, eccentric, extroverted movement of embrace, to include even enemies in a communion of peace.

Ever since the systems of the sixteenth century, it has been commonplace in confessional Reformed theologies to emphasize the Trinitarian pattern as the implication of a covenant theology based fundamentally on the eternal *pactum* between the divine persons. This also allowed them to recognize better the inner coherence of and integral relationships between the forensic and transformative aspects of redemption as distinctively displayed in the operation of each divine person.[6] As Geerhardus Vos expresses it, "Just as the blessedness of God exists in

---

4. William Perkins, "The Golden Chain," in Ian Breward, ed., *The Work of William Perkins,* The Courtenay Library of Reformation Classics (Appleford, England: The Sutton Courtenay Press, 1970), 169–260.

5. Herman Bavinck, *Reformed Dogmatics,* ed. John Bolt, trans., John Vriend, vol. 3 (Grand Rapids: Baker Academic, 2006), 194. On the structural significance of the *pactum salutis,* see, e.g., Heinrich Heppe, *Reformed Dogmatics,* rev. and ed. E. Bizer, trans. G. T. Thomson (London: G. Allen & Unwin, 1950; repr., London: Wakeman Trust, 2002), 373–83.

6. See R. Scott Clark and David VanDrunen, "The Covenant Before the Covenant," in *Covenant and Justification,* ed. R. Scott Clark (Phillipsburg: P&R Publishing, 2007).

the free relationship of the three Persons of the adorable Being, so man shall also find his blessedness in the covenantal relationship with God."[7] "There is room for an order of salvation in a scriptural, Christian, and Reformed sense," Bavinck wrote, "only on the foundation of the trinitarian confession."[8]

It is beyond our scope, but a historical case can be made that wherever the covenant of redemption remained firmly in place not only as a tacit affirmation but also as an organizing principle, a robust Trinitarian faith flourished in Reformed circles, and where this rubric was lost, ignored, or rejected, rigor mortis set in, and eventually the Trinity itself was either marginalized or rejected in the faith and practice of the churches.[9]

The Sovereignty of Grace

Furthermore, by grounding God's historical purposes in an eternal pact between the persons of the Godhead, covenant theology could affirm the priority of God's initiative and constancy above the exigencies and contingencies of human faithfulness in history. The basis for the inviolability of Zion as opposed to Sinai, which I have already explored by heavy reliance on Jon Levenson, finds its ultimate source in this eternal covenant.

The uniqueness of the divine persons is highlighted in the different ways that each contributes to every external work of the Godhead. At the same time, the unity of the Godhead is underscored by the fact that, with respect to the historical covenants, the conditional covenant of creation is contrasted with the covenant of grace precisely in that the latter has God alone as the guarantor of the promise. The Sinai covenant was "appointed through angels by the hand of a mediator. Now a mediator does not mediate for one only, but God is one" (Gal. 3:19–20 NKJV). This is crucial to Paul's argument that the Abrahamic covenant is not canceled by the Sinai covenant: God unilaterally promised Abraham the inheritance, while Sinai required two parties with a mediator (Moses). Paul's point is that while the Sinai treaty was in form and content a bilateral agreement between Yahweh and human partners, mediated by Moses, the covenant of grace rests upon a divine oath without human mediation. God alone is the oath-maker.[10] We have seen this

7. Richard B. Gaffin Jr., ed., *Redemptive History and Biblical Interpretation: The Shorter Writings of Geerhardus Vos* (Phillipsburg, NJ: P&R Publishing, 1980), 245; originally printed as "Doctrine of the Covenant in Reformed Theology," in Dutch: *De verbondsleer in de Gereformeerde theologie* (Grand Rapids: "Democrat" Drukpers, 1891), 68 pp., rectoral address at the Theological School of the Christian Reformed College in Grand Rapids.

8. Bavinck, *Reformed Dogmatics*, 3:569.

9. This is particularly evident in the sixteenth- and seventeenth-century debates between Reformed orthodoxy and Socinianism, Arminianism, and what John Owen and others called "neonomianism," as represented by Richard Baxter and John Goodwin. Obviously, these aberrations could be challenged without any direct reliance on the covenant of redemption (viz., Lutheranism), but I am suggesting that in Reformed circles at least, the *pactum salutis* and Trinitarian dogma were inextricably connected.

10. On this point, see S. M. Baugh, "Galatians 3:20 and the Covenant of Redemption," *Westminster Theological Journal* 66 (2004): 49–70.

in the covenant with Abraham (Gen. 15), but it is itself the historical outworking of the eternal covenant made not between God and human beings but between the persons of the Trinity.

"There is no gift that has not been earned by Him," Vos writes.[11] "The covenant of redemption does not stand by itself," he adds, "but is the basis of the economy of salvation. It is the great prelude which in the Scriptures resounds from eternity on into our own time and in which we can already listen to the pure tones of the psalm of grace."[12]

Keeping the covenant of grace *gracious*, so to speak, the intratrinitarian pact is the context in which *union with Christ* obtains such clear identity. It was because of the love displayed in the covenant of redemption that the Son willingly committed himself to fulfill all righteousness (the covenant of creation) so that he might bestow this righteousness and all other benefits in a covenant of grace. Thus, both historical covenants, law and gospel, meet in Christ. As Wilhelm Niesel pointed out, even the third (normative) use of the law is supposed to lead us back to Christ. Although "Reformed theology recognises the contrast between Law and Gospel, in a similar way to Lutheranism," Niesel adds, "law"—in its third use—now becomes adapted to the character of the covenant of grace.

> If we enjoy union with Christ, not only we ourselves but even our works too are just in God's sight. This doctrine of the justification of works (which was developed in the Reformed Church) is of the greatest consequence for ethics. It makes clear that the man who belongs to Christ need not be the prey of continual remorse. On the contrary he can go about his daily work confidently and joyfully.[13]

Along similar lines, Vos says that Reformed theologians "who strictly separate law and gospel and make the latter to consist wholly of promises—as a matter of fact, those theologians more than others—put emphasis on the fact that the law, as the comprehensive norm for the life of man, also determines man's relation to the gospel."[14]

Thus it is not only through the doctrine of justification that we are able to assure disquieted consciences that God is gracious to them, but on the wider basis of the Abrahamic covenant of grace. "The covenant," notes Vos, "is neither a hypothetical relationship, nor a conditional position; rather it is the fresh, living fellowship in which the power of grace is operative."[15] The new covenant

11. Vos, in Gaffin, *Redemptive History and Biblical Interpretation*, 248.

12. Ibid., 252.

13. Wihelm Niesel, *Reformed Symbolics: A Comparison of Catholicism, Orthodoxy and Protestantism*, trans. David Lewis (Edinburgh and London: Oliver & Boyd, 1962), 217, 220–21.

14. Vos, in Gaffin, *Redemptive History and Biblical Interpretation*, 254.

15. Ibid., 256. In Lutheran dogmatics, "everything depends on this justification, which is losable, so that the believer only gets to see a little of the glory of grace and lives for the day, so to speak. The covenantal outlook is the reverse. One is first united to Christ, the Mediator of the covenant, by a mystical union, which finds its conscious recognition in faith. By this union with Christ all that is in Christ is simultaneously given" (256).

promises not only forgiveness, but also a true circumcision (regeneration) that will result not only in genuine trust but a love for the law that is now inscribed on hearts of flesh rather than tablets of stone (Ezek. 11:19; Jer. 31:32–34, with its New Testament gloss in 2 Cor. 3). The Sinai covenant itself commands the Israelites to obey everything in the law, loving and serving Yahweh without reserve (Deut. 4:29; 6:5; 10:12–13; 15:10; 30:6, 10). Indeed, Israel is called to circumcise its own heart: "Circumcise, then, the foreskin of your heart, and do not be stubborn any longer" (10:16). Yet even when Israel's violation of this pact is presaged, the promise is present that God will, on the basis of the covenant with Abraham, be merciful (4:30–31). In fact, in that day, we are told, "the LORD your God will circumcise your heart and the heart of your offspring, so that you will love the LORD your God with all your heart and with all your soul, that you may live," replacing the curse with blessing (30:6–9 RSV).

Even in the documents in which the Sinai covenant is enshrined, therefore, the Abrahamic covenant—in anticipation of the new covenant—is not forgotten. Sinai itself pines for Zion, and God's eternal purpose is the source of that longing that can never be extinguished by historical circumstances. Yet God's unilateral promise in history is not arbitrary; it does not appear out of nowhere. Rather, it is anchored in the eternal pact between the persons of the Trinity.

Historical Rather Than Speculative Focus

Because God's electing purposes could only be realized in history, covenant theology drew attention away from speculation on the eternal decree to the promise delivered to humanity after the fall and constantly renewed in the covenant of grace. We do not fly upward or turn inward to discover God's electing grace. The covenant of redemption guards against the abstraction of election from its Trinitarian basis and, specifically, from Christ, who in Calvin's words is "the mirror of our election." We find the same language used by Bullinger in the Second Helvetic Confession (1561):

> Let Christ, therefore, be the looking glass in whom we may contemplate our predestination. We shall have a sufficiently clear and sure testimony that we are inscribed in the Book of Life if we have fellowship with Christ, and he is ours and we are his in true faith. In the temptation in regard to predestination, than which there is scarcely any other more dangerous, we are confronted by the fact that God's promises apply to all the faithful, for he says: "Ask, and everyone who seeks shall receive" (Luke 11:9f.). This finally we pray, with the whole Church of God, "Our Father who art in heaven" (Matt. 6:9), both because by baptism we are ingrafted into the body of Christ, and we are often fed in his Church with his flesh and blood unto eternal life.[16]

16. The Second Helvetic Confession, chap. 10, in *The Book of Confessions* (Louisville, KY: General Assembly of the PC[USA], 1991).

Believers are not to search out this secret decree, but to come to know God and the divine purposes by the external *works* of the Trinity, especially the historical and revealed covenants that God has made with his creatures. With its promulgation in word and ratification in sacrament, the covenant of grace provides the concrete context within which believers are assured of being chosen in Christ and belonging to the one elect people of God. While the eternal covenant anchors God's redeeming purposes in the Trinity rather than in human beings, we can only discern its features as it unfolds in the historical economy of grace.

Apart from this treatment of election in its relation to the covenant of redemption, abstract doctrines of election and divine sovereignty have often cropped up that yield to rationalistic speculations. Such approaches to the question were wisely excoriated by the Reformers as an attempt to search out the hidden God, which can only lead believers into a maze or "labyrinth." Employing this image repeatedly, Calvin calls the attempt to discern one's election in God's hidden counsels rather than in Christ "seeking outside the way."[17] We find God where he has found us: in the gospel. The covenant of redemption keeps our discussion of election tethered to the Trinity and to the historical economy, as revealed in Scripture through God's promulgation and development of his covenant of grace.

A Communicative Paradigm

Finally, the covenant of redemption suggests a communicative approach to God's triune operations *ad extra*. Specifically, the covenant of redemption provides the proper backdrop for an appeal, with Kevin J. Vanhoozer, to the correlation between the locutionary, illocutionary, and perlocutionary aspects of speech (as formulated in speech-act theory) and the Father, the Son, and the Spirit.[18] Appropriated in an ad hoc manner, we easily recognize its fruitfulness for interpreting a vast array of biblical passages. The Father speaks in the Son through the Spirit. We see this repeatedly in the works of the Godhead *ad extra*, where creative, providential, and redemptive actions are referred to the Father's (or "God's") utterance, the Son is identified as the hypostatic Word, and the Spirit is treated as the person who makes that utterance effective for its intended purposes.

Scripture is replete with references to covenantal speech yielding its effect through distinct operations of the divine persons, and this has been implicitly

17. John Calvin, *Institutes* 3.24.4: "I call it 'seeking outside the way' when mere man attempts to break into the inner recesses of divine wisdom, and tries to penetrate even to highest eternity, in order to find out what decision has been made concerning himself at God's judgment seat. . . . For just as those engulf themselves in a deadly abyss who, to make their election more certain, investigate God's eternal plan apart from his Word, so those who rightly and duly examine it as it is contained in his Word reap the inestimable fruit of comfort" (3.24.4 [2:968–69]). In the next two sections he emphasizes that one is to discern one's election in Christ alone, as he is revealed and given in the gospel (3.24.5–6).

18. Kevin Vanhoozer, *First Theology: God, Scripture and Hermeneutics* (Downers Grove, IL: InterVarsity Press, 2002), 154–57.

recognized in the history of Christian interpretation. Colin Gunton pointed out, in fact, the similarity between Basil's identification of Father, Son, and Spirit as original, creative, and perfecting cause respectively and Calvin's formula.[19] Throughout his work Calvin also assumes this classical notion of perichoresis, especially in relation to divine speech. God's Word remains what it is by virtue of its source (the Father) and its content (the Son). The Spirit does not bring a different word than the one spoken by the Father in the Son. Nevertheless, Calvin writes, "it seriously affects us only when it is sealed upon our hearts through the Spirit."[20] "As has been clearly explained, until our minds become intent upon the Spirit, Christ, so to speak, lies idle because we coldly contemplate him as outside ourselves—indeed, far from us."[21] Indeed, "the promise of salvation," apart from the Spirit, "would otherwise only strike the air or beat upon our ears."[22] The Father's promise is the origin of faith, the Son is the object of faith, and the Spirit is the giver of faith.[23] Christ communicates his Father's benefits to his coheirs by the Spirit.[24] In terms almost identical to Basil's, the French Confession declares its faith in "the Father, first cause, principle, and origin of all things. The Son, his Word and eternal wisdom. The Holy Spirit, his virtue, power and efficacy."[25]

Although such statements are replete in the history of theology, after centuries of modern theology's at least implicit unitarianism (and binitarianism) the revival of Trinitarian theology, including a fresh emphasis on pneumatology, has awakened interest in the Son and the Spirit as the "two hands" of the Father.[26] I will be appealing to this model at appropriate places throughout the rest of this volume.

The Exegetical Basis for the Covenant of Redemption

For all of its systematic-theological virtues, is the covenant of redemption exegetically tenable? In the ministry of Christ, the Son is represented (particularly in the Fourth Gospel) as having been given a people by the Father (6:39; 10:29; 17:2, 6–10; Eph. 1:4–12; Heb. 2:13, citing Isa. 8:18), who are called and kept by the Holy Spirit for the consummation of the new creation (Rom. 8:29–30; Eph. 1:11–13; Titus 3:5; 1 Pet. 1:5). In fact, to affirm the covenant of redemption was little more than to affirm that the Son's self-giving and the Spirit's regen-

---

19. Colin Gunton, *Father, Son and Holy Spirit: Toward a Fully Trinitarian Theology* (Edinburgh: T&T Clark, 2003), 81. He also points out in the same place the practically identical formulation of John Owen (81 n. 9).

20. Calvin, *Institutes* 1.8.5.

21. Ibid., 3.1.3.

22. Ibid., 3.1.4.

23. Ibid., 3.1.4–3.2.1.

24. Ibid., 3.2.1.

25. Gallican (French) Confession, art. 6, cited in Richard Muller, *Post-Reformation Reformed Dogmatics*, vol. 3, *The Divine Essence and Attributes* (Grand Rapids: Baker Academic 2003), 93

26. Although this revival of Trinitarian theology in mainstream Protestantism can be traced to Barth, the contributions of T. F. Torrance and especially of Colin Gunton have provided renewed impetus for a fully Trinitarian theology that includes the Spirit along with the Son as the Father's "two hands," an Irenaean analogy that Gunton put to such effective use.

erative work were the execution of the Father's eternal plan. (In this sense even the Son can be said to have been destined before the foundation of the world, as in 1 Pet. 1:20). Consequently, while it is an intratrinitarian arrangement and each person is perichoretically involved in the action of the other, it all takes place "in Christ"—hence, the emphasis in covenant theology on the theme of "Christ the Mediator." Even before creation and the fall, the elect are "in Christ" in terms of the divine *purpose* for history, though not yet *in history* itself.[27]

Thus, whatever unfolds in history with respect to the covenants of creation ("in Adam") and grace ("in Christ") will ultimately serve God's electing purposes in creating and redeeming his church (cf. Eph. 3:1–13; Col. 1:15–20). In such a covenantal understanding of election, soteriology and ecclesiology become inextricably linked.

A lodestar for reflection on the covenant of redemption is found in John's Gospel, where the language of "giving" and "receiving" a people from the Father is explicitly mentioned (6:39; 10:29; 17:2, 6–10). Commenting on John 17, Calvin observed, "Thine they were, and thou hast given them to me" (v. 6) means "that the elect always belonged to God."

> God therefore distinguishes them from the reprobate, not by faith, or by any merit, but by pure grace; for, while they are alienated from him to the utmost, still he reckons them as his own in his secret purpose. The certainty of that election by free grace lies in this, that he commits to the guardianship of his Son all whom he has elected, that they may not perish; and this is the point to which we should turn our eyes, that we may be fully certain that we belong to the rank of the children of God; for the predestination of God is in itself hidden, but it is manifested to us in Christ alone.[28]

When Jesus says, "I do not pray for the world, but for those you have given me" (v. 9 NKJV), Calvin comments that we ought to pray for the salvation of every person, "and thus include the whole human race, because we cannot yet distinguish the elect from the reprobate. . . . We pray for the salvation of all whom we know to have been created after the image of God, and who have the same nature with ourselves; and we leave to the judgment of God those whom he knows to be reprobate."[29]

> Now Christ expressly declares that they who *are given to him* belong to *the Father*; and it is certain that they are *given* so as to believe, and that faith flows from this act of *giving*. If the origin of faith is this act of giving, and if election comes before it in order and time, what remains but that we acknowledge that those whom God wishes to be saved out of the world are elected by free grace?[30]

27. For our purposes we will leave to one side the variations within this concept between so-called infralapsarianism and supralapsarianism (either of the orthodox or Barthian varieties).
28. John Calvin, *Commentary on the Gospel according to John*, trans. William Pringle (1847; repr., Grand Rapids: Baker, 1996), 170–71, on John 17:6.
29. Ibid., 172–73.
30. Ibid., 173.

The mutual giving between the persons of the Trinity extends outward *ad extra* to their acts of giving to creatures: gift-giving *between* them is the ground for the gifts *from* them to us.

We do not have the space here to treat the development of the Reformed understanding of election and reprobation, except to note that if the Reformed scholastics deviated at all from Calvin's teaching on the subject, it was in the direction of more clearly distinguishing between these two aspects of predestination. For example, William Ames states, "Election is the cause not only of salvation but everything causally connected with salvation; reprobation is not properly a cause of either damnation or sin (which deserves damnation) but an antecedent only."[31] In other words, the subjects of God's electing grace are, like the rest, those whom God regards as sinners lost in Adam even before creation and fall. While reprobation is a "passive decree" (simply leaving people to their freely chosen separation from God), election is God's "active decree," a determination to reconcile enemies.[32]

Decreed to be "in Christ" from all of eternity in the intratrinitarian covenant of redemption, the elect are redeemed by Christ in history, and are united to Christ by the Spirit in a covenant of grace: now they are children of the Father rather than transgressors before a judge. Holding the *ordo salutis* and *historia salutis* together, the seventeenth-century theologian William Ames summarizes:

> The judgment was, first, conceived in the mind of God in a decree of justification (Gal 3:8). Second, it was pronounced in Christ our head as he rose from the dead (2 Cor 5:19). . . . Third, it is pronounced in actuality upon that first relationship which is created when faith is born (Rom 8:1). . . . Fourth, it is expressly pronounced by the Spirit of God witnessing to our spirits our reconciliation with God (Rom 5:5). . . . This testimony of the Spirit is not properly justification itself, but rather an actual perceiving of what has been given before as if in a reflected act of faith.[33]

In this understanding, justification is not simply one doctrine among others; it is the Word that creates a living union between Christ, the believer, and the communion of saints. Far from severing soteriology from ethics and ecclesiology, justification inaugurates the new creation in its transformative and corporate as well as judicial and personal dimensions.

We also recognize in Ames's representative statement the Trinitarian and communicative character of this forensic Word: a judgment decreed by the Father, pronounced upon us in Christ through the resurrection, and declared to us in hearing the gospel, even as the Spirit brings its assuring effect within us. In the

31. William Ames, *The Marrow of Theology*, trans. and ed. John D. Eusden, from the 3rd Latin edition of 1629 (Boston: Pilgrim, 1968; repr. Durham, NC: Labyrinth, 1983), 156.

32. Although Calvin, especially in his disputes with Bolsec, was unwilling to recognize this sort of distinction, and both the Synod of Dort and the Westminster Assembly purposely left elbow room for infra- and supralapsarian positions, the former was (happily, to my mind) more dominant in Reformed scholasticism. Both sides cited Calvin, but it is anachronistic (for them or for us) to expect the reformer to offer a refined position on this question.

33. Ames, *The Marrow of Theology*, 161.

next several chapters I will argue that, especially when interpreted in its covenantal context, justification does not allow us to set a forensic and extrinsic verdict over against an ontological account of participation but rather establishes a forensic ontology whose reverberations can be felt and echoes heard across the entire landscape of the so-called *ordo salutis*, and not only in theory but also in corporate and individual experience and praxis. This does not mean that justification itself *includes* its effects, but that it *generates* them. Justification is exclusively juridical, yet it is the forensic origin of our union with Christ, from which all of our covenantal blessings flow.

REFORMATION VIEWS ON PARTICIPATION IN CHRIST

Concerning the Reformers' emphasis on union with Christ, much has been written, and this is because the theme of mystical union was profoundly important for their understanding of "the marvelous exchange" between Christ and the believer. We may put it in the following way:

- "We in Christ"—sharing in his election, flesh, life of obedience, atoning death, resurrection, justification, holiness, and glorification. We are in the family (*inheritance*).
- "Christ in us"—regeneration and sanctification, "the hope of glory." The family is in us (*resemblance*).

Union with Christ's Person and Work

According to Luther, everything that can be considered good in us is so because Christ lives in the believer and the believer in Christ. Far from rejecting the believer's actual righteousness (sanctification) in favor of a merely imputed righteousness (justification), Luther says that Christ's imputed righteousness "is the basis, the cause, the source of all our own actual righteousness."[34] Far from separating these distinct works of God, justification is made the ground and animating principle of sanctification.

> We conclude, therefore, that a Christian lives not in himself, but in Christ and his neighbor. Otherwise he is not a Christian. He lives in Christ through faith, in his neighbor through love. By faith he is caught up beyond himself into God. By love he descends beneath himself into his neighbor. Yet he always remains in God and in his love.[35]

Faith suffices not only for justification, but is also the constant source of the believer's renewal and service toward others.

---

34. Martin Luther, *Two Kinds of Righteousness,* in *LW* 31, ed. Harold J. Grimm (repr., 1971), 298.

35. Luther, *LW* 31:371; cf. Cornelius P. Venema, "Heinrich Bullinger's Correspondence on Calvin's Doctrine of Predestination," *Sixteenth Century Journal* 17 (1986): 335–350.

Drawing, like Luther, on the wide range of biblical analogies for this union, Calvin's judicial emphasis with respect to *justification* is complemented by the organic imagery of union and ingrafting in relation to the *inner renewal* and communion with Christ, including his holiness. Thus, commenting on John 17, Calvin explains, "Having been ingrafted into the body of Christ, we are made partakers of the Divine adoption, and heirs of heaven."[36] "This is the purpose of the gospel," he says, "that Christ should become ours, and that we should be ingrafted into his body."[37]

Calvin's pneumatological emphasis, familiar to us especially in his formulation of the way in which Christ is communicated to us in the Supper, is already apparent in his treatment of the mystical union. The Spirit's mediation of Christ's person and work, not an immediate participation in the divine essence, is a critical aspect of his account. We are "one with the Son of God; not because he conveys his substance to us, but because, by the power of the Spirit, he imparts to us his life and all the blessings which he has received from the Father."[38]

Significant for our interaction especially with the New Finnish (Helsinki) school and its Reformed corollaries, this statement displays the subtlety of Calvin's view. On one hand, he does not believe that there can be a communion with Christ's benefits apart from his person (more explicitly argued below). On the other hand, it is not his substance that is conveyed to us, but "his life and all the blessings which he has received from the Father." The link between difference and affinity is the Spirit.

On John 17:23 ("I in them and you in me . . .") he draws the image of a vast ocean with innumerable tributaries and channels, which "waters the fields on all sides."[39] The foundation of our assurance that we are loved by God is "that we are loved because the Father hath loved his Son."[40] "With such a love did the Father love him before the creation of the world, that he might be the person in whom the Father would love his elect."[41] In verse 26 the phrases "and I in them" "deserves our attention," he says, "for it teaches us that the only way in which we are included in that love which he mentions is that Christ dwells in us; for, as the Father cannot look upon his Son without having likewise before his eyes the whole body of Christ, so, if we wish to be beheld in him, we must be actually his members."[42]

On the "vine and branches" in John 15:1 he notes that this union is a gift of electing grace, not natural or universal. It is not an abstract participation in being, "as if it had been implanted in them by nature," but a personal union with the

---

36. Calvin, *Commentary on the Gospel according to John*, 166, on John 17:3.
37. Ibid.
38. Ibid., 183–84.
39. Ibid., 185.
40. Ibid., 186.
41. Ibid., 187.
42. Ibid., 189.

mediator of the covenant: "But Christ dwells principally on this, that the vital sap—that is, all life and strength—proceeds from himself alone."[43]

The mystical union of believers with Christ (and therefore with his body) is the wider field within which the Reformers recognize the integral connection of justification and sanctification, the imputation of righteousness, and the impartation of Christ's holy love in the lives of those united to him through faith. Faith looks to Christ for justification and "puts on" Christ for renewal and life. In this way, not only justification but also sanctification and glorification are assured in Christ alone, through faith alone.

Also in agreement with Luther, as well as Bernard of Clairvaux (to whom he directly appeals), Calvin emphasizes that salvation—as a general category comprehending all of the benefits of Christ from election to glorification—is secure precisely because it is not simply something that occurs at a distance, as if the gifts could be separated from the giver: "As if we ought to think of Christ, standing afar off and not rather dwelling in us!"[44] By virtue of this mystical union, we can be assured that we are already accepted in Christ, and everything that belongs properly to him is given freely to us:

> For we await salvation from him not because he appears to us afar off, but because he makes us, ingrafted into his body, participants not only in all his benefits but also in himself. So I turn this argument of theirs back against them: if you contemplate yourself, that is sure damnation. But since Christ has been so imparted to you with all his benefits that all his things are made yours, that you are made a member of him, indeed one with him, his righteousness overwhelms your sins; his salvation wipes out your condemnation; with his worthiness he intercedes that your unworthiness may not come before God's sight. Surely this is so: We ought not to separate Christ from ourselves or ourselves from him. Rather we ought to hold fast bravely with both hands to that fellowship by which he has bound himself to us. So the apostle teaches us: "Now your body is dead because of sin; but the Spirit of Christ which dwells in you is life because of righteousness" [Rom. 8:10].

In fact, Calvin appeals to this familiar patristic and medieval theme of mystical union *against* his opponents:

> According to these men's trifles, he ought to have said, "Christ indeed has life in himself; but you, as you are sinners, remain subject to death and condemnation." But he speaks far otherwise, for he teaches that the condemnation which we of ourselves deserve has been swallowed up by the salvation that is in Christ. And to confirm this he uses the same reason I have brought forward: that Christ is not outside us but dwells within us. Not only does he cleave to us by an indivisible bond of fellowship, but with a wonderful communion, day by day, he grows more and more into one body with us, until he becomes completely one with us. Yet I do not deny what I stated above: that certain interruptions of faith occasionally occur, according as its

---

43. Ibid., 107, on John 15:1.
44. Calvin, *Institutes* 3.2.24.

weakness is violently buffeted hither and thither; so in the thick darkness of temptations its light is snuffed out. Yet whatever happens, it ceases not its earnest quest for God.[45]

Calvin then expounds Bernard's discussion of "the two aspects of faith":

So indeed, *before* thee, not *within* thee: so in the judgment of thy truth, but not so in the intention of thy faithfulness. So, indeed, thou "callest those things which are not as though they were" [Rom. 4:17]. And they are not, therefore, because it is the things that are not that thou callest, and they are at the same time because thou callest them. For although, as regards themselves, they are not, nevertheless with thee they are; but, as the apostle says, "Not of their works" of righteousness, "but of him who calls" [Rom. 9:12]. Then he says that this connection between the two considerations is wonderful. Surely those things which are connected do not destroy one another![46]

So when we consider ourselves, there is nothing but despair; when we consider ourselves *in Christ*, there is faith, which brings hope and love in its train. Again Calvin quotes Bernard: "Surely if we think, 'If he has decreed to save us, we shall be immediately freed' [cf. Jer. 17:14]; in this, then, we may take heart." We are therefore raised from the status of transgressors to that of dignified heirs, "but by his dignifying us, not by our own dignity."[47]

This is one of the reasons that the Reformers were so critical of the scholastic notion of preparation for grace, with its frequent analogies to getting one's house in order for the arrival of a distinguished guest.[48] By contrast, the Reformers insisted that through this mystical union the guest himself dignifies the house by his own arrival and then begins its renovation. A strange guest this is indeed.

Earlier, Calvin writes:

Although we may distinguish them [justification and sanctification], Christ contains both of them inseparably in himself. Do you wish, then, to attain righteousness in Christ? You must first possess Christ; but you cannot possess him without being made partaker in his sanctification, because he cannot be divided into pieces [1 Cor. 1:13]. Since, therefore, it is solely by expending himself that the Lord gives us these benefits to enjoy, he bestows both of them at the same time, the one never without the other. Thus it is clear how true it is that we are justified not without works yet not through works, since in our sharing in Christ, which justifies us, sanctification is just as much included as righteousness.[49]

45. Ibid.
46. Ibid., 3.2.25. For an intriguing account of the relationship between Calvin and Bernard, see Dennis E. Tamburello, *Union with Christ: John Calvin and the Mysticism of St. Bernard* (Louisville, KY: Westminster John Knox, 1994).
47. Ibid.
48. One of many examples is Calvin's passage in the *Institutes* (3.3.2) where he argues against the medieval notion of "preparatory fear" as the engine that gets the Christian life going. Instead, Calvin insists, one can never bring about the fruit of repentance until one first trusts in God as a merciful Father, and this can only be derived from the confidence that we are fully accepted in Christ.
49. Ibid., 3.16.1.

Calvin recognizes here that justification need not be *confused* with sanctification by means of an all-encompassing ontology of union in order to recognize the *inseparability* of both legal (forensic) and organic (effective) aspects of that union. When discussing justification, Calvin emphatically cautions that "the question is not how we may become righteous but how, being unrighteous and unworthy, we may be reckoned righteous. If consciences wish to attain any certainty in this matter, they ought to give no place to the law."[50] Regardless of whether union temporally preceded justification, Calvin is clear that the latter is the basis for the former: "Most people regard partaking of Christ (*Christi esse participem*) and believing in Christ as the same thing. But our partaking of Christ (*participatio quam habemus cum Christo*) is rather the effect of believing (*fidei effectus*)."[51] The same act of faith that constantly looks to Christ alone for justification looks to Christ alone for sanctification and glorification. There are not two sources of the Christian life: one forensic and found in Christ alone, with the other being moral and found within us. Forensic justification through faith alone is the fountain of union with Christ in all of its renewing aspects.

Union without Fusion

In Calvin's view, it made little difference to say that one was justified by cooperation with an infused righteousness or by the "essential righteousness" of Christ indwelling the believer, since in either case the ground of justification would be an internal act of making righteous, rather than the imputation of an alien righteousness. This latter position was taken by the Lutheran reformer Andreas Osiander, although it was explicitly rejected in the Book of Concord. Since Osiander's position is so similar in some respects to accounts of participation that one finds in recent proposals that we will consider, it is worth summarizing Calvin's critique of Osiander, which takes up eight sections in the final edition of the *Institutes*.

We too speak a great deal of mystical union, says Calvin. In fact, he complained that Erasmus's rendering of *koinōnia* as *societas* and *consortium* fell far short of the mystical union, so he chose *communio*.[52] "But Osiander has introduced some strange monster of 'essential' righteousness by which, although not intending to abolish freely given righteousness, he has still enveloped it in such a fog as to darken pious minds and deprive them of a lively experience of Christ's grace."[53] Besides indulging in "speculation" and "feeble curiosity," Osiander is faulted for "something bordering on Manichaeism, in his desire to transfuse the

50. Ibid., 3.19.2.
51. John Calvin, *Commentary on Ephesians*, in *CO* 51 (CR 79): 186–87, on Eph. 3:17.
52. B. A. Gerrish, *Guilt and Grace: The Eucharistic Theology of John Calvin* (Minneapolis: Augsburg Fortress, 1993), 83. See John Calvin, *Commentary on 1 Corinthians* in *CO* 49 (CR 77): 313, on 1 Cor. 1:9.
53. Calvin, *Institutes* 3.11.5, in refutation of Andreas Osiander's *Disputation on Justification* (1550). Osiander was a Lutheran theologian whose views were finally rejected in the Book of Concord. Similarities with the view of justification advanced especially by the New Finnish Perspective on Luther have been noted and will be discussed in chap. 12.

essence of God into men," with the additional speculation "that Adam was formed to the image of God because Christ had already been destined as the prototype of human nature before the Fall."[54] We may summarize Calvin's critique of Osiander as follows. First, Osiander's view confuses Christ's essential righteousness with our own. He does not understand justification as the imputation of "that righteousness which has been acquired for us by Christ's obedience and sacrificial death, but pretends that we are substantially righteous in God by the infusion both of his essence and of his quality." Second, "he throws in a mixture of substances by which God—transfusing himself into us, as it were—makes us part of himself." This not only introduces a Creator-creature confusion; it also fails to recognize that "it comes about through the power of the Holy Spirit that we grow together with Christ, and he becomes our Head and we his members." The upshot is that justification is confused with regeneration, and the believer is confused with the divine essence. We can still affirm a communion with Christ's person, Calvin counters, without surrendering the doctrine of forensic justification.[55] In Osiander's treatment, "to be justified is not only to be reconciled to God through free pardon but also to be made righteous, and righteousness is not a free imputation but the holiness and uprightness that the essence of God, dwelling in us, inspires."[56]

Justification and rebirth, Calvin counters, must be joined but never confused.[57] He also criticizes Osiander's view (repeated today by the Helsinki school, as we will see) that "faith is Christ," rather than, as Calvin believes, an empty vessel that receives Christ.[58] Faith is the instrument through which we receive Christ, not to be confused with Christ (the material cause) himself.[59]

Conflating the new birth with justification, faith with Christ, and the believer with God, Osiander, a Lutheran, is also accused by Calvin of separating the two natures of Christ—an interesting twist on the running christological debates between these two traditions. "Osiander's opinion is that, since Christ is God and man, he is made righteousness for us with respect to his divine nature, not his human nature." What then of Paul's statement "With his blood God purchased the church for himself"? This could hardly refer merely to the divine nature of Christ.[60] It is not the Father or the Spirit—or even the Son merely according to his deity—but Jesus Christ as the incarnate Word who is the mediator of the covenant and therefore of justification.[61] Consequently, there can be no saving deity of Christ apart from the covenantal obedience that he rendered in his

54. Ibid.
55. Ibid.
56. Ibid., 3.11.6.
57. Ibid.
58. Ibid., 3.11.7. The reference to Osiander is from his *Confession of the Only Mediator and of Justification by Faith* (1551). Faith is itself of no inherent worth, Calvin adds in this section; it only receives, yet "can justify us by bringing Christ, just as a pot crammed with money makes a man rich."
59. Calvin, *Institutes* 3.11.6.
60. Ibid., 3.11.8.
61. Ibid., 3.11.9.

humanity as the Second Adam. "For if we ask how we have been justified, Paul answers, 'By Christ's obedience' [Rom. 5:19]. But did he obey in any other way than when he took upon himself the form of a servant [Phil. 2:7]? From this we conclude that in his flesh, righteousness has been manifested to us."[62]

Calvin notes that Osiander's view not only leads to a Nestorian Christology and an atonement doctrine that eliminates the saving humanity of Christ as mediator, but also to a docetic sacramental theology. Even though the apostles direct "our faith to the whole Christ and not to a half-Christ, they teach that the matter both of righteousness and of salvation resides in his *flesh*; not that as mere man he justifies or quickens by himself, but because it pleased God to reveal in the Mediator what was hidden and incomprehensible in himself" (emphasis added).[63] Not even Christ was justified by his essential righteousness as divine, but by his obedience as a servant under the law.[64] So once again we see that, far from representing antitheses to be negotiated, covenant and participation are integrally related themes.

In conclusion, Calvin observes "that mystical union" is "accorded by us the highest degree of importance, so that Christ, having been made ours, makes us sharers with him in the gifts with which he has been endowed." While our righteousness is indeed external to us—an alien righteousness that belongs properly to Christ rather than to us—Christ himself does not remain alien, but joins himself to us and us to him. "We do not, therefore, contemplate him outside ourselves from afar in order that his righteousness may be imputed to us but because we put on Christ and are engrafted into his body—in short, because he deigns to make us one with him."[65] Osiander, Calvin complains, has demanded a false choice between a forensic and a participationist scheme.

> Osiander laughs at those who teach that "to be justified" is a legal term; because we must actually be righteous. Also, he despises nothing more than that we are justified by free imputation. Well then, if God does not justify us by acquittal and pardon, what does Paul's statement mean: "God was in Christ, reconciling the world to himself, not imputing men's trespasses against them" [2 Cor. 5:19]? "For our sake he made him to be sin who had done no sin so that we might be the righteousness of God in him" [v. 21]?

Calvin compares a number of New Testament texts to ordinary legal usage and then concludes, "Osiander objects that it would be insulting to God and contrary to his nature that he should justify those who actually remain wicked." To this Calvin replies with the familiar *simul iustus et peccator* (at the same time just and sinful), reminding Osiander that according to their own righteousness, "they are always liable to the judgment of death before his tribunal." The key, he says, is to distinguish justification and inward renewal without divorcing them. Sanctification is

---

62. Ibid.
63. Ibid.
64. Ibid., 3.11.12.
65. Ibid., 3.11.10.

always partial in this life. "But [God] does not justify in part but liberally, so that they may appear in heaven as if endowed with the purity of Christ. No portion of righteousness sets our consciences at peace until it has been determined that we are pleasing to God, because we are entirely righteous before him."[66] According to Calvin, it is this comfort that Osiander, no less than Rome, denies to believers.[67] Only because justification is constituted by an imputed rather than an inherent righteousness are believers able "not to tremble at the judgment they deserve, and while they rightly condemn themselves, they should be accounted righteous outside themselves."[68]

So we discern complementary emphases in Calvin's account: the righteousness of Christ that justifies us is "outside of us," although by virtue of the mystical union Christ himself—including his righteousness—cannot remain outside of us. He avoids both a strict realism on one side and an arbitrary nominalism on the other.

The Spirit's Role in Mystical Union

Interestingly, Calvin begins his treatment of the Holy Spirit's work (the application of redemption) in the *Institutes* by returning to the mystical union. Christ's work for us must be distinguished but never separated from his union with us and work within us, both of which are accomplished by the Spirit. "First, we must understand that as long as Christ remains outside of us, and we are separated from him, all that he has suffered and done for the salvation of the human race remains useless and of no value for us. Therefore, to share with us what he has received from the Father, he had to become ours and to dwell within us." It is by "the secret energy of the Spirit" that "we come to enjoy Christ and all his benefits. . . . To sum up, the Holy Spirit is the bond by which Christ effectually unites us to himself."[69]

Thus, where medieval scholasticism concentrated on the infusion of supernatural habits (something done within the believer but at a distance), and some Protestants like Osiander simply collapsed faith into regeneration (as sanctification), the believer into Christ, Christ's humanity into his deity, and everything into God, Calvin focuses on the role of the Holy Spirit as the bond of our union with Christ. Difference and affinity are always simultaneously affirmed, and pneumatology provides the crucial link. Just as only the Son could be the Mediator, so also only the Spirit could bring about our actual union with his person and work. Throughout Calvin's commentaries, sermons, and treatises, as well as the *Institutes*, he places a special emphasis on the distinct personal properties of the Father, the Son, and the Spirit, revealed in the redemptive economy.

---

66. Ibid., 3.11.11.
67. Ibid.
68. Ibid.
69. Ibid., 3.1.1.

All supernatural gifts are found in Christ alone by the Spirit alone, by working through means. That we are in Christ *and* that Christ is in us are both due to the mediation of the Spirit. "But faith is the principal work of the Holy Spirit."[70] After all, it is faith that receives justification and is also active in love, yielding the fruit of good works. Since we are united to Christ through faith, this faith is the source not only of justification but also of sanctification and glorification. Echoing Luther's "marvelous exchange," Calvin writes:

> For in Christ he offers all happiness in place of our misery, all wealth in place of our neediness; in him he opens to us the heavenly treasures that our whole faith may contemplate his beloved Son, our whole expectation depend upon him, and our whole hope cleave to and rest in him. This, indeed, is that secret and hidden philosophy which cannot be wrested from syllogisms. But they whose eyes God has opened surely learn it by heart, that in his light they may see light [Ps. 36:9].[71]

Through the gospel that creates justifying faith, therefore, the Spirit brings about the death of the old self of pretended autonomy and the birth of the new self, created to belong to Christ and therefore to Christ's body. While a great deal more than justification is included as a result of being in Christ, Reformed theology has emphasized with Lutheran doctrine that justification is the judicial ground of it all.

Justification as the Judicial Basis for Mystical Union

Ever since Osiander and widely revived today, there have been attempts even in Protestant theologies to make this incorporation the basis for justification rather than vice versa. However, they always end up eliding the crucial distinction between Christ *for* us and Christ *in* us. According to classic Reformed treatments of this connection, Christ alone is the basis both for justification and union, but the act of justification is logically prior to union. Louis Berkhof nicely summarizes the classic Reformed interpretation:

> The mystical union in the sense in which we are now speaking of it is not the judicial ground, on the basis of which we become partakers of the riches that are in Christ. It is sometimes said that the merits of Christ cannot be imputed to us as long as we are not in Christ, since it is only on the basis of our oneness with Him that such an imputation could be reasonable. But this view fails to distinguish between our legal unity with Christ and our spiritual oneness with Him, and is a falsification of the fundamental element in the doctrine of redemption, namely, of the doctrine of justification. Justification is always a declaration of God, not on the basis of an existing condition, but on that of a gracious imputation—a declaration which is not in harmony with the existing condition of the sinner. The judicial ground for

70. Ibid., 3.1.4.
71. Ibid., 3.20.1.

all the special grace which we receive lies in the fact that the righteousness of Christ is freely imputed to us.[72]

Nevertheless, once justification has provided the legal ground, all of the gifts of God's grace are freely given in union with Christ.

Forensically secured, this mystical union is organic (John 15:5; 1 Cor. 6:15–19; Eph. 1:22–23; 4:15–16; 5:29–30) and is therefore a vital union (Rom. 8:10; 2 Cor. 13:5; Gal. 4:19). Mediated by the Spirit (1 Cor. 6:17, 19; 12:13; 2 Cor. 3:17–18; Gal. 3:2–3), it implies reciprocal action (John 14:23; 15:4–5; Gal. 2:20; Eph. 3:17) that is appropriate in covenantal relationships. It is also a personal union (John 14:20; 15:1–7; 2 Cor. 5:17; Gal. 2:20; Eph. 3:17–18) and therefore a transforming union (Matt. 16:24; Rom. 6:5; Gal. 2:20; Col. 1:24; 2:12; 3:1; 1 Pet. 4:13).[73]

One need not deny forensic justification nor absorb it into some wider scheme of participation (including mystical union) in order to affirm that there is more to *salvation* than this judicial dimension. Berkhof contrasts the Reformed understanding of this union with the rationalistic error ("immanence of God in all human spirits"), the mystical error ("union of essence"), the Socinian/Arminian error ("moral union of love and sympathy, like that existing between a teacher and his pupils or between friends"), and the sacerdotal error (God's grace as "something substantial").[74]

UNION WITH CHRIST AND COVENANT MUTUALITY

Resting as it does on the covenant of redemption, the covenant of grace is in its basis unconditional, inviolable, and irrevocable. Even repentance and faith are gifts of this royal grant, not conditions that human beings fulfill in order to receive grace. However, the gifts of this union include not only election, but also calling, redemption, justification, sanctification, and glorification. In the transition from election to calling, we also move from the covenant of redemption to the covenant of grace. Absolute and unconditional in its basis, the new covenant nevertheless promised the restoration of genuine obedience. On the basis of a forgiveness to which we have contributed nothing but sin and resistance, we are given a new heart that begins already to yield its "amen" both to God's promise and command in Christ.

It is one thing to say that the covenant of redemption, as an eternal and intra-trinitarian pact, is an exclusively divine oath, and quite another thing to say that the covenant of grace is unconditional as well. After all, are there not conditions held out for salvation, such as repentance and faith? In fact, is not the final glorification of God's elect in some sense conditioned on their perseverance in repentance and faith?

---

72. Louis Berkhof, *Systematic Theology*, new ed. (Grand Rapids: Eerdmans, 1996), 452.
73. Ibid., 450–51.
74. Ibid., 451–52.

Herman Bavinck summarizes a common distinction in Reformed systems between the unconditional and absolute character of the covenant of grace in its *essence* and its conditions in its *administration*:

> When in Genesis 15:8f. God makes a covenant with Abraham, it is not really a compact but a pledge. God gives his promise; he obligates himself to ful- fill it and passes between the pieces of the sacrificial animal. . . . This uni- lateral character had to come out with ever-increasing clarity in the course of history. True, the covenant of God imposed obligations also on those with whom it was made—obligations, not as conditions for entering into the covenant (for the covenant was made and based only on God's compassion), but as the way the people who had by grace been incorporated into the covenant henceforth had to conduct themselves.[75]

"In distinction from and contrast to the covenant of works, God therefore estab- lished another, a better, covenant, not a legalistic but an evangelical covenant."[76] Since the covenant in its essence is made with Christ and not with us, it is, as to its basis or essence, unconditional.

> In the covenant of grace, that is, in the gospel, which is the proclamation of the covenant of grace, there are actually no demands and no conditions. For God supplies what he demands. Christ has accomplished everything, and though he did not accomplish rebirth, faith, and repentance in our place, he did acquire them for us, and the Holy Spirit therefore applies them. Still, in its administration by Christ, the covenant of grace does assume this demanding, conditional form.[77]

Unlike the covenant of creation/works, the covenant of grace is unilateral in its basis. "But it is destined to become bilateral, to be consciously and voluntarily accepted and kept by humans in the power of God."[78] Just as God imposed oblig- ations on Abraham as consequences rather than conditions of the covenant, so new-covenant believers are merely recipients of the blessings that nevertheless engender for the first time a genuine longing for covenantal loyalty on our part.

In all of this we must remember that the cross, law and gospel, the flesh and the Spirit are not abstract categories, but are covenantally and eschatologically con- ditioned. The obsolescence of the age governed by the nexus of law, flesh, sin, and death, as it gives way to the reign of grace, the Spirit, righteousness, and life, is a redemptive-historical and not simply an existential fact. "Law," for example, func- tions differently in different covenants, as we have already seen. The law can con- demn us or simply guide us, depending on whether it is operating as the condition for life or as the rule of life. Beyond this covenantal conditioning, there is the fact that commands—although in many cases the same in content—are issued this

75. Bavinck, *Reformed Dogmatics,* 3:203–4.
76. Ibid., 225.
77. Ibid., 230.
78. Ibid.

side of the resurrection and Pentecost. Although the covenant of grace is woven throughout both testaments, its realities are more fully realized in this era.

Paradoxically, it is the announcement that because the blessings of the covenant come to us as a result of Christ's personal obedience rather than our own, and by virtue of the fact that the Spirit who unilaterally bestows new life has now been liberally poured out, that a return of grateful obedience on our part is even possible. Grace inevitably engenders a return of thankful obedience, so that the covenant is always entirely gracious in its basis. Even when responsibilities are laid upon the covenant partner, they are never the conditions for inheriting life but the characteristics of the life that they have inherited from the Father, in the Son, by the Spirit's effective operation. Only by refusing to embrace these blessings as one's own inheritance can a visible member of the covenant be estranged from the reality of participation in the covenant of grace: "For if we have died with him, we will live with him. If we endure, we will also reign with him. If we deny him, he will also deny us. If we are faithless, he remains faithful—for he cannot deny himself" (2 Tim. 2:11–13).

To be autonomous is really to be imprisoned "in Adam," but to be "in Christ" is to "be free indeed" (John 8:36). This side of the fall, bondage to the law and bondage to sin amount to the same thing. "Apart from the law sin lies dead. . . . For sin, seizing an opportunity in the commandment, deceived me and through it killed me. . . . Did what is good, then, bring death to me? By no means! It was sin, working death in me through what is good, in order that sin might be shown to be sin, and through the commandment might become sinful beyond measure" (Rom. 7:8, 11, 13). "Under the law" and therefore "under sin," the self is, as Augustine observed, curved in on itself. Whether by seeking to justify our morality or immorality, we are evading the judgment that would force us to look outside of ourselves for security. By itself, "law" merely deepens incurvation, guilt, death, and a troubled conscience, which provoke us to self-deception and conceit, alternating between self-righteousness and self-condemnation, and leading to the "fruit of the flesh" in interpersonal relationships that Paul lists in Galatians 5. The Spirit-grace-promise-gospel-faith matrix introduces us to a new Word (gospel) and with it a new world (the new creation).

It is precisely this contrast that, according to the Reformed theologians, energizes so much of Pauline theology especially. In Galatians 2:19–20 there is a close connection between being dead to the law, alive to God, and so identified with Christ that the identity of the self that lives by faith is defined by Christ's circumcision-death and resurrection. Similarly in Romans, Paul meets the objection to forensic justification as offering no ethics by appealing to our union with Christ (Rom. 6).

The theme of participation is therefore given a strikingly Trinitarian and christocentric expression in covenant theology. Grounded in God's eternal purposes, this identity "in Christ" becomes realized in both the history of redemption broadly (*historia salutis*) and in the individual incorporation of believers through mystical union (*ordo salutis*). Union with Christ does not displace justification; on the contrary, it emphasizes that everything that God gives to believers—not only justification but also sanctification and glorification subsist properly "in him," not "in us." The gains of being in Christ are so great that even Paul's suffering is not, properly speaking, his own—in which he might either glory or because of which he might despair, but is a matter of suffering *with Christ*. There is no ostensibly autonomous Paul any longer, not because he has lost his selfhood in contemplative ascent, or has had his finite ego absorbed into an infinite Ego, or surrendered it to ecclesial identity, or attained mastery over his "lower" appetites. These would simply be different (Greek) ways of pursuing the goal by works.

Rather, law-logic itself has been part of the problem. Due to sin, the law as a covenant of life simply makes one more deeply egocentric. In Paul's understanding "boasting" in one's own righteousness, far from unseating the reign of sinful autonomy, is the throne from which the autonomous self spreads its dominion. However, when its real intentions and demands are announced, the law begins to break up this autonomy at its heart by exposing our delusions of grandeur and stability, allowing the gospel to do its work of taking us entirely outside of ourselves and locating our existence in Christ alone. In this sense the law in its wrath even serves as a merciful accomplice to the gospel:

> For through the law I died to the law, so that I might live to God. I have been crucified with Christ; and it is no longer I who live, but it is Christ who lives in me. And the life I now live in the flesh I live by faith in the Son of God, who loved me and gave himself for me. I do not nullify the grace of God; for if justification comes through the law, then Christ died for nothing. (Gal. 2:19–21)

"For to me, living is Christ and dying is gain" (Phil. 1:21). With the same notion of participation he can comfort the struggling saints: "For he has graciously granted you the privilege not only of believing in Christ, but of suffering for him as well" (v. 29).

Not even our suffering is allowed to be simply "our own," but is something that we share with Christ. Calvin offers the following litany of implications of this union:

> We see that our whole salvation and all its parts are comprehended in Christ. We should therefore take care not to derive the least portion of it anywhere else. If we seek salvation, we are taught by the very name of Jesus that it is "of him." If we seek any other gifts of the Spirit, they will be found in his anointing. If we seek strength, it lies in his dominion; if purity, in his conception; if gentleness, it appears in his birth. For by his birth he was made like us in all respects that he might learn to feel our pain. If we seek redemption, it lies in his passion; if acquittal, in his condemnation; if remission of the curse, in his cross; if satisfaction, in his sacrifice; if purification, in his blood; if reconciliation, in his descent into hell; if mortification of the flesh, in his tomb; if newness of life, in his resurrection; . . . if inheritance of the heavenly kingdom, in his entrance into heaven; if protection, if security, if abundant supply of all blessings, in his kingdom; if untroubled expectation

of judgment, in the power given him to judge. In short, since rich store of every kind of good abounds in him, let us drink our fill from this fountain, and from no other.[79]

Christ, therefore, is the new creation. To be in Christ is to be exiled from this age and to be relocated in the age to come.

Wedged by the Spirit between Pentecost and Parousia, pilgrims are no longer what they were or where they were, but they have not yet arrived at the place that is being prepared for them and for which they are themselves being prepared. From this summary, we can see that the *unio mysticus* theme has a prominent place in Reformed (covenant) theology. However, does it have the conceptual resources to generate its own ontology? In the next chapter my goal is to develop some suggestions, from the preceding account of union with Christ, for a covenantal ontology, in conversation with alternative proposals, and then to return to the other gifts of union with Christ.

79. Calvin, *Institutes* 2.16.19.

Chapter Eight

Neoplatonic Participation (*Metathexis*)

"Overcoming Estrangement"

Charged by its forensic core, union with Christ encompasses not only justification, but also the organic, transformative, and moral aspects as well. In fact, it is possible to say that covenant theology *is* a theology of participation (*koinōnia*). But what *kind* of participation? Mystical union and participation have been put forward as an alternative to forensic justification by proponents of the New Perspective on Paul (NPP). In addition, Radical Orthodoxy (RO), Robert Jenson, and the New Finnish interpretation of Luther represent broader theological challenges by advocating a certain version of participation (*metathexis*) as a central dogma. Interacting with these perspectives, this chapter will flesh out the claim that a forensic-covenantal ontology can yield a more satisfying scheme of participation.

CONTRASTING ONTOLOGIES OF PARTICIPATION

Launching my previous volume in this series (*Lord and Servant*) by building on Paul Tillich's typology of *overcoming estrangement* versus *meeting a stranger*, I argued that covenant theology exhibits strong preferences for the latter type.[1] Implicit in a covenantal account of anything is the presupposition that otherness is not something to be overcome, but to be accepted and welcomed. At the same time, otherness is no more a univocal concept than being: God is not an Other alongside others, but, to draw upon an overused and overinterpreted Pauline citation from a pagan poet, "In him we live and move and have our own being" (Acts 17:28). Nevertheless, the Lord of the covenant is always represented in this unfolding drama as holy in an absolute and utterly distinct sense that can only be applied analogically to creatures—the other side of Paul's speech that is less often cited.

However, sin—the condition and specific acts of covenant-breaking—introduces an otherness that is founded not in creational integrity, but in *ethical enmity*, a crisis of interpersonal communion. Since the fault is first of all juridical (covenant-breaking), the restoration begins with the forensic word and work of the Trinity, on the basis of which the ontological effects of the curse are finally overcome, and the consummation (beyond the possibility of sin and death) is assured. The *covenant*, not a general metaphysical scheme, specifies what kind of alienation and reconciliation are in view.

Consequently, the *reconciliation* that covenant theology has in mind when it reads the Scriptures is not a mediation of such binaries as finite/infinite, visible/invisible, corporeal/spiritual, sensible/intelligible, and so forth, but the divine act of bringing about a *koinōnia* with enemies—even while they are still in an active state of hostility toward God—in a peace treaty out of which is forged a new kingdom. Apart from sin, ontological distance required divine condescension by way of the covenant of creation, but now God has condescended still further, mediating ethical distance in a covenant of grace. The person in whom he meets us is simultaneously the Covenant Lord (Yahweh) and the covenant servant (the last Adam): everything in this relationship between God and human beings is mediated in Christ by the Spirit.

By contrast, the paradigm of "overcoming estrangement" does not prepare us to meet a stranger who may or may not be a friend, but tends to assimilate the foreign experience. To borrow additionally from Avery Dulles's helpful typology in *Models of Revelation*, this ontological approach promises a "new awareness" in salvation as in revelation.[2] According to this pattern, emphasis falls not on the surprising arrival of good news (a genuine *novum* in history), but on remembering what we have always known and repeating what has always been true (*mimēsis*). Salvation is assimilated basically to epistemology and ethics—realization and empowerment—with a corollary suspicion of the notion of divine rescue and intervention as a violent intrusion upon autonomy. Tillich keenly recognized that these two types of philosophy of religion do not simply color var-

---

1. Michael Horton, *Lord and Servant: A Covenant Christology* (Louisville, KY: Westminster John Knox, 2005), chap. 1.
2. Avery Dulles, S.J., *Models of Revelation* (Maryknoll, NY: Orbis Books, 1992), 28, 99–113.

ious doctrines but also provide substantially different paradigms for every theological locus. To put it simply, the one paradigm promises enlightenment and an elevation of nature beyond itself; the other promises a rescue *extra nos* and a liberation of nature from its bondage to sin and death.

To be sure, such typologies run the risk of oversimplification. Undaunted, I suggest that the view that Tillich identifies as the "ontological way" (overcoming estrangement), which seems to dominate much of contemporary theology, has frequently yielded a worldview with implications across the entire system of Christian theology. Of course, like all typologies, Tillich's suggests *tendencies* rather than stated goals or positions, and I intend my own sweeping generalization to be taken in the same manner.

Although such contrasting ontologies will be detected especially in my interaction with RO and the New Finnish school (below), George Hunsinger nicely contrasts Hans Urs von Balthasar's and Karl Rahner's theologies in similar terms, focusing especially on the person and work of Christ. Rahner's soteriology and therefore his Christology are oriented toward "reempowerment" more than redemption, which is consistent, I suggest, with a view of revelation as "new awareness" within the paradigm of overcoming estrangement. Hunsinger describes Rahner's transcendental outlook in similar terms:

> Because our plight is one of *estrangement* from God more nearly than of enmity and condemnation, the solution is more nearly one of our being reunited with God *through an inner experience* of spiritual re-empowerment. The cross of Christ is significant, not because of vicarious expiatory suffering, but because it shows that Jesus fully took part in the *brokenness* of the human condition without forsaking his spiritual union with God. We are saved *not* so much by something fundamentally unique and *unrepeatable* that took place apart from us on our behalf as by a certain communion with Christ which allows *some measure* of his perfected spirituality and destiny to be *repeated or re-enacted* in our lives. We are saved by the effect *in us* for which the work apart from us functions as little more than the precondition for its possibility. (emphasis original)

For this one does not require a "high Christology."[3]

In a manner similar to John Milbank, as we will see, the bogeyman for Rahner is "extrinsicism" or "forencism," notes Hunsinger:

> Rahner's rejection of all high views of Christ's work under the label of "the satisfaction theory" or of "extrinsicism" and so on would seem to land him squarely in the middle [Christology] camp, as would also many of his corresponding affirmations. . . . For the very essence of middle soteriology is the idea of salvation by spiritual *repetition*.[4]

---

3. George Hunsinger, *Disruptive Grace: Studies in the Theology of Karl Barth* (Grand Rapids: Eerdmans, 2000), 264–65.
4. Ibid., 265.

Yet the view that Rahner rejects as extrinsicism does not deny participation:

> The real question is how these factors [intrinsic and extrinsic] are related, and how they are defined in the first place. *Koinōnia* with Christ for the middle conception [of Rahner] is essentially our participation in and appropriation of Christ's "spirituality," no matter whether it is called his God-consciousness, or the kingdom of God, or the new being, or authentic being-towards-death, or experiential religion, or the hermeneutical privilege of the poor, or woman-spirit rising, or the rejection of violence, or the original blessing, or perhaps simply faith, or even faith formed by love. The list goes on and on, but the structure is always the same. What took place *extra nos* is no more than the condition for the possibility of what takes place *in nobis*. The *decisive locus of salvation* is not fixed in what took place in the cross of Christ there and then, but in what takes place in us or among us here and now. Salvation essentially encounters us as a *possibility* that is not actual for us *until* it is somehow actualized in our spiritual and social existence, and the process of actualization proceeds by degrees. Though primarily a divine gift, salvation is always *also* a human task.[5]

In fact, Hunsinger observes, this "is really the question around which the entire Reformation pivoted. . . . In sum, in a high soteriology it is not Christ who points us to spirituality but spirituality that points us to Christ, who as God with us is the *exclusively unique* object of our worship and our faith."[6]

I will engage directly with RO and the New Finnish or Helsinki school as representing the "overcoming estrangement" version of participation, and then offer my own proposal. In brief, that proposal will suggest that only a covenantal ontology with God's judicial word at the headwaters of the new creation can encompass the forensic and transformative, personal and cosmic, historical and eschatological fullness of redemption.

RADICAL ORTHODOXY

Introducing their program, John Milbank, Catherine Pickstock, and Graham Ward explain, "The central theological framework of radical orthodoxy is 'participation' as developed by Plato and reworked by Christianity, because any alternative configuration perforce reserves a territory independent of God."[7] Radical Orthodoxy is convinced that the univocity of being—that is, the view that "existence" means the same thing for God and for creatures—drains the world of transcendence. From Scotus and his nominalist successors to Kant, all the way to Derrida and Deleuze, the notion of an autonomous space of "being" alongside God quite naturally led to atheism, as the *nihil* of nihilism expanded. Hence, RO wants

5. Ibid., 266.
6. Ibid., 267.
7. John Milbank, Catherine Pickstock, and Graham Ward, eds., *Radical Orthodoxy: A New Theology* (New York and London: Routledge, 1999), 3, in the introduction.

to recover "an intrinsic link between sign and thing signified," recognizing that created corporeality is "suspended" in uncreated incorporeality, thus demonstrating
that in order for something to be, it must exceed itself.[8] Due to the denial of an
essential participation of signs in the signified, all that is left is a radical voluntarism
in which reality becomes a mere construction of a despotic and arbitrary will.

The tradition that RO seeks to renew is Christian Neoplatonism—specifically,
the theurgic Neoplatonism of Proclus and Iamblichus rather than the philosophy of Plotinus himself. The key term in this lexicon is *metathexis*, an ontological participation of the natural in the supernatural. The visible, material, and
mutable creation is not only dependent on God's Word (the Son) and power (the
Spirit), but also exists only to the extent that it participates in invisible, immate-
rial, and immutable being. While Plato anticipated a Christian *metathexis*,
according to Milbank, "for him there remains a chaotic material residue that does
not participate," while for Plotinus there can only be a fall *away from* being (since
there can be no participation in the One). There remains a "tension between the
pure source and the imperfect copying of that source which generates the next
lower level, and this tends to a dialectical dissolution of participation." In theurgic Neoplatonism, however, *metathexis* involves "a kind of kenotic descent of the
divine powers into the cosmos."[9] It was this heritage that one finds appropriated,
for example, by Aquinas, for whom everything in creation "is already as itself
more than itself, and this more is in some sense a portion of divinity. (Everything
is therefore 'engraced.')"[10] In sharp contrast, modern philosophy (with its sources
in late medieval nominalism) snaps the analogical cord of this participatory
ontology with its doctrine of the univocity of being. The space occupied by
autonomous human being and thought is given the name "pure nature."[11]

The RO Analysis of Covenant Theology

Owing to the appearance of published essays in conversation with the Reformed
tradition, Milbank was able to state for himself what he regards as the principal
differences.[12] Milbank surmises that RO may be "the first ecumenical theology
in modern times."[13] Just as Judaism, Christianity, and Islam find remarkable convergence in their early medieval Neoplatonic versions, Milbank locates a similar

---

8. Ibid., 4–5.
9. John Milbank, *Being Reconciled: Ontology and Pardon* (London and New York: Routledge,
2003), 114–15; cf. John Milbank, "Can a Gift Be Given? Prolegomena to a Future Trinitarian Metaphysics," *Modern Theology* 2, no. 1 (January 1995): 119–61; John Milbank and Catherine Pickstock,
Truth in Aquinas (London: Routledge, 2001), esp. chap. 2, and for a more extensive survey of the RO
project, see Milbank, Pickstock, and Ward, *Radical Orthodoxy*.
10. Milbank, *Being Reconciled*, 115.
11. Ibid., 114.
12. John Milbank, "Alternative Protestantism," in *Radical Orthodoxy and the Reformed Tradition:
Creation, Covenant, and Participation*, ed. James K. A. Smith (Grand Rapids: Baker Academic, 2005),
25–42. I also interact with RO at greater length in an essay in the same volume, 107–34, "Participation and Covenant."
13. Milbank, "Alternative Protestantism," 25.

stream in Calvinism (Ames to Edwards) that he finds more congenial to this ecumenical project.[14] Yet whatever Milbank thinks is inimical to this Platonic legacy
he attributes to Scotism, as, for example, the Reformed attachment to the doctrine of concursus (despite its clear articulation in Thomas and prenominalist
scholasticism generally).[15] I will restrict my analysis of Milbank's proposal to the
relationship between justification and union with Christ.

With respect to justification, Milbank allows that the Reformers got off on
the right foot, by reverting "to a patristic concern with participation in Christ,"
against the flow of late medieval (nominalist) theology. However, in general
Calvin was fairly naive philosophically, while Luther's more explicit and thorough
metaphysics was, at the end of the day, "univocalist-nominalist," "more or less
monophysite," which leads also to a near fusion of Christ and the believer rather
than a participation that is somewhere between identity and difference.[16] Furthermore, the Reformers' earlier emphasis on union was eventually displaced in
their thinking by "imputationism" and "extrinsicism."[17]

"Participation is present, therefore, in Calvin's thought, but primarily in a
christological context," which Milbank thinks may nevertheless be extended "to
a more general metaphysical theory of participation that expounds the doctrine
of creation." "A parallel extrapolation could be made from Calvin's eucharistic
theology: if God is not in the elements by local spatial presence, as in Luther's
doctrine of consubstantiation, but nonetheless the Eucharist conveys a spiritual
sharing in Christ's body in heaven, then is not this also a kind of participation of
the finite in the infinite?"[18] The suggestion seems to be that our eucharistic participation in Christ serves as an instance of a more general metaphysical truth—
namely, the ontological participation of being in God, rather than as an event

14. Ibid., 9, 26. There is no basis for regarding Ames as a Platonist. In fact, he was a Ramist. The
Cambridge Platonists sharply rejected Reformed orthodoxy, and although Edwards represents the
closest thing to a synthesis of Platonism/idealism and Reformed theology, it has been subjected to
criticism within the tradition at those very points. The Protestant scholastics displayed various influences: Aristotelian-Thomist, Platonist, Ramist, and a few Scotists. However, these influences do not
seem to have played any significant role in their systems and certainly failed to provoke any serious
debates. In any case the proscription of any magisterial role given to philosophy (adopted by all of
these theologians) cautioned against anything more than an ad hoc appropriation of such terminology. Edwards, however, does seem to be an exception, giving more space to philosophical speculation
in theology—and with conclusions that are more explicitly Platonic than the tradition would affirm.
For example, he writes, "Matter . . . is truly nothing at all, strictly and in itself considered. The nearer
in nature beings are to God, so much the more properly are they beings, and more substantial; and
that spirits are as much more properly beings, and more substantial than bodies" (*The Mind*, in *The
Works of Jonathan Edwards*, vol. 6, *Scientific and Philosophical Writings*, ed. Wallace E. Anderson [New
Haven: Yale University Press, 1980], 338).
15. Milbank, "Alternative Protestantism," 27.
16. Ibid., 28: "This is because the univocalist-nominalist metaphysic will not allow for a sharing
that falls between identity and difference and only imitates by sharing (since it imitates being as such),
but equally only shares by imitating (since we cannot really be a part of being as such, which is God,
who is utterly simple)."
17. Ibid., 27–28.
18. Ibid., 29.

determined by its covenantal context and specific to the covenantal actions of proclaiming and sealing the gospel.

Covenant and participation are not antithetical concepts, Milbank allows, but only after he has redefined the former in a manner that assimilates it to his account of the latter. "There is, in consequence," says Milbank, "no mileage whatsoever in pitting covenant against participation; this is simply a conceptual error, unless one has a faulty concursive notion of covenant, which thinks of divine and finite causes as contributing half-shares to an outcome, as if they lay on the same ontic plane (the two horses pulling the one barge)."[19] In fact, only by integrating covenant within Platonic participation does one avoid "a creeping Pelagianism," he says, despite the fact that the covenant theology that emerged from the Reformation, quite apart from Platonism, directly challenged the concursive notion of covenant to which Milbank refers.[20] At the hands of Ockham, Biel, and Holcot, nominalism certainly did represent what Milbank accurately describes as "a creeping Pelagianism," with its *facientibus quod in se est deus non denigat gratiam* (God will not deny his grace to those who do what lies in them). As I will argue, however, in this respect Milbank is much closer than is Reformation theology to the covenantal nomism of late medieval thought.

From Milbank's perspective, however, it is the Reformation and the covenant theology arising from the Reformed tradition that belongs to the nominalist heritage. First, Calvin's thought (and Reformed theology generally) is too wedded to Hebraic ways of thinking. Along with an inflexible genealogy of Western decadence, consigning Reformation theology to a malignant Scotism, Milbank attributes the "extrinsicism" of Protestant covenant theology to the "oriental despotism" of ancient Near Eastern treaties, which the Hebrew Bible carried over, evidently as a precursor to late medieval nominalism.[21] At the end of the day, Milbank asserts, Calvin sees too much continuity between old and new covenants, leading him to believe that Jews participated in Christ and his covenant as truly as Christians, which leads to "a certain kind of Philo-Semitism."[22]

Second, Calvin advocates an extrinsic justification that is impossible, in Milbank's view, since reality is already participating in being. Calvin's doctrine of justification "is still not acceptable. It paradoxically offends the idea of the divine glory." After all, "if the creation is not univocally 'alongside' God, as if God and creation were both individual entities, then there is no ontological limbo in which the divine decree of justification can hover. . . . We must indeed receive, as Aquinas taught, an infused *habitus* of *justitia*."[23]

---

19. Ibid., 30. This is a salutary point, and Reformed theology indeed clears this hurdle precisely by strongly affirming analogy rather than univocity. I will suggest ways in which this important point can be more clearly expressed in relation to divine and human agency in chap. 10.

20. Ibid.

21. Milbank, *Being Reconciled*, 48–49.

22. Milbank, "Alternative Protestantism," 32.

23. Ibid., 32–33.

Rejecting the Thomistic concept of justification as an infused habit, Calvin failed to realize that faith is actually love, Milbank judges:

> If I had any indictment to make of the magisterial Reformation, it would be that it qualifies the one most crucial thing about Christianity, namely, that it is the religion of love. It tends to displace the centrality of love in favor of themes of trust and hope, even if Luther is far more guilty in this regard than Calvin. And in many ways, this is the *gravest imaginable heresy*. (emphasis original)[24]

Yet once again, this criticism measures the gulf between a Platonic account of participation and a covenantal one. It also faces us again with another false choice between faith and love, since Calvin (like Luther) did not downplay the importance of the latter, but insisted that faith alone can engender love.[25] "How shall the mind rise up to taste the divine goodness," asks Calvin, "and not at once be wholly set on fire with answering love for God?"[26]

General Analysis and Critique of Milbank's Proposal

Once more, I am convinced that the greatest divide between RO and the traditions of the magisterial Reformation, as Milbank and his colleagues suggest, is a substantially different metaphysical-ontological paradigm.

The Genealogy of Nihilism

Although space does not allow an adequate treatment here, it is perhaps worth pointing out that neither Calvin nor the Reformed tradition can be explained away as easily as Ward and Milbank assume in their sweeping genealogy of nihilism from Scotus to Deleuze. The covenant theology espoused by Reformed thinkers is antithetical to the contractual thinking of nominalism—which is the target of Luther's critique in the Heidelberg Disputation. If the Lubacian/RO reading of Scotus is contested by specialists,[27] then the attempt to sweep Calvin into the Scotist/nominalist stream is even more dubious.[28]

---

24. Ibid., 33.
25. Calvin, *Institutes* 3.2.41.
26. Ibid.
27. See, among others, the illuminating essay by Richard Cross, "'Where Angels Fear to Tread': Duns Scotus and Radical Orthodoxy," *Antonianum* 76, no. 1 (2001): 7–42.
28. In relation to Calvin especially, the historical link to nominalism has been decisively refuted by Catholic historian Alexandre Ganoczy, in his *The Young Calvin*, trans. David Foxgrover and Wade Provo (Philadelphia: Westminster, 1987), 173–78. See also David Steinmetz, "Calvin and the Absolute Power of God," *Journal of Medieval and Renaissance Studies* 18, no. 1 (Spring 1988): 65–79; Susan Schreiner, *Where Shall Wisdom Be Found? Calvin's Exegesis of Job from Medieval and Modern Perspectives* (Chicago: University of Chicago Press, 1994); Jelle Faber, "Nominalisme in Calvijns preken over Job," in *Een sprekend begin*, ed. R. ter Beek et al. (Kampen: Uitgeverij Van den Berg, 1993), 68–85. See also several summaries of the primary and secondary literature in Richard Muller, *The Unaccomodated Calvin: Studies in the Foundation of a Theological Tradition* (New York and Oxford: Oxford University Press, 2000), 40–41, 48, 52–53; cf. Heiko Oberman, *The Harvest of Medieval Theology* (Durham, NC: Labyrinth, 1985), 30–57; idem, "Some Notes on the Theology of Nominalism," *Harvard Theological Review* 53 (1960): 47–76.

Nominalism's radically voluntaristic concept of God's "absolute power" Calvin called "a diabolical blasphemy" that could only render us balls that God juggles in the air.[29] As B. B. Warfield, Émile Doumerge, and B. A. Gerrish have demonstrated, God's "fatherly beneficence and liberality," even more than his sovereignty, dominate Calvin's horizon.[30] Gerrish notes, "To claim that the notion of arbitrary, despotic will is the key to [Calvin's] doctrine of God does scant justice either to Calvin's own explicit statements about where the primacy lies or to the implications of his careful systematic order."[31]

With respect to the "proper seat of faith," Calvin shows no evidence of being a voluntarist, much less a radical one.[32] He argues for a more holistic approach than the Thomist-Scotist debate allows, faulting both sides for failing to recognize that faith is not merely assent but also "confidence and assurance of heart." [33] Nevertheless, if forced to choose, he prefers the Thomist approach.[34] On all the relevant points that might mark Calvin as a nominalist, he is seen to adopt rather traditional prenominalist assumptions. Irenaeus, the Cappadocians, Augustine, Anselm, Hilary, and Bernard exercised a greater influence on Calvin than either Thomas or Scotus, although the former has a clear edge in his thinking.[35]

Projecting nominalism (anachronistically) back into the ancient Near Eastern context, Milbank also assumes the same conflation of Abrahamic and Sinaitic covenants that we have seen with respect to the NPP. If my argument in part 1 is accurate, then the suzerainty treaty-type (Sinaitic) was a kind of corporate covenantal nomism, yet distinct from the royal grant that in both form and content matches the covenant of grace.

As I have already indicated, there are similarities between the covenantal nomism described by Sanders and the covenant theology of medieval nominalists (Ockham, Biel, Holcot). Both collapse the two covenants into a single covenant of law that is nevertheless somewhat "relaxed" by gracious elements: "Do what you can," as opposed to the Sinaitic "Do this and you shall live." Milbank does not

29. Calvin, *Institutes* 1.17.2. Cf. the editor's note on the same page (n. 7), referring to Calvin's extended criticism of this nominalist position in *De aeterna Dei praedestinatione* (in *CO* 8 [CR 36]: 361), as well as his *Sermons on Job* lxxxviii, in *CO* 34 (CR 62): 339ff. on Job 23:1–7.

30. B. B. Warfield, "Calvin's Doctrine of God," in the *Princeton Theological Review* 7 (1909): 381–436; reprinted in idem, *Calvin and Calvinism* (New York: Oxford University Press, 1931); Émile Doumergue, *Jean Calvin: Les homes et les choses de son temps*, vol. 4 of *La pensée religieuse de Calvin* (Lausanne: Georges Bridel, 1910); B. A. Gerrish, *Grace and Gratitude: The Eucharistic Theology of John Calvin* (Minneapolis: Augsburg Fortress, 1993), 23–24.

31. Gerrish, *Grace and Gratitude*, 24.

32. Calvin, *Institutes* 3.2.1; 3.2.7. Calvin was simply not all that interested in such debates, except to the extent that they promoted or undermined an evangelical understanding of faith as assured confidence of God's goodwill toward us in Christ. One could chalk this up to naïveté or to a propensity to determine the relevance of philosophical questions in theology by their relevance to the gospel.

33. Richard Muller, *The Unaccomodated Calvin: Studies in the Foundation of a Theological Tradition* (New York and Oxford: Oxford University Press, 2000), 49.

34. Ibid., 165, citing Calvin's 1539 *Institutio* (1.15.7), roughly identical in the 1559 edition (1.15.8). See Muller's discussion on pages 162–73.

35. See A. N. S. Lane, *John Calvin: Student of the Church Fathers* (Edinburgh: T&T Clark, 1999); Johannes Van Oort, "John Calvin and the Church Fathers," in *The Reception of the Church Fathers in the West: From the Carolingians to the Maurists*, ed. Irena Backus (Leiden: E. J. Brill, 1997), 685–86.

seem to recognize any such distinction in covenant types, and therefore he tends to lump all covenant theologies with the suzerainty type, which he designates as "oriental despotism." It is easy to gain the impression from Milbank's work that anything valuable in the Old Testament must be salvaged from its Hebraic soil and be transplanted in Hellenic thought (usually, by way of allegorization).

Ontology: Nature and Grace

The RO paradigm of participation remains committed to ontological dualism in the creaturely realm. Neoplatonic *metathexis* and covenantal *koinōnia* seem to me to represent different worldviews, and "covenant" can be assimilated within the former paradigm only at the price of losing both its definition and its hermeneutical significance for Christian faith and practice.

Although Milbank repeats a common Roman Catholic criticism that Reformed theology sets nature and grace in antithesis, Reformed theology has typically held Rome in suspicion on just this account. According to Reformation theology, there is no need to suspend the material in the spiritual or the visible in the intelligible, because there is no such binary in the Scriptures. In both its visible and invisible variety, the whole creation is equally distinct from God, equally valued, equally fallen, and equally redeemed. The only qualitative divides are those between God and creation (on the ontological register) and sin and grace (on the ethical-covenantal register). Sin, evil, "the flesh," are located across the entire ontic field: the mind as well as the body, thought as well as passions, spirit as well as matter. Matter does not need to be saved (or suspended) by spirit; rather, the entire creaturely realm requires salvation from sin and death: the curse for the broken covenant.

Reflecting the characteristically Reformed suspicion of dualistic ontologies, Adrienne Dengerink Chaplin points out that RO still works within the scheme of "visibility versus invisibility, corporeality versus incorporeality, sensibility versus intelligibility, body versus soul."[36] She adds:

> I will suggest that the biblical notions of reconciliation and transformation can instead serve this project more fruitfully. Reconciliation does not imply a mediation between two different creational realms or spheres (e.g., between the physical and the nonphysical), but rather a restoration of a broken relationship or covenant between God and his people. Transformation likewise points to a changed creation without having to abandon its finite, physical character. On such an understanding, the finite, visible, physical world is not a world of nihilism, a worthless void, but rather a deeply broken and wounded world that is in need of redemption, in need of a savior. Though finite, creation is not incomplete. It is without original lack or need. It is already blessed. Hence, it is not because of its finitude or physicality that the world is in need of redemption or mediation—it is because of its fall into sin.[37]

36. Adrienne Dengerink Chaplin, "The Invisible and the Sublime: From Participation to Reconciliation," in Smith, *Radical Orthodoxy and the Reformed Tradition*, 90.
37. Ibid., 91.

Here Buber's contrast between religions of epiphany and religions of proclamation (or Ricoeur's between manifestation and proclamation) complement the contrast between "overcoming estrangement" and "meeting a stranger."[38] There is symbolism, allegory, new awareness, sacralization of being, manifestation, full presence, and glory on one side. On the other side, there is history, dramatic narrative, new events, a covenantal designation of "sacred" (not in relation to its place in the scale of being but in relation to the use that God makes of creaturely reality in revelation and redemption), proclamation, eschatological tension, and the way of the cross.

The difference can be seen, for example, in the running debate between Hans Urs von Balthasar and Karl Rahner, as we have seen above. "My main argument," says Balthasar, "—not only against Rahner but [also] against the entire transcendental school which already existed before him and spread alongside him—is this: It might be true that from the very beginning man was created to be disposed toward God's revelation, so that with God's grace even the sinner can accept all revelation. *Gratia supponit naturam.*"

> But when God sends his own living Word to his creatures, he does so, not to instruct them about the mysteries of the world, not primarily to fulfill their deepest needs and yearnings. Rather he communicates and actively demonstrates such unheard-of things that man feels not satisfied but awestruck by a love which he never could have hoped to experience. For who would have dared describe God as love, without having first received the revelation of the Trinity in the acceptance of the cross by the Son?[39]

It is one thing to say that God condescends to establish a relationship with creatures—even with those who have turned their backs on him—and quite another to say that creation involves a divine *kenōsis*, a self-emptying that makes room as it were in God. Of the various versions of panentheism revived in our day, Moltmann's is perhaps the most explicit in drawing upon the kabbalistic idea of *zimzum*.[40] Yet the metaphysical assumption in most theories of *kenōsis* (even after all of the disclaimers) seems to be emanation, which in either Plotinian or Proclean versions of Neoplatonism stands in sharp contrast to creation ex nihilo.

To be sure, at least in RO's version of Christian Platonism, everything that exists has real value all the way down the scale precisely because it participates in being, especially in the Dionysian image of higher modes of being descending to pull the lesser modes up into a never-ending exchange of plenitude. Nevertheless,

38. Michael Horton, *Covenant and Eschatology* (Louisville, KY: Westminster John Knox, 2002), 143–44.

39. Hans Urs von Balthasar, "Current Trends in Catholic Theology," *Communio* 5, no. 1 (1978): 79.

40. The major figure here is Isaak Luria. See Jürgen Moltmann, *The Trinity and the Kingdom: The Doctrine of God*, trans. Margaret Kohl (San Francisco: Harper, 1991), 109–11; idem, *God in Creation: A New Theology of Creation and the Spirit of God*, trans. Margaret Khol (Minneapolis: Fortress, 1992), 86–93. Hans Urs von Balthasar also appeals to the *zimzum* notion in *Theo-Drama: Theological Dramatic Theory*, vol. 2, *The Dramatis Personae: Man in God*, trans. Graham Harrison (San Francisco: Ignatius Press, 1990), 260–71.

no matter how benevolent the hierarchy of created being, it remains ontologically reified. In the covenant theology of Scripture, however, there are two distinct kinds of reality: divine and nondivine. This is the only ontological dualism that is finally decisive for Christian theology. However analogically they are related (creation depends at every moment on the God whose attributes it reflects), creation is suspended by the freedom of God's word (energies) not in God's being or essence. It does not exist alongside God, as an independent entity floating in an ontological desert, but it is, as Gunton argues, "outside" of God:

> If the world is truly to be the world, it needs to be "outside" of God, not in such a relationship according to which it is in some way enclosed within God. For this reason, panentheism cannot finally be distinguished from pantheism, because it does not allow the other space to be itself. . . . It tends to generate an idea of creation out of God rather than out of nothing. Similarly, those doctrines which in some way make time eternal, or read our temporality and spatiality up into God's eternity and infinity, confuse the creature with the creator.[41]

Creation can be said to be a divine gift, dependent on the Trinity both in its origin and its existence in every moment, without concluding that this dependence derives from participation in God's being. That, it seems to me, is one of the remarkable consequences of the analogy of being; although Milbank champions this doctrine, I cannot escape the impression that his account of participation is a form of univocity after all, with the Creator-creature difference being quantitative rather than qualitative.

Turning from critique to construction, I should point out that Reformation theology has an ontology of participation for creation as well as redemption. Just as the covenant of creation included every person "in Adam," and the covenant of grace includes all of the elect "in Christ," so also all things hold together (participate) in Christ, yet in different ways. In every act of the Trinity *ad extra*, the Father speaks, the Son mediates that speech, and the Spirit brings about its intended effect within the creaturely realm. Eliding the distinction between the covenants of creation and grace, RO easily risks conflating creation and redemption, election and providence. In this view, the generic "en-gracing" of creation that is synonymous with ontological participation (*metathexis*) differs from salvific reconciliation only in degree. Grace is viewed as a substance rather than as God's favor shown to those who are at fault. However, in our account creation and redemption are alike the result of Trinitarian speech-acts. I agree with Milbank's insistence that covenant and participation are not themselves incommensurable concepts.[42] However, I remain unconvinced that a *covenantal* account of participation can be assimilated into the metaphysics of Platonism/Neoplatonism.

Justin Holcomb also contends that participation and covenant are not antithetical motifs and, although indicating areas where Reformed theology can learn

---

41. Colin Gunton, *The Triune Creator* (Grand Rapids: Eerdmans, 1998), 142.
42. Milbank, "Alternative Protestantism," 25–26.

from RO, Holcomb recognizes that the metaphysics of participation itself needs a more concrete christological focus:

> To avoid endless elasticity, Radical Orthodoxy needs to give a central role to Christ's enduring identity, and this will require filling the conceptual gestures with exegesis and covenant theology. . . . Radical Orthodoxy strongly emphasizes what is universal, general, and speculative at the expense of affirming and defending the particularity of divine redemption in Christ. The scope of participation is wide, but the center is unfocused.[43]

In my view, however, the deeper problem is not that RO is unfocused at its center, but that it simply has another center. As speculative metaphysics (specifically, the theme of ontological participation) swallows the horizon, Christology is swallowed by ecclesiology, and redemptive mediation has to do with overcoming metaphysical binaries (finite/infinite, material/spiritual, visible/invisible, corporeal/incorporeal, temporal/eternal, and so forth) rather than ethical and eschatological ones (sin/grace, death/life, condemnation/justification, estrangement from God/reconciliation and renewal, "this age" and "the age to come").

The proper antithesis is therefore not between participation and covenant, but between different accounts of both. Just as there are different covenants (broadly grouped under the covenants of creation and grace), there are different kinds of participation (God's providential care of creation and God's redemptive acts). Obviously, the concept of covenant is inherently participatory, but covenantal participation (*koinōnia*) is different from *metathexis*. Platonic *metathexis*, with its scale of being, affirms mere appearances (finite, material, visible, temporal) only as they are suspended in the real (infinite, spiritual, invisible, eternal).[44]

Whatever formal Jewish-Christian revisions to Platonism may be endorsed, the *model* itself is emanation rather than creation, which generates univocity after all. However, to say, as the Protestant orthodox did, that God was the *principium essendi* (ground or source of being) was not the same as saying that created reality existed by participating in God. As Dennis Bielfeldt has written in a different connection, "That the created order has its ground outside itself does not entail a 'participation' in that ground."[45] Covenant is not simply a theme that can be assimilated to a preexisting metaphysical map; it *is* the map. What Plato calls *appearances* the church calls *creation*.

Even in RO's attempt to offer a more body-affirming Plato, we eventually encounter the Plato we have known all along and have refused to follow. Milbank

43. Justin Holcomb, "Being Bound to God: Participation and Covenant Revisited," in Smith, *Radical Orthodoxy and the Reformed Tradition*, 250.

44. James K. A. Smith's essay, "Will the Real Plato Please Stand Up?" in Smith, *Radical Orthodoxy and the Reformed Tradition*, offers a very useful summary of the different versions of Plato and Platonism in play with respect to these current debates between RO and the immanentist moves of Nietzsche and his heirs (particularly Deleuze).

45. Dennis Bielfeldt, "Response to Sammeli Juntunen, 'Luther and Metaphysics,'" in *Union with Christ: The New Finnish Interpretation of Luther*, ed. Carl E. Braaten and Robert W. Jenson (Grand Rapids: Eerdmans, 1998), 165.

and Pickstock speak of the beatific vision as the consequence of our having been "freed from our bodily carapace," and at last mediation will no longer be necessary.[46] James K. A. Smith responds, "That, however, does not sound like the new or real Plato they have introduced to us; rather, it sounds like the traditional Plato who has been the object of Reformed critique."[47] In *Truth in Aquinas*, they even seem to follow the traditional Plato in concluding that our existence in the eschaton will transcend embodiment, which would "seem to suggest that embodiment is accidental to human creatures, whereas the Reformed tradition wants to assert the essential—and essentially good—character of embodiment that persists in the eschaton (even if the conditions of materiality are modified)."[48]

Although the RO writers often take Plato through the (quite un-Platonic) hermeneutical turn, emphasizing the linguisticality of being, the principal motive is the *eros* for a depth in being that can only be suspended in what exceeds it rather than a depth that belongs to it essentially by virtue of the fact that it is the product of the Trinity's effective Word.

In the account I am offering, we were created by language, in language, for language, and unto language. As the eternal Word mediates the external works of the Trinity to creation, and this mediation does *not* end in the eschaton, the liturgical consummation is an unending discursive and hermeneutical interplay.[49] Our theology of the Word is not an implication of our ontology, but vice versa. We are "worded" creatures, the result of a Triune speaking. Both our creation and our redemption are speech events, and the particular kind of discourse we are talking about is covenantal all the way down.

The RO circle does claim to begin with concrete Christian praxis: namely, the Eucharist. However, as George Vandervelde reminds us, it is, in Ward's expression, "an *understanding* of the eucharist" (emphasis added)[50]—specifically, "the notion of transmutation."[51]

> It is this understanding that governs all else, including, I contend, Christology. . . . In Ward's system this transmutation consists in some kind of ontic change by which we (and all creation) come to participate analogically in the Godhead. This central understanding of soteriology explains the focus on the few words of institution as key to all else. In Ward's soteriology, the axis of redemption does not turn on alienation-guilty-enmity and reconciliation-forgiveness-friendship. The basic situation that requires

46. Milbank and Pickstock, *Truth in Aquinas*, 28.

47. Smith, "Will the Real Plato Please Stand Up?" 70.

48. Ibid., 72, referring to Milbank and Pickstock, *Truth in Aquinas*, 124 n. 76, 43.

49. The seventeenth-century Reformed theologian Francis Turretin, for one, held that Christ's mediatorial kingdom is eternal, against the Socinians. Our union with Christ will never end: he will always remain the covenant head of his church (Turretin, *Institutes of Elenctic Theology*, ed. J. T. Dennison Jr., trans. G. M. Giger, vol. 2 [Phillipsburg, NJ: P&R Publishing, 1994], 490–99).

50. Graham Ward, *Cities of God* (London: Routledge, 2000), 6.

51. George Vandervelde, "'This Is My Body': The Eucharist as Privileged Theological Site," in Smith, *Radical Orthodoxy and the Reformed Tradition*, 273–74.

redemption lies in finitude, fragmentation, atomism (or certain constructions of finitude, some of which fall into nihilism). Accordingly, redemption is understood within the framework of ontological oneness by virtue of analogical participation in the being of the triune God.[52]

"Whereas for Radical Orthodoxy suspension of the material saves the 'appearances by exceeding them,'" notes James H. Olthuis, "the Reformed tradition fears that the suspension of the material with its privileging of the invisible over the visible, in the end, can mean only the loss of creational integrity and the denial of creational goodness."[53] As further evidence of this denial, he cites RO writer Philip Blond: "'Invisibility as a possibility represents a higher dimension of actuality.' Again, 'every natural visible rests on an infinitude of participation' in God and 'his ideality.'"[54] Therefore, it seems that a choice indeed must be made between a covenantal and an ontological account of participation, since each paradigm generates different questions as well as answers.

Ontology and Pardon

The differences between medieval and modern ontologies are surely greater than their similarities, but the latter may be overlooked especially in the genealogical opposition between patristic/early medieval and early modern-nominalist thought drawn by RO. As part of the *ad fontes* movement of the humanists, Calvin and his heirs believed that they were simply recovering and articulating the best of patristic heritage.[55] On the other hand, Erasmus also thought he was leading a patristics revival, as have the English Latitudinarians, the Catholic Tübingen school, nouvelle théologie, and the Lux Mundi circle, which have profoundly shaped RO. In fact, the last three influences on RO display obvious signs of a Hegelian mediation and interpretation of this heritage. Neither the Reformed tradition nor RO has sought merely to repristinate the first five centuries, and each in its own way may at times have exploited the ancient sources for its own purposes as well as followed them. The stream that runs from theurgic Neoplatonism through Pseudo-Dionysius, Erigena, and Eckhart to modern idealism will naturally interpret the patristic sources differently from the Reformed tradition. To invoke Tillich's contrasting typologies again, "overcoming estrangement" is the ontological current of the RO stream. Reformed theology has consistently emphasized that union with Christ is simultaneously forensic and organic, legal and relational, but only in a covenantal framework can these be seen as mutually reinforcing rather than as antitheses to be reconciled (ultimately, by assimilating the first in each pair to the second).

---

52. Ibid., 274.

53. James H. Olthuis, "A Radical Ontology of Love: Thinking 'with' Radical Orthodoxy," in Smith, *Radical Orthodoxy and the Reformed Tradition*, 280.

54. Ibid., 280 n.4; referring to Milbank, Pickstock, and Ward, *Radical Orthodoxy*, 221, 238.

55. See especially Calvin's "Prefatory Address to King Francis" in the *Institutes*, where he argues this point. A cursory glance at the major Reformed systems displays a profound grasp of and appreciation for the formative work of the ancient Christian writers.

Between justification and glorification lie the vast benefits of adoption and sanctification. Yet a crucial question is how we relate these elements in the *ordo*. Is justification the prerequisite and foundation for sanctification and glorification, or is it the outcome of sanctification? Karl Adam supplied a representative summary of the Roman Catholic answer to this question:

> But since, according to the Catholic conception, justification does not consist in an external imputation of the merits of Christ . . . , but in the gracious operation of the creative love of Christ within us, and in the supernatural emergence of a new love for goodness and holiness, therefore justification of its nature demands sanctification and perfection, and is only complete and finished in this sanctification. Strictly speaking, therefore, a man in a state of grace is not already a saint (*homo sanctus*), not, that is, until he has given this grace free scope in his life and under its awakening impulse overcome every evil tendency, even to his most intimate thoughts and most subtle inclinations, and having brought all that is good to dominance has become the perfect and unalloyed man. Only such a one, whose being is in its every part transfigured by love of God and his neighbour, only such a one will see God. Are there such men on this earth of ours? "Who shall be able to stand before the LORD, this holy God?" (1 Kings [Sam.] vi, 20).[56]

Since no such people exist (except for Mary and Jesus), purgatory exists for "passive punishment" and "suffering for sin."[57] There is always a superabundance of grace, streaming down the ladder of ecclesial being from the merit of Christ and the saints all the way down to the laity.[58] However, final justification is the outcome of human cooperation with this infused grace. The Reformation separated justification and sanctification, Adam says. In fact, judging from his narrative, one might conclude that Luther and Calvin denied the new birth and sanctification.[59]

In contrast to the Roman Catholic conception, covenantal union preserves identity through organic and federal headship and difference through its emphasis on the personal incorporation of individuals in Christ's body through election, calling, justification, and glorification. Since grace is not a commodity or substance managed by the church as the image of the celestial hierarchy, but God's favor on account of Christ, the *gift* (Christ and all of his benefits) is the same for all believers, even if different *gifts* are granted by the Spirit for service to the body.

Covenantal union also preserves the evangelical character of the mystical participation: every gift shared by all believers together is "in Christ." However, Adam insists that we not only receive Christ's merits but also contribute our own. "We have not only the certainty of forgiveness, but also the severe imperative, the commandments and the doctrine of merit."[60] Justification is not mere imputa-

---

56. Karl Adam, *The Spirit of Catholicism*, trans. Dom Justin McCann, O.S.B. (1924; repr., New York: Crossroad, 1977), 101.
57. Ibid., 104.
58. Ibid., 126.
59. Ibid., 108.
60. Ibid., 149.

tion and forgiveness; "nay, [grace] forgives him *for the very reason that it has already inwardly sanctified him*" (emphasis added).[61]

In sum, the real difference between Roman Catholic and confessional Protestant positions does not lie in whether the reality of the new birth and sanctification is affirmed. Rather, the difference lies in whether forensic justification is affirmed along with renewal, and whether the former is regarded as the sponsor of the latter. According to Rome, the new life "is a sort of overflow of the eternal and infinite life within the soul."[62] Intrinsic righteousness is the basis for the external verdict, and the righteous deeds of the new self are "meritorious."

Of course, none of this could happen apart from God's grace—which preserves the account from the charge of legalism, Adam holds (as the NPP maintains in relation to Judaism). Nevertheless—and despite the obvious contradiction of the words that he quotes from Romans 4:4, he concludes that "eternal life becomes, as St. Paul expresses it, a wage and a reward."[63] The believer has "certainty of faith," but not "certainty of salvation," since "he does not know with unconditional certainty whether he is permanently worthy of love or of hatred."[64]

Elaborating this basic approach in a slightly new key, John Milbank argues that the "fall" is not primarily located in the corruption of will, but "is revealed first and foremost as loss of the vision of God and as physical death and incapacity of the body."[65] Further, he interprets Augustine in at least semi-Pelagian terms, rejecting the doctrine of original sin as our participation in Adam's guilt and the bondage of the will as well as the Augustinian doctrine of election. Redemption is not really about rescuing the ungodly from divine judgment, but about restoring the *visio Dei*.

The drama of redemption, as it is worked out in history through amazing paradoxes, is exchanged for a theurgic religious philosophy of grace-assisted human striving for the beatific vision, in which paradoxes surrender to explanatory theodicies. Contemplation (theory) displaces drama (theater). It is unclear how the gospel as good news would figure into his account of redemption, since "news" implies an extrinsic announcement of something new, something that does not derive simply from the nature of things. The grace that redeems, he insists, does not consist in the radical liberation of a supposedly depraved will or "extrinsicist" imputation of an alien righteousness. "Instead, the gift of grace consists in a miraculously restored desire for God, despite the loss of original vision and capacity."[66] While Reformation theology understands grace as God's verdict (*favor*) and a gift (*donum*) of new life, Milbank restricts grace to the latter and treats it as an infused substance. At the heart of the notion of infused grace lies an ontological dualism, which assumes that there is a substantial deficiency in

61. Ibid., 180.
62. Ibid., 181.
63. Ibid., 182.
64. Ibid., 183.
65. Milbank, *Being Reconciled*, 9–10.
66. Ibid.

nature that must be supplemented by grace. In Reformed theology, however, grace justifies, sanctifies, and glorifies creatures without adding anything substantial to their nature.

Missing the distinction that Luther and Calvin make between the freedom of the will in things indifferent (i.e., choosing one's vocation, home, spouse, etc.) and its bondage in relation to "things heavenly," Milbank once again draws a straight line from the Reformation to modernity.[67] Instead, he insists that we need to recover the view that forgiveness is "mediated only through the sacrament of penance," a "public sign, a gesture, an offering which somehow 'makes up' for a past error." It is "to make a restitution so complete that one is utterly reconciled with the one wronged (here God himself) and one's relationship with him can flow in future so smoothly that it is exactly, as Kierkegaard later put it, as if it had never suffered any 'jolt' whatsoever." Thus is it "a positive means of recompense."[68]

> In so far as many modern Christian versions of forgiveness, as exemplified by Kierkegaard, recommend a unilateral act of ontological cancellation, then they would seem to be long-term legatees of this oriental despotism [of the ancient Near East], protracted to infinity in the late medieval reconception of God as a reserve of absolute, infinite untrammeled power and will.[69]

Evidently the Hebrew prophets are also indicted for this "oriental despotism" that leads to the *potentia dei absoluta* of nominalism when Milbank adds,

> After the Incarnation, *contrary to Jewish expectation*, there is held to begin not a reign of realized forgiveness, but a time when divine forgiveness can be somewhat mediated by human beings: a time for which justice is infinitized as forgiveness. . . . By contrast, the negative and unilateral post-late-mediaeval and Reformation sense of forgiveness perverts this constitution into *a despotism now to be exercised as anarchy*. If there is something legitimate in forgiveness as negation, then this surely is but a negation of negation, an absorption into the positive through suffering of evil, which is of its nature privative in the first place. (emphasis added)[70]

Understandably, given his understanding of sin as mere privation of goodness, Milbank wonders what forgiveness can actually forgive. If sin does not actually exist, but is in fact a negation of the good, God can only love "what remains positively loveable in [the sinner] despite his sin, not pretending to love what is not loveable and does not deserve love. (The reverse view is actually yet more post-late-mediaeval distortion of the Gospel.)"[71]

Divine impassibility is given an almost Stoic cast in Milbank's construction. "Indeed, one mystical theologian of the late mediaeval period, Julian of Norwich,

67. Ibid., 20.
68. Ibid., 45–46.
69. Ibid., 48.
70. Ibid., 49.
71. Ibid., 52.

roundly declared that God does not forgive, since he cannot be offended, but only continues to give, despite our rejection of his gift."[72] In fact, so threatened would God's immunity to offense be by a literal attribution of forgiveness to God that Milbank finally denies that it really is God who forgives (even analogically). "Such an eternal divine gift only becomes forgiveness when in Christ it is *not* God forgiving us (since he has no need to) but humanity forgiving humanity. *Therefore divine redemption is not God's forgiving us, but rather his giving us the gift of the capacity for forgiveness*" (emphasis added).[73] Of course, this interpretation is radical, but given the catholic consensus concerning the forgiveness of sins, its orthodoxy is more questionable.[74]

In place of such forensic views, Milbank directs his vision toward the eternal process of giving and returning gifts in an endless exchange in which God always gives *more*, but never gives *uniquely*, which again raises the question as to whether his account is more univocal than analogical. Is the Creator-creature distinction in redemptive gift-giving, as well as in creation, merely quantitative, or is it qualitative? Rather than being understood above all as an offense against *God* that draws sanctions against the covenant servant, according to Milbank sin simply interrupts the *human receiving* (which always includes in its very nature a return that brings intrahuman forgiveness and reconciliation). The incarnation is in excess of the gift, to inaugurate this intrahuman cycle of gift-giving after sin has thwarted it.[75]

The result is an entirely subjective theory of atonement. The sense of sin-and-grace as personal and covenantal, at least between God and humans, is all but lost in favor of metaphysical harmony (the intrahuman cycle of gift-giving) restored after it has been refused. Yet after suggesting something close to a Nestorian separation of the humanity (which forgives) and the Deity (which does not need to forgive), Milbank (purporting to follow Aquinas, though through a certain reading of Maximus) verges on monophysitism, even in terms for which he criticized Luther: "Forgiveness, therefore, perfects gift-exchange as *fusion*."[76] It involves "even the appropriate blending together in one idiom or *tropos* of the one with the other."[77] Thus, both the plight of humans before God and the solution are in metaphysical and ontological rather than in covenantal and historical terms.

Instead of interpreting the New Testament as the fulfillment of the Old Testament types (with obvious sacrificial themes), Milbank assimilates it to Greek *metathexis*, leaving very few traces of the Hebraic (covenantal) element. "Hence

72. Ibid., 60.
73. Ibid., 62.
74. Ironically, in order to circumvent the impact of sin on God, Milbank's account actually sounds quite voluntaristic, particularly when he asserts that the atonement was in no way required (even if God had determined to redeem) because of any essential characteristic of God's nature. God might have chosen another way (since satisfaction of divine justice is not required), but he chose to do so (ibid., 66–67).
75. Ibid., 67.
76. Ibid., 70.
77. Ibid., 71.

the New Testament does not speak of Jesus's death as a sacrifice in the rabbinic sense of a death atoning for sins, nor as something lost to earth to compensate for what we have taken from God. *Nothing can be taken from the impassible God,* and nothing can be added to his sum" (emphasis added).[78] One wonders how God's love, which Milbank charges Reformation theology with having displaced with trust, can even be seriously affirmed in such a radical account of divine impassibility.

Blissfully preserved from genuine covenantal relationships with creatures, God cannot be offended by human fault, and even if this were possible, sin is actually "nothing whatsoever." Therefore, sacrifice and satisfaction have no foothold in being, according to Milbank, because sin and evil have none. The relationship between sin and divine judgment as well as grace and divine justification is entirely submerged in favor simply of a restored *human* capacity for forgiving others.

> St Paul therefore speaks not of the offering of Christ to the Father, with whom he is really identical, but, instead, of our dying to sin and purely finite obsessions, including negative legality, *with Christ,* in order that we might immediately pass with him into a new sort of life. Christ and we ourselves are both killed by evil which is nothing, and so in dying to evil, we die to nothing whatsoever. . . . If any "ransom" is offered by Christ, then it seems indeed that for St Paul, as the Fathers divulged, it is granted to the chthonic gods who are really demons, and to the demonic intermediate powers of the air.[79]

Christ is assimilated to the Father, the church to Christ, the believer to the church, and the believer's works to Christ's.

Once again we recognize the false choice offered here. By contrast, Paul sees no discrepancy between vicarious atonement—indeed, *propitiation* (Rom. 5:6–21) and union with Christ in his death and resurrection (Rom. 6). "Much more surely then," says Paul, "now that we have been *justified by his blood,* will we be saved through him *from the wrath of God.* For if *while we were enemies,* we were reconciled to God through the death of his Son, much more surely, having been reconciled, will be saved by his life" (Rom. 5:9–10). While Paul sees the profound dimensions of cosmic conflict and the renewal of gift-exchange, he not only fails to set these in opposition to "juridical" models, but also treats the divine outcome of the covenant lawsuit as the source for dealing with all of the wider dimensions of redemption.

Yet Milbank can only resist such conclusions on a priori grounds. Deducing what must be from his metaphysical commitments, he says that since the powers are really nothing, "only in a comical sense was Christ, strictly speaking, a sacrifice."[80] In Hebrews, Christ puts an end to sacrifice.

---

78. Ibid., 99.
79. Ibid.
80. Ibid., 100.

He does this not really by offering a one all-sufficient sacrifice (this is to read over-literally and naively) but by passing into the heavenly sanctuary as both priest and victim, and making an "atoning offering" there—in the one place where it is absurdly unnecessary, since offerings are only sent up to this altar from earthly ones. The point is that Christ's earthly self-giving death is but a shadow of the true eternal peaceful process in the heavenly tabernacle, and redemption consists in Christ's transition from shadow to reality—which is also, mysteriously, his "return" to cosmic omnipresence and irradiating of the shadows (Hebrews 9: the Middle Platonic element here is essential).[81]

Milbank has taken a masterful exploitation of Platonic language in the service of quite un-Platonic conclusions and turned it back into a Platonic allegory of the ascent of mind from the shadowy realm of appearances. Just as John's Gospel exploits Greek categories only to radically revise their content ("The Word became flesh" as the most obvious category mistake in Greek thinking), a Platonist could only balk at the recurring theme in Hebrews of Christ's entering the heavenly sanctuary with his own *blood*.

For Hebrews, the point of Christ's entrance into the true temple is that his sacrifice is final because it is the true sacrifice of which all other divinely appointed offerings were mere tokens. It reaches all the way to God's throne, not simply as a proleptic or typological sharing, but as the reality that brings all types to an end. Not merely a sign sharing in the signified, the cross is the reality itself. The types could never secure permanent forgiveness, not because they were sacrifices, but because they were not Christ's sacrifice. Given the emphasis of Hebrews on Christ's sacrifice as the reality and therefore the end of all redemptive substitutions, it is difficult to imagine a less suitable source for Milbank's argument that Christ's work simply reenergizes an intrahuman cycle of reconciliation.

Surrendering the dynamic historical and eschatological ontology of redemption for a timeless allegory of ascent, Milbank judges, by contrast, "The heavenly altar that is purified is, for the author of the *Epistle to the Hebrews*, the psychic realm: 'your conscience'; and purification of this realm consists not in one more sacrificial 'work'—even a final such work—but rather in the final removal of the illusion of the need for such works."[82] While the writer to the Hebrews is transforming the ostensibly psychic realm of conscience into the very visible realm of blood and agony in the very citadel of heaven itself, Milbank misses the irony and therefore (I suggest) the principal strategy, ontology, and argument of this epistle. In fact, it is precisely because the forensic and juridical have a logical priority that Hebrews can speak of the cleansing of the conscience as the effect of a far-from-illusory sacrifice.

Like any version of overcoming estrangement I can think of, RO offers a subjective theory of the atonement, one in which the problematic of sin and grace becomes submerged in a synergistic vision of a church that heals all ontic fissures.

81. Ibid.
82. Ibid., 100–101.

As in Dionysius, Eckhart, and Hegel, one detects in RO (and Milbank in particular) the danger of assimilating the concrete event of the cross into a speculative philosophy.

What then are we to make of Milbank's charge that the priority of trust over love constitutes "the greatest heresy of all"? According to a covenantal account of participation, it follows that trust is precisely the appropriate result of reconciliation and response of transgressors, and that hope is the appropriate stance of pilgrims, with love as the fruit of such divine reconciliation. Love receives its due within a framework of actual covenantal relationships between the persons of the Trinity, between the triune God and his covenant people, and among the covenant people themselves, extending outward to the whole creation. However, for genuine love to arise within those who are not only at fault, but remain hostile to the offended party, forgiveness and justification can be the only basis. Precisely because we are not justified by love are we paradoxically freed to love simply out of gratitude to God and concern for our neighbor—beyond any economy of debt that has been satisfied by Christ. In my view a covenantal account offers a richer context for love as an intrinsically interpersonal matter rather than directing our attention to an abstract hierarchy of being.

THE NEW FINNISH SCHOOL:
LUTHER AGAINST THE LUTHERANS

I have focused on Radical Orthodoxy (RO) and Milbank's account in particular. Other versions of Neoplatonic participation have been advanced, especially what has come to be called the New Finnish interpretation of Luther. Associated particularly with Tuomo Mannermaa, this school has put forward a radical reinterpretation of Luther that sharply contrasts with traditional interpretations, including those of the Lutheran confessions themselves. Evolving largely from dialogues with the Russian Orthodox Church, this working group has been introduced to English-speaking audiences through the work of Carl E. Braaten and Robert W. Jenson, particularly their collection of essays *Union with Christ*.[83] Although Luther's interest in the *unio mysticus* is well-recognized, the Helsinki circle argues that Luther held a radically ontological concept of participation that was quickly muted by the Lutheran tradition, as evidenced by the strictly forensic concept of justification found in the Book of Concord.

Mannermaa argues that in Luther's ontology, being and act are identical: one cannot separate the person from the work of Christ. "This ontological basis has its epistemological side as well: the act of knowing and the object of knowledge are identical. . . . God is both the object and subject, the actor and act, of faith."[84]

83. See n.45.
84. Tuomo Mannermaa, "Why Is Luther So Fascinating?" in Braaten and Jenson, *Union with Christ*, 12.

Justification and all other saving graces are not acts done by God at a distance, therefore, but the result of the divine indwelling. However, according to Mannermaa, confessional Lutheranism abandoned Luther's view by separating Christ's person and work: justification as a purely forensic act before indwelling.[85]

The move that we have indicated in Reformed theology—that is, treating justification as the forensic basis of mystical union—was made in Lutheran orthodoxy as well.[86] Therefore, while the *inhabitatio Dei* was affirmed, it was "considered a consequence of this 'righteousness of faith,' i.e., the forgiveness of sins."[87]

However, Mannermaa is convinced that for Luther the believer's righteousness (justification) is constituted not by imputation but by an actual ontological participation in Christ's inherent righteousness. Faith *is* Christ, according to the Helsinki school, imputing to Luther what seems more appropriately said of Osiander: "According to the Reformer, justifying faith does not merely signify a reception of the forgiveness imputed to a human being for the sake of the merit of Christ, which is the aspect emphasized by the Formula of Concord. Being a real sharing (participation) in Christ, 'faith' stands also for participation in the institution of 'blessing, righteousness and life' that has taken place in Christ."[88]

For his own part, Robert Jenson is attracted to this thesis for its ecumenical potential. "My interest in Luther is not that of a *Lutherforscher*, but that of a systematic theologian and ecumenist. As a systematician, I have found I can do very little with Luther as usually interpreted. And the sort of Lutheranism that constantly appeals to that Luther has been an ecumenical disaster."[89] He approvingly summarizes the Finnish interpretation of Luther's *Christian Liberty*, which does not mention "anything about imputation or unconditional acceptance of the unacceptable or the other 'Lutheran' items."

> Faith makes righteous (1) because believing what God says fulfills the first and great commandment; (2) because the soul that hearkens to the word becomes what the word is, holy and right; and (3) because in faith the soul is united with Christ as a bride with the groom, to be "one body" with him and so possess his righteousness.[90]

---

85. Tuomo Mannermaa, "Justification and *Theōsis* in Lutheran-Orthodox Perspective," in Braaten and Jenson, *Union with Christ*, 28.

86. Tuomo Mannermaa, *Christ Present in Faith: Luther's View of Justification*, ed. Kirsi Stjerna (Minneapolis: Fortress, 2005), 4; quoting *The Book of Concord: The Confessions of the Evangelical Lutheran Church*, trans. and ed. Theodore Tappert (Philadelphia: Muhlenberg, 1959), 548–49.

87. Ibid.

88. Ibid., 32.

89. Robert W. Jenson, "Response to Tuomo Mannermaa, 'Why Is Luther So Fascinating?'" in Braaten and Jenson, *Union with Christ*, 21.

90. Ibid., 23. There is a great difference, however, between saying that the soul becomes what the Word is with respect to holiness and righteousness, and the view that the soul becomes essentially what the Word is. According to the former, we are conformed to Christ's likeness or image; according to the latter, to Christ's essence. Confessional Protestants have always held to a distinction between God's communicable and incommunicable attributes, affirming that God can communicate his holiness and righteousness to creatures, though not the divine essence (omniscience, omnipresence, omnipotence, etc.).

While RO (especially Milbank) sees Luther's "forensicism" as a product of an allegedly nominalist commitment, the Finnish school insists that Luther was anything but a nominalist. "In contrast to Ockham, a human being is not an *ens per se*, but rather an *ens per participatum* in the sense that the ground of its being lies outside itself."[91] Yet this is only a criticism of Milbank's interpretation of Luther. Both projects are aiming at a similar ontological paradigm, but the Helsinki school is convinced that an ostensibly Neoplatonist Luther can be snatched from the "forensicism" of Lutheranism.[92]

Although closer to the Roman Catholic understanding of justification than confessional Protestantism, Mannermaa's provocative thesis reflects a more "Byzantine" Luther. If faith is seen by Rome as assent to truths concerning the object of love, which only becomes active by love through the infusion of grace (*gratia infusa*), Luther sees love as identical to law. Love striving upward to God is the same as works-righteousness, Mannermaa accurately interprets on this point. Even grace-elevated love remains human love.[93]

The *fides caritate formata* (faith formed by love) position of Rome "rests on Greek ontology, and its notion of striving love only signifies a partial, incomplete, and insufficient divinization."[94] By contrast, Luther replaced love with the grace of God in Christ as the "substance" rather than the mere "accident."[95] Thus, we are always justified by Christ's righteousness, not by our own. "Even Christ *in nobis* is Christ *extra nos*."[96] Indeed, in Mannermaa's construal of Luther's teaching, not even in sanctification does it appear that the believer is actually the subject of good works. "Because of the Christian's union with Christ," writes Mannermaa, "his or her works are works of Christ himself."[97] For this reason, "*The strict distinction between justification and sanctification that came to characterize later Lutheran theology is not at all a central or constitutive distinction in the theology of Luther*" (emphasis added).[98] In a similar conflation, in the sacraments, "contrary to other signs, the essence of the representation and the essence of what is being represented are identical. The essence of the representation is the essence of what is being represented."[99] The synthesizing tendency is as comprehensive in Mannermaa's interpretation as in Osiander's: a conflation of justification and sanctification, the act and object of faith, the believer with Christ; Christ's humanity is collapsed into his divinity, and the sacramental signs simply *are* the reality signified.

91. Ibid., 164.
92. However, the contrast that Mannermaa draws between Ockham and Luther is also obvious in Lutheran and Reformed systems, in their routine identification of God as the *principium essendi*.
93. Mannermaa, *Christ Present in Faith*, 23–24.
94. Ibid., 45.
95. Ibid., 25.
96. Ibid.
97. Ibid., 50.
98. Ibid., 49. On the same page, Mannermaa refers to the Osiander debate as provoking such "later Lutheran" positions.
99. Ibid., 83.

Finally, Mannermaa's interpretation, like Osiander's, makes faith identical with God's essential righteousness. Aside from the fact that even in his direct citations on this point Luther actually says that faith *clings* to Christ (which assumes an instrumental-material distinction),[100] Mannermaa offers a doctrine of justification that N. T. Wright quite properly refuted, though assuming (erroneously) that this was the Protestant doctrine. God's essential righteousness is never said in Scripture to be imputed or transferred to believers. Rather, it is Christ's active and passive obedience that are imputed, on the basis of which he then personally indwells believers by his Spirit. Christ is indeed present *in* faith, but not *as* faith.

While critics of the confessional Lutheran (and Reformed) position are finding the Finnish perspective appealing, Luther scholars as well as many Lutheran theologians often suspect this interpretation of Luther to be so determined by metaphysical and ecumenical concerns that it runs roughshod over the reformer's own writings. Robert T. Kolb, for example, surveys the weaknesses of this view, relating it to the Osiandrian controversy. "From his training in the Kabbala, Osiander acquired neoplatonic presuppositions similar to the metaphysical foundation that appears to lie behind Peura's and Mannermaa's position."[101] Timothy Wengert judges, "Here one sees what happens when modern ecumenical agendas and old-fashioned pietism become the chief spectacles through which to view an historical figure."[102] Dennis Bielfeldt wonders whether the Finnish circle is overstating its case for Luther as an advocate of *theōsis*.

> The Finns are adept at discovering key passages (often from the early Luther), and ingenious in interpreting them in support of a comprehensive systematic theological vision built around deification. While this certainly has its theological benefits (especially for ecumenical work), I sometimes am disquieted by the thought that the results of their research may reflect their own presuppositions almost as much as the findings of the neo-Kantian Luther scholars obviously reflected theirs.[103]

Challenges have also come from outside the Lutheran tradition. New Testament scholar Mark Seifrid asks, "Am I wrong in thinking that this 'participatory' approach starts looking very much in the end like the 'substantial' conceptions which most

---

100. See, for example, the quotation of Luther on ibid., 26: "Therefore faith justifies because it takes hold of and possesses this treasure, the present Christ." Or another: "Christ is present in the faith itself." The grammatical construction (*in ipsa fide Christus adest*) militates against simply identifying faith (the subjective act) with Christ (the object). Faith is not the treasure, but takes hold of it. Or another example on 43: "Faith has (possesses) Christ 'as a ring has a gem.'" Mannermaa does not offer a single citation that demonstrates the more radical thesis that the ring *is* the gem.

101. Robert T. Kolb, "Contemporary Lutheran Understandings of the Doctrine of Justification," in *Justification: What's at Stake in the Current Debates*, ed. Daniel Treier and Mark Husbands (Downers Grove, IL: InterVarsity, 2004), 156 n. 9.

102. Timothy Wengert, review of *Union with Christ*, in *Theology Today* 56 (1999): 432–34, cf. Timothy Wengert, "Melanchthon and Luther/Luther and Melanchthon," *Lutherjahrbuch* 66 (1999): 55–88.

103. "Response to Sammeli Juntunen, 'Luther and Metaphysics,'" in Braaten and Jenson, *Union with Christ*, 163.

are rightly concerned not to absolutize? Luther's refusal to enter into the ontological question as to 'how' Christ is present in the believer surely provides a warning against playing 'participatory' or 'substantial' ideas off against 'relational' ones."[104]

As Reformed historical theologian Carl R. Trueman points out, nearly all of the Luther writings to which the Finnish school appeals are "pre-Reformation" works, such as the *Dictata super Psalterium* (1513–16) and the 1515–16 *Romans*, thus failing to interact with Luther as a historical figure whose thinking matures and develops.

> To return, however, to Mannermaa's quotation from the Romans commentary: when read in the context in which the passage occurs, Luther is in fact not here discussing the joyful exchange of sins and righteousness as Mannermaa claims but rather the paradoxical reality of the believer being both old and new man. Indeed, the passage contains no explicit reference to or discussion of the union between the believer and Christ and is simply not relevant to the argument Mannermaa is trying to make.[105]

The use to which Luther's *Galatians* is put similarly advances an interpretation of his teaching on righteousness (especially concerning the heavenly/earthly distinction) in the main body of the text that is exactly at odds with "the larger theological framework laid out in the preface."[106]

Trueman is referring to Luther's discussion of righteousness before God (*coram deo*) and civil righteousness (*coram hominibus*), external righteousness imputed and internal righteousness imparted, and related distinctions that the reformer regarded as paradigmatic for evangelical theology. In that preface Luther emphasizes that the only righteousness that can be said to justify the ungodly is the *iustitia alienum* that is imputed to the believer rather than being formed within. "The obvious question is: if participation in Christ in a manner akin to *theōsis* is so crucial to Luther, why is there no major prolegomenal discussion of this in the preface to Galatians, and why is there so much discussion of these other distinctions?" In response to Trueman's critique, Robert Jenson writes:

> By no means does "impute" here [in Galatians] have to denote an act of judicial discretion. To impute or not to impute something is to make a judgment, and most judgments, also in court, are judgments of fact. . . . God judges the sinner righteous because in ontic fact the sinner and Christ make one moral subject, in whom Christ's divine righteousness overwhelms the sinner's unrighteousness, relegating it to the past tense of the old Adam, even though the sinner cannot sense this. . . . Surely Luther is right and majority Protestantism is wrong.[107]

104. Mark Seifrid, "Paul, Luther, and Justification in Gal 2:15–21," *Westminster Theological Journal* 65, no. 2 (2003): 227.
105. Carl R. Trueman, "Is the Finnish Line a New Beginning? A Critical Assessment of the Reading of Luther Offered by the Helsinki Circle," *Westminster Theological Journal* 65, no. 2 (2003): 236.
106. Ibid., 238.
107. Robert W. Jenson, "Response to Mark Seifrid, Paul Metzger, and Carl Trueman on Finnish Luther Research," *Westminster Theological Journal* 65, no. 2 (2003): 249.

Remarkably, Jenson interprets Luther as teaching what he explicitly rejects in the Galatians preface and elsewhere: namely, that justification is a "judgment of fact" (analytic) concerning a state of affairs rather than a verdict that creates a new state of affairs.

Especially given the fact that many of the "Lutheran" elements of the Book of Concord were written by Luther and drafted under his supervision by those close to him, it is not surprising that we find growing refinement rather than discontinuity. While it is quite possible that Osiander developed a full-blown theology of substantial union in part from some statements in Luther's earlier writings, it seems fairly clear that Luther's mature teaching was decisively opposed to any attempt to find a righteousness *in us* (even that which one had by virtue of union with Christ) that could stand in the divine judgment. Nevertheless, minus the Nestorian tendencies, Osiander's position seems to be identified by the Helsinki circle as Luther's, and neo-Hegelian theologies understandably discover in such a position a fecund source for a speculative reconciliation of being that is quite different from the reconciliation of the ungodly that is found in the New Testament.[108]

In his response to Trueman, Jenson concludes by changing the subject, as if the real motive of Trueman's critique is indicative of the Lutheran-Reformed divide:

> Here, I think, we simply hit an old confessional wall: is being hyper-Cyrillean a good or a bad thing? I do not think the Christological and sacramental differences that have for all these centuries divided Calvinists and Lutherans—Zwinglians are beyond the pale—should be church-divisive. But the differences are real and important in themselves; in my judgment nothing less than two entire interpretations of reality clash here, which do not seem patient of mediation. I thought perhaps I had made some progress in that direction in my *Systematic Theology*, but critique from my Reformed friends has continued unabated.[109]

While there certainly are different metaphysical assumptions at work in Lutheran and Reformed theologies, the greater divide is between the great dogmatic systems

---

108. See Robert Jenson, *Systematic Theology*, vol. 1 (New York: Oxford University Press, 1997), 309, 311, 340–44. Even the "Nestorian" implications of Osiander's doctrine are not completely obviated in the Finnish school. For example, Mannermaa interprets Luther as holding to "a most profound contradiction" in Christ's person at the site of the "happy exchange." "By his divine nature Christ is the 'Divine Power,' Righteousness, Blessing, Grace, and Life.' The divine attributes fight against sin, death, and curse—which also culminate in his person—and overcome them" (Mannermaa, *Christ Present in Faith*, 16). Thus, the Christus Victor theme is brought into the person of Christ himself: a battle between the two natures, one of which is essentially the devil, sin, law, and damnation, while the other is divine, righteousness, and life. Todd Billings has pointed out to me the importance of the cross in Calvin's rebuttal of Osiander. Christ's work on the cross is rendered unnecessary if God's essential righteousness poured into the believer, rather than forgiveness of sins, is the goal of union with Christ. See his superb treatment of this debate in J. Todd Billings, *Calvin, Participation, and the Gift: The Activity of Believers in Union with Christ* (Oxford: Oxford University Press, 2007), chap. 2.

109. Jenson, "Response on Finnish Luther Research," 250.

of modernity (including Jenson's) and the premodern confessional traditions, as well as between the Orthodox/Roman Catholic ontological paradigm and the forensic emphasis of Lutheran/Reformed theologies. Jenson and Mannermaa themselves realize that their interpretation of Luther stands against the confessional Lutheran tradition.

One can certainly find in the Reformers and in their successors remnants of a medieval ontology. Nevertheless, it is questionable whether Mannermaa's Luther would have provoked the controversy that he did any more than the New Perspective's Paul. Through external and internal debate, traditions refine the insights provoked by paradigm shifts. In the next chapter I will be arguing that our tradition needs to be more deeply refined as a result of the Reformers' critical insights. However, this means for me a movement away from Neoplatonism while for the New Finnish school (as for RO), it means a more Neoplatonic interpretation of Luther.

Barth characterized much of modern theorizing about the new birth in terms of either a "subjectivism from above" or a "subjectivism from below." In the first view (which Barth wryly designates "christomonist"), "the *in nobis*, the liberation of man himself, is simply an appendage, a mere reflection, of the act of liberation accomplished by Jesus in His history, and hence *extra nos*. Jesus Christ, then, is fundamentally alone as the only subject truly at work."[110]

In the anthropocentric "subjectivism from below," human decision and conversion are themselves salvific. "This understanding allows no place for a concrete Other which acts with power towards him and which speaks to him in the word of promise. Hence the change does not really have the character of a response to the action of another, of an answer to his word, of an act of gratitude."[111]

Both of these rival types of subjectivism are essentially monistic.[112] Broadly speaking, they seem to me to be representative of the proposals of Mannermaa and Milbank respectively. Against both Milbank's and Mannermaa's Neoplatonic concept of participation, the Reformers and especially their successors understood such *ens per participatum* to be mediated by God's word and Spirit.

I have argued that a forensic and covenantal ontology grounded in God's justifying verdict represents a fundamentally different paradigm than a Platonic ontology. However, this thesis will be put to the test as we move through the gifts of union with Christ in the following chapters. Moving from critique back to construction again, the next chapter will suggest the broad outlines of a covenantal ontology with justification as its forensic source.

---

110. Karl Barth, *CD* IV/4:19. Of course, this is how many have characterized Barth's own position. To what extent this last fragment of his *Church Dogmatics* reflects some movement I will leave to the Barth scholars.
111. Ibid., 20.
112. Ibid.

Chapter Nine

Covenantal Participation (*Koinōnia*)

"Meeting a Stranger"

As the place where strangers meet, covenant highlights nearness as well as distance. "The fear of the LORD is the beginning of wisdom" (Prov. 1:7). We need to have the sense to keep our distance, "for indeed our God is a consuming fire" (Heb. 12:29). "It is a fearful thing to fall into the hands of the living God" (10:31). Hence, the constant warning of the Reformers and their heirs to find God where God has found us: in Christ, offered in the covenant of grace, and not by seeking out God's hidden majesty.

Nevertheless, we dare not refuse the invitation of the Great King to "draw near" in faith.

> Therefore, my friends, since we have confidence to enter the sanctuary by the blood of Jesus, by the new and living way that he opened up for us through the curtain (that is, through his flesh), and since we have a great high priest over the house of God, let us approach with a true heart in full assurance of faith, with our hearts sprinkled clean from an evil conscience and our bodies washed with pure water. Let us hold fast to the confession of our hope without wavering, for he who has promised is faithful. (10:19–23)

Union with Christ and the covenant of grace are not simply related themes, but are different ways of talking about one and the same reality. Therefore, not only are the forensic and transformative dimensions comprehended; soteriology and ecclesiology are also seen as inseparably related. Whether we speak of being in Christ or being in the covenant, Christ is the mediator, and there is a distinction between being internally united to Christ in a covenant of grace and belonging in merely an external and visible sense. "For not all Israelites truly belong to Israel" (Rom. 9:6). The covenant in its outward administration is wider than election. Nevertheless, it is only within the covenant of grace that the eternal covenant of redemption is realized in history.

Having introduced a covenantal account of union (chap. 7) and contrasted it with Neoplatonic versions (chap. 8), this chapter will explore the potential for a covenantal ontology in relation to the *ordo salutis*.

A COVENANTAL ONTOLOGY: IS IT POSSIBLE?

It is one thing to argue for a covenantal perspective on election, justification, and sanctification—perhaps even other loci in dogmatics. However, are we expecting too much of a biblical-theological motif by suggesting that it generates its own ontological framework? There are challenges, to be sure.

First, there is always the threat of naïveté. After Kant, theology has been living in denial, assuming that it could transcend metaphysics. However, the issue is not whether one is asking metaphysical questions, but whether theology is a species of philosophical analysis. The seventeenth-century Reformed theologian Francis Turretin pointed out that even when treating the same topics, theology considers them in a different mode than metaphysics. On holy ground it is not safe to follow the light of nature; one must be led by the revelation of God as redeemer in Christ, as he is given to us as the mediator of the covenant. "This mode of considering, the other sciences either do not know or do not assume."[1]

Second, there is little doubt that a covenantal ontology, funded by the history of God's revelation to and through Israel, will be less sophisticated and speculative than many of its rivals. It will not offer satisfying philosophical resolutions to a host of problems that have vexed the learned of all ages. It will draw us down from the dizzying heights of abstract thinking to the messiness of mundane history. A covenantal ontology will appear somewhat spartan in comparison with its rivals, yet it is precisely in its restricted genus, scope, and criteria that theology deserves to be called a science rather than the musings of the spiritually and intellectually gifted.

---

1. Francis Turretin, *Institutes of Elenctic Theology*, ed. J. T. Dennison Jr., trans. G. M. Giger, vol. 1 (Phillipsburg, NJ: P&R Publishing, 1992), 17. In their zeal "to bring the Gentiles over to Christianity by a mixture of philosophical and theological doctrine," Turretin adds, the systems of "Justin Martyr, Origen, Clement of Alexandria, and the Scholastics" are "philosophical rather than theological since it depends more upon the reasonings of Aristotle and other philosophers than upon the testimonies of the prophets and apostles. The Socinians of this day strike against the same rock, placing philosophy in the citadel as the foundation of faith and interpreter of Scripture." So Turretin says that the Reformed strike a "middle way" between those "who hold that philosophy is opposed to theology" and should never be used and those who confuse theological and philosophical systems (44).

With these qualifications, I think that it is not only possible but also of importance today to develop our ontology from the materials of Christian doctrine: particularly in this context, the gospel itself. Has the Reformed tradition gone far enough with its rethinking of ontology and metaphysics in the light of its covenant theology?

OUTLINES OF A COVENANTAL ONTOLOGY

Contemporary emphasis on participation has reminded us that we are united to Christ's person. Like Luther, Calvin emphasized this point: there can be no participation in Christ's work apart from his person.[2] We are heirs not only of Christ's gifts, but also of his very life, which we enjoy now through the indwelling of the Spirit, and in the consummation as we see him "face to face" in resplendent majesty (1 Cor. 13:12). United with Christ in God's eternal election (Eph. 1:4, 11; 2 Tim. 1:9; etc.), doubly so in his incarnation (Heb. 2:14–18; 4:14–5:10), as well as his death and resurrection (Rom. 6:1–23; cf. 1:3–4; 4:25; 1 Cor .15:35ff.), we are assured that one day the bride will become a wife in the marriage feast, whose reality is already made tangible in Word and sacrament.

Nevertheless, this union that we enjoy is effected for and in us not by an impersonal process of emanations, by a ladder of participation, or by infused habits, but by the Holy Spirit, who gives the ungodly the faith both to cling to Christ for justification and to be united to Christ for communion in his eschatological life. Mediation is not a principle or a process, but is located in a person. Jesus himself is Jacob's ladder, with angels descending and ascending (cf. Gen. 28:10–22; John 1:43–51). "For there is one God; there is also one mediator between God and humankind, Christ Jesus, himself human, who gave himself a ransom for all—this was attested at the right time" (1 Tim. 2:5–6). Creation and redemption are mediated by this one hypostatic Word, whose unique and unrepeatable descent and ascent secures our participation in the new creation that has already appeared in his resurrection.

Covenantal Union (*Koinōnia*)
and Neoplatonic Participation (*Metathexis*)

Fellowship, communion, sharing, and participation belong to the covenantal sphere in the Scriptures. In the New Testament, *echō* (to have) is often used for possessing someone or something. *Metechō* means "to share or participate."[3] In

---

2. For example, see the citations in chap. 7 of the present volume, as well as John Calvin's *Institutes* 1.13.14; 1.13.6; 3.2.24.

3. J. Eichler, "Fellowship, Share, Have, Participate," in *The New International Dictionary of New Testament Theology: A–F*, ed. Colin Brown, a translation and revision of Lothar Coenen, Erich Beyreuther, and Hans Bietenhard, *Theologisches Begriffslexikon zum Neuen Testament* (Grand Rapids: Zondervan, 1975), 636.

Plato, particulars (appearances) are related to the eternal ideas or forms by way of participation (*metochē*), while in Plotinus, J. Eichler notes, "the idea broadened out into the pantheistic and mystical having of the divine One." "In later philosophy the *nous* (mind) became the world-soul which no longer had personal characteristics. It was no longer said that man had *nous* or *logos* (reason). Instead he was said to participate (*metechō*) in them."[4]

Especially through Origen and the Alexandrian school (with roots in Philo), Christian theology was influenced by the notion of the cosmic ladder of being, with lower forms of existence participating in higher forms, deriving ultimately from the absolute. Creation, in this scheme, is an emanation (for Origen, eternal) of divinity from the one God reaching all the way out to the extremities of being. Specific scriptural teachings challenged or qualified aspects of the metaphysical heritage, but the worldview was essentially that of Middle Platonism, Stoicism, and Neoplatonism.

These expressions (*echō* or *metechō*) are absent from the Greek translation of the Hebrew Scriptures (LXX), although they begin to appear in hellenized Palestine. According to J. Eichler, "The word *echō* does not in fact appear in any of these OT passages apart from the late reference in Esther. On the other hand, the relationship described there which God guarantees to his people through the covenant provides the basis for what the NT describes in its theological use of the idea of having."[5]

It is with the New Testament, and especially with Paul, that the notion of "having"—particularly, God's having us and we him in Christ—becomes expressed.[6] We now read, for example, of having eternal life (John 5:24; 1 John 5:12; 2 John 9, as also in Paul and Hebrews).

> In this way John takes up the prophetic, eschatological message of John the Baptist which saw the promised time of salvation break in with Christ. This is a theme which links Jn. with the Synoptics and Paul. Behind it is the thought of late Jewish apocalyptic that the present is void of salvation. For salvation is revealed only to a few gifted visionaries; it is to be expected in its fullness only in the future. However, Jn. and the other NT writers reject this idea. For here and now in the present believers have peace with God (Rom. 5:1), redemption through his blood (Eph. 1:7; Col. 1:14), and access to God's gracious purpose in salvation (Eph. 3:11). Now is the day of salvation (2 Cor. 6:2). Life as full salvation in Christ (Jn. 3:16, 36) is entered into now.[7]

For Paul especially, this eschatological "having" is the result of possessing the Spirit of Christ as the *arrabōn* (deposit) or firstfruits of the consummation.[8] Thus

4. Ibid.
5. Ibid., 637.
6. Ibid. The Gospels also use *echō* in relational references to demonic possession, to have a demon (*daimonion echein*) (Matt. 11:18; Luke 4:33), and in a few other contexts, such as having children, the claim of the religious leaders that they have God as their faith (etc.).
7. Ibid., 638.
8. Ibid.

the Spirit is not only the key to sharing in Christ here and now, but also in the realities of the age to come.

Metechō and *koinōneō* are synonymous, and Paul uses the terms interchangeably.[9] To share or participate (*koinōneō*) is to have someone or something in common (*koinos*), forming a communion or fellowship of sharers (*koinōnia*) and making of each participant a partner, companion, or sharer (*koinōnos/synkoinōnos*).

It is not surprising that this word would figure prominently in covenant theology. Although it was used in Hellenistic literature to refer to the relationship between humans and the gods, it was never used in the LXX for this relationship.[10] The term is most commonly used in Greek literature in reference to the close bonds of friendship and of citizens in the state.[11] With the advent of the eschatological kingdom in Christ, it became an important way of describing the communion of the saints, as coheirs with Christ of all of the Father's blessings. Paul uses the word thirteen times, and it is used in Acts 4:32ff. for the communal sharing of material goods as well as in Acts 2:42, where it points to the common worship of the covenant *qāhāl* in festive assembly.

According to J. Schattenmann, Paul's notion of *koinōnia* differed both from Hellenism and Judaism. In contrast to the former, the fellowship that Paul has in mind is not equivalent to any earthly society, but is always "the fellowship of his Son" (1 Cor. 1:9), "the fellowship of the Holy Spirit" (2 Cor. 13:13), "fellowship in the gospel" (Phil. 1:5), "fellowship of faith" (Phlm. 6), and in 1 Corinthians 10:16, "a participation in" the body and blood of Christ. "This new existence," notes Schattenmann, "is not a divinization in the sense of mysticism and the mystery religions, but incorporation into Jesus' death, burial, resurrection, and glory."

> It is not the elimination or fusion of personality but a new relationship based on the forgiveness of sins. Paul expressed this in paradoxes, new expressions that he coined and mixed metaphors which he used to present *koinōnia* and guard against mystical understanding. These include: *syzēn,* to live with (Rom. 6:8; 2 Cor. 7:3); *sympaschein,* to suffer with (Rom. 8:17); *systaurousthai,* to be crucified with (Rom. 6:6); *synegeiresthai,* to be raised with (Col. 2:12; 3:1; Eph. 2:6); *syzōopoiein,* to make alive with (Col. 2:13; Eph. 2:5); *syndoxazein,* to glorify with (Rom. 8:17); *synkleronomein,* to inherit with (Rom. 8:17); *symbasileuein,* to reign with (2 Tim. 2:12).[12]

In none of the New Testament contexts (including 2 Pet. 1:4) does *koinōnia* (or its cognates) "refer to a mystical fusion with Christ and God, but to fellowship in faith."[13]

There is a close connection in the New Testament between faith, baptism, the Spirit, and union with Christ (Rom. 6:1ff.; 1 Cor. 10:1ff.; 12:13; Col. 2:11–13).

---

9. J. Schattenmann, "Fellowship," in *The New International Dictionary of New Testament Theology: A-I,* 639.

10. Ibid., 640.

11. Ibid.

12. Ibid., 643.

13. Ibid., 644.

Thus, Christ's obedience is ours: a legal, corporate solidarity (Rom. 5:12–21). But it is also a dynamic effect in us: the same power by which Christ was raised from the dead is *at work in us* (Rom. 6:1–9; Eph. 1:18–22). *Koinōnia* involves, therefore, a mutual indwelling of believers in each other in that place that is called Christ's body, an analogical participation in the mutual indwelling of the persons of the Trinity (John 14:20–23; 17:20–23). Christ indwells us not immediately or essentially, as if our natures were somehow transfused or mingled, but by his Spirit (Col. 1:27). This is the sense in which, through God's "precious and very great promises," we now "participate in the divine nature" (2 Pet. 1:4). The Lord's Supper is a communion/participation (*koinōnia*) in his incarnate body and blood, and in each other as his covenantal body (1 Cor. 10:16–17).

As a result, the New Testament writers refer not to a general participation in being but to union with Christ as the locus of our redemption. Representative is Calvin's encouragement to find our purity in Christ's virginal conception, our anointing with the Spirit in his baptism, our mortification in his tomb, our life in his resurrection, and the gifts of the Spirit in his sending of the Spirit at Pentecost, which is echoed also in the Great Litany of the Book of Common Prayer.[14]

N. T. Wright observes that Paul almost always uses the preposition *eis* in reference to *Christos*. The best explanation is that "The usage of Χριστός is incorporative" of Christ as the representative of his people. This particular *person*, Jesus, is Israel's *Messiah*. That is the point. "But why should 'Messiah' bear such an incorporative sense? Clearly, because it is endemic in the understanding of kingship, in many societies and certainly in ancient Israel, that the king and the people are bound together in such a way that what is true of the one is true in principle of the other."[15] This is what it means to be baptized into Christ.[16] In Romans 6:3, "Χριστός is basically shorthand for 'the people of the Messiah.'"[17] There is therefore no question of any fusion of persons or even of a participation that falls somewhere between identity and difference.

In a covenantal understanding, both individualism and collectivism are resisted as the plane shifts from beings-and-being to the ethical relations between a suzerain and a vassal-representative who stands for (and in his office incorporates) the vassal-people, mediating their relation to the suzerain. Daniel 7; Psalm 8; Genesis 1; and Isaiah 45 (esp. v. 23), as Wright adds, "all point towards the nexus of thought which we have seen . . . : the obedience of Israel, the obedience of Adam, the exaltation of the human figure and/or the Israel-figure to a position of pre-eminence in virtue of that obedience."[18] Paul is basically working out the theme of the Servant Songs of Isaiah.[19]

14. Calvin, *Institutes* 2.16.19.
15. N. T. Wright, *The Climax of the Covenant: Christ and the Law in Pauline Theology* (Edinburgh: T&T Clark, 1991), 46.
16. Ibid., 47ff.
17. Ibid., 48.
18. Ibid., 58.
19. Ibid., 60.

Consistent with the story I have offered so far, Morna D. Hooker concludes, "Israel should have been obedient to God; this obedience has now been fulfilled, so Paul argues, in the person of Jesus Christ."[20] Thus, union with Christ through faith is the only way of obtaining the status that Israel was, according to Paul, still seeking through the law. This covenantal understanding of union with Christ is consistent also with the interpretation of Passover in the Jewish literature. In the Mishnah tractate *Pesaḥim* 10:5, we read a well-known guideline for celebration of Passover: "In every generation a person is duty-bound to regard himself as if he has personally gone forth from Egypt."[21] Our modern democratic sensibilities bristle at such a strong identification of representative solidarity as Israel's collective guilt for Achan's theft or humanity's collective guilt "in Adam." (Premodern thinkers like Pelagius bristled at such federal concepts as well.) Nevertheless, its welcome correlate is the collective participation of the wicked in the obedience and victory of the Second Adam, which forms the heart of the gospel.

Particularly in Paul's interpretation, union with Christ corresponds to the new world of grace, faith, promise, justification, and life, in contrast to the old world of sin, unbelief, law, condemnation, and death. As we have seen, the Old Testament believers share with us in the reality for which they hoped in type and shadow. In fact, this *koinōnia* between the old and new covenant saints is so strong that the writer to the Hebrews can say of the Old Testament heroes, "Yet all these, though they were commended for their faith, did not receive what was promised, since God had provided something better so that they would not, apart from us, be made perfect" (Heb. 11:39–40).

Differences between Platonic participation (*metathexis*) and New Testament communion (*koinōnia*) are also delineated by Eastern Orthodox theologian John Zizioulas. First, Zizioulas points out that patristic theology did not simply treat participation (*metochē*) and communion (*koinōnia*) as interchangeable: "Participation is used only for creatures in their relation with God, and never for God in his relation to creation. . . . If we consider what this distinction entails for the idea of truth, our conclusion has to be: the truth of creation is a *dependent* truth, while the truth of God's being is *communion* in itself" (emphasis original).[22] The truth is not found in the "nature" of things (after Kant, we might say, the *Ding-an-sich*), but in the communion of beings—the communion of the creature with God by participation (which, again, does not work in reverse).[23]

Revealing the close parallels between Irenaeus and covenant theology, Zizioulas notes that in contrast to the classical Greek heritage, the biblical understanding of history and truth is eschatological: not a return to an original state, but a "fulfillment" ahead of us.[24] Thus, "history is true, despite change and decay, not just

20. Cited in ibid., 61, from Morna D. Hooker, *Pauline Pieces* (London: Epworth Press, 1979), 66.
21. Cited in Mark Seifrid, *Christ Our Righteousness: Paul's Theology of Justification* (Downers Grove, IL: InterVarsity Press, 2000), 24, from Jacob Neusner's translation (1988).
22. John Zizioulas, *Being as Communion* (Crestwood, NY: St. Vladimir's Seminary Press, 1985), 94.
23. Ibid.
24. Ibid., 95–96.

because it is a movement towards an end, but mainly because it is a movement from the end, since it is the end that gives it meaning."[25] According to Maximus, "The things of the Old Testament are shadow (σκιά); those of the New Testament are image (εἰκών); and those of the future state are truth (ἀλήθεια)."[26] Only in Platonism (and Origenism) is the icon "less real" than the truth. Whereas Platonism is always concerned with the past remembered (*anamnēsis*)—that is, a connection with the world of ideas (as it is also in Origen and Augustine), it is otherwise for the wider patristic consensus. "This tradition presents truth not as a product of the mind, but as a 'visit' and a 'dwelling' (cf. Jn. 1:14) of an eschatological reality entering history to open it up in a communion-event. This creates a vision of truth not as Platonic or mystical contemplation understands it but as picturing a new set of relationships, a new 'world' adopted by the community as its final destiny."[27]

Thus truth, as being, is *constituted* as communion, and the essence of our fallen state is to place being and truth *before* communion.[28] "Idolatry, i.e. turning created existence into an ultimate point of reference, is the form that the fall takes, but what lies behind it is the fact that man refuses to refer created being to communion with God," which means "a rupture between truth and communion," which "results automatically in the *truth of being* acquiring priority over the *truth of communion*" (emphasis original).[29]

Where Milbank is interested in comparisons between the Platonic tradition and Christian teaching, Zizioulas emphasizes contrast. However, the problem in Zizioulas's analysis is that he too constantly refers this problem to nature itself, to the creation as somehow fallen in its very essence already (especially in his genealogy of "individual" and "person," the former essentially bearing the characteristics of fallenness even before the fall itself). Therefore, the "problem" that Christianity addresses is once again ontic rather than covenantal. Zizioulas thinks that there is first of all the brute datum of being—the individual who subsequently enters into communion, but this logic cannot escape the death-drive of nihilism.[30]

However, I would argue that this "brute datum of being" is an epistemological (ultimately, ethical) rather than an ontological problem. No one actually exists as an "individual" according to Zizioulas's definition (self-enclosed, unrelated, merely biological). That we tend to *live* that way is evidence of our sinful condition, falling back not into our biological state but denying the covenantal character of our created existence in relation to both God and fellow-creatures. Baptism into Christ therefore does not entail an ontological transition from created existence (inherently fallen) to redeemed personhood, but a liberation of creatures by the covenant of grace to fulfill their created telos *as* covenantal persons-in-communion.

25. Ibid., 96.
26. Quoted in ibid., 99.
27. Ibid., 100.
28. Ibid., 101.
29. Ibid., 102.
30. Ibid., 103.

As a result, the covenantal antithesis is ethically and soteriologically conditioned: sin-and-grace rather than individual-and-person. The goal of redemption (union with Christ and communion with his body) is to restore rather than to transcend created nature. Therefore, the entity that Zizioulas refers to as an "individual" is an imagined self, with no ontological reality, but part of the suppression of the truth in unrighteousness, identified with a humanly willed breach of covenant.

Forensic Grace with Transformative Effects

After the fall, creaturely existence is no longer *regarded* as constituted ontologically in *koinōnia*, although it *is* such, as a communion in death, condemnation, and the war of all against all. This existence is only a story that can be told, not an ontology that can be mapped. Our story becomes inserted into God's story, however, as it is revealed in the history that culminates in Christ. "Many human events and developments may have other origins and beginnings," wrote Barth concerning the new birth. "The Christian life, faithfulness to God as the free act and attitude of a man, begins with that which in the days of Augustus and Tiberius, on the way from the manger of Bethlehem to the cross of Golgotha, was actualised as that which is possible παρὰ Θεῷ, with God." "The fact that the change" in which one becomes a Christian "has its ground and commencement in the history of Jesus Christ characterises it as a divine happening, in distinction from all the other natural or supernatural changes which are notable enough in their own way."[31]

Disrupting Ontology: Breaking Away from the Notion of Infused Habits

Just as fresh covenant-making events mark new and sometimes radically different directions in redemptive history, so also eschatology points up the surprising and unsettling newness of God's gracious work. A century ago Geerhardus Vos observed that eschatology had been sidelined by, among other things, "the extensive application of the principle of evolution to the history of God's kingdom, the preeminently practical bent of modern Christianity, the spread of a one-sided moralizing conception of the Christian religion, and, perhaps more than anything else, the general anti-supernaturalism by which present-day thinking is colored." "Evolution," he noted, "means constant transformation, in the present case constant spiritual growth, but without any crisis or catastrophe. Eschatology, on the other hand, means a break in the process of development, suspension of the continuity, a sovereign termination of the historical process by the intervention of God."[32]

31. Karl Barth, *CD* IV/4:17.
32. Geerhardus Vos, "Our Lord's Doctrine of the Resurrection," in *Redemptive History and Biblical Interpretation: The Shorter Writings of Geerhardus Vos*, ed. Richard B. Gaffin Jr. (Phillipsburg, NJ: P&R Publishing, 1980), 317.

To be sure, the covenant concept can also underscore unity, such as that between the one economy of grace running across both testaments. However, eschatology consistently steps forward to remind us that this forward movement has a transcendent rather than immanent source, keeping us on the edge of our seat for the next "new thing" in the redemptive drama. Even the differences between particular covenants (such as the law-covenants of creation and Sinai, distinguished from the promissory covenants issued in Genesis 3 and in the covenants with Abraham and David, issuing in the new covenant realized in Christ) are precipitated by new eschatological events. Reformed theology cannot therefore help being a form of narrative or dramatic theology: the doctrine can only arise in the process of performance. It is a story that is told, a drama that is staged in the middle of history.

By contrast, the paradigm of overcoming estrangement does not really anticipate the *novum*. In the medieval paradigm, grace is less disruptive than elevating. Although this approach may seem at first sight to be more affirming of nature (grace healing rather than abolishing), the idea that creation requires "elevation" suggests that its problem is ontic: some deficiency in created reality itself. From a Reformed perspective, however, nature needs no elevation or participation in the supernatural realm in order to be what God's Word has said and continues to say it should be. Creation needs something new in history, a real turning point on earth, and not deeper or stronger suspension of the natural in the supernatural or infusions of new habits. We need a decisive transition not from the finite to the infinite, matter to spirit, natural to supernatural, or biological individuals to ecclesial persons, but from "this age" to "the age to come."

Whether in Plato's striving toward timeless contemplation of eternal, unchanging forms, or in Hegel's striving toward the Absolute's self-realization in history, nothing new really happens. Events are either temporal appearances of an eternal idea or finite instances of an infinite process that unfolds according to an immanent determinism from acorn to oak tree. Greek ontologies continue to enthrall us, distracting us from the economy of grace and the eschatological inbreaking of the kingdom of God. In my view we cannot simply build an eschatological emphasis on the foundation of any of these alien ontologies. Like covenant, eschatology—the particular eschatology of the prophets and apostles—must be allowed to disrupt and reorient our theology, like grace itself.

Recently, Bruce McCormack has argued that in spite of their remarkable rediscovery of the gospel of free justification, the Reformers ignored theological ontology and therefore never challenged the medieval one "which could, logically, *only fund a Catholic ordering of regeneration and justification* (to the detriment of their own definition of justification" (emphasis original).[33] "For Thomas, considered on the most general level of reflection, grace is two things: it is the action of God

---

33. Bruce McCormack, "What's at Stake in Current Debates over Justification?" in *Justification: What's at Stake in the Current Debates*, ed. Mark Husbands and Daniel J. Treier (Downers Grove, IL: InterVarsity Press, 2004), 84.

upon the soul and the effect of that action"—namely, a "healing."[34] This healing results from the infusion of grace in the soul.[35] If theology retains the category of infused habits at all, then a certain logical priority would seem to be owed to regeneration as the beginning of the process of ontological healing. Before summarizing and evaluating McCormack's intriguing thesis, it is worthwhile to offer a brief account of the traditional Reformed critique of this medieval ontology with respect to infused habits.

Grace, Habits, and Infusion

The notion of infused grace is part of a wider ontology that is applied to the original created state. Augustine had maintained that Adam was upheld in righteousness by an enabling grace that was added to an ontologically unstable nature. The fall occurred with the withdrawal of this *donum superadditum* and the consequent shift of vision from the invisible and intellectual to the visible and corporeal. Following Augustine, the early medieval scholastics distinguished between an operative grace (liberating the will from its bondage) that always precedes human effort and a cooperative grace that assists human effort.[36] Following Aquinas, the Council of Trent decreed that through prevenient grace God prepares the soul, while it is "through his stimulating and assisting grace [that individuals] are disposed to convert themselves to their own justification."[37] It is worth noting Wilhelm Pauck's observation that the verb *ekkechutai* in Romans 5:5 ("the love of God *is shed abroad* in our hearts by the Holy Spirit" [KJV alt.]) was rendered *diffusa est in* (was diffused) by the Vulgate, and this became a key basis for the doctrine of infused habits.[38]

At the same time, this prevenient (operative) grace is not itself an infused habit or actual indwelling, but is rather "an operation of God by which the soul is turned toward" God.[39] It is not an infused grace (i.e., indwelling grace or the Holy Spirit indwelling us), but "a grace that arouses and assists extrinsically."[40] Yet, unlike Augustine, Bellarmine and other post-Tridentine theologians held that this prevenient grace provides the capacity but does not actually confer the gift of faith itself.[41]

---

34. Ibid., 85; cf. Thomas Aquinas, *ST* 1a2ae, Q. III, art. 2; 1a2ae, Q. III, art. 3. Joseph P. Wawrykow offers a careful analysis and defense of Aquinas on this point in *God's Grace and Human Action: "Merit" in the Theology of Thomas Aquinas* (Notre Dame, IN: University of Notre Dame Press, 1995).

35. Ibid., 87.

36. Peter Lombard, *Sent.* II., dist. 26, 1; cited by Herman Bavinck, *Reformed Dogmatics*, ed. John Bolt, trans. John Vriend, vol. 3 (Grand Rapids: Baker Academic, 2006), 512.

37. Council of Trent, session VI, canon 5, in Heinrich Denzinger, *The Sources of Catholic Dogma*, trans. Roy J. Deferrari (London: Herder, 1955), 250. This view is developed in Thomas Aquinas, *ST* 1a2ae 1121.

38. Wilhelm Pauck, introduction to Karl Barth, *Christ and Adam: Man and Humanity in Romans 5*, trans. T. A. Smail (New York: Harper & Bros., 1956); a translation of *Christus und Adam nach Römer 5* (Zollikon-Zurich: Evangelischer Verlag, 1952), 5.

39. Thomas Aquinas, *ST* I, Q. 62, art. 2, ad 3; cf. ibid., II, 1, Q. 109, art. 6; II, 1, Q. 112, art. 2; III, Q. 89, art. 1, ad 2.

40. Robert Bellarmine, *De justificatione*, in *Controversiis*, I, c. 2, cited by Bavinck, *Reformed Dogmatics*, 3:513.

41. Bavinck, *Reformed Dogmatics*, 3:514.

Bavinck points out that the differences here go to the very heart of ontology, particularly in the understanding of grace.

> Concerning this grace, there is an important difference between Rome and the Reformation, particularly in its Reformed development. In Catholic theology, the grace referred to here is called *gratia gratum faciens*, the grace that makes humans pleasing to God, and it is further differentiated into actual and habitual grace. The former is granted humans to enable them to engage in saving activities. For the natural human, the human without the superadded gift, though still capable of performing many naturally and morally good works, cannot perform the works that belong to a higher order and are linked with supernatural, heavenly blessedness.[42]

The categories are clearly those of nature and grace rather than sin and grace:

> By actual grace, Catholic theology means not merely the external call of the gospel with its moral influence on the human intellect and will, but thinks in this connection of an illumination of the intellect and inspiration of the will that communicates to humans not only moral but even natural (physical) powers. At this point already we need to note that Rome bases the absolute necessity of habitual grace not so much on the sinful state of humankind as on the thesis that humans, having lost the superadded gift, are now purely natural beings who in the nature of the case cannot perform supernatural good works or saving acts, for "it is fitting that acts leading to an end should be proportioned to that end" [Aquinas].[43]

Thus, actual grace "not only morally but also 'physically' elevates our faculties so that they are capable of acting supernaturally, and it is therefore entitatively (essentially) supernatural, 'transcending the entire natural order,' forming, with merely natural grace, a contrast that is no less sharp than that between nature and supernature."

> Of habitual (infused) grace it is stated even more sharply that it is a gift of God by which humanity "is elevated to the supernatural order and in some manner made a participant of the divine nature." It is a "divine quality inhering in the soul; like a kind of brightness and light it removes all stains from our souls and renders these same souls more beautiful and more bright."[44]

Thus, grace "divinizes" individuals and "elevates them 'into the divine order.'" The assumption is that grace makes us something *more* than human instead of liberating us *for* the full humanity for which we were created.

> It "lifts us not merely above human nature but above every nature, above the highest choirs of heavenly spirits, . . . not merely above the whole exist-

42. Ibid., 574.
43. Ibid., 575, quoting Aquinas, ST II, 1, Q. 109, art. 5.
44. Ibid., 576, quoting C. Pesch, *Praelectiones dogmaticae*, 3rd ed., 9 vols. (Freiburg: Herder, 1906), 5:19, 21; and Roman Catechism, II, 2, Q. 38.

ing creation but also above all possible beings, the most perfect beings conceivable not excepted." And since only God stands above all possible beings, "this grace-filled elevation must transpose us into a divine sphere."[45]

This grace "seeks to elevate and to make well."[46] Bavinck judges, "The forgiveness of sins is secondary here. Faith has only preparatory value. The primary thing is the elevation of human beings above their nature: divinization, 'both becoming like God and union with him' [Pesch]."[47]

In contrast, says Bavinck, "the Reformation rejected this Neoplatonic mysticism, returned to the simplicity of Holy Scripture, and consequently gained a very different concept of grace."

> Grace serves, not to take up humans into a supernatural order, but to free them from sin. Grace is opposed not to nature, only to sin. In its real sense, it was not necessary in the case of Adam before the fall but has only become necessary as a result of sin. . . . The "physical" opposition between the natural and the supernatural yields to the ethical opposition between sin and grace.[48]

Bavinck allows that this terminology was borrowed by the Reformers and Protestant orthodoxy from medieval theology for describing the gift of salvation.

> The Reformation did confess that it is not only external but also internal, that it bestows not only moral but also "hyperspiritual" (supernatural) powers, that it is a quality, a disposition. But even though it sometimes expressed itself in the same terminology as Rome, it put a different meaning in it. . . . In the view of the Reformation, the operation of grace is and remains ethical.[49]

In other words, grace does not elevate nature, but liberates it from its bondage to sin and death.

For Rome, grace "is an aid to humans in their pursuit of deification." "In the Reformation, however, grace is the beginning, the middle, and the end of the entire work of salvation; it is totally devoid of human merit. Like creation and redemption, so also sanctification is a work of God."[50] Healing has an important place within a covenantal account of participation in Christ, but in reducing the *ordo salutis* to this motif, the Roman Catholic paradigm does not accommodate the forensic element. Furthermore, in a covenantal ontology "healing" is effected by the Spirit through the gospel, not by the infusion of a gracious substance.

Even with Augustine's introduction of the notion of a *donum superadditum* (superadded gift), one discerns a marked contrast with a covenantal understanding

---

45. Ibid., quoting J. Heinrich and C. Gutberlet, *Dogmatische Theologie*, 2nd ed., 10 vols. (Mainz: Kirchheim, 1881–1900), 8:588ff.
46. Ibid.
47. Ibid., 577.
48. Ibid.
49. Ibid., 579.
50. Ibid.

of this situation. According to the federal theologians, Adam and Eve were never in a state of grace before the fall.[51] Endowed in their creation with all of the requisite gifts necessary for fulfilling God's eschatological purposes, there was nothing lacking requiring a gracious supplement.

This reveals a fundamentally different understanding not only of the original condition of humanity in Adam (under a covenant of works), but of grace itself. After all, "the image of God is not a superadded gift but integral to the essence of humanity," as Bavinck observes.

> The covenant of grace differs from the covenant of works in method, not in its ultimate goal. It is the same treasure that was promised in the covenant of works and is granted in the covenant of grace. Grace restores nature and takes it to its highest pinnacle, but it does not add to it any new and heterogeneous constituents. From this it follows that in Reformation theology, grace cannot in any respect bear the character of a substance.[52]

If grace is a spiritual substance infused into a person in order to perfect nature, rather than divine favor shown to those who are at fault, we have a perfect example of the contrast between ontological-metaphysical and ethical-covenantal construals of the problem.[53]

Reformed writers noted further problems with the Augustinian interpretation at this point: (a) it located the fall in an inherent weakness in the constitution of humanity as such (viz., having the lower appetites), and (b) posing God's withdrawal of a *donum superadditum* made God responsible for the fall.[54] To this extent at least Augustine, for all of his great accomplishments as a theologian of

51. For example, Peter van Mastricht says that God's grace is "nothing but grace towards the wretched" (cited by Heinrich Heppe, *Reformed Dogmatics*, rev. and ed. E. Bizer, trans. G. T. Thomson [London: G. Allen & Unwin, 1950; repr., London: Wakeman Trust, 2002], 96); the same view of grace as synonymous with mercy (i.e., God's favor shown to those at fault and not simply without merit) can be found in Rollock, Ussher, Perkins, Ursinus, Olevianus, Zanchi, Owen, and others. The Westminster Confession deliberately uses the terms "voluntary condescension" rather than "grace" to describe God's original relation to humankind. Grace is always shown not only to those who do not deserve favor, but also to those who "have deserved otherwise" (Amandus Polanus, cited by Heppe, *Reformed Dogmatics*, 96).
52. Ibid.
53. After affirming the goodness of the original creation, specifically, of the creature made in God's image, the Heidelberg Catechism teaches that God is not unjust in requiring perfect performance of his law, "for God so made man that he could perform it; but man, through the instigation of the devil, by willful disobedience deprived himself and all his descendants of this power" (Q. 6, 9, in *Ecumenical Creeds and Reformed Confessions* [Grand Rapids: CRC Publications, 1987]). Similarly, the Belgic Confession (art. 14) states, "We believe that God created man out of the dust of the earth and made and formed him after His own image and likeness, good, righteous, and holy, capable in all things to will agreeably to the will of God. *But being in honor he understood it not* [cf. Ps. 49:20 KJV], neither knew his excellency, but willfully subjected himself to sin and consequently to death and the curse, giving ear to the words of the devil. For the commandment of life [another term for the covenant of works], which he had received, he transgressed" (also in *Ecumenical Creeds and Reformed Confessions*, cited above).
54. On this point, see for example William Ames, *The Marrow of Theology*, trans. John D. Eusden (Boston: Pilgrim, 1968; repr., Durham, NC: Labyrinth, 1983), I, XI, 8.

grace, introduced the legacy of an ontology significantly determined by Neoplatonic sensibilities, a legacy that was refined by Thomas Aquinas. Anthony Kenny explains Thomas's position. Unlike animals, human beings have certain capacities—for instance, to learn languages or a capacity for generosity.

> These capacities are realized in action when particular human beings speak particular languages or perform generous actions. But between capacity and action there is an intermediate state possible. When we say that a man can speak French, we mean neither that he is actually speaking French, nor that his speaking French is mere logical possibility. . . . States such as knowing French . . . are dispositions. A disposition . . . is halfway between a capacity and an action, between pure potentiality and full actuality.[55]

Thus, for Aquinas, regeneration is an infused habit or disposition that is somewhere between a mere logical possibility and a realized action: prevenient, but not actual grace.

McCormack interprets the Thomistic anthropology in relation to justification:

> In a human nature properly ordered after the image of God—the mind (which Thomas regarded as the highest part of human nature) is in subjection to God and the lower (appetitive) powers of the soul are in subjection to the mind. It is this right ordering of human nature which Thomas defined as "justice." . . . It is this essential derangement of nature that is addressed in divine justification. For Thomas, justification is the process by which God makes us to *be* just.[56]

Accordingly, writes Aquinas, God "infuses the gift of justifying grace in such a way that, at the same time, He also moves the free choice to accept the gift of grace," for the forgiveness of sins.[57] "There is (1) the infusion of justifying grace; (2) a movement of free choice directed toward God by faith; (3) a movement of free choice against sin; and (4) the forgiveness of sins."[58]

The case of infants in baptism was paradigmatic for this process from infused justification to forgiveness of sins.[59] Regeneration replaces imputation: God's work *in* us is the basis of forgiveness.[60] For Calvin, by contrast, "we say that [justification] consists in the remission of sins and the imputation of Christ's righteousness."[61] McCormack surmises:

> If, for example, we make regeneration to be the basis of the non-imputation of sin—as Thomas had it—there remains no reason to distinguish between

55. Anthony Kenny, ed., introduction, in Thomas Aquinas, *Summa theologica*, "Dispositions for Human Acts," Blackfriars edition (New York: McGraw-Hill, 1964), 22:xxi.

56. Ibid., 88; cf. Thomas Aquinas, *ST* 1a2ae, Q. 113, art. 1.

57. Ibid., 88; see Thomas Aquinas, *ST* 1a2ae, Q. 113, art. 3.

58. Ibid., 88–89.

59. McCormack, *What's at Stake*, 89.

60. Ibid., 90.

61. Calvin, *Institutes* 3.2.2.

the two. Regeneration, after all, is sanctification viewed from the angle of an initiating moment rather than as part of a larger process. Hence, Calvin insists on the imputation of Christ's righteousness. . . . In this development, the decisive role was played—for both the Reformed and the Lutherans— by Calvin's response to the challenge of a one-time Lutheran by the name of Andreas Osiander.[62]

Sometimes Luther sounds as if faith has priority over imputation, notes McCormack, which then raises the question as to how one comes to believe. At least if one insists on the priority of grace in any sense, it would seem that regeneration must precede faith. So even in the process of defending *sola gratia* within a medieval ontology, the *sola fide* could be easily compromised.

> The residual problem created by Luther's analysis (and one he bequeathed to later generations of Protestant theologians) lies in the fact that the priority of the giving of faith over the act of divine imputation would seem clearly to require a certain logical priority of regeneration (a work of God "in us") over justification. And to the extent that that were so, the "break" with Catholic understandings of justification like Thomas's would be less than complete.[63]

No wonder the Finnish school takes it a step further, seeing salvation as "more ontological and mystical than ethical and juridical." This new interpretation "brings as much to Luther as it reads out of him," with a relation to Luther's writings that's "tenuous . . . at best."[64] The same problems are involved, says McCormack, in the Joint Declaration on Justification between the Lutheran World Federation and the Vatican.[65]

While these recent interpretations fail to do justice to Luther, much less the confessional position on justification, McCormack judges that the failure of the Reformers and their heirs to critique the ontological presuppositions underlying the rejection of justification is itself part of the problem. "Already at Augsburg, . . . Osiander showed himself to be unhappy with Melanchthon's defense of a forensic understanding of justification."[66] For his own part, Calvin felt obliged to add a new section against Osiander's position in the 1559 *Institutes*.

McCormack correctly points out that for Calvin the righteousness of Christ is not a substance but is his active obedience in fulfillment of the law and passive obedience on the cross:

62. McCormack, *What's at Stake*, 92. I have already summarized Calvin's critique of Osiander's view of justification as the transfer of Christ's "essential" righteousness to the believer. Evaluations of Osiander vary, but his status has been somewhat rehabilitated especially by the New Finnish interpretation of Luther.
63. Ibid., 94.
64. Ibid., 95, referring to Carl Braaten and Robert Jenson, eds., *Union with Christ: The New Finnish Interpretation of Luther* (Grand Rapids: Eerdmans, 1998). See the discussion of this view below.
65. Ibid., 95–96.
66. Ibid., 96.

In making this distinction between "essential righteousness" and "acquired righteousness," Calvin made a significant contribution not only to the Reformed understanding of justification but also to Protestantism in general. . . . In saying, "Whomever, therefore, God receives into grace, on them he *at the same time* bestows the spirit of adoption [Rom. 8:15], by whose power he remakes them to his own image," Calvin makes justification to be logically prior to—and the foundation of—that bestowal of the Spirit of adoption by means of which the believer is regenerated. On this view, regeneration would have to be seen as the logical consequence of the divine verdict registered in justification. In sum, Calvin's understanding of justification is strictly forensic or judicial in character. It is a matter of a divine judgment, a verdict of acquittal. And the means by which it is accomplished is imputation.[67]

I agree with the thrust of McCormack's argument. However, we should bear in mind that for the magisterial Reformers "regeneration" encompassed conversion and sanctification. Thus, regeneration could not possibly be described by the Reformers in any other terms than as a consequence of justification. However, later Reformed theology, particularly in its confrontation with Arminianism, came to distinguish regeneration from conversion and sanctification. Consequently, we cannot simply compare and contrast Calvin with his heirs on regeneration, given the narrowing definition. Lutheran and Reformed theologies were at one in affirming that *sanctification* followed from justification rather than vice versa—even if *regeneration* in the narrow sense was prior to both.

That being said, McCormack's thesis presses us to ask whether the logical priority of regeneration even in the narrow sense opens the door to a nonforensic basis of justification, with an infusion of habits. To be sure, the Reformers and their heirs continued to use the language of new qualities infused. However, as Bavinck points out above, they gave such terminology a new meaning. With McCormack, I am suggesting that the terminology of infused habits should be abandoned.

In chapter 7, I referred to Louis Berkhof's summary of the Reformed position on mystical union as the result rather than the source of justification. At the same time, Berkhof, after considerable analysis of the options, adopts the later Reformed consensus that regeneration precedes effectual calling and justification. This reveals the inner tension in Reformed (and, I would add, Lutheran) soteriology. Against all attempts to assimilate the forensic character of justification to inner transformation, it sharply distinguishes justification from regeneration and sanctification. Yet, against synergistic theologies (such as Arminianism), it insists upon the priority of regeneration as a definitive change in disposition. In doing so, the Reformed theologies carefully refined the definition of regeneration to an infused habit precisely because a habit is not yet an act (as conversion and sanctification certainly are). Therefore, they could assert the necessity of a divine work of regeneration before human decision (against Arminianism) without returning to the Roman Catholic confusion of justification with sanctification.

67. Ibid., 100–101.

However, the danger is that by appealing to the medieval ontology of infused habits, the "implanting" of the seed that will yield repentance, faith, and all other graces can become just as separated from the forensic word of justification (i.e., the gospel) as it is in medieval ontology. Recognizing this danger, Protestant orthodoxy *walled off* justification from any inward change, but then (with varying degrees of success) continued to appeal to traditional medieval categories for regeneration and sanctification.

Although I affirm everything that they were after in the formulation, I am arguing that justification should be seen more clearly not merely as ontologically *different* from inner renewal, but also as the ontological *source* of that change (regeneration in both its narrower and broader senses). In that case, we need not formulate a doctrine of regeneration as immediate and direct or even as subconscious and nontransformative, but treat justification as an illocutionary speech-act (*verbum externum*) that, when identified with the Spirit's perlocutionary act of effectual calling, issues in repentance and faith. Developing this particular argument will be a central aim of the next chapter.

For Calvin, not only is justification entirely forensic; union with Christ is also regarded as first of all forensic and only consequently transformative. "At several points in the *Institutes*," argues McCormack, "Calvin appears to make 'union with Christ' to be logically, if not chronologically, prior to both justification and regeneration."[68] But if so, how do we distinguish regeneration from justification? Are we justified by an inner work after all (Christ dwelling in our hearts)? "Only the strict emphasis upon imputation is capable of closing the door with finality upon the Medieval Catholic view."[69]

McCormack's concern seems valid, with Osiander as a test case. However elevated their realistic language concerning the *unio mystica*, the Reformers and Protestant orthodoxy still regarded imputation as the judicial basis of the entire *ordo salutis*, refusing to collapse imputation into an essential union. It is true that one can find references in Luther and Calvin to justification through union with Christ; this was only to affirm that all of our righteousness before God is in Christ and not in us. When considering the relation between faith (justification) and the renewing gifts (sanctification) of that union, however, we have seen that they treat the former as the basis for the latter. The indisputable point is that they understood imputation as the sole basis for their objective righteousness, regardless of how they spoke of the order.

That being said, McCormack's point seems all the more plausible. While the Reformers' doctrine of justification ran against the grain of medieval ontology, placing the whole *ordo salutis* on an entirely different ontological map redrawn by forensic justification remains an unfinished task even beyond the superb refinements of the Reformation and post-Reformation era. The question is whether we can articulate an *ordo* without *any* appeal to infused habits. Is a foren-

68. Ibid., 101; see Calvin, *Institutes* 3.2.1 and 3.2.10.
69. Braaten and Jenson, *Union with Christ*, 102.

sic ontology capable of generating its own account not only of justification, but also (on that basis) of calling, sanctification, and glorification? In other words, does God's Word, rendered effectual by the Spirit, have the illocutionary and per-locutionary force to bring about the world of which it speaks?

Where the Reformers' teaching concerning justification underscores the divisions between Eastern Orthodoxy/Roman Catholicism and confessional Protestantism, contemporary ecumenism often turns to other topics in the Reformers' writings that remain less determined by forensic categories. McCormack relates that when he presented a similar paper in an Orthodox-Reformed colloquium, Thomas Torrance objected, drawing attention to Calvin's teaching on the eucharistic feeding in the *Institutes* (4.17), where Eastern motifs (especially the Cyrillian) are more prominent, urging that we should "only then turn to 2.15–17," where atonement and justification are treated directly.[70] But McCormack finds this "hermeneutically odd." Shouldn't we start with the place where Calvin directly treats it?[71] Ontological healing over penal substitution was Torrance's point, and therefore he chose to interpret (marginalize) Calvin's treatment of the latter in the light of his eucharistic reflections on the former rather than follow Calvin's own order of direct treatment.[72] We have already encountered a similar approach in the New Finnish interpretation of Luther: developing his doctrine of justification from his treatment of the sacraments rather than by more direct consideration of his writing on justification itself.

According to McCormack, there is a tension in Calvin's teaching on imputation on the one hand "and the more nearly patristic understanding of those themes which are suggested by a good bit of rhetoric that Calvin employs in speaking of the eucharist."[73] The latter seems at odds with rejection of communication of attributes, but Calvin does not recognize the ontological perils of Cyril's rhetoric.[74]

> Had he done so, he might have realized that he could not reasonably affirm Cyril's rhetoric of the life-giving character of Christ's "body" without accepting Cyril's soteriology of divinization, as well as the (largely) Platonic ontology of "participation" which made that soteriology possible in the first place. He might also have seen that he was creating serious problems for his doctrine of justification.[75]

McCormack, of course, is not the first to be perplexed by Calvin's appropriation of Cyrillian christological notes in his eucharistic teaching. Especially in more Zwinglian-leaning sacramental theologies of American Presbyterians such as Hodge, Warfield, Thornwell, and Dabney, Calvin's repeated references to the

70. Ibid., 103.
71. Ibid.
72. Ibid., 104.
73. Ibid.; see Calvin, *Institutes* 4.17.9.
74. Braaten and Jenson, *Union with Christ*, 104.
75. Ibid., 104–5.

communication of Christ's life-giving flesh in the Eucharist has elicited criticism as a hangover from the mystical theologies otherwise alien to Calvin's system.[76]

In my next volume I will address this question more directly in consideration of the Supper. It will suffice for our purposes here merely to state my conclusion. This mystical notion was not a foreign element in Calvin's system—a hangover from his inherited ontology, but was explicitly defended as integral to his eucharistic teaching, which was itself part of a broader emphasis on union with Christ. While this union is not justification but is rather the consequence of justification, the Spirit truly unites believers to Christ—not simply to his benefits, but to his person. The *unio mysticus* was already significantly reinterpreted in covenantal rather than essentialist terms, especially after his dispute with Osiander. Although more refinement was (and is still) needed, and one must interpret Calvin's understanding of justification from his explicit treatment of justification rather than his eucharistic teaching, I do not believe that the latter is at all inimical to a covenantal model. Although there will be different ways of parsing what is meant by a communion of Christ's life-giving substance in the Supper, Calvin and the Reformed tradition seem to me to be perfectly justified in concluding, with a broader consensus, that apart from union with the life-giving *person* of Christ, there can be no communication of his *benefits*.

It is therefore not participation or mystical union per se that are problematic terms in Reformed theology. The important question is whether these themes are articulated within a more Platonic or a more covenantal ontology. McCormack recognizes the appeal of these alternative ontologies, particularly given the situation in mainline Protestantism. "We live in a time in which the churches of the Reformation are in doctrinal chaos. Many there are who, appalled by the gnosticism and even paganism of a good bit of the theology to be found on the left wing of their churches, have turned longing eyes towards Rome and Constantinople."[77] Consequently,

> I think it is accurate to say that there are no hotter topics in Protestant theology today than the themes of *theōsis*, union with Christ, the de Lubacian axiom "the Eucharist makes the church," etc. . . . In the process, the churches are slowly coming under the influence of a concept of "participation" in Christ that owes a great deal to the ancient Greek ontologies of pure being. . . . *In truth, forensicism (rightly understood!) provides the basis for an*

76. Charles Hodge, "Doctrine of the Reformed Church on the Lord's Supper," in Charles Hodge, *Essays and Reviews*, selected from *The Princeton Review* (New York: Robert Carter & Bros., 1857). With John Williamson Nevin in his sights, Hodge characterizes even Calvin's understanding of Christ's whole vivifying person being communicated in the Supper (which he acknowledges to be taught in some of the Reformed confessions) as "an uncongenial foreign element" drawn from patristic sources, a too-literal reading of John 6, and a desire to placate the Lutherans (363–66). Even sharper views were expressed by James Henley Thornwell, R. L. Dabney, and William G. T. Shedd, the last of whom attempted to assimilate Calvin's view to his own Zwinglian conception (*Dogmatic Theology*, ed. Alan W. Gomes, 3rd ed. [Phillipsburg, NJ: Presbyterian & Reformed, 2003], 814–15). I will interact directly with these views in vol. 4.

77. McCormack, *What's at Stake*, 105.

alternative theological ontology to the one presupposed in Roman and Eastern soteriology. Where this is not seen, the result has almost always been the abandonment of the Reformation doctrine of justification on the mistaken assumption that the charge of a "legal fiction" has a weight, which in truth, it does not. (emphasis added)[78]

It is especially this bold suggestion that I wish to advocate along with McCormack. In his comment on Romans 8:15 cited earlier, Calvin makes justification that which brings everything else, including regeneration (again, the whole process of inward renewal), in its wake. Unlike a human judge who can only call them as he sees them, God's declaration, McCormack concludes, "creates the reality it declares." "God's declaration, in other words, is itself constitutive of that which is declared."[79]

Once more we see the superiority of communicative and covenantal over purely causal and metaphysical grammars. In the latter case, justification becomes a debate over the mechanics of the inner life, while in the former it has to do with a Covenant Lord pronouncing a courtroom verdict upon the servant that issues in a completely new ontological, ethical, and eschatological orientation—including the inner life in its sweep. No less than God pronounced "Let there be . . . !" when there was nothing, Abram "the father of many" while he was childless, Sarah fruitful while she was barren, and a young woman pregnant while she was a virgin, God pronounces believers to be righteous while they are unrighteous. Thus, the entire reality of the new creation—not only justification but also renewal, and not only the renewal of the individual but also of the cosmos—is constituted by the covenantal speech of the Trinity.

McCormack appeals to John Murray's comment that "the declarative act of God in the justification of the ungodly is constitutive. In this consists its incomparable character." However, he faults Murray for restricting this to being constitutive only of our righteous state rather than of regeneration and everything else.[80] The reason for this, McCormack suggests, is that Murray, *unlike* the Westminster Confession, treats regeneration as distinct from and prior to effectual calling—a point to which I will return in the next chapter. The point to be made here is that the notion of regeneration (as a new habit infused or implanted) before effectual calling (through the gospel's forensic announcement) is precisely what keeps justification from being constitutive across the entire *ordo salutis*.

While McCormack is more sweeping in his criticism of such moves, I share his concern to see justification as that forensic, declarative, covenantal Word that simultaneously creates the new status *and* the new being of those who are in Christ. Justification itself is not to be confused with regeneration and sanctification, but is to be regarded as their Word-constituting source. "The divine imputation is a verdict

---

78. Ibid., 106.
79. Ibid., 107.
80. Ibid., referring to John Murray, *Redemption Accomplished and Applied* (Grand Rapids: Eerdmans, 1955), 123.

whose final meaning can only be grasped when it is seen in the framework of a teleologically-oriented covenant of grace" grounded in election, McCormack argues.

> The eschatological dimension is even more important for my purposes here. The regeneration, which flows from justification as its consequence, is the initiation of a work that is completed only in the eschaton, only in the glorification of the saints. . . . To be "clothed with Christ's righteousness" in time, means to be clothed with the saving efficacy of his death (which addresses the problem of guilt) and the saving efficacy of his life of obedience (in which the new humanity is inaugurated).[81]

He concludes:

> Now if I am right up to this point in my reflections, then the ground has been taken out from beneath the charge of a "legal fiction" without recourse to the vexed problem of our union with Christ. Imputation, understood as a judicial act with transformative consequences, is adequate to handle the problem. . . . I do not participate in the historical humanity of Christ (a thought which would require a unity on the level of "substance" if it is really to move beyond the thought of a unity of wills); rather I participate in the *kind* of humanity which Jesus instantiated and embodied through his life of obedience.[82]

Already we are beginning to see how different ontologies give rise not only to different views of the individual's experience of redemption (the *ordo salutis*), but also to different ecclesiologies. As the Word assumed our humanity rather than a preexisting human person, we participate in Christ as the head of this new humanity rather than in his unique personal identity. One's conception of the mystical union of the believer with Christ is inextricably related to one's view of the mystical body, his church. If the ascension of Christ in the flesh is ontologically constitutive for this time between the times, then the church cannot be equivalent to the incarnate Christ because not even the believer's "person" fused with his person. Rather, the believer participates in the covenantal body of which he is the head. We can still affirm that we participate ontologically in the person as well as the benefits of Christ, but a covenantal ontology suggests that this is more like the relation of a commonwealth and its monarch or a husband and wife or parents and children in a family than a fusion of essences, personalities, or even wills. To be sure, this union is not merely legal or even relational, but spiritual, mystical, and real—since the Spirit accomplishes a more vital *koinōnia* than any natural community. Nevertheless, unity in covenant (even the covenant of grace) is different from unity in essence, and the essence of generic humanity is different from the essence of a specific historical person.

In this formulation, it is impossible to view justification as a "legal fiction," since the righteousness that is imputed is Christ's actual ("acquired") obedience,

---

81. McCormack, *What's at Stake*, 109.
82. Ibid., 110.

performed not merely by a fellow human but by the representative head of the covenant people, acting officially not just for himself but as a public person.

Yet there is a further benefit. There is a tendency in evangelical theology to treat justification as one doctrine among others to which the effective and transformative aspect must be added in order to have a "balanced" soteriology. Implicitly, justification is treated as necessary for one problem: how we receive a new status before God, while regeneration and sanctification are treated as the solution to a different (and often, it seems, more important) problem: how we are transformed morally. I share McCormack's concern to see forensic justification as the communicative source of the new creation *as a whole*. That judicious language of the Westminster Confession (chap. 13) reminds us that believers are justified "not for anything wrought in them or done by them, but for Christ's sake alone." Not even Christ's indwelling of the believer can be the basis for justification, but merely his active and passive obedience on our behalf. Treating justification as the legal ground of mystical union helps to preserve the point, and the elimination of any notion of infused habits pulls up the last remnants of medieval ontology.

As I elaborated in the previous chapter, Paul not only makes the believer's moral renewal an inevitable consequence of the forensic absolution pronounced in justification (linking Rom. 5 and 6); he also treats justification specifically as a speech-act analogous to ex nihilo creation itself in Romans 4 (v. 17). God creates a new world by speaking the gospel into unbelief, not only in justification but also in every aspect of our individual and corporate life, and not only once but also throughout our pilgrimage. The Word that is spoken in effectual calling is not only a discourse *about* justification, but *is* God's announcement of the justification of the sinner, received by faith. Yet, as in creation, there is both the initiating ex nihilo fiat, "Let there be . . . !" and the Spirit's agency within creation, bringing about the declaration's perlocutionary effect: "Let the earth bring forth . . . !"

This point is hardly unique to McCormack, of course; it is emphasized by Lutheran and Reformed theologies generally.[83] Nevertheless, it demands a more thorough critique of the "infused habits" ontology, as McCormack suggests. It is precisely in the covenant of grace that we come to participate in this kind of humanity that Christ mediates, not by mere imitation nor by an ontological participation that would make the believer or the church an extension of the incarnation, but by sharing an inheritance that belongs to Christ by right and to us by gift. It is an inheritance communicated not directly (by imitation or fusion), but by the Spirit through the means of grace.

83. The Canons of Dort (in *Ecumenical Creeds and Reformed Confessions*) express this view of regeneration, especially in the Third and Fourth Heads of Doctrine, arts. 11–12, comparing it to creation and the resurrection from the dead. Although art. 11 says that the Spirit "infuses new qualities into the will," this is not a medieval notion of infused habits, but simply a manner of expressing the impartation of new life from a source external to the person who is "dead in sins." This source is identified as the Spirit, and while regeneration is not "effected *merely* by the external preaching of the gospel, by moral suasion, or such a mode of operation that, after God has performed His part, it still remains in the power of man to be regenerated or not," it is not represented here as accomplished apart from or prior to the external preaching of the gospel.

Therefore, we can affirm with McCormack that "the horticultural/organic images employed in the New Testament" for our union and participation with Christ "should be understood, I think, as metaphors that successfully bear witness to the intimacy of that relation but mislead if taken more literally."[84] Of course, *all* of the terms that Scripture employs for justification and union are metaphors. The juridical, accounting, and clothing metaphors as well as the organic, familial, political, and bodily ones are analogies. Only a misunderstanding of the role of analogies would lead us to conclude that any of them are less than true, but they must all be equally affirmed without reducing one set to the other.

There is indeed an initiating moment of new life, but it is the result of the justifying verdict that one receives through faith, by the effectual calling of the Spirit. It is not as if Paul has no ontology; for him "the ethical is itself ontological," which requires a "covenant ontology."[85] Instead of playing the ontological and the forensic off against each other, McCormack insists that forensicism itself is "deeply ontological."

> At the very root of forensic thinking lies the recognition that human being is the function of a decision which gives rise to a willed relation. Human being is the function of a decision God *made* in eternity past in his electing grace. And it is a function of a decision God *makes* in time in justifying the ungodly. The former is the ground of the latter; the latter actualizes the content of the former in time.[86]

Doubtless, such a covenant ontology can only represent a misguided reversion to an alleged Scotist voluntarism from the RO perspective. However, a theology that attempts to give due attention to the biblical emphases of creation ex nihilo, election, covenant, and free grace will necessarily interpret the Creator-creature relationship in terms of God's sovereign freedom to enter into relationships that are not necessary or natural but willed—not in absolute freedom, understood as unmotivated by God's nature, but apart from any external conditions.[87]

A FINAL COMPARISON AND CONTRAST

Drawing together my principal critique of more Neoplatonist versions of participation, I will conclude this chapter with a brief discussion of analogy, organi-

84. Ibid.
85. McCormack, *What's at Stake*, 113.
86. Ibid., 115. This will no doubt add fuel to the fire of Milbank's critique of Reformation theology as hopelessly enmeshed in Scotist voluntarism, but by itself this point was also affirmed by Lombard and Aquinas, in contrast to an Origenist and Erigenist theory of a necessary ontological participation of creation (at least the intellectual or spiritual aspect) in God's being (i.e., emanationism).
87. However, if this were a radical (nominalist-univocalist) voluntarism, there would be no connection between God's being and God's willing. By contrast, I would maintain that while God can only will that which is consistent with the divine nature, this leaves open a whole range of free decisions for God that are not absolutely necessary to that nature.

cism, the relation of nature and grace, essence and energies, and justification and union.

Analogy and Participation

The doctrine of analogy runs like a thread throughout my proposal, as a challenge to any blurring of the Creator-creature distinction. RO also advocates analogy over univocity. However, whereas theologians like Erich Przywara and Balthasar view analogy as a guardian of creation ex nihilo against Neoplatonism's scale of being, RO interprets analogy more in the direction of affinity and Neoplatonism.[88] For example, Przywara states the implication of the doctrine of analogy that Milbank might (wrongly, I suggest) associate with a nominalist conception of the God-world relation: "Creation, in spite of its innermost dependence upon God, is endowed with its own separate essence and separate existence. God is wholly real, and yet the creation is in its own way real also."[89]

At the end of the day, RO seems to represent a different kind of univocity than nominalism, but a univocity just the same, since created being participates ontologically in uncreated being as such. Where RO treats univocity as a *separation* of the creation from the Creator, this move has typically been treated in the history of theology as a *confusion* of uncreated and created reality.

The RO school (especially Milbank) is bold in its exhortation to return to the wells of Christian Neoplatonism. By contrast, Lossky and Ware attempt to exonerate the East from Neoplatonic taint, and for all of his sympathetic and learned contributions to patristic research, Balthasar nevertheless held that the Platonic legacy often provided a scheme alien to the economy of grace. Balthasar explained:

> The deepest longing of man is to ascend to God, to become like God, indeed to become equal to God. . . . In all peoples an estate, a class, a caste, has formed that was meant to give visible, representative and, as it were, sacramental expression to this general longing. But we know that the snake got a hold of this very innermost drive of man to press on to God, and poisoned it. Original sin does not sit somewhere on the periphery of human nature.

88. In his definitive study of the doctrine of analogy, E. L. Mascall noted that on one hand, analogy "postulates between God and the world a distinction than which none could be more ultimate and unconditional, in another sense it brings them into a relation more intimate than any other doctrine has ever postulated. In its unqualified assertion that God is self-existent and that every other being depends entirely on him, it leaves no room for any semi-divine intermediaries between God and the world. No system of hierarchically graded aeons cascading down in a series of steadily diminishing divinity, no *nous* or World-Soul neither fully divine nor yet exactly finite, no Arian Logos near enough to God to be able to make a world and yet far enough from God to demean himself to so lowly a work, nothing whatever to bridge the gulf between Being that is self-existent and being that is altogether dependent, except the sheer omnipotent fiat of God himself" (*Existence and Analogy* [London: Longmans, Green, 1949], 124). I am grateful to Edward T. Oakes, S.J., for pointing this out in his *Pattern of Redemption* (New York: Continuum, 1994), 25–26 n. 17.

89. Erich Przywara, *Polarity*, trans. A. C. Bouquet (Oxford: Oxford University Press, 1935), 54; quoted by Oakes, *Pattern of Redemption*, 37.

206 Covenant and Salvation

Rather, the very promise *"eritis sicut dii"* [You shall be like gods (Gen. 3:5 Vulg.)] is the perversion of the original core of this nature itself.[90]

This false promise lies at the heart of Plato's Divided Line.[91] In this approach, the soul becomes the site of divinity. Balthasar continues:

> Thus one finds in one's human nature a place—perhaps only a point, but this point suffices—where one can, as it were, traffic with God "religiously," on the same footing, a place where a mystical *identity* obtains between Creator and creature. Now to reach this mysterious point of identity requires all kinds of strenuous effort: the earthly and temporal now seems in the schema to be only an external husk that envelops and hides the inner kernel—a husk which must be shattered ascetically, "denied," and made transparent. The perfected and knowing exercitant looks through all this [outer husk] as mere appearance, for all non-identity with the divine is basically a non-being; and this applies as well therefore to the constricted ego and its individuality.[92]

Only the doctrine of analogy can preserve us from this fatal error of Platonism.[93]

The church fathers were also infected by this virus, too enthusiastic about the potential of Greek philosophy as preparation for the gospel, according to Balthasar.[94] For Dionysius and Maximus, despite a formal adherence, "the Trinity plays almost no role whatever in the living-out of the Christian life. In fact what Maximus does is to get past the Cappadocians and Nicea and consciously link up with the Origenist schema of Logos theology."[95]

> Closely bound up with this is their version of the incarnation, which despite the Antiochenes and Nestorius, constantly was inclined to a docetic and Eutychian view. The incarnation is consequently thought of as the most extreme point of the "egression" of God from himself. The self-emptying (*kenōsis*) appears as God's self-alienation in the service of fetching the world back home to the Godhead. . . . In this schema the incarnation must appear as something provisional and transitional. The resurrection of the flesh, formally confessed and maintained, appears like a disturbance of the systematic lines and usually was subtilized in one or another form.[96]

Hence come "its asceticism and mysticism, . . . a movement of the ascending, step-by-step return of the world potencies into God, unambiguously away from the material to the spiritual. Spiritualization, presented in a thousand different

---

90. Oakes, *Pattern of Redemption*, 110, quoting Hans Urs von Balthasar, "Patristik, Scholastik und wir," *Theologie der Zeit* 3 (1939): 65–104, esp. 69 ("The Fathers, the Scholastics, and Ourselves," trans. Edward T. Oakes, in *Communio* 24 [Summer 1997] and online).
91. Oakes, *Pattern of Redemption*, 112.
92. Ibid.
93. Ibid., 113.
94. Ibid., 115.
95. Ibid., 116.
96. Ibid., 119.

colorations, is the basic tendency of the patristic epoch," with early monasticism already providing "the peril of this movement."[97]

In the face of these dangers, analogy kept theology from the shoals of pantheism.[98] However, to the extent that Platonic notions of participation dominate, as in "Russian Sophia speculation," the Creator-creature distinction is blurred. (It is worth noting that John Milbank draws extensively on Sergius Bulgakov, one of the chief thinkers in this circle to which Balthasar refers.)[99] Balthasar continues:

> In this way the fundamental deficiency of the whole Platonic schematic is revealed: it is able to be an excellent expression of the *supernatural* relation between the God of grace and the engraced creature (to put it in Christian terms). Grace is of course essentially "participation" in the divine nature, but [the Platonic schema] is not able sufficiently to clarify the relationship of the two *natures* [divine and human] that lies at the basis of every act of grace.[100]

"And so it happens that in all forms of Platonic-Christian thinking creation (nature) and the Fall of sin have a secret, if often mostly unspoken, affinity." Nature and grace become identified with the matter-spirit dualism, and this danger is present in patristic theologies.[101]

Organicism

Organic analogies of insemination and growth, vine and branches, head and body, are replete in Reformed treatments of this union, but they are recognized as *analogies* for a covenantally constituted union. By contrast, theologies of participation that set the organic against the forensic or simply absorb the latter into the former often end up interpreting "organic" in literal, substantialist terms.

The description that Charles Hodge offered of Schleiermacher's "Christian pantheism" seems all too relevant with respect to contemporary theologies (however radically orthodox by name) that set the organic and intrinsic against the forensic and extrinsic. According to Hodge's summary,

> The incarnation of God is continued in the Church; and this new principle of "divine-human life" descends from Christ to the members of his Church, as naturally and as much by a process of organic development, as humanity, derived from Adam, unfolded itself in his descendants. Christ, therefore, saves us not so much by what He did, as by what He is. He made no satisfaction

97. Ibid., 120.
98. Ibid., 122.
99. See John Milbank, *Being Reconciled: Ontology and Pardon* (London and New York: Routledge, 2003), 113, 128, and esp. his appeal to sophiology on xii, 131–35, 208. Sergius (Sergeï Nikolaevich) Bulgakov's principal works, now available in English, are his dogmatic trilogy *On Divine Humanity. The Lamb of God* (2007), *The Bride of the Lamb* (2002), and *The Comforter*, trans. Boris Jakim (Grand Rapids: Eerdmans, 2004), which is perhaps the most significant, especially on the issues addressed here.
100. Oakes, *Pattern of Redemption,* 125, quoting von Balthasar, "Patristik, Scholastik und wir," 90.
101. Oakes, *Pattern of Redemption,* 125, quoting von Balthasar, "Patristik, Scholastik und wir," 91.

to the divine justice; no expiation for sin; no fulfillment of the law. There is, therefore, really no justification, no real pardon even, in the ordinary sense of the word. There is a healing of the soul, and with that healing the removal of the evils incident to disease. Those who become partakers of this new principle of life, which is truly human and truly divine, become one with Christ. . . . What the Scriptures and the Church attribute to the Spirit working with the freedom of a personal agent, when and where he sees fit, this system attributes to the "theanthropic-life" of Christ, working as a new force according to the natural laws of development. . . . This system may be adopted as a matter of opinion, but it cannot be an object of faith. And therefore it cannot support the hopes of a soul conscious of guilt.[102]

Remarkably similar to McCormack's characterization of Torrance's approach (appealing to Calvin's more Cyrillian eucharistic teaching to interpret his forensic doctrine of justification), Hodge notes that the Erlangen theologian J. H. A. Ebrard "finds his doctrine of regeneration, not in what Calvin and some few of the Reformed theologians taught under that head, but in what they teach of the Lord's Supper, and of the mystical union."[103] "But they depart from Scripture and from the faith of the Church universal," Hodge judges, "in substituting 'the theanthropic nature of Christ,' 'his divine-human life,' 'generic humanity healed and exalted to the power of a divine life' (i.e., deified), for the Holy Ghost. . . . The Christ within (as some of the Friends also teach), is, according to this system, all the Christ we have. Ebrard, therefore, in one view, identifies regeneration and justification": we are pronounced just on the basis of this new life infused.[104]

Milbank's affinity for the Catholic Tübingen school and the Lux Mundi movement, and the revival of Osiandrian tendencies in the New Finnish perspective, reflect some common influences, particularly those of conservative neo-Hegelianism. Similar to Hodge's characterization of the mediating theologians, Berkhof summarizes:

> The view of the mediating theologians . . . is cast in a pantheistic mold. After the incarnation there are no two natures in Christ, but only a divine-human nature, a fusion of divine and human life. In regeneration a part of that divine-human life passes over into the sinner. This does not require a separate operation of the Holy Spirit whenever a sinner is regenerated. The new life has been communicated to the Church once for all, is now the permanent possession of the Church, and passes from the Church into the individual. This view ignores the legal aspect of the work of Christ entirely. Moreover, it makes it impossible to hold that any one could be regenerated before the divine-human life of Christ came into existence. The Old Testament saints cannot have been regenerated. Schleiermacher is the father of this view.[105]

---

102. Charles Hodge, *Systematic Theology*, 3 vols. (New York: Charles Scribner's Sons, 1872), 3:21–25.
103. Ibid., 23.
104. Ibid., 24. It is worth noting that this identification of justification and regeneration is also maintained by N. T. Wright in *What Saint Paul Really Said: Was Paul of Tarsus the Real Founder of Christianity?* (Grand Rapids: Eerdmans, 1997), 113–29.
105. Louis Berkhof, *Systematic Theology*, 4th ed. (1939; Grand Rapids: Eerdmans, 1941), 478.

For Schleiermacher, the Holy Spirit is "the spirit of the community," but given his modalism, it is not surprising that the Spirit is simply collapsed into Christ.[106] In Schleiermacher, notes Herman Bavinck, conversion and justification are comprehended under regeneration as two sides of the same coin, seen from the human and divine perspectives.[107] A. Neander, C. E. Nitzsch, H. Martensen, J. Lange, J. Ebrard, J. Beck, and others held that justification was "on the basis, not of the imputed, but of the infused righteousness of Christ, so that it is not only a judicial but also a communicative and sanctifying act of God and a preview (πρόληψις) of the future."[108]

I realize that the dogmatic conclusions of neo-Protestantism and the mediating theologies differ at important points from the views of many today who advocate a participatory over a forensic system. However, they share some of the same ontological assumptions. Although "meeting a stranger" versus "overcoming estrangement" can serve as no more than heuristic devices, the typology does at least point to different habits of thought that confront each other in these current (indeed, recurring) debates. Tuomo Mannermaa and his circle have with great erudition explored the Kantian and neo-Kantian assumptions of the so-called Luther renaissance led by Karl Holl. However, it is anachronistic to suggest that confessional Lutheranism departed from Luther as a result of Kantian sympathies.[109] John Milbank, of course, presses it back to nominalism's "extrinsicism," where God is a reality alongside creaturely reality rather than its ground of existence.[110]

However, in a covenantal ontology, the divine-human relation can be no more easily reduced to the "Kantian" ethical than to the "Platonic" essential. For us to belong to God, and for God to belong to us, there must indeed exist not only an extrinsic relation of Justifier and justified, but also a divine indwelling that is as personal and organic as it is forensic and judicial. From beginning to end, in creation and redemption, in justification and sanctification, in the new birth and glorification, grace is God's energetic Word at work both in making pronouncements in the Son and bringing about their intended effect in the Spirit.

Nature and Grace

Finally, it should be pointed out that Milbank and RO generally are indebted not only to a broader medieval ontology for their definition of grace, but are particularly shaped by the work of Maurice Blondel and Henri de Lubac. Reacting against the implicit semi-Pelagianism of late medieval (nominalist) theology, these French Catholic theologians were formative for the thinking that led up to the Second Vatican Council.

---

106. Ibid., 467.
107. Bavinck, *Reformed Dogmatics*, 3:552.
108. Ibid., 553.
109. Tuomo Mannermaa, *Christ Present in Faith: Luther's Doctrine of Justification*, ed. Kirsi Stjerna (Minneapolis: Fortress, 2005), 1.
110. Milbank, *Being Reconciled*, 223 n. 4.

To summarize all too briefly, their argument was that by positing, alongside the supernatural, a "pure nature" of purely human ends achieved through purely human efforts, which somehow might mysteriously save those who failed to do what lies within them, post-Tridentine theologies were still susceptible to charges of semi-Pelagianism even though their distinction between pure nature and supernatural grace was designed to refute that Reformation critique. Instead, de Lubac insisted, human nature is itself oriented to the supernatural. Nature is already "engraced."[111] "Yet," as Robert Jenson points out, "an ambiguity remains, of the very sort over which a Western theology of grace has so often come to grief. De Lubac is compelled to say, 'The idea of the possible gift presupposes . . . the idea of a certain fundamental and interior aptitude for receiving that gift.'"[112] Positing "two initiatives of grace," one that "brings [humans] into being" and another that "calls" them, deepens a fundamentally problematic ontology of grace, Jenson observes.

> De Lubac, with most theology Protestant or Catholic, thus presumes that creation is itself effected not by a divine call but by a prior divine act of other sort. . . . So long as this presumption is maintained, the problem about nature and grace is insoluble. If we suppose with de Lubac that a human nature itself uncalled is antecedently apt for the call of grace, we will eventually be brought to one or another "semi-Pelagianism." If we suppose, with those de Lubac rebuked, that a nature itself uncalled is antecedently neutral to the call of grace, we will, as de Lubac showed, still be brought to a kind of "semi-Pelagianism," only by a more circuitous route.[113]

However, de Lubac himself opens his own door to "semi-Pelagianism" by proposing that we are not only "open" to grace by nature, but also possess an "aptitude" for it as well.

By contrast, Jenson rightly argues, "it is not only our salvation that is accomplished by God's address, but our being as such." Both in creation and in redemption, nature is "open" to God, but this does not imply aptitude. Jenson has put his finger on the more fundamental ontological problem: the failure to recognize that "both nature and grace are aspects of one conversation conducted by God with us."[114]

I would only add further that Reformed theology has always affirmed that nature is "open" to God in this sense. There is no autonomous "nature" with its own immanent telos. Augustine's maxim, "You have made us for yourself, and our hearts are restless till they find their rest in you,"[115] finds clear expression in the first question and answer both of Calvin's Geneva Catechism and the Westminster Shorter Catechism: "Man's chief end is to glorify God and to enjoy him

---

111. See especially Henri de Lubac's magisterial work, *The Mystery of the Supernatural*, trans. R. Sheed (New York: Herder & Herder, 1967).
112. Robert Jenson, *Systematic Theology*, vol. 2 (New York: Oxford University Press, 1999), 67.
113. Ibid., 68.
114. Ibid.
115. Augustine, *Confessions*, 1.1.

forever." Yet the Reformed scholastics distinguished between natural and moral ability, so that human nature as such is transcendentally oriented, yet morally incapable of realizing that aim. Hence, the idolatry, lack of meaning, boredom, and other effects of a frustrated natural telos. The gospel comes not to give humans a supernatural aim, but to liberate them from the state of sin, fear, alienation, and condemnation, which keep them from realizing their created telos. This is accomplished not by a supernatural elevation of nature (as in the medieval ontology advanced by Milbank), but by the liberation of nature—adding nothing new, while making all things new. The Word does this, which is to say, the Father does this in the Son and by the Spirit. As Jenson adds, "'Let there be . . .' and 'Christ is risen' are but two utterances of God within one dramatically coherent discourse. A creature who exists by hearing the first is indeed open to the second, in a straightforward way that requires no dithering about 'aptitudes' [habits]."[116] Jenson's characteristically Lutheran emphasis on the Word as communicative power helpfully qualifies (perhaps at some points even contradicts) other aspects of his system that seem closer to the paradigm of overcoming estrangement in its neo-Hegelian version.

In the Roman Catholic understanding, shared by RO, the ontological is reduced to the ethical after all, since final justification is understood as the result of one's cooperation with grace, although "ethical" in this case refers to our own works. However, if love is equivalent to law—its apt summary, as Jesus, Paul, and John have told us—then justification by love is the same as justification by our personal fulfillment of the law-covenant. From the covenantal perspective, however, the divine stranger comes to us not as an essence to be participated in but as a Father, a Son, and a Spirit, who each in their own unique and unrepeatable way initiate us into "the mystery hidden for ages in God who created all things; so that through the church the wisdom of God in its rich variety might now be made known to the rulers and authorities in the heavenly places. This was in accordance with the eternal purpose that he has carried out in Christ Jesus our Lord, in whom we have access to God in boldness and confidence through faith in him" (Eph. 3:9–12).

Although the ontological boundary will never be breached, it is precisely by overcoming the ethical enmity that results from being law-breakers that a new relationship of intimate and organic union can emerge. In other words, *justification establishes the legal basis without which our relationship with God could only remain ethical and merely legally defined, as under the curse of the law.*

Essence and Energies

At least in Eastern Orthodox theology there is a distinction between God's essence and energies, which has close parallels to the formulation that one typically finds in the classic Reformed systems, namely, that God cannot be known

---

116. Jenson, *Systematic Theology*, 2:68.

in his essence, but only in his works. It is not the being of God, but the economy of God—specifically, God as he is known in Christ according to the covenant of grace—that presents the only safe passage to a God who is hidden in inaccessible glory. However, the Eastern doctrine helpfully reminds us that God's "works" are not restricted to the creaturely effects of divine power, but include God's "workings"—for example, the speech-acts that are neither an emanation of the divine essence nor created entities, but divine actions.

Vladimir Lossky argues that the priority that Western Trinitarianism places on the divine essence over the divine persons gives rise to a somewhat different mystical theology of union:

> If one speaks of God it is always, for the Eastern Church, in the concrete: "The God of Abraham, of Isaac and of Jacob; the God of Jesus Christ." It is always the Trinity: Father, Son, and Holy Ghost. When, on the contrary, the common nature assumes the first place in our conception of Trinitarian dogma the religious reality of God in Trinity is inevitably obscured in some measure and gives place to a certain philosophy of essence. Likewise, the idea of beatitude has acquired in the West a slightly intellectual emphasis, presenting itself in the guise of a vision of the essence of God. . . . Indeed, in the doctrinal conditions peculiar to the West all properly theocentric speculation runs the risk of considering the nature before the persons and becoming a mysticism of "the divine abyss," as in the *Gottheit* of Meister Eckhart; of becoming an impersonal apophaticism of the divine-nothingness prior to the Trinity. Thus by a paradoxical circuit we return through Christianity to the mysticism of the neo-platonists.[117]

By contrast, says Lossky,

> In the tradition of the Eastern Church there is no place for a theology, and even less for a mysticism, of the divine essence. The goal of Orthodox spirituality, the blessedness of the Kingdom of Heaven, is not the vision of the essence, but, above all, a participation in the divine life of the Holy Trinity; the deified state of the co-heirs of the divine nature, gods created after the uncreated God, possessing by grace all that the Holy Trinity possesses by nature.[118]

Of course, Reformed theology would cast a suspicious glance at the last sentence in Lossky's quote. Yet the distinction between essence and energies itself may reflect a point of convergence. Just as the rays are not the sun itself, yet are not mere effects of the sun, the energies of God are neither God's essence nor simply creaturely realities. "Thus, according to St. Gregory Palamas, 'to say that the divine nature is communicable not in itself but through its energy, is to remain within the bounds of right devotion.'"[119] "In the same way, St. Basil talks of the

117. Vladimir Lossky, *The Mystical Theology of the Eastern Church* (Crestwood, NY: St. Vladimir's Seminary Press, 1976), 65.
118. Ibid., 70.
119. Ibid.

role of the energies in manifesting, opposing them to the unknowable essence: 'It is by His energies'—he says—'that we say we know our God; we do not assert that we can come near to the essence itself, for His energies descend to us, but His essence remains unapproachable.'"[120] "St. Maximus the Confessor expresses the same idea when he says: 'God is communicable in what He imparts to us; but He is not communicable in the incommunicability of His essence.'"[121]

However, the Western concentration on the divine essence recognizes only that which either belongs to this essence or that which is merely the creaturely effect of which he is the cause. "The philosophy of God as pure act cannot admit anything to be God that is not the very essence of God. From this point of view God is, as it were, limited by His essence; that which is not essence does not belong to the divine being, is not God." Thus deification is rendered impossible.[122] Instead of locating union at the level of energies, the West was forced to think in terms of union with the divine essence (often leading to pantheistic conceptions) by means of a causal scheme of infused habits.

Lossky points out that whereas the West eschews the essence-energies distinction, focusing on the essence, it introduces its own distinctions between nature and supernature, "the infused virtues, and habitual and actual grace." The West talks about "created grace," as if there is some supernatural realm somewhere between the Creator and creation.

> Eastern tradition knows no such supernatural order between God and the created world, adding, as it were, to the latter a new creation. It recognizes no distinction, or rather division, save that between the created and the uncreated. For eastern tradition the created supernatural has no existence. That which western theology calls by the name of the *supernatural* signifies for the East the *uncreated*—the divine energies ineffably distinct from the essence of God.[123]

On the basis of these moves, the West, according to Lossky, adopted a causal paradigm in its doctrine of grace.

> The difference consists in the fact that the western conception of grace implies the idea of causality, grace being represented as an effect of the divine Cause, exactly as in the act of creation; while for eastern theology there is a natural procession, the energies, shining forth eternally from the divine essence. It is in creation alone that God acts as cause, in producing a new subject called to participate in the divine fullness; preserving it, saving it, granting grace to it, and guiding it towards its final goal. In the energies *He is, He exists*, He eternally manifests Himself. Here we are faced with a mode of divine being to which we accede in receiving grace; which, moreover, in the created and perishable world, is the presence of the uncreated and eternal

120. Ibid., 71–72.
121. Ibid., 72–73.
122. Ibid., 77.
123. Ibid., 88.

light, the real omnipresence of God in all things, which is something more
than His causal presence—"the light shineth in the darkness, and the darkness comprehendeth it not" (John i, 5).[124]

According to this paradigm, the divine-human relationship is not conceived in
terms of cause and effect, but in a more pneumatologically oriented gift of "interior light." Although casual analogies are replete in Eastern as well as Western
reflection (and we can hardly dismiss such terminology entirely), I share Lossky's
concern for a more relational (Trinitarian) account. Instead of seeing God as a
sole agent acting upon the world, we should recognize the Spirit as the one at
work within creation to bring about the perlocutionary effect of the Word spoken by the Father in the Son. Similarly Lossky argues:

> The energies, bestowed upon Christians by the Holy Spirit, no longer
> appear as exterior causes, but as grace, an interior light, which transforms
> nature in deifying it. "God is called Light," says St. Gregory Palamas, "not
> with reference to His essence, but to His energy." . . . Perfect vision of the
> deity, perceptible in its uncreated light, is "the mystery of the eighth day";
> it belongs to the age to come. But those who are worthy attain to the vision
> of "the Kingdom of God come with power" even in this life, a vision such
> as the three apostles saw on Mount Tabor.[125]

I will return to the synergism that is a key component of the Eastern doctrine in
chapter 12, but the point to be made here is that the view that Lossky presents
is more richly pneumatological and eschatological—and the distinction between
essence and energies is an essential reason for that emphasis.

In my view, it is this essence-energies distinction (instead of nature-supernature),
the emphasis on the personal properties of each member of the Godhead (rather
than that a tendency to isolate the essential unity), and the consequently vital pneumatological mediation that represents convergences with Reformed theology and
preserves Orthodox *theōsis* from the always-immanent threat of pantheism that we
encounter in the history of Western mysticism, which I have identified with RO
and the New Finnish perspective (including Jenson's treatment).

For his own part, Jenson concludes, "Now I myself think that Palamas's wall
between the energies and the essence is disastrous, finally also to Palamas's own
chief concern, but that is beside the present point."[126] Although the infinite cannot be predicated of the substance of the finite, Mannermaa argued, "the infinite
is present in, permeating the substance of the finite in a nonaccidental way."[127]
It is not clear what is meant by "in a nonaccidental way," but if it means that the

124. Ibid., 88–89.
125. Ibid., 220.
126. Robert W. Jenson, "Response to Mark Seifrid, Paul Metzger, and Carl Trueman on Finnish
Luther Research," *Westminster Theological Journal* 65, no. 2 (2003): 246.
127. Dennis Bielfeldt, "Response to Sammeli Juntunen, 'Luther and Metaphysics'," in Carl E.
Braaten and Robert W. Jenson, eds., *Union with Christ: The New Finnish Interpretation of Luther*
(Grand Rapids: Eerdmans, 1998), 165–66.

substance of the finite is permeated by the infinite in a necessary and essential manner, then the *analogia entis* seems threatened with pantheistic implications.

Elsewhere, Mannermaa writes, "When a human being is united with God, he or she becomes a participant not only in the human but also in the divine nature of Christ. At the same time, a kind of 'communication of attributes' occurs: the attributes of the essence of God—such as righteousness, life, power, etc.—are communicated to the Christian."[128] Aside from the seemingly arbitrary communication of some attributes of divinity ("such as righteousness, life, power, etc.") rather than all of them (such as omnipresence, omniscience, omnipotence, etc.), the weakness of this typically Western account is that one must either choose participation in essence or nonparticipation.

Once a distinction is drawn between essence and energies, the latter conceived as works of God that are nevertheless *God-at-work* (and not just creaturely effects of divine causal action), there is a greater possibility for convergence with a covenantal account of participation. The next chapter will explore this assertion more concretely with respect to effectual calling.

To conclude, I will repeat the point that for all of its philosophical sophistication, the ontology proposed by RO seems, at the end of the day, too thin. Like its medieval predecessors, RO knows only of a *gratia gratum faciens* (a grace that makes us righteous), while Reformation theology recognizes both a purely forensic justification *and* a mystical union that results in a decisive renewal and lifelong process of mortification and vivification: dying and rising with Christ. Infusionism has never generated a forensic space in its ontology, but under the forensic canopy of Trinitarian speech-acts, the transformative has been regarded as a necessary correlate to that justification which brings all of God's good gifts in its wake.

---

128. Mannermaa, *Christ Present in Faith*, 8.

Chapter Ten

Covenantal Ontology
and Effectual Calling

With effectual calling or the new birth, we encounter the first site of impact from the justifying Word as it moves through the *ordo*, from the juridical to the transformative. As I have already intimated, it is under this locus that the contest over contrasting ontologies can be won or lost. Even if it is granted that justification is an exclusively forensic declaration, the rest of the *ordo* has sometimes been treated even in Reformed theology as the consequence of an entirely different event—namely, an infusion of a new *habitus* (disposition) prior to effectual calling.

My argument in this chapter is that this later formulation reintroduced a medieval ontology of infused habits at this point in the *ordo*, however much it was distinguished from justification. As a consequence, the potential for a schizophrenic ontology presented itself: justification was still regarded as strictly forensic, but just for this reason had to be securely walled off from the rest of the *ordo*, which was attributed to regeneration. Building on McCormack's suggestions in the previous chapter, I contend here that we should recover the earlier identification of the new birth with effectual calling and treat justification as the forensic source for all of the benefits that flow from union with Christ. Eliminating the distinction between regeneration and effectual calling entails the elimination of any appeal to the category of infused habits. Effectual calling *is* regeneration (the new birth), and although the Spirit brings about this response when and where he will, it is brought about through the ministry of the gospel, as Romans 10:17; James 1:18; and 1 Peter 1:23 explicitly state. Through the announcement of the external Word, declaring the absolution, the Spirit gives us the faith to receive the verdict, which in turn begins in us from that moment on the fruit of *faith*: evangelical repentance, mortification, vivification, sanctification, and works of love. There is no justification apart from faith, but this faith itself is given by God through the external ministry of the gospel that the Spirit makes inwardly effective. The gospel does what it says, because it is not simply a saving message concerning Christ (illocutionary act) but is attended by the Spirit's vivifying agency (perlocutionary effect).

First, drawing on Kevin Vanhoozer's suggestive appropriation of speech act theory for understanding the effectual call, I propose that *a communicative paradigm offers richer possibilities for affirming the monergistic and Trinitarian conclusions of traditional Reformed theology than are possible in a purely causal scheme.* Second, challenging the ontology of infused habits that funds a later Reformed distinction between regeneration (direct and unmediated) and effectual calling (mediated by the Word), I will argue that *the doctrine of justification gives rise to a rival ontology that is communicative and covenantal all the way down.*[1]

"THOSE HE PREDESTINED HE ALSO CALLED": SOVEREIGN COMMUNICATION

In its defense of *sola gratia*, in its controversies with Rome, Socinianism, and Arminianism, Reformed theology was emphatically monergistic: that is, salvation in its entirety can be ascribed to God and his grace alone. Given the inherited ontology shared by all parties, which was essentially causal (patterned on physics: the movement of objects in space), Reformed theologians went to great pains to insist that regeneration or effectual calling was not an impersonal operation of one object upon another, nor coercive.

Effectual but Not Coercive

The connection between election and calling is well-attested, both within the Pauline corpus (Rom. 9:6–24; Eph. 1:4–13; 2 Thess. 2:13–15; 2 Tim. 1:9) and elsewhere (John 6:29, 37, 44, 63–64; 15:16, 19; Acts 13:48; 1 Pet. 1:2; 2 Pet. 1:10), and it proceeds as the execution of an eternal covenant of redemption within the context of a historical covenant of grace. As Kevin Vanhoozer relates, "By the seventeenth century, the effectual call had gained privileged status in the

---

1. I have already presented this case with respect to the God-world relation in creation and providence (see Michael Horton, *Lord and Servant: A Covenant Christology* (Louisville, KY: Westminster John Knox, 2005), chap. 3.

ordo salutis, for the call effects one's union with Christ and is the beginning from which all other blessings flow."[2]

From the beginning Reformed theology has also understood the divine call in terms of an outward call, by which God summons the whole world to Christ through the preaching of the gospel, and an illumination by the Spirit, drawing the elect inwardly to embrace it. Yet it is crucial to recognize that, according to this view, the internal call is not distinguished from the external call in either content or form.[3] The inseparability of the preached Word and the Spirit is grounded in the ontological unity of the living Word and the Spirit. The Father preaches; the Son is preached, and the Spirit is the "inner preacher," who illumines the understanding and inclines the will to receive him.

Although the relationship between union with Christ and the means of grace (preaching and sacrament) will be explored in my next volume, it is important to add here that the gift of faith is delivered and strengthened by the Spirit through the outward means of preaching and sacrament.[4] Yet some are attracted to the light, others repelled by it. Those who do come to trust in Christ are represented as "dead in sins" (Eph. 2:1–5), unable to respond until God graciously grants them the gift of faith to freely embrace what they would otherwise reject (Isa. 65:1; John 1:13; 3:7; 6:44; Acts 13:48; 16:14; 18:10; Rom. 9:15–16; 1 Cor. 2:14; Eph. 2:1–5; 2 Tim. 1:9–10; 2:10, 19).

While on guard against synergism, Reformed theologians wanted to avoid the opposite danger of treating humans as blocks of stone, setting creation and redemption in dualistic opposition. Against any kind of Manicheism, they emphasized that grace liberates rather than destroys nature. Of course, the battleground for such debates was often a strong libertarian notion of free will wedded to covenantal nomism insisting that God could not command anything of which human beings were incapable. In this context, the Reformers and their successors offered some useful distinctions, some of which were announced in Luther's preface to his Galatians commentary. First, one had to distinguish between "things heavenly" and "things earthly." According to the former, even those destitute of new life and therefore given to idolatry and confusion were nevertheless capable of remarkable accomplishments in the arts and sciences. In

2. Kevin J. Vanhoozer, "Effectual Call or Causal Effect? Summons, Sovereignty and Supervenient Grace," in *First Theology: God, Scripture and Hermeneutics* (Downers Grove, IL: InterVarsity Press, 2002), 99.

3. The Reformed scholastic, Johann Heinrich Heidegger, for example, writes, "The word is the same which man preaches and which the Spirit writes on the heart. There is strictly one calling, but its cause and medium is twofold: instrumental, man preaching the word outwardly; principal, the Holy Spirit writing it inwardly in the heart." Quoted by Heinrich Heppe, *Reformed Dogmatics*, rev. and ed. E. Bizer, trans. G. T. Thomson (London: G. Allen & Unwin, 1950; repr., London: Wakeman Trust, 2002), 518. Heidegger adds, "The first effect of calling is regeneration" (ibid.).

4. See, for instance, the Heidelberg Catechism, Q. 65: "It is by faith alone that we share in Christ and all his blessings; where then does that faith come from? A. The Holy Spirit produces it in our hearts by the preaching of the holy gospel and confirms it through our use of the holy sacraments" (*Ecumenical Creeds and Reformed Confessions* [Grand Rapids: CRC Publications, 1987], 41).

fact, Calvin labors this point in the *Institutes* against the "fanatics," whom he charges with disparaging the gifts of God in creation and the common grace of the Spirit.[5]

A second and related distinction was made between righteousness before fellow humans (*coram hominibus*) and righteousness before God (*coram deo*). To these the Reformed particularly added the distinction between natural and moral ability. With respect to free will, sin has so blinded the hearts and minds of human beings that they do not desire God, at least the God who is revealed in his Word and on the terms he gives. Yet precisely because they freely will this rejection of God's covenant, they are responsible. Can they do otherwise? In one sense, they can: they have the *natural* ability. In other words, the fall has not eliminated any human faculty or natural capacity. The problem is not the power to will and to do, but the *moral* determination of that willing and doing by slavery to sinful autonomy. Wills do not exist in isolation, but are the acts of the whole person, who is shaped by convictions, desires, and preferences revealing ultimate dispositions. Before God can evoke attraction rather than repulsion, the will must be freed, the mind illumined, the heart of stone turned to a heart of flesh.

For example, the Second Helvetic Confession teaches, "Therefore, in regard to evil or sin, man is not forced by God or by the devil but does evil by his own free will, and in this respect he has a most free will." In "heavenly things," he is bound in sin. "Yet in regard to earthly things, fallen man is not entirely lacking in understanding." While subjects are passive in this initial regeneration, they work actively and not passively in good works. "For they are moved by God that they may do themselves what they do. . . . The Manichaeans robbed man of all activity and made him like a stone or a block of wood. . . . Moreover, no one denies that in external things both the regenerate and the unregenerate enjoy free will," as in deciding whether to leave the house or remain at home.[6]

More precisely, the Westminster Confession states, "God hath endued the will of man with that natural liberty that it is neither forced, nor by any absolute necessity of nature determined to good or evil." Before the fall the will was entirely free to choose good or evil, but after the fall humanity "has wholly lost all ability of will to any spiritual good accompanying salvation," rendering every person "dead in sin, . . . not able, by his own strength, to convert himself, or to prepare himself thereunto."

> When God converts a sinner and translates him into the state of grace, he frees him from his natural bondage under sin and, by his grace alone, enables him freely to will and to do that which is spiritually good; yet so as that, by reason of his remaining corruption, he does not perfectly or only will that

5. Calvin, *Institutes* 2.2.15.

6. Second Helvetic Confession, chap. 9 (Free Will), in *The Book of Confessions* (Louisville, KY: General Assembly of the PC[USA], 1991).

which is good, but does also that which is evil. The will of man is made perfectly and immutably free to good alone in the state of glory only.[7]

Such statements reflect a basic Augustinian consensus, filtered through the Reformation. The Westminster divines add that God is pleased "in his appointed and accepted time, effectually to call, by his Word and Spirit," all of the elect "out of that state of sin and death in which they are by nature, to grace and salvation by Jesus Christ." He accomplishes this by "enlightening their minds, . . . taking away their heart of stone, . . . renewing their wills, . . . and effectually drawing them to Jesus Christ; *yet so as they come most freely, being made willing by his grace*" (emphasis added).[8]

The Synod of Dort affirmed that God's inward calling always meets with success. However, just as the fall "did not abolish the nature of the human race" but "distorted" it and led to spiritual death, "so also this divine grace of regeneration does not act in people as if they were blocks and stones; nor does it abolish the will and its properties or coerce a reluctant will by force, but spiritually revives, heals, reforms, and—in a manner at once pleasing and powerful—bends it back."[9] The will is liberated, not violated. "If it be compelled," says John Owen, "it is destroyed."[10] The classic terminology of effectual calling (rather than the more recent term, "irresistible grace") already indicates a more communicative model of divine action than causal grammars allow.

Speech-Act Theory and Effectual Calling

Unlike most conceptual schemes drawn from philosophy, communicative theory, first of all, tends to be modest in its metaphysical claims, which allows wider berth to a theological determination of metaphysical conclusions; second, it actually fits well with the kind of world that we find described for us in Scripture, namely, a reality that is from beginning to end a creation of the Word. This way of thinking, as I have already indicated, is hardly innovative: for example, as Calvin expressed it, "To the Father is attributed the effective principle of what is done, and the fountain and wellspring of all things; to the Son, wisdom, counsel, and the ordered arrangement of what is done; but to the Spirit is assigned the power and efficacy of the action."[11] Yet I wonder, with Kevin Vanhoozer, whether recent explorations in communicative theory display advantages over and beyond a traditional causal scheme in further realizing the potential for such Trinitarian and Word-oriented instincts.[12]

---

7. Westminster Confession of Faith, chap. 11, in *The Book of Confessions* (PC[USA], 1991).
8. Westminster Confession of Faith, chap. 12 (Effectual Calling), in *The Book of Confessions* (PC[USA], 1991).
9. Canons of the Synod of Dort (1618–19), in *Ecumenical Creeds and Reformed Confessions*, 135–36.
10. John Owen, *The Works of John Owen*, ed. William H. Gould, 16 vols. (Edinburgh: Banner of Truth Trust, 1965–68), 3:319.
11. Calvin, *Institutes* 1.13.18.
12. Vanhoozer, "Effectual Call or Causal Effect?

Causal or Communicative?

Two dangers to be avoided are, on the one hand, to assume that philosophical language and concepts are merely linguistic vessels that do not affect the content and, on the other, to suppose that whenever certain terms are employed, they bear the same meaning that they have in their original philosophical context. Theology has found Aristotle's categories of causality useful for a variety of reasons, but each tradition has used them for quite different conclusions.

However, medieval (especially post-Thomist) theology evidences direct dependence not only on Aristotelian *categories*, but also on the philosopher's *concept* of cause in his *Physics*. "Hence grace is," observes Vanhoozer concerning Aquinas, "'the work of God in human beings raising them above their human nature to the point where they become sharers in the divine nature.' . . . In this case [as divine assistance], grace acts on the soul 'not in the manner of an efficient cause but in the manner of a formal cause; so whiteness makes something white and justice makes someone just.'"[13]

Obviously, the Reformation represents a significant challenge to this medieval interpretation of Aristotelian causality. Yet the causal ontology that yielded the notion of infused habits has never been seriously challenged. Again, this was so for very good reasons. Distinguishing between efficient, instrumental, formal, material, and final causes allowed Reformation theologians to show the relations between, for instance, the efficient cause of grace (God), the material or meritorious cause (Christ's person and work), the means of grace (Word and sacrament), the instrumental cause (faith), and the goal or final cause of grace (God's glory in human redemption). At the same time, every conceptual toolbox comes with its own surprises, and in this case the question to be asked is whether other vocabularies can help us get the same job done somewhat better.

As we have seen, the Reformed labored the point that grace renews rather than destroys nature, that God does not operate on us as one works on stone, so that God overcomes the bondage of the will not through force but through liberation. Yet can the vocabulary of cause-and-effect make that point well? Or does it require perpetual defensive strategies against charges that they in fact deny in practice what they affirm in principle? On one hand, there is a legitimate suspicion of synergism, yet on the other, a concern to avoid a Manichean dualism between God and the world, grace and nature. Criticism of classical theism's concept of the God-world relation (which directly affects the doctrine of effectual calling) is hardly limited to those from the Arminian tradition, which is radicalized in the contemporary evangelical project known as "open theism." Moltmann also says that "we 'have to stop thinking in terms of causes at all.'"[14]

---

13. Vanhoozer, *First Theology*, 101; citing Thomas Aquinas, *ST* Ia2ae.110.2 and 112.1.

14. Vanhoozer, *First Theology*, 105, referring to Jürgen Moltmann, *God in Creation: A New Theology of Creation and the Spirit of God*, trans. Margaret Kohl (Minneapolis: Fortress, 1993), 14.

For modern theology (Schleiermacher and Tillich especially), Vanhoozer notes, we are always already related to God, so as Schleiermacher puts it, "All divine grace is always prevenient."[15] This is "overcoming estrangement"—or going the "ontological way" with a vengeance. By making everything divine, pantheism in effect acknowledges no divinity (thus reducing itself to atheism). As its corollary, a grace that is always everywhere in the same way ends up being little more than a subjective human awareness of the "sacredness" of all things. Vanhoozer continues, "For much modern theology, then, prevenient grace has become a matter of ontology." Grace is not regarded simply as a willed relation, shown to those at fault, but is simply the way things are.

> Process theology represents what is perhaps the logical conclusion of the way many non-Reformed theologians now construe the God-world relation. God is a creative participant in the course of world history, the leader of a cosmic community who seeks to persuade beings to choose the good, namely, that which leads to greater self-realization. . . . God is not the ruler of the universe but its wooer, working not with causal power but with the power of love and persuasion.[16]

Drawing on a recent concept in the philosophy of mind, Vanhoozer suggests *supervenience* as a more fruitful category. Rather than simply *intervening*, "where one kind of reality enters into another kind of reality to produce an effect that would not otherwise come about," Vanhoozer writes, "(1) the effectual call supervenes on the external call; (2) the effectual call is a speech act with a unique communicative force." Thus, God is neither "a mere physical cause" nor "an ineffectual influence."[17] In the classical model, there seems to be not only an ontological distinction but also "a fundamental dualism between Creator and creation, grace and nature."[18]

I am not sure that this does sufficient justice to the classic formulations at least of Reformed theology, which repeatedly singled out Manichean dualism and resisted quasi-deistic pictures of the God-world relation. As we see in the quotes above, Aristotelian categories were stretched, precisely to avoid any suggestion of coercion. The gap was ethical, not ontological: free will in "things earthly" was clearly affirmed, but not in "things heavenly" because of the voluntary bondage to sin and unbelief. These older theologians never conceived of the effectual call in anything other than personal terms and regarded it as the work of the Spirit *within*, not merely *upon*, the believer, winning consent and not coercing compliance. Unlike Aristotle's Unmoved Mover, the triune God was recognized as the living and active agent of regeneration. Yet even with these qualifications, one wonders if the causal model itself is to blame for the confusion.

---

15. Cited in Vanhoozer, *First Theology*, 105.
16. Ibid., 104.
17. Ibid., 106, 109.
18. Ibid., 109.

Surveying possible contemporary analogies for effectual calling (such as "downward"/"top-down"/"whole-part" or "supervienient" causation in theology-and-science discussions), and Clark Pinnock's emphasis on prevenient grace, Vanhoozer concludes that, among other deficiencies, these get us "no further than a 'general call,'" not an effectual one.[19] For example, "The incarnation, for [Arthur] Peacocke, is not a matter of God's entering a closed nexus from the outside as a stranger but of certain divine properties emerging in the man Jesus from within the natural processes of creation."[20]

So what is Vanhoozer's proposal? "In brief, I propose thinking of the God-world relation in terms of communicative rather than causal agency. The call exerts not brute but communicative force."[21] Drawing on John Searle as well as Nicholas Wolterstorff's theological applications of speech-act theory in his *Divine Discourse*, Vanhoozer says:

> A speech act has two aspects: propositional content and illocutionary force, the "matter" and "energy" of communicative action. . . . We may distinguish, with Jürgen Habermas, speech acts from strategic acts; whereas the former aim to communicate, the latter aim only to manipulate. It is one thing to bring about a result in the world, quite another to bring about understanding. My claim is that God's effectual call is not a causal but a communicative act. . . . Jesus commands, "Lazarus, come out!" (Jn 11:43), a speech act that literally wakes the dead. . . . Only God, of course, has the right to say certain things, such as "I declare you righteous." . . . Is the grace that changes one's heart a matter of energy or information? I believe it is both, and speech act theory lets us see how. God's call is effectual precisely in bringing about a certain kind of understanding in and through the Word. The Word that summons has both propositional content (matter) and illocutionary force (energy).[22]

In this scheme, the parallels between creation and redemption to which Scripture makes frequent allusion are more apparent.

Given the significance that speech plays in the God-world relation, Vanhoozer seems entirely justified in concluding,

> Humans are indeed "ontologically constituted" by language, and this insight puts a wholly different spin on the question of how the effectual call works a change in the human heart. . . . The doctrine of the effectual call prompts us to change pictures and think not of a causal but a communicative joint and to identify the point at which communication takes place as interpretation. The effectual call thus provides the vital clue as to how God interacts with the human world. In my opinion, the Reformers were right to stress the

19. Ibid., 115–16.
20. Ibid., 116–17, citing Arthur Peacocke, "The Incarnation of the Informing Self-Expressive Word of God," in *Religion and Science: History, Method, Dialogue*, ed. W. M. Richardson and W. J. Wildman (New York: Routledge, 1996), 331.
21. Vanhoozer, *First Theology*, 117.
22. Ibid., 118; citing Nicholas Wolterstorff, *Divine Discourse: Philosophical Reflections on the Claim That God Speaks* (Cambridge and New York: Cambridge University Press, 1995).

connection between God's Word and God's work of grace. . . . Perhaps the
most adequate way to view the God-world relation is in terms of *advent*.[23]

Thus, instead of trying to situate a doctrine like effectual calling within a pre-
existent ontology, we should ask what kind of ontology such doctrines might
engender and require. "Advent" also fits better with the covenantal paradigm of
"meeting a stranger." The effectual call especially illustrates the point that the subjective event of reconciliation is not the result merely of a new awareness or the
projection of a new way-of-being in the world, but of a personal encounter from
"outside." The very term "calling" is itself redolent of this advent of the stranger
who effectually summons us to his side.

Vanhoozer refers to the case of the conversion of Lydia, for example, in Acts
16:14 ("The Lord opened her heart to listen eagerly to what was said by Paul"):
a communicative act changes her heart.[24]

> Yes, God "bends and determines" the will, but even the seventeenth-century
> theologians knew that God "moves the will to attend to the proof, truth and
> goodness of the word announced" [Canons of Dort]. Divine communica-
> tive action is thus of a wholly different sort from instrumental action, the
> kind of action appropriate if one were working on wood or stone. God's
> work of grace is congruous with human nature. Jesus immediately qualifies
> his statement "No one can come to me unless the Father . . . draws him"
> with a quote from Isaiah 54:13: "And they shall all be taught by God." On
> this he provides the following gloss: "Every one who has heard and learned
> from the Father comes to me" (Jn 6:44–45). The Father's drawing, in other
> words, is not causal but communicative. The Word itself has a kind of force.
> One might say, then, with regard to grace, that the *message* is the medium.[25]

It is significant that Vanhoozer can appeal to the traditional confessional formulations in support of his communicative model, while quite properly raising the
question as to whether these instincts are better served by eschewing a causal paradigm altogether.

As Vanhoozer and I have both argued, drawing on the Reformed emphasis on
redemptive history as a divine drama, that revelation cannot be reduced to timeless principles or mere information.[26] In effectual calling, the Spirit draws us into
the world that the Word not only *describes* but also *brings into existence*. Specta-

23. Vanhoozer, *First Theology*, 119.
24. Ibid.
25. Ibid., 120, citing Heppe, *Reformed Dogmatics*, 520.
26. For my programmatic use of drama, see Michael S. Horton, *Covenant and Eschatology* (Louisville, KY: Westminster John Knox, 2002), 9–12. Of course, I am not the first to use this metaphor. Calvin frequently wrote of the world and the church as "the glorious theater," and my own use of the model was probably suggested by the many references to "the drama of redemption" that I came across in my seminary education by reading Herman Bavinck, Geerhardus Vos, Herman Ridderbos, M. G. Kline, and Edmund Clowney, among others. In recent years, drama has become a staple for theological models, as in Hans Urs von Balthasar's *Theo-Drama*, 5 vols. (San Francisco: Ignatius Press, 1988–98); and Kevin J. Vanhoozer's *The Drama of Doctrine* (Louisville, KY: Westminster John Knox, 2005); the latter also displays its debt to the Dutch Reformed tradition while enriching and extending it.

tors become participants in the unfolding drama. When the Spirit brings about in the audience the perlocutionary effect of the divine drama's performative utterance, effectual calling does not mean mere influence or coaxing, but a thoroughly effective speech-act.

It is particularly when *God* is the dramatist, in command of both the plot (redemption) and the casting (effectual calling), that we can conclude that in this case at least, the "new creation" is simultaneously effective and uncoerced.[27] Ezekiel's vision of the valley of dry bones (Ezek. 37) provides a striking example of this approach. So indeed does God's original fiat in creation and the resurrection of Christ, to which both Scripture and the Reformed confessions appeal in describing effectual calling. "Persuasion" is too weak a term to express this analogical connection. God did not *persuade* creation into being or lure Christ from the dead, but summoned, and it was so, despite all the odds. At the same time, one can hardly think of these acts of creation and resurrection as *coerced*.

Clifford Geertz also points out that the dramatic model is inherently holistic, rather than singling out a particular faculty: "'The great impact [of the theater],' Morgan writes, 'is neither a persuasion of the intellect nor a beguiling of the senses. . . . It is the enveloping movement of the whole drama on the soul of man. We surrender and are changed.' Or at least we are when the magic works."[28] Yet the "magic" in the case of effectual calling is always the result of the wisdom of the playwright (Father), the content of the drama itself (Son), and—something that cannot be duplicated by any theater company of creatures—the charisma of the casting director (Spirit), who makes sure that the Word never returns empty, without having accomplished everything for which it was sent.

As useful as communicative theory is for enriching our concept of effectual calling—and, more generally, delineating a covenantal account of the God-world relationship—what we need is a richer account of causality, not to simply dispense with the analogy itself. After all, every speech-act involves *causes*, and to the Spirit we have even attributed the perlocutionary *effect* of all divine works. Vanhoozer has himself spoken of speech-acts as bearing both "matter" and "energy," *bringing about* not only understanding but also the appropriate response. Therefore, to say that "God's effectual call is not a casual but a communicative act" seems to overstate the case. Even to suggest that humans are "'ontologically constituted' by language" implies some notion of cause. Like the analogies of creation and resurrection, then, speech-act theory does not do away with causality, but redefines it in more interpersonal and so covenantal terms.

In my view what is transcended is a certain construal of causality that is too closely associated with physics: the movement of bodies from one place to another

---

27. For this reason, anthropomorphic theologies (such as Moltmann's) actually end up deepening the causal scheme, as if God (or each divine person) is a humanlike subject acting on or in relation to another. God's omniscience, omnipresence, wisdom, eternity, immutability, aseity, as well as trinity, ensure that his omnipotence is *not* like the overpowering of one person by another.

28. Clifford Geertz, *Local Knowledge: Further Essays in Interpretive Anthropology* (New York: Basic Books, 1983), 27–28.

through force rather than the movement of persons from enmity to reconciliation through speech. While this sort of an account will not bring to an abrupt end debates over divine and human freedom, it may at least situate this long discussion within a more productive paradigm. Bringing about a new relationship through communication is different from simply causing movements between objects.

Pneumatology and Perlocutions

Yet, as the Reformed tradition has especially emphasized, the Spirit alone makes the Word effective. At this point, Vanhoozer makes the connection "between pneumatology and perlocutions."

> Now, the primary role of the Holy Spirit, I believe, is to *minister the Word*, . . . applying both the propositional content and the illocutionary force of the gospel in such a way as to bring about perlocutionary effects: effects that in this case include regeneration, understanding and union with Christ. Not for nothing, then, does Paul describe the Word of God as the "sword of the Spirit" (Eph 6:17). It is not simply the impartation of information nor the transfer of mechanical energy but the impact of a total speech act (the message together with its communicative power) that is required for the summons to be efficacious.[29]

Rather than say that the Spirit *supervenes* on the preached gospel (since regeneration is not always given with it), Vanhoozer prefers to say that the Spirit *advenes* on it, "when and where God wills," to make it effective.[30] We are at some remove now from the causal ontology of infused habits, which are wordless events inviting the criticism that they are merely violent subversions of creaturely integrity.

God as sovereign speaker avoids both panentheistic and merely causal approaches that usually land us in stalemates over who has the greatest degree of volitional power to make things happen.

> What God says makes a difference, but it would be perverse to describe this difference in terms of impersonal causation. . . . God comes to the world in, and as, Word. To be precise, God relates to the world with both "hands": Word and Spirit. . . . While perlocutions do "emerge" from illocutionary acts, they do not do so necessarily.[31]

This protects the important doctrinal point that while the Spirit works through the Word, the general call is broader than the effectual call. The classical dogmatics are far from endorsing "impersonal causation," yet the *grammar* of causation itself grew out of an *ontology* that in fact did (viz., Aristotle's Unmoved Mover).[32] This does not vitiate their conclusions or even their formulations, but

---

29. Ibid., 121.
30. Ibid., 122.
31. Ibid., 123.
32. See R. S. Clark, "The Authority of Reason in the Later Reformation: Scholasticism in Caspar Olevian and Antoine de la Faye," in *Protestant Scholasticism: Essays in Reassessment*, ed. Carl Trueman

it does raise the question as to whether the communicative rather than the observational analogies of physical causes can more adequately make the points that theologians have rightly wanted to draw out from exegesis.

Vanhoozer offers, "God's self-communication is 'advenient.' Jesus came to his own, though the world knew him not. It follows that the advent of God's Word is not a foreign intervention. On the contrary, if God is a stranger it is only because humanity has turned its back and made him so."[33] This throws light once again on the point that grace overcomes ethical separation, not ontological binaries.

Communication does not work like brute causes, but it also is not mere information or exhortation. Scripture already assumes a communicative approach. "The word of God is living and active" (Heb. 4:12). We are reminded in Isaiah 55:10–11,

> For as the rain and snow come down from heaven, and do not return there until they have watered the earth, making it bring forth and sprout, giving seed to the sower and bread to the eater, so shall my word be that goes out from my mouth; it shall not return to me empty, but it shall accomplish that which I purpose, and succeed in the thing for which I sent it.

God's speech not only reaches its addressee, but because the Spirit is always already present in creation to bring that speech to fruition, its illocutionary stances, which are always deployed in a covenantal context (commands, promises, curses, blessings, etc.), also actually bring about the reality they announce.

In my view, the very points that the Reformed confessions defended by appealing (in however ad hoc a manner) to causal categories can be better expressed in communicative terms. We do not need infused habits prior to speech, since God's speech itself comes from the Father in the Son and reaches its appointed goal through the Spirit.

Interesting possibilities converge when we bring together speech-act theory, a Trinitarian perspective, a covenantal ontology, and the doctrine of analogy. The infinite-*qualitative* distinction between God and creation is the antidote to the infinite-*quantitative* dualisms that haunt theology and philosophy. God is neither "up there" and far away nor a needy member of the community of persons: Paul tackles both of these views in his speech to the philosophers (Acts 17). Rather, God is radically present as the Father in the Son and by the Spirit, yet for that reason utterly distinct from that creation. The God who relates to the world is therefore a Trinity; the means of that relationship is the Word, and the context of that relationship is the covenant.

---

and R. S. Clark (Carlisle: Paternoster, 1999), 111–26. See also, in the same volume, D. V. N. Bagchi, "Sic et Non: Luther and Scholasticism," and David C. Steinmetz, "The Scholastic Calvin." A number of other essays in this collection are quite helpful for assessing Reformed appropriations of Aristotelian terminology.

33. Clark, "The Authority of Reason," 124.

Despite his Trinitarian emphasis, Barth's identification of revelation and redemption obscures the pneumatological conditioning of divine communication. Conflating the external and internal call inevitably tends to collapse the Spirit's perlocutionary agency into the Son's existence as the illocutionary act. In classical Reformed formulations, by contrast, revelation remains what it is regardless of whether it is received, and it is only saving when it is received by Spirit-given faith.

In consequence of this understanding, freedom is not a magnitude that God possesses as a monopoly to be negotiated or to be ceded in part to the creature. Just as the Creator-creature relation is not one of greater and lesser being, so also it is not one of greater and lesser freedom, as if God and creatures existed on the same ontic plane. To put it crassly, there is no "freedom pie" to be divided up between God and creatures: God fully possesses divine freedom, and creatures fully possess the free agency that is appropriate to their nature. God does not simply have *more* freedom than we have, but the *kind* of freedom that only God—specifically, the triune God of Scripture, can have. A univocity of being underlies all hyper-Calvinistic and Arminian assumptions of a freedom and a willing that is unhinged from the nature of the agents of whom these are predicated. When freedom is predicated of both God and creatures, it must be understood analogically, and this creates space for genuine freedom appropriate to independent-necessary and dependent-contingent agents, God and humans respectively.

Divine *Poēsis*

The triune God, then, is the consummate poet in the original sense, making by speaking. Effectual calling is a divine *poēsis*, a drama that not only is *about* something but also *itself* bears the reality. Words are no longer seen as signs of a longed-for signified, nor as identical to the signified, but as mediating an advent.

Abraham is not only *told about* a promise; he is also *called out* by the covenant God from a moon-worshiping family in Ur and given a promise that is not grounded in anything that already exists. That promise creates a new history. In fact, the promise is given in opposition to the ontological realities already in play: old age, Sarah's barrenness, and the law of inheritance. Yet, looking back to creation ex nihilo, and forward to the justification of the ungodly, Abram is given a past, present, and future that he and Sarah could not secure by their own skillful conniving. The eternal covenant of redemption breaks into history, issuing in the promise of a new creation. Abram embraced the promise "in the presence of the God in whom he believed, who gives life to the dead and calls into existence the things that do not exist" (Rom. 4:17b). The calling itself creates a new world to be inhabited by covenant partners. It is understandable that Paul can only compare this evangelical advent of the Word to another ex nihilo creation.

This divine *poēsis* is the opposite of Nietzsche's nihilistic self-creation. Reflecting the neurosis that psychologist Robert Jay Lifton has identified as the "Protean style," always striving to reinvent a self from the materials of marketing ads and consumer products, the postmodern person is driven by meaningless choice. This leads to a situation, he says, in which cases formerly diagnosed as pathologies are considered normal.[34] It is not the freedom to be what we were intended for, but freedom as an abstract power of choosing, always unsure of its existence, striving to authenticate itself by new choices, that defines this nihilistic self-creation.

By contrast, effectual calling is the death of the self-*poēsis* of the autonomous modern self and the aimless postmodern wanderer. It is nothing less than the merciful reconstitution of the self as *pilgrim*. Called away from whatever narratives of sin, death, exile, oppression, vanity, and violence defined their existence, the New Testament disciples too are made willing characters in an unfolding plot of the new creation in Christ. It is not because of a new awareness, amounting to turning over a new leaf, but a complete metamorphosis that can only be explained by reference to God's sovereign speech-action and the concrete reality of the kingdom that it inaugurates in Christ, who is no longer simply the Jesus of history, but is simultaneously the Christ of faith.

> From now on, therefore, we regard no one from a human point of view; even though we once knew Christ from a human point of view, we know him no longer in that way. So if anyone is in Christ, there is a new creation: everything old has passed away; see, everything has become new! All this is from God, who reconciled us to himself through Christ, and has given us the ministry of reconciliation. (2 Cor. 5:16–18)

Instead of thinking merely of a sole agent (God) acting upon another agent (humans), greater conceptual space is given to the noncoercive yet always effectual working of the divine persons upon, for, and within people. Since Scripture itself treats God's effectual working as communicative (primarily, speaking), and Reformation theology has emphasized this point, the categories of speech-act theory appear promising. It is always through his Word and Spirit that God brings about intended results in the created order—an important premise in challenging the notion of a subconscious and unmediated work of the Spirit prior to a communicatively mediated effectual calling.

So the question is not *whether* God causes things, but *how*. Even when acting miraculously, God is an employer of means. The Son and the Spirit mediate the Father's speech in their distinctive manner, and they also employ creaturely means. The Son becomes incarnate in history, and the Spirit brings about within us the appropriate response to his Word. Christ is not only promised; he also *is* the promise. "For in him every one of God's promises is a 'Yes.' For this reason it is through him that we say the 'Amen,' to the glory of God" (2 Cor. 1:20). Christ as the Father's illocutionary act restores the liturgical exchange that the fall has turned into a disordered Babel of confusion and discord. The natural creation still manages to utter its liturgical lines even under the curse: "The heavens are telling the

---

34. Robert Jay Lifton, "The Protean Style," in *The Truth about Truth: De-confusing and Reconstructing the Postmodern World*, ed. Walter Truett Anderson (New York: G. P. Putnam's Sons, 1995), 130–35.

glory of God; and the firmament proclaims his handiwork. Day to day pours forth speech, and night to night declares knowledge" (Ps. 19:1–2). In the meantime, those who are created in God's image sing Walt Whitman's "Song of Myself" in bondage to individual and collective narcissism. Yet once the one who "suppresses the truth in unrighteousness" (Rom. 1:18 NKJV) are swept into the story that God is telling the world, they find themselves "born anew, not of perishable but of imperishable seed, through the living and enduring word of God. . . . That word is the good news that was announced to you" (1 Pet. 1:23, 25b).

> By his great mercy he has given us a new birth into a living hope through the resurrection of Jesus Christ from the dead, and into an inheritance that is imperishable, undefiled, and unfading, kept in heaven for you, who are being protected by the power of God through faith for a salvation ready to be revealed in the last time. (1 Pet. 1:3–5)

More like being overwhelmed by beauty than by force, the call is effectual because of its *content*, not because of an exercise of absolute power independent of it. And yet the appropriate "amen" cannot be attributed to the recipient, since it is the Father's communication of the Son and the Spirit's effective agency within the natural processes of even truth-suppressing consciousness that brings it about.

The doctrine of effectual calling helps to unseat the sovereign self from its pretended throne by emphasizing that this new creation, including the new birth, is a divine *poēsis*, not a self-making. And yet, it does not unseat through violence anymore than through mere moral persuasion. We receive our new selves as we are baptized into the new creation of which Christ is the firstfruits, becoming joint heirs with Christ as a power and right that is not inherent in us but as those "who were born, not of blood or of the will of the flesh or of the will of man, but of God" (John 1:13). "Worded" by this Word, or as I have described it elsewhere, "rescripted" into God's drama of redemption, we simply find ourselves new creatures in a new world that we freely chose, though not *because* we freely chose it. And our own grace-enabled "amen" becomes as much a part of the covenantal liturgy as the Word to which it responds.

CHALLENGING THE DISTINCTION BETWEEN REGENERATION AND EFFECTUAL CALLING

Now we move to the second part of my argument: If we are thinking more in line with interpersonal speech that issues first in a creation/new creation fiat ("Let there be . . .") and then in a covenantal conversation ("Let the earth bring forth . . ."), we no longer need to appeal to infused habits. The argument thus far would suggest that regeneration is not a direct and immediate act of God on the soul, but the perlocutionary effect of the illocutionary act pronounced by the Father in the Son through the Spirit. As the hypostatic Word, Christ himself is present as the content of this Word of the gospel as it is preached. Thus, the effectual Word is not merely a created thing acting on a created person. It also is the energetic working of the Father in the Son and by the Spirit, bringing about the "amen" within the creature.

Here we once again call upon the essence-energies distinction advocated by the East, but with a specific focus on the Word. There is always a distinction between the incarnate Word (consubstantial with the Father and the Spirit) and the spoken and written Word. Yet the Word in its spoken and written form is not only a creaturely witness that may or may not correspond to God's Word at specific moments; it is the *working* of God. Combining this distinction with speech-act theory, we may say that in this respect God's *working* is God's *wording*.

Nor is regeneration something done at a distance; instead, it is already the presence of Christ mediating the voice of the Father in the power of the Spirit, who not only works upon us but also within us. Calvin comments, "We must also observe that form of expression, *to believe through the word*, which means that faith springs from hearing, because the outward preaching of men is the instrument by which God draws us to faith. It follows that God is, strictly speaking, the Author of faith, and men are *the ministers by whom we believe*, as Paul teaches (1 Cor. 3:5)."[35] Commenting on Romans 10:17 ("Faith comes from what is heard, and what is heard comes through the word of Christ"), Calvin writes:

> And this is a remarkable passage with regard to the efficacy of preaching; for he testifies that by it faith is produced. He had indeed before declared that of itself it is of no avail; but that when it pleases the Lord to work, it becomes the instrument of his power. And indeed the voice of man can by no means penetrate into the soul; and mortal man would be too much exalted were he said to have the power to regenerate us; the light also of faith is something sublimer than what can be conveyed by man: but all these things are no hindrances, that God should not work effectually through the voice of man, so as to create faith in us through his ministry.[36]

Against both the medieval doctrine of justification according to infused habits and the Anabaptist emphasis on a direct and immediate work of the Spirit within, the Reformers insisted upon the mediation of the Word—specifically, the gospel. "For faith and the Word belong together," Wilhelm Kolfhaus argues concerning Calvin's view. "The foundation of both expressions is always the faith produced by the Spirit through the Gospel."[37] In Dennis Tamburello's fine summary of Calvin's *ordo*, "The Holy Spirit brings the elect, through the hearing of the gospel, to faith; in so doing, the Spirit engrafts them into Christ."[38]

---

35. John Calvin, *Commentary on the Gospel according to John*, trans. William Pringle (1847; repr., Grand Rapids: Baker, 1996), 181, on John 17:20.

36. John Calvin, *Commentary on the Epistle of Paul the Apostle to the Romans*, ed. and trans. John Owen, *Calvin's Commentaries*, vol. 19 (Edinburgh: Calvin Translation Society, 1844; repr., Grand Rapids: Baker Books, 1993), 401, on Rom. 10:17.

37. Quoted and translated by Dennis Tamburello, *Union with Christ: John Calvin and the Mysticism of St. Bernard* (Louisville, KY: Westminster John Knox, 1994), 86.

38. Ibid.

Although the Word is just as truly communicated to hearers (the external call), the further act of the Spirit (the inward or effectual call) is necessary for bringing about the response of faith. A person in a crowded theater that is engulfed in flames may hear the locution "Fire!" and even recognize it as an illocutionary act of warning, without being persuaded to evacuate the room. However, anyone who does evacuate owes his or her safety to that warning. In the case of effectual calling, it is not only what is said but the one who says it that gives this particular utterance its perlocutionary force. Given the right circumstances, crying "Fire!" will yield evacuation, no matter who says it. However, in the case of bringing those who are spiritually dead to life, Jesus says, "No one can come to me unless drawn by the Father who sent me; and I will raise that person up on the last day" (John 6:44). It is always effectual: "Everyone who has heard and learned from the Father comes to me" (v. 45). Yet even in this case, as in the analogy, it is not a direct and immediate exercise of divine power that creates faith, but the Word that is uttered by the Father, in the Son, through the Spirit. Through his creaturely word the Spirit acts within us through media accommodated to our capacity, not simply upon us in an immediate show of force.

Once again, Reformed confessions and systems have never held that *effectual calling* is direct and immediate. It has been generally agreed that faith comes from the preaching of the gospel. However, in the postconfessional era it became common to speak of *regeneration* as a work of the Spirit in the heart prior to effectual calling; a direct and immediate work of the Spirit infusing a new disposition or habit, planting the principle of new life, so that one would respond favorably to that external ministry. So while effectual calling was indeed mediated by the preached gospel, regeneration was a subconscious operation of sovereign grace. Having anticipated this question in the previous chapter, here I want to offer a more direct challenge to the distinction between regeneration and effectual calling.

SETTING UP THE PROBLEM: REGENERATION *AND* EFFECTUAL CALLING

It seems that the notion of regeneration as a habit infused immediately and prior to effectual calling took up residence in the shell left by its vacated inhabitant: baptismal regeneration. Turretin explains that the Reformed "deny actual faith to infants against the Lutherans and maintain that a seminal or radical [root] and habitual faith is ascribed to them against the Anabaptists."[39] Like Jeremiah and John the Baptist, infants may receive the Spirit before they actually believe.[40] "Although infants do not have actual faith, the seed or root of faith cannot be

39. Francis Turretin, *Institutes of Elenctic Theology*, vol. 2, ed. J. T. Dennison Jr., trans. G. M. Giger (Phillipsburg, NJ: P&R Publishing, 1994), 583.
40. Ibid., 585–86.

denied to them, which is ingenerated in them from early age and in its own time goes forth in act (human instruction being applied from without and a greater efficacy of the Holy Spirit within)."[41]

Thus, against the Lutheran view, Reformed theology does not necessarily tie regeneration to the moment of baptism, while also rejecting the Anabaptist position that children not yet capable of the act of faith are therefore incapable of receiving the seed of faith. Calvin taught much the same thing.[42] On one hand, especially against the Anabaptists, Calvin argues for infant baptism along covenantal lines: The children of the believers are to be baptized because they already are the heritage of the Lord. Therefore, baptism is a sign and seal of the covenant, God's pledge, which emphasizes the role of the church as mother of the faithful, nurturing the visible body from infancy.[43] On the other hand, he still speaks of baptism as somehow being the instrument through which the Spirit plants the seed of faith and repentance.[44]

At the very least, there is tension between these two quite different defenses of infant baptism. The first, underscoring the covenantal continuity between Old and New Testament saints (circumcision and baptism), sees the sacraments as signs and seals of the covenant, ratifying God's promise to the child. The second appeals to something like infused habits.[45] Therefore, there is already a tension that is tacitly at work between a covenantal ontology and the inherited medieval ontology.

Even by Turretin's time, Reformed theologians were not entirely at one as to whether regeneration preceded (or could be distinguished from) effectual calling. As the tradition moved steadily away from any notion of baptismal regeneration (though still maintaining that baptism is a means of grace), this space was sometimes filled by the concept of a direct and immediate regeneration—the implanting of the *seeds* of faith and repentance—that would in due time be exercised by the elect through their hearing the gospel. As we will see, this formulation was not universally accepted among the Reformed, but it did come to occupy a privileged position in later Reformed theology. Rejecting this ontology of grace with respect to justification, some Reformed theologians increasingly inserted it back into the *ordo* in discussion of the new birth.[46]

The formulation of the *ordo salutis* was to a large extent provoked by challenges, from Rome but also especially from other Protestants. Where the principal concerns (*sola gratia, sola fide*, monergism) were considered sufficiently looked

---

41. Ibid., 586.

42. Calvin, *Institutes* 4.16.17.

43. Ibid., 4.15.14–15.

44. Ibid., 4.16.20.

45. In chap. 4 of *Grace and Gratitude: The Eucharistic Theology of John Calvin* (Minneapolis: Augsburg Fortress, 1993), B. A. Gerrish also marks these different trajectories in Calvin's treatment.

46. See, for example, Hermann Bavinck's discussion of the various positions in *Reformed Dogmatics*, ed. John Bolt, trans. John Vriend, vol. 3 (Grand Rapids: Baker Academic, 2006), 582–83. Reformed positions in the sixteenth and seventeenth centuries were still quite fluid on this question. Luther and Calvin even spoke of regeneration and repentance interchangeably.

after, the rest of the issues related to the *ordo* were left somewhat fluid.[47] Direct encounters with Arminianism and Amyraldianism provoked greater refinement, but the logical priority of regeneration and justification (and the distinction between regeneration and effectual calling) remained flexible. In fact, a century ago Bavinck could summarize the Reformed view in a way that places regeneration *after* imputation and the gift of the Spirit.[48] This is hardly a unanimous position, as we will see.

Nicely summarizing the rationale for an evolving distinction between initial regeneration (insemination) and the new birth, Charles Hodge begins with the potential for confusing justification and regeneration even in the Lutheran Formula of Concord (xv. Quaes. iv. 13). Especially with the rise of debates within early Lutheranism (associated with Osiander and Flacius Illyricus), this relation required greater clarification. In line with the caution of the Reformed scholastics, Hodge challenges us to eschew speculation concerning the mechanics of this new birth. "Its metaphysical nature is left a mystery. It is not the province of either philosophy or theology to solve that mystery."[49]

Still, errors had to be confronted. On one hand, Hodge continues, "Regeneration does not consist in any change in the substance of the soul" (contra Flacius), a position that smacks of a Manichean dualism between nature and grace.[50] At the same time, there was the perennial concern to avoid synergism (regeneration as a process of divine-human cooperation). Therefore, this regeneration, Hodge repeated, is *physical* rather than merely *moral* in nature, which simply meant that it was not something that was offered or presented to the will and understanding, but an effectual operation upon both that immediately imparted a new disposition or *habitus*—although *habitus* does not mean exactly the same thing here as it does in Roman Catholic theology.[51] Nor is a "physical cause" the same thing for Hodge that it is for Aristotle. The point was to say that in regeneration the Spirit actually changes one's disposition, so that the preaching of the gospel will be received rather than resisted.

47. For example, in the last quarter of the sixteenth century, William Perkins spoke even of "first and second regeneration," roughly corresponding to regeneration (in which the subject is passive) and conversion (in which the subject is active) (William Perkins, *The Workes of That Famous and Worthy Minister of Christ*, 3 vols. (London: John Legatt, 1612–18), 1:717. Significantly, van Mastricht acknowledges that until his time most Reformed writers had treated the topic of regeneration more broadly, as including "vocation, spiritual quickening, conversion, and sanctification, while we have taken it in a stricter sense, as denoting only the bestowing of the first act or principle of spiritual life" (Peter van Mastricht, "Regeneration," in *Theologia theoretica-practica*, new ed., 2 vols. [Utrecht: Thomae Appels, 1699], 1:58).

48. Bavinck says, "Hence the imputation of Christ precedes the gift of the Spirit, and regeneration, faith, and conversion do not first lead us to Christ but are taken from Christ by the Holy Spirit and imparted to his own" (*Reformed Dogmatics*, 3:525).

49. Charles Hodge, *Systematic Theology*, 3 vols. (New York: Charles Scribner's Sons, 1872), 2:6.

50. Ibid.

51. As we will see below, the Reformed understood this infused *habitus* to be an entirely subconscious operation of the Spirit. It was not yet active in faith or repentance, but simply disposed one to them.

In Hodge's own day the challenge of synergism was particularly pronounced, especially in the New Haven theology of Nathaniel Taylor and Charles Finney, for whom regeneration was basically equivalent to repentance. (One of Finney's most celebrated sermons was titled "Sinners Bound to Convert Their Own Hearts," which sounds oddly like the imperative of the Sinai covenant in contrast to the promise of the new covenant.) Consistent with the eudaemonistic theory (people always seek the goal that is calculated to bring them maximum happiness), they maintain that regeneration "is a change from selfishness to benevolence."[52]

By contrast, says Hodge, "according to the common doctrine of Protestants, i.e., of Lutherans and Reformed," are the following points: "Regeneration is an act of God." Further, it occurs subconsciously; it is "not a new purpose created by God. . . . Nor is it any conscious exercise of any kind." Therefore, justification can in no way be said to follow any actual moral renovation. Further, it is not a change of substance, which would be Manichean—as if creation were *essentially* flawed rather than ethically fallen.[53] Positively, "it is a new life," a new birth, and a new heart.[54] Not even one's act of faith could therefore be said to effect the new birth.

Nor is this notion of a subconscious regeneration (direct and immediate) distinct from effectual calling unique to the British-American tradition, but represents the emerging consensus of the later Reformed scholasticism on the Continent as well, as Louis Berkhof explains. However, Berkhof recognizes that even as late as the Westminster Assembly, Reformed theology had typically treated effectual calling and regeneration as synonymous.[55] In fact, if a distinction was allowed, the former was even given logical priority over the latter.[56] "This view," Berkhof concedes, "finds some justification in the fact that Paul, who uses the term 'regeneration' but once, evidently conceives of it as included in calling in Rom. 8:30." He adds, "The extensive use in Post-Reformation times of the term 'calling' rather than 'regeneration,' to designate the beginning of the work of grace in the life of sinners, was due to a desire to stress the close connection between the Word of God and the operation of His grace." Yet Berkhof concludes that the emerging tendency of some to distinguish regeneration and calling was a profitable refinement: "In a systematic presentation of the truth, however, we should carefully discriminate between calling and regeneration."[57]

---

52. Hodge, *Systematic Theology*, 2:12.
53. Ibid., 52.
54. Ibid., 33–35.
55. Louis Berkhof, *Systematic Theology*, 4th ed. (1939; Grand Rapids: Eerdmans, 1941), 466–69.
56. Ibid., 470–71: "It is a well known fact that in seventeenth century theology effectual calling and regeneration are often identified, or if not entirely identified, then at least in so far that regeneration is regarded as included in calling. Several of the older theologians have a separate chapter on calling, but none on regeneration. According to the Westminster Confession, X. 2, effectual calling includes regeneration."
57. Ibid.

Berkhof adduces the rationale offered by the late-nineteenth-century Presbyterian theologian William G. T. Shedd: "It is the influence of spirit upon spirit; of one of the Trinitarian persons upon a human person. Neither the truth, nor a fellow-man, can thus operate directly upon the essence of the soul itself."[58] Aside from the metaphysical dualism, Shedd's statement also isolates the Spirit in the new birth, rather than recognizing that in every external work the persons of the Trinity cooperate in their unique ways, with the Word always included as the "matter" of the Spirit's work. Further, the medieval ontology is clearly in view when regeneration is treated as an operation upon "the essence of the soul itself." Berkhof acknowledges potential texts against this conclusion: the parable of the sower (Matt. 13:1–9); James 1:18 ("He gave us birth by the word of truth"); and 1 Peter 1:23 ("born anew . . . through the living and enduring word of God"); yet he finally accepts the logic of Shedd's argument.[59]

Therefore, in opposition to Rome, when the central question was justification—Reformation theologies were suspicious of the language of infused habits, while encounters with various forms of synergism drove the Protestant scholastics back to the traditional categories of infused habits in order to affirm the logical priority of grace. So we can identify two moves here: first, to speak of the new birth as effected through the Word yet in terms of a new habit implanted; second, to distinguish this new birth from effectual calling through the Word. The first move could be explained simply in terms of using a familiar analogy employed in 1 Peter 1:23. *The danger of the second move, however, was that justification and regeneration/sanctification were not only properly distinguished, but also were given different ontological fields of discourse that allowed them to drift apart like tectonic plates.*

Typical of many later Reformed scholastics, Peter van Mastricht seems to accept this distinction, although he still sometimes speaks of the Word's mediation of regeneration. Regeneration infuses a new habit, not actually creating faith and repentance, but disposing one to the effectual call. In fact, his description of regeneration as an infused *habitus* distinct from any *actual act* of faith, hope, love, or repentance is identical to that of Aquinas.[60] To be sure, this leaves a lot for effectual calling through the Word to accomplish, since a disposition (habit) still requires mediation (the Word) for its realization in act. Furthermore, regeneration, thus defined, is not yet conversion, much less sanctification, so there is no actual moral growth before justification.

Nevertheless, the question remains: Are there adequate exegetical and theological grounds for distinguishing regeneration from effectual calling, much less for identifying the former with an infused habit? And is such a move susceptible

58. Quoted in ibid., 474.
59. Ibid.
60. Van Mastricht, "Regeneration," in *Theologia theoretica-practica* (1699), anonymous English translation revised by Brandon Withrow, in Peter van Mastricht, *A Treatise on Regeneration* (Morgan, PA: Soli Deo Gloria Publications, 2002), 26. The only difference is that this regeneration is not effected by baptism.

to leaving justification to stand alone, however centrally, on a forensic island surrounded by a sea of inner operations that take place apart from the declaratory Word?

Like the Westminster Confession, the other major Reformed confessions and catechisms shared the view illustrated in question and answer 65 of the Heidelberg Catechism: "The Holy Spirit creates it [saving faith] in our hearts by the preaching of the holy gospel and confirms it by the use of the holy sacraments." The later theologians were not denying that this is how *effectual calling* occurs, but inserted the distinct event of regeneration prior to it. Passages such as 1 Peter 1:23 and James 1:18, which directly assert that the new birth comes by the Word, were taken by some in the tradition as referring to the act of faith rather than to regeneration itself.

Again, part of the problem is that these writers link the Word to "moral persuasion," to which Arminians (not to mention Socinians and Pelagians) had reduced regeneration. In other words, *the ministry of the Word was understood simply in its illocutionary function of presenting the content of the gospel.* At that point, one could either challenge this moral-influence theory of the Word, reasserting the Reformation's strong conception of the Word's efficacy, or one could insert an immediate, subconscious regeneration prior to hearing and believing. From my account thus far, it should be obvious that I prefer the former option. If we treat the instrumentality of the Word in terms of both illocutionary and perlocutionary acts, then the monergism that these writers rightly insist on affirming can be firmly defended without appeal to a regeneration that is logically prior to and separate from effectual calling through the gospel. To borrow Vanhoozer's expression above, we could say that effectual calling *advenes* on the external preaching of the gospel. With the older Reformed writers, we still affirm the necessity of the Spirit's sovereign work of inwardly regenerating hearers while affirming that this operation *beyond* the mere hearing of the external Word nevertheless occurs *with* it and *through* it.

The ability to respond to the gospel is indeed given to us by the Spirit, but this is even more explicitly and clearly affirmed by referring the act to the Spirit's working through the Word rather than to either subconscious operations or infused habits. Scripture repeatedly identifies God's "creating power" with the Word that is spoken. Like the original creation, the new birth is the result of a mediated speech-act.

Not even during this later period was everyone agreed on this question. In the second half of the seventeenth century, Herman Witsius argued, "Regeneration is that supernatural act of God whereby a new and divine life is infused into the elect person, spiritually dead, and that *from incorruptible seed of the word of God, made fruitful by the infinite power of the Spirit*" (emphasis added).[61] In this, Witsius is

61. Herman Witsius, *The Economy of the Covenants*, trans. William Crookshank, 2 vols. (London: Edwards Dilly, 1763; lithographed in 1990 from an 1822 edition by the den Dulk Christian Foundation and distributed from Phillipsburg, NJ: P&R Publishing, 1990), 357.

simply following the Canons of Dort (Third and Fourth Heads), which is consistent with the Westminster Confession's assumption that regeneration and effectual calling are one and the same event.[62] In my view we can even speak of "new qualities infused," as long as it is simply a figure of speech for the unilateral gift of faith and new birth through the gospel. Peter van Mastricht concludes, "The Father in this case is God; hence we are said to be born of God (Jn 1:13), and the regenerate are called 'the sons of God' (1 Jn 5:1–2). The mother in whose womb, as it were, we are conceived and nourished is the Church (Gal 4:26). *The seed, the Word of God, which 'liveth and abideth forever' (1 Pet 1:23), is received by the external call of the gospel*" (emphasis added).[63]

Even after vigorously challenging the nominalist (semi-Pelagian) and Arminian view that regeneration by mere "moral persuasion" was tantamount to a child giving birth to itself, John Owen writes,

> We grant that in the work of regeneration, the Holy Spirit, towards those that are adult, doth make use of the word, both the law and the gospel, and the ministry of the church in the dispensation of it, as the ordinary means thereof; yea, this is ordinarily the whole external means that is made use of in this work, and an efficacy proper unto it is accompanied withal.[64]

Yet these are means in God's hand, not our own; they do not enable us to regenerate ourselves by our own will, but are made effectual by the Spirit's "physical" agency.[65]

Therefore, why do we need to posit a distinct work of grace prior to any external Word, particularly when the New Testament typically relates the new birth to that Word? In my view, this distinction between regeneration apart from means and effectual calling through the Word is both exegetically untenable and theologically unnecessary. Although the distinction between a general call and an effectual call (regeneration) can be easily sustained by exegesis, a further distinction between regeneration (unmediated) and effectual calling (mediated) seems to contradict the explicit references to regeneration by the Word cited above.

Berkhof certainly acknowledges the impressive exegetical credentials of the older view: Luke 1:13, 57; 23:29; John 1:14; 16:21; Galatians 4:24; James 1:18; 1 Peter 1:23, as well as the parable of the sower, for example.[66] Furthermore, the Reformed confessions (Belgic 24–25; Heidelberg Q 54; Dort III and IV, articles 11, 12, 17) "speak of regeneration in a broad sense, as including both the origin of the new life and its manifestation in conversion."

---

62. This was also van Mastricht's and several others' preferred term for this immediately implanted potentiality.

63. Van Mastricht, *A Treatise on Regeneration*, 12–13.

64. Owen, *The Works of John Owen*, 3:316.

65. Ibid.

66. Van Mastricht, *A Treatise on Regeneration*, 475.

We are even told that faith regenerates the sinner [Belgic 24]. There are passages which seem to say that the Word of God is instrumental in the work of regeneration [Belgic 24 and 26; Dort III and IV, arts. 12, 17]. Yet they are couched in such language that it still remains doubtful, whether they actually teach that the principle of the new life is implanted in the soul by the instrumentality of the Word. They fail to discriminate carefully between the various elements which we distinguish in regeneration.[67]

However, these confessional statements are doubtful or imprecise on this point only if one presupposes a distinction between regeneration and effectual calling.

Nevertheless, Berkhof finally draws his conclusion from the organic analogy itself rather than from the specific way in which the New Testament employs it: "Two elements must be distinguished in regeneration, namely, generation or the begetting of the new life, and bearing or bringing forth, by which the new life is brought forth out of its hidden depths. Generation implants the principle of the new life in the soul, and the new birth causes this principle to begin to assert itself in action."[68] Berkhof uses "principle" (and the phrase, "implanting of the principle of the new spiritual life") the way the older theologians (Catholic and Protestant) spoke of the implanted *habitus*.[69] Yet when it comes to effectual calling, "it is the same Word that is heard in the external call, and that is made effective in the heart in the internal calling."[70]

If this is the case, why do we need an immediately infused *habitus* to intervene between these mediated events? Why not just say that the Spirit regenerates through the proclaimed gospel, albeit when and where the Spirit chooses, just as the Reformed confessions and catechisms affirm? Do we really need to appeal to the medieval category of infused habits, however revised in content, in order to refute synergism? Does such a formulation save us from synergism only to open the door again to a dualism between God's person and Word? Crucially, *what* is implanted, according to the passages we have cited: a principle of new life or the living and active and life-imparting Word? Does the Spirit ever implant a seed other than his Word? And is that Word ever a mere principle or silent operation rather than a vocal, lively, and active speech? Is it not the case that in attributing all efficacy to the Spirit's power, Scripture typically represents this as occurring through the word of God that is "at work" in its recipients (1 Thess. 2:13; cf. Rom. 8:14–16; 1 Cor. 2:4–5; 4:12–13; 2 Cor. 4:13; Gal. 3:2; Eph. 1:17; 1 Thess. 1:5; Titus 3:5)—specifically, that message of the gospel, which is "the power of God for salvation" (Rom. 1:16; 10:17; 1 Thess. 1:5)?

67. Ibid., 476.
68. Ibid., 465. Whether this overliteralizes the analogy of insemination-and-birth in our ordinary experience remains an open question. However, the intention is to retain the medieval and Protestant scholastic language of infused principles or dispositions (a new *habitus*) while insisting on the priority of divine agency in effecting this new life. Of course, Aquinas and the traditional Roman Catholic view also defended this priority in terms of the "first justification" in baptism, yet required human cooperation for completion of the process.
69. Ibid., 468.
70. Ibid., 469.

Regeneration *as* Effectual Calling

Neither side in this debate confused justification with sanctification nor denied that effectual calling is mediated through the Word. Nevertheless, I am suggesting that speech-act theory is better suited to amplifying both the monergistic principle of *sola gratia* and the forensic principle of even an inward regeneration mediated by the external Word than a causal framework that requires infused habits apart from that mediation.

In my view, the separation of regeneration and effectual calling set up the possibility for a schizophrenic soteriology according to which part of the *ordo* is radically forensic in its source and the other remains trapped in the medieval ontology that the former was struggling to overcome. Instead of seeing the whole series of events as the result of God's effectual word of speaking a new world, issuing in both justification and sanctification, it forces us to think of these two events as resting on their own independent ontological foundations.

I suggest, therefore, that the external call *includes the locutionary act of the Father's speaking and the Son as the illocutionary content. The* internal call *(effectual calling), synonymous with regeneration, is the Spirit's perlocutionary effect.* As in all of God's works, the Spirit brings to fruition the goal of divine communication. The Father objectively reveals the Son, and the Spirit inwardly illumines the understanding to behold the glory of God in the face of Christ (2 Cor. 4:6; cf. John 1:5; 3:5; 17:3; 1 Cor. 2:14), liberating the will not only to assent to the truth but also to trust in Christ (Jer. 32:39–40; Ezek. 36:26; Eph. 2:1–9; Heb. 8:10). Regeneration or effectual calling is something that happens to those who do not have the moral capacity to convert themselves, yet it not only happens *to* them; it also happens *within* them, winning their consent. The source of this inward renewal is not an infused principle, but the Spirit working through the Word. The notion of regeneration as mediated by the preached gospel leads inevitably to mere "moral persuasion" (i.e., offering an external enticement that the will may either accept or reject) only if the Word is mere information or exhortation rather than the "living and active" energy of God.

While my differences with Balthasar fall along the usual Roman Catholic/ Reformed fault lines, his thorough integration of the transcendentals, particularly *beauty*, suggests areas of common conviction. As we have seen, the Reformed symbols emphasize that effectual grace does not "coerce a reluctant will by force, but spiritually revives, heals, reforms, and—in a manner *at once pleasing and powerful*—bends it back."[71] In *Two Say Why*, Balthasar elaborates the experience of "falling in love."[72] Here, desire is directed outward, toward the other. It is the other who elicits this response, not something that is worked up within oneself. Similarly, with God, the truth, goodness, and beauty that are manifested in Christ's liv-

---

71. Canons of the Synod of Dort (1618–19) in *Ecumenical Creeds and Reformed Confessions*, 135–36.
72. Hans Urs von Balthasar and Joseph Ratzinger, *Two Say Why* (London: Search Press, 1971; Chicago: Franciscan Herald Press, 1973).

ing, dying, rising, interceding, and reigning on behalf of his people are inherently overwhelming in their testimony. It is never a weakness in the object but rather the depravity of the subject that keeps one from recognizing and embracing Christ in the gospel. Therefore, when that veil is taken away and those who are "dead in trespasses and sins" are "made alive" (Eph. 2:5), it is always effectual. Yet that which is effectual is not merely brute power, but especially the personal revelation of Christ himself, working his Father's eternal will according to the Spirit's convincing testimony. As Balthasar says elsewhere, God is "a seducer of hearts."[73]

It is not *immediacy* that guards regeneration from synergism, but its divine *source*. The Father never speaks apart from the Son, and the Spirit makes that Word, not another, bear fruit. It is the triune God who accomplishes all of this, yet always in a mediated manner. To be sure, not everyone receives the saving Word, as we learn in various places in the Gospels (e.g., Matt. 13:1–30, 36–43; John 3:3, 5–12). The Spirit must draw one inwardly to embrace the external Word:

> "The Spirit gives life; the flesh profits nothing. The words that I speak to you are spirit and they are life. But there are some of you who do not believe." For Jesus knew from the beginning who they were who did not believe and who would betray him. And he said, "Therefore, I have said to you that no one can come to me unless it has been granted to him by my Father." (John 6:63–65, NKJV)

Jesus promised, "My sheep hear my voice. I know them, and they follow me. I give them eternal life, and they will never perish. No one will snatch them out of my hand. What my Father has given me is greater than all else, and no one can snatch it out of the Father's hand. The Father and I are one" (John 10:27–30).

As Paul observes in his discourse on election and calling in Romans 9–11, the current condition of Jews in relation to this gospel is not due to a failure of the Word. In fact, no one would believe apart from God's electing, redeeming, and regenerating grace. The Spirit inwardly convinces one of the gospel, yet whenever and wherever the Spirit chooses. "Those whom he predestined he also called" (Rom. 8:30). We were "dead through trespasses and sins." "But God, who is rich in mercy, out of the great love with which he loved us even when we were dead through our trespasses, made us alive together with Christ—by grace you have been saved—and raised up with him and seated us with him in the heavenly places in Christ Jesus" (Eph. 2:1, 4–5).

If this account is accurate, we are "worded" all the way down: in election, through the covenant of redemption; in creation, and now in the covenant of grace. There is simply no place for infused habits in this kind of covenantal ontology.

I am suggesting that a covenantal paradigm, rather than distinguishing between a forensic event (justification) and infused habits (regeneration), renders the entire *ordo* forensically charged, without confusing justification with sanctification or denying that union with Christ includes organic and transformative

---

73. Hans Urs von Balthasar, *Heart of the World* (San Francisco: Ignatius Press, 1980), 117–18.

as well as forensic aspects. Furthermore, even regeneration and sanctification are effects of God's performative utterance: a declaration on the level of ex nihilo creation: "Let there be . . . !" While union with Christ and the sanctification that results from that union are *more than* forensic, they are the *consequences* of God's forensic declaration. Both justification ("Let there be . . . !") and inner renewal ("Let the earth bring forth . . . !") are the result of the speaking God: Father, Son, and Spirit. There is always more to a relationship than communication, but it is always generated and sustained in its own particular manner by acts of discourse (including sacraments as well as verbal address).

Like ex nihilo creation, justification is not a process of transforming an already-existing state of affairs. In other words, it is a synthetic rather than analytic verdict, eschatological rather than organic. Nevertheless, when the Spirit brings about within creation the response appropriate to that pronouncement, an analytic judgment follows ("God saw all that he had made, and it was very good" [Gen. 1:31 NIV]). When God *externally* declares the wicked to be righteous only for the sake of Christ, he also *inwardly* declares those dead in sins to be alive in Christ by the Spirit. It is that double declaration that then issues in the actual transformation of a person from unbelief and rebellion to faith and repentance. No wedge can be legitimately driven between speech and action. God's speaking is active; the Word itself has the power, in the Spirit, to bring about its intended effect within creaturely reality without violating creaturely integrity.

Chapter Eleven

"Behold, I Make All Things New"

The Verdict That Does What It Says

"For the first time, with the Reformation, there appeared this conception of a grace that saves a man without changing him, of a justice that redeems corrupted nature without restoring it, of a Christ who pardons the sinner for self-inflicted wounds but does not heal them."[1] Such statements as this one by Etienne Gilson reflect a deep suspicion that the churches of the magisterial Reformation do not believe in the new birth or sanctification. Similarly, Milbank rejects "all Protestant accounts of grace as mere imputation (although there are many Protestant accounts not of this kind)"—when in actual fact, there are *no* Protestant accounts of this kind, at least of which I am aware. Therefore, Milbank announces that "an account of the arrival of grace must for me also mean an account of sanctification, and of ethics."[2]

The assumption seems to be that if one holds that *justification* is an exclusively forensic declaration on the basis of Christ's righteousness imputed through faith alone, then *salvation* (encompassing all the benefits of our union with Christ)

---

1. Etienne Gilson, *The Spirit of Medieval Philosophy* (London: Sheed & Ward, 1936), 421.
2. John Milbank, *Being Reconciled: Ontology and Pardon* (London and New York: Routledge, 2003), 138.

must exclude all intrinsic actions and effects. Not only does this second premise fail to follow necessarily from the first; it also has no standing in the history of confessional Protestantism, which has displayed extensive interest in sanctification and ethics as the inevitable fruit of justifying faith.

As relevant today as when he wrote it in the 1950s is G. C. Berkouwer's reply to those who deny Luther's interest in God's gracious renovation of believers: "To anyone who has had a whiff of Luther's writings this conception is incredible. Even a scanty initiation is enough to be convinced that justification for Luther meant much more than an external event with no importance for the inner man."[3] In fact, only in the Reformation view are both a purely forensic justification and a moral transformation simultaneously affirmed as two inseparable aspects of the salvation that we have in Christ.[4] The real question, then, is whether justification is the *source* of new obedience or its *result*. In this chapter, we turn our attention to sanctification as the perlocutionary effect of the evangelical Word pronounced upon us by the Father in grace.

ADOPTION: FORENSIC AND RELATIONAL, JUDICIAL AND TRANSFORMATIVE

Appealing to the research of Phyllis Bird, I pointed out in *Lord and Servant* (chap. 4) that Genesis 1–2 exploits Egyptian mythology for polemical purposes. While the Pharaoh was thought to be the son of the gods, in Genesis this royal sonship extends beyond the king, and not only to all sons but also to all human beings: "male and female" created in God's *image*, the language of sonship. To be adopted by the Great King, the vassal "puts on" the identity of the suzerain, including its regal glory. It is this lost glory that is recovered—and because it is no less than the glory of the God-Man, it is greater than the original glory of "the first man . . . from the earth, a man of dust" (1 Cor. 15:47). "Just as we have borne the image of the man of dust, we will also bear the image of the man of heaven" (v. 49).

As I argued in that chapter, the *imago Dei* does not subsist in a particular faculty (such as the soul), but in the totality of human existence as commissioned for glory. There I also noted M. G. Kline's observation that there are three principal elements of this image or likeness that are evident across redemptive history: the images of the temple (dominion, kingship), the ethical commission (the foundations of the temple are justice, equity, truth, righteousness, goodness), and glory (physical beauty). "To be the image of God is to be the son of God."[5] To "put on Christ" is to derive all of one's righteousness from him, both for justifi-

---

3. G. C. Berkouwer, *Studies in Dogmatics: Faith and Sanctification* (Grand Rapids: Eerdmans, 1952), 29.

4. In the Roman Catholic perspective, which Milbank adopts, the forensic category remains, but it is the meritorious acts of the saints, as well as our own, that dominate this aspect.

5. Michael S. Horton, *Lord and Servant: A Covenant Christology* (Louisville, KY: Westminster John Knox, 2005), chap. 4, citing M. G. Kline, *Images of the Spirit* (Eugene, OR: Wipf & Stock, 1999), 35.

cation and sanctification. That is not only because he is the eternal Son, but also because he is the justified covenant head of his people, "and was declared to be Son of God with power according to the spirit of holiness by resurrection from the dead" (Rom. 1:4). In Christ, our rags are exchanged for robes of regal splendor, and we are seated at the same table with Abraham, Isaac, and Jacob.

However, in common with the practices of its neighbors, Israel's law made the firstborn son heir of the estate, which was also the inheritance law of the Greco-Roman world. As we see in the case of Abraham's vexing concern, slaves could inherit the estate only if there were no son to inherit (Gen. 15:3), so daughters and slaves were in a precarious position, completely dependent on the generosity of their fathers, husbands, and masters. In the era of liberal democracy, we may find it difficult to imagine the dissonance of the announcement to ancient ears, "There is no longer Jew or Greek, there is no longer slave or free, there is no longer male and female; for all of you are one in Christ Jesus. And if you belong to Christ, then you are Abraham's offspring, heirs according to promise" (Gal. 3:28–29).

So the thing to notice, especially in Paul's treatment, is not an ostensible chauvinism in identifying the people of God as "sons" rather than "sons and daughters," but the radical discontinuity with both Judaism and Hellenism in identifying *daughters and slaves* as *sons*—that is, the legal heirs of the estate. In the process, the whole notion of who constitutes the right to "property" is subverted, at least in the communion of saints. This is another place where law cannot bring about the state of affairs that belongs to humanity's commission. It is faith, not law (whether Sinaitic or Hellenic), that determines the heirs of Abraham. The application is also made in 1 Peter 3:7: Not only in the church but also in domestic relations, husbands are told to "show consideration for your wives in your life together, . . . since they too are also heirs of the gracious gift of life."

A lodestar for justification, Galatians 3 and 4 are also crucial for our understanding of adoption. After all, the same logic that announces freedom from the bondage of the law for righteousness also pertains to the right of inheritance, which is a question of "sonship." Paul unfolds his argument redemptive-historically: with the law (here intending the whole old covenant administration) as the "disciplinarian until Christ came, so that we might be justified by faith" (3:24).

> My point is this: heirs, as long as they are minors, are no better than slaves, though they are the owners of all the property; but they remain under guardians and trustees until the date set by the father. So with us; while we were minors, we were enslaved to the elemental spirits of the world. But when the fullness of time had come, God sent his Son, born of a woman, born under the law, in order to redeem those who were under the law, so that we might receive adoption as children. And because you are children, God has sent the Spirit of his Son into our hearts, crying, "Abba! Father!" So you are no longer a slave but a son, and if a son then also an heir through God. (4.1–7 NRSV/RSV)

Furthermore, these brothers and sisters are not only heirs of whatever is left over from the spoils of the firstborn son's inheritance. In fact, the very passage we are

using for the structure of these chapters (Rom. 8:30) begins first with the statement, "For those whom he foreknew he also predestined to be conformed to the
image of his Son, in order that he might be the firstborn within a large family"
(v. 29). Jews and Gentiles alike are "fellow heirs, members of the same body, and
sharers in the promise in Christ Jesus through the gospel" (Eph. 3:6). Properly
speaking, it is Christ who is the "heir of all things" (Heb. 1:2; cf. Luke 20:14),
but precisely because he possesses all things not only as a private but as a public
person, union with him means communion with each other.

In this economy, Moses is a servant in God's house, while Jesus Christ is the
firstborn son (Heb. 3:1–6).

> For the one who sanctifies and those who are sanctified all have one Father.
> For this reason Jesus is not ashamed to call them brothers and sisters, say-
> ing, "I will proclaim your name to my brothers and sisters, in the midst of
> the congregation I will praise you." And again, "I will put my trust in him."
> And again, "Here am I and the children whom God has given me." Since,
> therefore, the children share flesh and blood, he himself likewise shared the
> same things, so that through death he might destroy the one who has the
> power of death, that is, the devil, and free those who all their lives were held
> in slavery by the fear of death. . . . Therefore he had to become like his broth-
> ers and sisters in every respect, so that he might be a merciful and faithful
> high priest in the service [cf. 8:6, *leitourgia*] of God, to make a sacrifice of
> atonement for the sins of the people. (2:11–15, 17)

As with justification, this adoption is not a legal fiction, since the law is fulfilled:
the firstborn Son has won the entire estate by his victorious service to the crown,
but every adopted child has an equal share. At this point, the character of
the covenant of grace as founded on a royal grant becomes especially obvious.
Having merited his estate by his loyal service to the Great King, the inheritance is passed on in perpetuity to all of those coheirs included in his last will
and testament. Jesus' high-priestly prayer in John 17 is pregnant with this
covenantal grant, even to the point of linking his own fulfillment of his earthly
mission to the intratrinitarian covenant of redemption, referring to "those whom
you gave me" (v. 9), who are now to be included in the *koinōnia* of the Trinity
itself.

As in creation, the covenant of grace is therefore founded in excess rather than
lack. Unlike the principle of scarcity that rules in the economy of sin and death,
or a Neoplatonic emanation in which "being" diminishes as it is diffused down
the ladder, in this family the wealth is distributed to all alike without any loss of
assets. After all, this inheritance is grounded not merely in the one divine essence
but also in the shared wealth of the Trinity according to the covenant of redemption. The children need not worry about their future or jockey for their Father's
favor (as Jacob and Esau). After all, "He who did not withhold his own Son, but
gave him up for all of us, will he not with him also give us everything else?" (Rom.
8:32). As Calvin comments on Ephesians 1:23,

This is the highest honour of the Church, that, until he is united to us, the Son of God reckons himself in some measure imperfect. What consolation is it for us to learn, that, not until we are along with him, does he possess all his parts, or wish to be regarded as complete! Hence, in the First Epistle to the Corinthians, when the apostle discusses largely the metaphor of a human body, he includes under the single name of Christ the whole Church.[6]

If union with Christ in the covenant of grace is the matrix for Paul's *ordo*, justification remains its source, even for adoption. We do not move from the topic of justification to other (more ostensibly interesting) ones, but are always relating the riches of our inheritance to this decisive gift. In William Ames's words, "Adoption of its own nature requires and presupposes the reconciliation found in justification. . . . The first fruit of adoption is that Christian liberty by which all believers are freed from the bondage of the law, sin, and the world."[7]

Once again we can see that the antithesis between forensic and effective or legal and transformative is unwarranted. Adoption, like justification, is simultaneously legal and relational, as is the obverse: alienation and condemnation. The tendency to replace the legal exchange with some notion of a transfer of substance, properties, or habits in justification would have as its corollary a concept of adoption in which the adoptee, no longer adopted, receives a transfer of DNA.

To be sure, there are organic as well as legal images for complementary aspects of the wider *ordo*. Particularly when we exchange a causal paradigm for a communicative one, however, false choices are eliminated. Reformation theology does not leave us in the courtroom, but it is the basis for our relocation to the family room. "For Luther," writes Oswald Bayer, "the customary alternative of 'forensic' or 'effective' is no alternative at all. The forensic is effective, the effective forensic. That is his answer to the much-debated question. What God says, God does. The reverse is also true. . . . God's work is God's speech. God's speech is no fleeting breath. It is a most effective breath that creates life, that summons into life."[8]

Justification is not an inert but a living Word, on a par with creation ex nihilo, according to Paul (Rom. 4:17, with Ps. 33:6)—not only the Word *about* God, but also the Word *of* God, which creates the reality that it announces. The Word that pronounces us rightful heirs immediately begins to work in us the family resemblance that has the firstborn Son as its archetype. Justification need not be conflated with sanctification in order to render it operative; the Word that justifies also sanctifies, through the same faith, as I will argue more fully now.[9]

6. John Calvin, *Commentaries on the Epistles of Paul to the Galatians and Ephesians*, trans. William Pringle (Grand Rapids: Eerdmans, 1957), 218.

7. William Ames, *The Marrow of Theology*, trans. John D. Eusden (Boston: Pilgrim, 1968; repr. Durham, NC: Labyrinth, 1983), 165.

8. Oswald Bayer, *Living by Grace: Justification and Sanctification*, trans. Geoffrey W. Bromiley (Grand Rapids: Eerdmans, 2003), 43.

9. The results of the second Anglican–Roman Catholic International Commission (ARCIC II), published in *Growth in Agreement II: Reports and Agreed Statements of Ecumenical Conversations on a World Level 1982–1988*, ed. Jeffrey Gros, Harding Meyer, and William G. Rusch (Geneva: World

ORGANIC ASPECTS OF UNION

Before warring nations can enter into an era of peaceful relations, they must formally and legally conclude a peace. Before orphans can enjoy the love and care of a new family, they must be legally adopted. What security would the weaker have in relation to the stronger if they did not know that the legal obstacles that might withdraw their status have been finally and forever resolved? The status being settled once and for all, our new relationship to God and the promised inheritance is a terminus a quo (starting point) of divine accomplishment and not a terminus ad quem (goal) of our striving. To insist upon the logical priority of legal justification is simply to recognize that God's love is consistent with God's justice, righteousness, holiness, and beauty.

Just as the metaphor of adoption, in the *covenantal* context, stresses the legal and relational together, the organic metaphors associated with regeneration and sanctification underscore the power of that justifying Word to actually insert the believer into the world that it announces. Here we encounter the familiar vocabulary of vine and branches, tree and fruit, head and body, firstfruits and full harvest, living stones being built into a temple. Thus, the reference point for sanctification remains Christ's person and work, mediated by the Spirit through Word and sacrament, received through faith alone—but not by a faith that is alone. Furthermore, sanctification is treated in the New Testament in terms of the already–not yet, justifying to my mind at least a distinction between definitive and progressive sanctification.[10] Just as the temple vessels were not intrinsically holy before they were set aside for holy purposes, there is no preparation on our part that can make us holy.[11]

However, we should beware of turning the distinction into a separation, where our status as holy in Christ (definitive sanctification) is one thing and our own holiness (progressive sanctification) is another. In our pilgrimage, we are not, strictly speaking, growing in *our* holiness, but we are also bearing the fruit of our union with Christ and his holiness. The flesh (*sarx*) is not given a new lease on life, improved, elevated, and revived. Rather, the Adamic self is put to death, and the person thus raised is now a participant in the Spirit, sharing with Christ in the powers of the age to come. Thus, our justification and union with Christ (which includes definitive sanctification) cannot be seen merely as the starting point for a life of personal transformation, but as the only source of any fecun-

---

Council of Churches; Grand Rapids: Eerdmans, 2000), in par. 15, appealing to 1 Cor. 6:11, stated that "justification and sanctification are two aspects of the same divine act": "God's grace effects what he declares: his creative word imparts what it imputes. By pronouncing us righteous, God also makes us righteous. He imparts a righteousness which is his and becomes ours." In my estimation, ARCIC II, though still insufficiently attentive to the purely forensic character of justification, is more consistent with the Reformation perspective than is the Joint Declaration on Justification between the Lutheran World Federation and the Vatican.

10. See especially John Murray, *Collected Writings of John Murray* (Edinburgh: Banner of Truth Trust, 1977), 2:277–93.

11. For an excellent treatment of this topic, see John Webster, *Holiness* (Grand Rapids: Eerdmans, 2003), esp. chap. 4.

dity throughout the Christian life. Our mortification and vivification in sanctification are not our own contribution alongside justification and union with
Christ, but are the effect of that new relationship.

Calvin offers helpful insights on this point in his comments on John 17, in
Jesus' high-priestly prayer. Believers are "sanctified by the truth," which is God's
Word (v. 17), "for the word here denotes the doctrine of the Gospel": here Calvin
uses the opportunity to take a swipe at the "fanatics," who imagine a sanctification that comes from an "inner word" apart from the external Word.[12] "And for
their sakes I sanctify myself," Jesus prays (v. 19).

> By these words he explains more clearly from what source that sanctifica-
> tion flows, which is completed in us by the doctrine of the Gospel. It is
> because he consecrated himself to the Father that his holiness might come
> to us; for as the blessing on the firstfruits is spread over the whole harvest,
> so the Spirit of God cleanses us by the holiness of Christ, and makes us par-
> takers of it. Nor is this done by imputation only, for in that respect he is said
> to have been made to us righteousness; but he is likewise said to have been
> made to us sanctification (1 Cor 1:30) because he has, so to speak, presented
> us to his Father in his own person, that we may be renewed to true holiness
> by his Spirit. Besides, though this sanctification belongs to the whole life of
> Christ, yet the highest illustration of it was given in the sacrifice of his death;
> for then he showed himself to be the true High Priest, by consecrating the
> temple, the altar, all the vessels, and the people, by the power of his Spirit.[13]

The goal is "that they may all be one" (John 17:21).[14] Calvin is as much on home
ground in discussing the richness of the organic-horticultural metaphors as the
legal. While they are distinct, the organic and the legal are two sides of the same
covenantal coin.

The same harmony can be found in the confessional treatments, as in the Second Helvetic Confession, chapter 15: "Wherefore, in this matter we are not
speaking of a fictitious, empty, lazy and dead faith, but of a living, quickening
faith. *It is and is called a living faith because it apprehends Christ who is life and
makes alive, and shows that it is alive by living works*" (emphasis added). It is not
the quality of faith itself, but of the person it apprehends, that makes it the sufficient means of receiving both our justification and sanctification. Not because
of what faith is, but because of who Christ is, faith in Christ cannot fail to bring
forth good works. In fact, precisely because believers do not trust at all in their
own piety, the works that spring from faith are truly pious.[15]

12. John Calvin, *Commentary on the Gospel according to John*, trans. William Pringle (1847; repr.,
Grand Rapids: Baker, 1996), 179–80.

13. Ibid., 180–81.

14. Ibid., 183.

15. Second Helvetic Confession, chap. 15, in *The Book of Confessions* (Louisville, KY: General
Assembly of the PC[USA], 1991): "This all the pious do, but they trust in Christ alone and not in
their own works. For again the apostle said: 'It is no longer I who live, but Christ who lives in me;
and the life I now live in the flesh I live by faith in the Son of God, who loved me and gave himself
for me. I do not reject the grace of God; for if justification were through the law, then Christ died to
no purpose' (Gal 2:20[–21])."

The new creation into which believers have been inserted, far from the end of strife, is the beginning of inner conflict, since the will that was once bound to sin and death is now liberated to pursue righteousness yet not free from the presence of sin. Precisely because believers have been legally and eschatologically transferred from "this age," under the condemnation of the law, sin, and death; and transferred to "the age to come," under justification, righteousness, and life—because of this transfer, sanctification is not a mere moral improvement but the real effects of a qualitatively new kind of life. Paradoxically, it is this very liberation that issues in constant inner struggle. By contrast, the struggle of the unregenerate, says Ames, is "not the striving of the Spirit against the flesh but that of the flesh fearing flesh inordinately desiring."[16] Ames's statement points up the fact that however useful Aristotelian or Kantian conceptions of "ethics," "virtue," and "duty" may be, the definitive categories for theology are covenantal and eschatological: the tyranny of sin (flesh) versus the reign of life in righteousness (the Spirit). Natural ethics may check immoderate habits, but it cannot create a new world.

Once again, the communicative approach is not only more consistent with Scripture's own way of talking about God's effective Word; it is also clearly evident in the treatments offered by the Reformers. However, just as Paul's treatment of justification led logically to the question "Should we continue in sin in order that grace may abound?" (Rom. 6:1), the Reformation unleashed radical elements that went well beyond the views of the Reformers.

> Luther had hardly begun to proclaim the freedom of the Christian before he had to fight against abuse of the term. He did not do this in such a way as to speak about the good works that must be added to faith. Instead, he did so by calling people back to that faith that occurs "where the Holy Spirit gives people faith in Christ and thus sanctifies them."[17]

At this juncture Luther's response was precisely Paul's: To infer from justification that we are free to remain in sin is to ignore the vast scope of what justification actually accomplishes.

Although it is not itself a renovation, justification issues, as an effective Word, in a completely new reality. The God who declares the wicked righteous simultaneously (though distinctly) makes the dead alive. Acquittal and acceptance lead inevitably to new life and new obedience, not vice versa. While our first impulse is to return to the law and self-effort in order to stem the tide of antinomianism, Paul and the Reformers call us back to the gospel, whose power in the face of continuing sin we have not sufficiently weighed. Apart from the imputation of righteousness, sanctification is simply another religious self-improvement program determined by the powers of this age (the flesh) rather than of the age to come (the Spirit).

16. Ames, *The Marrow of Theology*, 171.
17. Gerhard Forde, *On Being a Theologian of the Cross: Reflections on Luther's Heidelberg Disputation, 1518* (Grand Rapids: Eerdmans, 1997), 56–57.

This gospel not only announces our justification, but also our participation in the power of Christ's crucifixion and resurrection. Again Forde is insightful:

> In our modern age, influenced by Pietism and the Enlightenment, our thinking is shaped by what is subjective, by the life of faith, by our inner disposition and motivation, by our inward impulses and the way they are shaped. When we think and live along these lines, sanctification is a matter of personal and individual development and orientation. It is true that we also find this approach in Luther. No one emphasized more sharply than he did our personal responsibility and irreplaceability. But this approach is secondary. "The Word of God always comes first. After it follows faith; after faith, love; then love does every good work, for . . . it is the fulfilling of the law."[18]

Even in sanctification "the focus is not upon the saints but upon sanctification, upon the Word of God in all its sacramental forms, and also upon secular institutions that correspond to the second table of the law. . . . Only God is holy, and what he says and speaks and does is holy. This is how God's holiness works, which he does not keep to himself, but communicates by sharing it."[19]

Far from creating a morbid subjectivity and individualism, as is often charged, this view frees us from being curved in on ourselves, fretting over our own souls. In a moving and friendly letter to Cardinal Sadoleto, Calvin made much the same point, arguing that only by being freed of having to love our neighbor in the service of our own salvation are we able to really love them for their own sake.[20] Sanctification is a life not of acquiring but of receiving from the excess of divine joy that then continues to overflow in excess to our neighbor. Thus, we are obligated to God only by gratitude, but to our neighbor also by debt. While we do not owe God anything, we owe our neighbors love and service through our vocations.

ESCHATOLOGY: *SIMUL IUSTUS ET PECCATOR*

While fully adopting Luther's *simul*, the Reformed have insisted that the radical announcement of the "already" is assigned to our ethical as well as legal relation to God. A definitive moral change has occurred that does not involve stages of development. We are decisively transferred from death to life, from the dominion of sin to the dominion of righteousness. Progress in the *realization* and outworking of that definitive change is incomplete in this life, but the *transfer* from the lordship of the old age to that of the new age is itself a completed event.

To be sure, the only righteousness with which we can appear before God is the perfect holiness that we have in Christ alone. Nevertheless, Paul answers antinomianism with the triumphant indicative that we are not only justified and

18. Ibid., 58; *LW* 36:39.
19. Forde, *On Being a Theologian of the Cross*, 59.
20. John Calvin, *A Reformation Debate: Sadoleto's Letter to the Genevans and Calvin's Reply*, ed. John C. Olin (Grand Rapids: Baker, 1966), 56.

then left to the tyranny of sin, but that we are also baptized into Christ's newness of life. Without the slightest retraction of the emphasis on forensic justification that elicited the accusation, Paul indicates that precisely *on the basis of* imputation, something *more than* an imputed righteousness is included in our union with Christ. Both justification and sanctification are found in Christ, not in us.

Luther follows the same course in countering antinomianism, yet elsewhere the absolute newness of the believer's identity in Christ is downplayed by what sometimes verges on an underrealized eschatology, as in Luther's statement, "I have heard of it but as yet have seen *nothing* of it. '*Not in essence*, but by promise, I have eternal life. I have it in obscurity. I *do not see it*, but I believe it and will *hereafter surely feel it*" (emphasis added).[21] While we do indeed live by faith rather than by sight, believing what we hear even when we do not see it, is it really the case that we have seen nothing of the age to come and have felt no impact of the new creation? Or is it that the age to come is even now breaking in on this present age, already beginning to transform everything from the inside out?

While our failures should send us back to Christ rather than to the law for safety, Reformed theology seems less reticent to encourage believers to be cheered by the newness that they actually experience. An underrealized eschatology loses the agonizing paradox of the *simul* just as surely as an overrealized perfectionism.[22] Exactly because Paul is the figure described in Romans 6—not only justified but also truly "alive in Christ" and definitively liberated from the tyranny of sin—he is disturbed by the discrepancy between this fact and indwelling sin that he discovers in himself in Romans 7.[23]

According to Jane E. Stohl, Luther has an "eschatological reserve." "For Calvin the transformation of the believer is measurably advanced and manifest, whereas for Luther the reality of redemption remains deeply hidden until the Last Day."[24] "Finally for Luther what matters most is not what the believer does in or for the world, but how he or she survives it."[25] While this is too facile a contrast between

21. Forde, *On Being a Theologian of the Cross*, 35; citing Luther, WA 16:52, 19–21.

22. As Tuomo Mannermaa points out, Luther speaks of the *simul* in two senses: the believer is totally sinner in herself and totally righteous in Christ (*totus-totus*), yet also partially sinful and partially righteous in terms of sanctification (*partim-partim*) (*Christ Present in Faith: Luther's Doctrine of Justification by Faith*, ed. Kirsi Stjerna [Minneapolis: Fortress, 2005], 58–60). It is that second sense that I am stressing here, although it must always keep the first in view.

23. There have been serious exegetical objections raised against the traditional Reformed and Lutheran interpretation of the "I" in Rom. 7, beyond those raised by Arminian theology. Werner G. Kümmel, *Römer 7 und die Bekehrung des Paulus* (Leipzig: Hinrichs, 1929), regarded the "I" in Rom. 7 as a stylistic device that is not to be read as autobiographical. Herman Ridderbos (*Paul: An Outline of His Theology*, trans. John Richard de Witt [1975; repr., Grand Rapids: Eerdmans, 1997]) also develops an intriguing line of exegesis. Nevertheless, I remain persuaded that there are good exegetical reasons to retain the autobiographical "I" while recognizing that it is illustrative also of a wider redemptive-historical reality—i.e., the transition from the era of "this age" (law, sin, condemnation, death) and "the age to come."

24. Jane E. Strohl, "God's Self-Revelation in the Sacrament of the Altar," in *By Faith Alone: Essays on Justification in Honor of Gerhard O. Forde*, ed. Joseph A. Burgess and Marc Kolden (Grand Rapids: Eerdmans, 2004), 107.

25. Ibid., 109.

the Reformers, it seems to me that the church desperately needs the maturity and wisdom of both emphases. In view of the eschatological tension, individual, ecclesial, and social activism often lead to either despair or self-righteousness (or both). "Surviving" the world seems not only to put us back in the position of receivers (who for that reason actually have more to offer others), but also helps the church to recognize what it seems easily to forget, namely, that we are not building a kingdom but receiving one (Heb. 12:28). Furthermore, it comports better with the rather inauspicious New Testament appeals to simply fulfill our secular callings and live godly lives (1 Thess. 4:11–12), in sharp contrast with our usual ecclesiastical pontifications on all matters political and social in pursuit of triumphalist world transformation. At the same time, just as the "new creation" must mean something not only for our justification but also for our sanctification, surely the existence of a colony of heaven in this present age involves more than mere survival.

We can avoid synergism and passivity at least in part by recognizing that the divine grace of sanctification does not render the subject immobile or passive, but definitively and progressively transforms the character of that agency. God's work renders us even more mobile and more active in righteousness than we were in unrighteousness. John Webster draws our attention to this point nicely:

> The sanctifying Spirit is *Lord*; that is, sanctification is not in any straight-forward sense a process of cooperation or coordination between God and the creature, a drawing out or building upon some inherent holiness of the creature's own. Sanctification is *making* holy. Holiness is properly an incommunicable divine attribute; if creaturely realities become holy, it is by virtue of election, that is, by a sovereign act of segregation or separation by the Spirit as Lord. . . . From the vertical of "lordship" there flows the horizontal of life which is truly *given*. Segregation, election to holiness, is not the abolition of creatureliness but its creation and preservation.[26]

Simultaneously justified and sinful, we are also simultaneously renewed and sinful. Though less complete, the renewal is no less definitive than justification.

In other words, I do not think that we properly understand the New Testament in general or Paul in particular if we think in terms of the believer being, paradoxically, the "old self" and the "new self" at one and the same time. Rather, we are *defined* by the age to come, as it has already dawned for us by virtue of the Spirit's act of uniting us to Christ through faith. That is why the persistence of indwelling sin provokes anguish. With each capitulation to temptation, we are acting *as if* the indicative announcement that "rewords" us were not true. Hence, Paul's call to "reckon" or "consider" ourselves "dead to sin and alive to God in Christ Jesus" (Rom. 6:11). Without the triumphant indicative of Romans 6, which gives rise to real imperatives to be what we are, Paul's struggle in Romans 7 seems, oddly enough, less paradoxical. We are not under the reign of sin and

---

26. John Webster, *Holy Scripture: A Dogmatic Sketch* (Cambridge: Cambridge University Press, 2003), 27.

death, yet we continue to sin and die. Although believers are no longer objectively "in Adam," the empirical evidence often falls far short of adducing convincing testimony of that fact. Still, we go on believing that sin's dominion over us has been toppled, going by the testimony of the Spirit (which is inseparable from the external world), on the basis of the resurrection of Jesus. Not only a theology of the cross but also a theology of the resurrection feed the New Testament soteriology. If we have been crucified and buried with Christ, then we have also been raised with him in newness of life.

A genuinely paradoxical logic requires in addition a genuine narrative and historical movement (before and after) in order to keep from being frozen in a timeless present. Sanctification is not an ontic process of transforming the natural into the supernatural, but God's identification with nature, his act of bringing it under the scope of his special, electing love. "However indispensable *sola fide* may be," Webster reminds us, "it should not be taken to mean that passivity is the only mode of Christian existence." "*Sola fide* means that in all its acts, the being of the sanctified sinner refers to the lordly creativity of God—to the Father's electing mercy before all time, the Son's finished work, and the Spirit's presence and promise."[27] Still, we can concur with Barth's pastoral wisdom: "If justification is a happening which we experience in ourselves, if we can find ourselves in it, so that there is no puzzle, but it can be readily conceived, then we must have made a mistake."[28] If, in the face of confidence in our own moral progress, Barth (like Luther) may sometimes downplay the *already* that the justifying Word has engendered, he is surely correct to remind us of the puzzle engendered by the *not yet*. George Hunsinger reminds us that despite the "high christology" that Barth and Balthasar share, when it comes to this question, given Balthasar's Roman Catholic emphasis on salvation as a "process," they part ways. "On the relation between the 'extrinsic' and 'intrinsic' aspects of soteriology, on what takes place *extra nos* and what takes place *in nobis* and on how they are related, Catholic theology often seems ambiguous at best."[29] This is not simply a difference in emphasis, Hunsinger reminds us. "The entire gospel, as understood by the Reformation, depends on the affirmation that Christ's righteousness and life become ours as a gift that is received not by works but by faith alone."[30] On this point, Lutheran and Reformed views are at one: sanctification as well as justification is the gift of God alone through faith in Christ alone.

If salvation cannot be reduced to a process (thereby surrendering justification), it can nevertheless hardly be denied that sanctification involves a process of gradual conformity to the image of Christ. Hunsinger recognizes this weakness in Barth's treatment of sanctification. Whatever Barth's appropriate criticisms of Roman Catholic soteriology, "von Balthasar rightly challenges Barth, it

27. John Webster, *Holiness* (Grand Rapids: Eerdmans, 2003), 88.
28. Karl Barth, *CD* IV/1:546.
29. George Hunsinger, *Disruptive Grace: Studies in the Theology of Karl Barth* (Grand Rapids: Eerdmans, 2000), 267–68.
30. Ibid., 273.

seems to me, for rejecting all talk of growth or progress in the Christian life."[31] In fact, Hunsinger concludes,

> My own hunch, for what it's worth, is that baptism may again provide a key. Insofar as baptism is both a gift and a vocation, it combines both the idea of a once-for-all saving event, which baptism attests by being administered to each believer (or in the case of infants, each "proleptic" believer) only once, with the idea that dying and rising with Christ is also our daily vocation. Barth knew how to highlight the "once-and-for-all" and the "again and again" aspects of our dying and rising with Christ, but unfortunately failed to do justice to the "more and more" aspect as well.[32]

The more thoroughly Trinitarian our soteriology, the more we will see the significance of the Spirit's work *within* us, on the basis of what the Father has given *to* us and the Son has done *for* us.[33]

In a covenantal perspective, there are always two parties, and while the Lord of the covenant is always the giver of justification and sanctification, the gift initiates a genuine responsiveness on the part of the covenant servant. This faith is always a gift, although it is always simultaneously a human decision.[34] As a result of *having been turned* toward the Word by the Word and Spirit, conversion (faith and repentance) is a decisive, once-and-for-all *human turning* that marks the believer's awareness of God's calling, and as Luther and Barth also emphasized along with Calvin, this conversion yields lifelong mortification and vivification, "again and again." The whole life is repentance, as Luther urged in the first of his Ninety-five Theses. Yet this lifelong conversion is indeed a process of growing into conformity with our "wording" in Christ. However much its degrees remain hidden to us, this is the "more and more" that Hunsinger properly highlights as

---

31. Ibid., referring to Hans Urs von Balthasar, *The Theology of Karl Barth: Exposition and Interpretation,* trans. Edward T. Oakes (San Francisco: Communio Books, Ignatius Press, 1992), 371.

32. Hunsinger, *Disruptive Grace,* 274.

33. In my view, Barth does give greater space to this very point in *CD* IV/4, in his discussion of "Baptism with the Holy Spirit," but his actualism (see esp. p. 39) and, as Hunsinger suggests, his sharp antithesis of Spirit baptism and water baptism (throughout this volume, but especially in the second half, 41–213) reflect his suspicions of organic growth. When God's work is always identified with that which is direct, immediate, and ever new, in contrast to human work (even as grateful response), any notion of a salvific process is seen as a threat to *sola gratia.* As I will develop more fully in vol. 4, the problem at this point turns not on monergism versus synergism, but on the notion of mediation.

34. Of course, Barth could emphasize this point, as he does throughout his final fragment of the *Church Dogmatics* (*CD* IV/4). On the other hand, Berkouwer properly indicates the problems involved in Barth's understanding of faith as not "the act of human belief, but the act of the original divine belief" (e.g., Karl Barth, *Erklärung des Philipperbriefes,* 6th ed. [Zollikon, Zurich: Evangelische Verlag, 1947], 42; quoted by G. C. Berkouwer, *Studies in Dogmatics: Faith and Sanctification* [Grand Rapids: Eerdmans, 1952], 122). On the other hand he affirms, "But free and sovereign grace does not abolish human subjectivity" (also cited by Berkouwer, 122). Furthermore, gradual growth and process seem inimical to the actualism that is so important for every locus. With Hunsinger, I argue that Barth's understanding of baptism is an important link in understanding his view of sanctification, but the commitment to this actualistic ("again and again") understanding of God's work more generally represents a deeper motive.

connected with our baptism. Even this gradual, actual growth in holiness must be an article of faith—a promise to which we cling regardless of appearances.

WHY SANCTIFICATION ALWAYS NEEDS JUSTIFICATION

The judicial and the mystical, forensic and organic, legal and transformative—these are neither separated nor confused in this view of justification and union with Christ. However, Vos states:

> In our opinion, Paul consciously and consistently subordinated the mystical aspect of the relation to Christ to the forensic one. Paul's mind was to such an extent forensically oriented that he regarded the entire complex of subjective spiritual changes that take place in the believer and of subjective spiritual blessings enjoyed by the believer as the direct outcome of the forensic work of Christ applied in justification. The mystical is based on the forensic, not the forensic on the mystical.[35]

Whether justification is collapsed into sanctification or separated from it, the results are the same: a moralism that can neither embrace the promise nor bring about any genuine transformation at the deepest level—namely, the struggle between the two ages. G. C. Berkouwer's observation is still relevant in our own day: "The problem of the renewal of life is attracting the attention of moralists."

> Amid numberless chaotic and demoralizing forces is sounded, as if for the last time, the cry for help and healing, for the re-organization of a dislocated world. The therapy prescribed perhaps varies, the call for moral and spiritual re-armament is uniformly insistent. . . . These are the questions we must answer. For implicit in them is the intent to destroy the connection between justification and sanctification, as well as the bond between faith and sanctification.[36]

Paul relates everything—including sanctification, the problems of ethics, and ecclesial harmony—to Christ's cross and resurrection.

Thus, when we move from justification to discussion of sanctification, "we are not withdrawing from the sphere of faith." "We are not here concerned with a transition from theory to practice. It is not as if we should proceed from a faith in justification to the realities of sanctification; for we might as truly speak of the reality of justification and our faith in sanctification." *Separating* justification from sanctification is as serious as *confusing* them, because it means that the latter is "cut loose or abstracted from justification."[37] When that happens, says Berkouwer, "the dis-

35. Geerhardus Vos, "'Legalism' in Paul's Doctrine of Justification," in *Redemptive History and Biblical Interpretation: The Shorter Writings of Geerhardus Vos*, ed. Richard B. Gaffin Jr. (Phillipsburg, NJ: P&R Publishing, 1980), 384.
36. Berkouwer, *Faith and Sanctification*, 11–12.
37. Ibid., 20.

tinction between justification and sanctification could then be traced to the subject of each act: God or man. Such an obvious division would have taken place; man—this would be our conclusion—is not called upon to justify but to purify himself. It is not hard to see that the Scriptures are intolerant of this division."[38] Paul teaches that believers are "sanctified in Christ Jesus" (1 Cor. 1:2, 30; 6:11; 1 Thess. 5:23; cf. Acts 20:32; 26:18). As Bavinck puts it, "Many indeed acknowledge that we are justified by the righteousness of Christ, but seem to think that—at least they act as if—they must be sanctified by a holiness they themselves have acquired."[39]

Of particular interest in the light of our last chapter's discussion, Berkouwer suggests that this problem goes back to "the Roman Catholic doctrine which teaches that justification must be understood as the infusion of supernatural grace."

> On this basis, sanctification can have meaning only as the successive development, with the cooperation of a free will, of the grace implanted. . . . Sanctification, on these terms, takes place in an atmosphere of forces and counter-forces, among which faith may then perform its now very modest function of preparing for justification; and justification itself becomes almost indistinguishable from sanctification. Once the sanctifying grace takes root, many forces throw in their weight.[40]

Instead we must see that faith always feeds "on the forgiveness of sins"; it does not just begin there. It is a life constantly grounded in promise, always received through faith.[41]

In this respect Berkouwer's insights, characteristic of confessional Reformed theology in the twentieth century, are similar to Barth's. "Despite Barth's measured approval of his work," notes Hunsinger, "[Hans] Küng never quite grasped what the Reformation meant by 'imputation' and by the centrality it assigned to passages like 1 Corinthians 1:30 and Colossians 3:3."[42] "The *sola-fide* is at the heart of justification but no less at that of sanctification," says Berkouwer.[43] Far from encouraging antinomianism in his advice to Melanchthon, "Sin bravely!" Luther used such provocative language to shift the focus back to Christ. "He does not say, 'Sin till you are blue in the face,' or 'Sin for all you're worth,'" notes Berkouwer, "but 'Sin bravely!'" "With this word—whatever the libertine may do with it—he intends to exorcise the terror of the believer who has discovered some sin in himself and has now lost sight of the grace of God. An abundance of grace can subdue the power of sin."[44]

Berkouwer warns that even when justification is affirmed, it can be separated from justification, so that what we call "the Christian life" comes to occupy its

38. Ibid., 21.
39. Cited ibid., 22.
40. Ibid., 27.
41. Ibid., 28.
42. Hunsinger, *Disrputive Grace*, 13.
43. Berkouwer, *Faith and Sanctification*, 33.
44. Ibid., 35.

own independent status. Justification may be affirmed as a past event, but its significance as the constant source for sanctification becomes lost. In Wesley's doctrine, "Sola-fide becomes a point of departure and breaks its connections with sanctification. Here lies the cause of Wesley's tendency toward synergism, in spite of his adherence to *sola-fide*."[45] The church is called not to "work for a second blessing," but to "feed on the first blessing, the forgiveness of sins."[46] Paul stresses that his goal is simply to "lay hold of that for which also I was laid hold of by Christ Jesus" (Phil. 3:12 NASB). The struggle of the church militant is not to envelope Christ in our faithfulness, but to be enveloped by Christ's faithfulness. In fact, Berkouwer goes so far as to say:

> Perfectionism is a premature seizure of the glory that will be: an anticipation leading irrevocably to nomism. The "second blessing" constitutes the link. . . . When Peter, stupefied by the wonderful catch of fish, confronts the goodness of his Master, he cries out: "Depart from me; for I am a sinful man, O Lord!" (Luke 5:8). Surrounded by the radiance of the Master, Peter can only bow his head. Later those other words were to cut through the night: "If all shall be offended in thee, I will never be offended" (Matt. 26:33). By these words Peter meant to envelop Christ with *his* fidelity and love. Christ must here bathe in Peter's glory, not Peter in Christ's. We know the outcome. Not these words, but rather those spoken over the bonanza of fish, belong to the Militia Christiana.[47]

Berkouwer therefore relates sanctification not to a divine work apart from justification (particularly implanted habits), but to justification itself. "Barth opposes especially the *habitus*-concept and denounces it as 'the unbiblical conception of a supernatural qualification of the believer,'" and Berkouwer finds the same judgment in Calvin.[48]

The real question, says Berkouwer, is whether justification is sufficient to ground *all* of the blessings communicated in the mystical union. "The same Catechism [Heidelberg, Lord's Day 24] which denies us even a partial righteousness of our own mentions the earnest purpose with which believers begin to live" according to all the commandments.

> It is this beginning which has its basis solely in justification by faith. . . . It is not true that sanctification simply succeeds justification. Lord's Day 31, which discusses the keys of the kingdom, teaches that the kingdom is opened and shut by proclaiming "to believers, one and all, that, whenever they receive the promise of the gospel by a true faith, all their sins are really forgiven them." This "whenever" illustrates the continuing relevancy of the correlation between faith and justification. . . . The purpose of preaching the ten commandments, too, is that believers may "become the more earnest

45. Ibid., 52.
46. Ibid., 64.
47. Ibid., 67.
48. Ibid., 76, citing KD 2/1:177; and Calvin, *Institutes* 3.14.13.

in seeking remission of sins and righteousness in Christ" [Heidelberg Cat-echism Q. 115]. . . . Hence there is never a stretch along the way of salva-tion where justification drops out of sight.[49]

"Genuine sanctification—let it be repeated—stands or falls with this continued orientation toward justification and the remission of sins." Therefore, "the vic-tim of this view" of sanctification as a human work subsequent to the divine work of justification "can arrive only at a sanctification that is a causal process, and he is bound, in the end, to speak as Rome of an infused grace and of a quantitative sanctification."[50]

Obviously, once again we meet the larger question above concerning ontolo-gies and conceptual vocabularies. Referring to the language of "new qualities 'infused' into the will" in the Canons of Dort, Berkouwer agrees with Barth's eval-uation: "Though the expression is not too fortunate, the thing intended is right."[51] We should beware of doing too much with the metaphors. Yet at the same time, Berkouwer adds, Scripture does speak of the Spirit being "poured out" at Pentecost, "shed abroad in our hearts" (Rom. 5:5 KJV), and of the Spirit's seed that is planted within believers (1 John 3:9). "All depends on whether it be under-stood that the operation of the Holy Spirit is to us an inscrutable mystery," says Berkouwer.[52]

This verdict seems about right. Rather than marginalize the horticultural imagery, we should take it at face value, recognizing that Christ truly communi-cates his life to us by his Spirit. The problem comes, I suggest, when we transform these analogies into quasi-scientific descriptions of inner mechanics. Berkouwer helpfully points out crucial differences between Roman Catholic and Reformed concepts of "infusion." While Bavinck, for example, defended the language of "infusion" for regeneration, he rejects the Roman Catholic interpretation.

> Of this doctrine he says that it completely alters the nature of grace, because grace is placed in physical, instead of in ethical, antithesis to nature. The ethical contrast of sin and grace yields to that of nature and super-nature. Grace, according to Rome, is not first of all the free favor of God in which He forgives our sins, but a quality injected into man by which he shares, to some extent, the divine nature. It is a supernatural, created, hyper-physical power—infused into man through the mediation of priest and sacrament—which elevates the recipient to the supernatural order. Opposed to this view is the Reformed teaching that grace is the favor of God which relieves the believer of his sins for the sake of Christ. But this confession does not imply that the forgiveness would be a remote kind of righteousness in the sense that human life would not be enriched by it.[53]

49. Berkouwer, *Faith and Sanctification*, 77.
50. Ibid., 78.
51. Ibid., 78–79, citing the Canons of Dort and Barth, *KD* 1/2.440.
52. Berkouwer, *Faith and Sanctification*, 81.
53. Ibid., 83.

Reformed theology "has always protested vigorously against the Catholic 'donum superadditum' as a new dimension in this sinful world."[54] Therefore, in using such terminology—however inadequate it may be at certain points—it is a matter of putting new wine in old wineskins. "And when the Canons and Bavinck speak about 'new qualities' and 'gratia interna,' they wish only to express the truth that the new life is not a product of flesh and blood. The judgment of charity would seem to be that theirs is a '*theologia crucis*' rather than a '*theologia gloriae*.'"[55] Thus there is nothing here that elevates a regenerated person over anyone else.[56]

Even with the medieval terminology, Reformed theology can maintain the following:

> The renewal is not a mere supplement, an appendage, to the salvation given in justification. The heart of sanctification is the life which feeds on this justification. There is no contrast between justification as act of God and sanctification as act of man. The fact that Christ is our sanctification is not exclusive of, but inclusive of, a faith which clings to him alone in all of life. Faith is the pivot on which everything revolves. Faith, though not itself creative, preserves us from autonomous self-sanctification and moralism.[57]

Building on Bavinck, Berkouwer verges on a direct rejection of the concept of infusion and habits. While heeding his caution not to assume that by using such language the Reformed were saying the same thing, I still think that the very concept should be eliminated entirely from the *ordo salutis*, including sanctification. It is the gospel that creates faith (as our confessional statements maintain, following esp. Matt. 13:1–9; John 6:63; Rom. 10:8–17; James 1:18; 1 Pet. 1:23), and this faith, engendered by the effectual call, lays claim to justification, sanctification, and all other blessings in Christ. The Spirit, working through the gospel, gives it all: faith, yielding repentance, love, and the fruit of the Spirit.

In this case the "preparation for justification" is neither performed by the sinner nor immediately by God, but by God through the gospel, and this is as true for the continuance of faith as it is for its inception. "Litanies of guilt are spoken on the way of salvation," Barth reminds us, "not only during the first stage of conversion, but, as Christ becomes more wonderful to us, in crescendo."[58] The

---

54. Ibid., 85. For a summary and defense of this view, see Johann Adam Möhler, *Symbolism: Exposition of the Doctrinal Differences between Catholics and Protestants as Evidenced by Their Symbolical Writings*, trans. James Burton Robertson (New York: Crossroad, 1997): "This relation of Adam to God, as it exalted him above human nature, and made him participate in that of God, is hence termed . . . a supernatural gift of divine grace, superadded to the endowments of nature." The fall, therefore, arises in the strife between "higher" (intellectual) and "lower" (sensual) powers of nature (27). Luther regarded this original acceptability of Adam before God natural rather than supernatural (30). Calvin followed suit, although he distinguished between free will in the prelapsarian and postlapsarian states (33–36). On justification, see chap. 3 of Möhler's work.

55. Berkouwer, *Faith and Sanctification*, 87.

56. Ibid., 93.

57. Ibid.

58. Ibid., 112, quoting Karl Barth.

preaching of the gospel that gave us a new birth unto a living hope in the first place continues to sustain our pilgrimage. We never move beyond justification, never beyond faith and the forgiveness of sins. On the contrary, as we grow in holiness, we become more acutely aware of our sin, and the struggle against it becomes increasingly intense.

The charge of "extrinsicism" is therefore unfounded as a general description of Reformation soteriology, and there is no need to appeal to infused habits in an effort to fend off that charge. We have seen that in Calvin's development of the *unio* motif, the objective person and work of Christ would mean nothing for us if the Spirit did not unite us subjectively to Christ. It is one thing to say that the work of Christ for us (*extra nos*) is the sole legal basis for his work in us (*in nobis*) by the Spirit, and quite another to deny either the legal basis (forensic justification) or its transformative effects (new birth and sanctification).

The alternative to "extrinsicism," according to many who level this charge against Reformation theology, is some version of the *imitatio Christi*. Berkouwer observes:

> Noteworthy in this peroration is the conclusion that we share in the conquest and redemption of the world. It is quite clear in this idiom of activism how inadequate is the disavowal of "copying" Christ. Even with this restriction the Gospel may recede into a moralistic haze—a danger for which the very word "*imitatio*" is largely to blame.[59]

Being a follower of Christ became reduced to imitation and example. "Influential, also, was Augustine's dictum: 'Quid est enim sequi nisi imitari?' (For what does it mean 'to follow' if not 'to imitate'?)"[60] I might add that in contrast to Kierkegaard's "learner," Augustine's more Platonic definition easily reduces the Christian life to a matter of mirroring that archetypal life of Christ in the realm of appearances.

"Disciple" in the New Testament, however, includes but is hardly reducible to imitation. Even the imitation to which we are called in the New Testament is related to the sufferings of Christ, which are not atoning but nevertheless contribute to the progress of the gospel in the world (1 Pet. 2:21, 24). As Berkouwer recognizes, "Hence those who follow do not have to repeat anything: they are healed." Imitation, in this scheme, "is to live conformably to, and on the basis of, the Atonement. . . . And they [the sheep] are to walk not on paths that will at length lead them to communion with Christ but on the path that lies open because of the communion with Christ which they enjoy by faith alone."[61]

At the same time, we should recognize that if even discipleship (much less soteriology) cannot be reduced to imitation, it certainly includes it, and once we recognize that Christ is first and foremost the one who heard and obeyed in our place,

59. Ibid., 138.
60. Ibid., 138 n. 2.
61. Ibid., 142–43.

we too, in organic and mystical as well as legal union with him, no longer "live by bread alone, but by every word that comes from the mouth of God" (Matt. 4:4). George Lindbeck reminds us that the proper category for discipleship and *imitatio Christi* is the third use of the law, not the atonement or justification.[62] Otherwise we are left with the moralism of salvation-by-following-Jesus'-example. In such theologies, writes Lindbeck, "not only does revelation subsume soteriology but, so the reformers would say, law absorbs gospel."

> This is what happens when the crucified God is first of all the prototype of authentic human existence so that it is by being prototype that Jesus Christ is Savior. From a traditional perspective, the error here is in the reversal of the order: Jesus is not first Example and then Savior, but the other way around. . . . Theologies of the cross that stress the *imitatio Christi* have their place, but that place is not with atonement, but with what Calvinists call the third use of the law, and with what Luther, if I may coin a phrase, might call a Christian's use of the first use of the law.

Theologies of the cross that focus on imitation are theologies of glory.[63]

Once we put the theme of imitation in its place, so to speak, we can speak again of the law, precisely because it returns this time (in its third use) after having pronounced its verdict on us as those who *in Christ* have already fully met its requirements. "Hence Paul can say without a qualm that he is 'under law to Christ' (1 Cor. 9:21)," notes Berkouwer. "For him there is no terror in the word 'law,' nor any tension between being under law and belonging to Christ."[64] "In numerous ways, throughout the history of the church, the true relationship between Gospel and Law has been obscured. Two opposite tendencies are apparent: the tendency to make the Gospel into a new law and the tendency to sever the Gospel from the law."[65] Yet this can only result in a confused mixture of legalism and antinomianism, both of which are opposed to God's grace.[66] "Some, among them Barth, have spoken of the law as the form of the gospel whose content is grace." However, says Berkouwer, "We protest against the reduction of the law to this status; by it the law is practically dissolved in the gospel."[67]

> In true faith the inner and outer aspect of life are harmoniously developed. The law drives the believer out into the world—to his neighbor, to his poor brother and sister (James 2:15), to his enemy, to his brother in prison, to the hungry and thirsty ones; and thrusts him into contact, for good or for ill, with earthly goods, marriage, and civil authority.[68]

---

62. George Lindbeck, "Justification and Atonement: An Ecumenical Trajectory," in *By Faith Alone: Essays on Justification in Honor of Gerhard O. Forde*, ed. Joseph A. Burgess and Marc Kolden (Grand Rapids: Eerdmans, 2004), 208.
63. Berkouwer, *Faith and Santification*, 209.
64. Ibid., 175.
65. Ibid., 188.
66. Ibid.
67. Ibid., 190.
68. Ibid., 192.

"The apostle Paul," Berkouwer writes, "preaches holiness with repetitive fervor, but in no way does he compromise his unequivocal declaration: 'For I determined not to know anything among you, save Jesus Christ, and him crucified' (1 Cor. 2:2)."

> Not for a moment would he do violence to the implications of that confession. Hence in every exhortation he must be relating his teaching to the cross of Christ. From this center all lines radiate outward—into the life of cities and villages, of men and women, of Jews and Gentiles, into families, youth, and old age, into conflict and disaffection, into immorality and drunkenness. If we would keep this center, as well as the softer and harder lines flowing from it, in true perspective, we must be thoroughly aware that in shifting from justification to sanctification we are not withdrawing from the sphere of faith. We are not here concerned with a transition from theory to practice. It is not as if we should proceed from a faith in justification to the realities of sanctification; for we might as truly speak of the reality of justification and our faith in sanctification.[69]

WHY JUSTIFICATION NECESSARILY ENTAILS SANCTIFICATION

In the Roman Catholic view, there is no *relating* of justification and sanctification because they are really one and the same.[70] As Berkouwer points out, "Sanctification, on these terms, takes place in an atmosphere of forces and counter-forces, among which faith may then perform its now very modest function of preparing for justification; and justification itself becomes almost indistinguishable from sanctification."[71] In Berkouwer's contrast between Rome's "field of forces" and the Reformation's emphasis on the gospel and faith as the radiating center, we see again the advantages of a more explicitly covenantal ontology:

> The "*sola-fide*" of justification made it possible, once for all, to regard justification and sanctification as almost identical acts of God, operative, in concentric circles of increasing radius, on the plane of individual human life. . . . In opposition to [Rome's] hypothetical field of forces, the Reformation again restored sanctification in its true relation to faith. . . . And we speak of faith, not as a point of departure for a fresh emission of power, or as a human function or potency producing other effects, but of faith as true orientation toward the grace of God and as the life which flourishes on this divine grace, on the forgiveness of sins.[72]

Thus Berkouwer finds it "incomprehensible" that the Reformation view could have ever been criticized as having no bearing on sanctification or the life of holiness. It has everything to do with it because it brings everything back to faith in

69. Ibid., 20.
70. Ibid., 27.
71. Ibid.
72. Ibid., 28.

Christic.[73] Faith is hardly an "external" thing with no subjective impact; rather, it links us to Christ along with all of his benefits. The covenant that is unilaterally given and always remains unconditional in its basis as pure gift gives rise to a genuinely bilateral relationship of hearing and answering, passive receiving and an active return of thanksgiving to God and service to neighbor.

Luther opposed the merit of works, "but in all his opposition he was fully conscious that Christ must assume form in the believer. . . ."[74] "Faith is not a competitor of love and good works but rather a sponsor, and gives foundation to them because it acknowledges the grace of God. Again and again, and for this reason, Luther pointed out the deep significance of the first commandment and accounted all works performed outside its sphere as nothing."[75] It can hardly be said that justification leaves faith and practice bereft of an ethic when "Luther argues emphatically from faith to love of one's neighbor: all one's works must promote the welfare of one's neighbor, since in his faith each has all the possession he requires and can therefore freely and lovingly devote his entire life to the service of his fellowman."[76]

Recalling the treatment of law and gospel that I offered in part 1, I suggest that the exhortations in Scripture, though they are indeed commands or laws, are not conditions in a law-covenant. Rather than say, "Do this and you shall live," the gospel says, "You have died and your life is hidden with God in Christ." On this basis, the imperative (third use of the law) is issued: "Therefore, live accordingly" (cf. Col. 3:3–17). The gospel tells us that God has fought too hard for us, given too much for us, suffered too deeply for us, to leave us forgiven and yet bleeding on the battlefield. In it, God promises to bind up our wounds, heal us, and restore us so that we can glorify and enjoy God and love and serve our neighbor.

According to the account thus far, justification is not the first stage of the Christian life, but the constant wellspring of sanctification and good works. Luther summarizes, "'Because you believe in me,' God says, 'and your faith takes hold of Christ, whom I have freely given to you as your Justifier and Savior, therefore be righteous.' Thus God accepts you or accounts you righteous only on account of Christ, in whom you believe."[77] Whatever other piece of good news (concerning the new birth, Christ's conquest of sin's tyranny and promise to renew us throughout our life, the resurrection of our body, and freedom from the presence of sin), much less the useful exhortations that we may offer, the announcement that Luther here summarizes alone creates and sustains the faith that not only justifies but sanctifies as well.

Good works now may be freely performed for God and neighbors without any fear of punishment or agony over the mixed motives of each act. Because of justification in Christ, even our good works can be "saved," not in order to improve either God's lot or our own, but our neighbor's. Calvin explains:

73. Ibid.
74. Ibid., citing *LW* 1:203, on Gal. 4:19.
75. Berkouwer, *Faith and Sanctification*, 32–33.
76. Ibid.
77. Martin Luther on Gal. 2:16, in *LW* 26:132.

But if, freed from this severe requirement of the law, or rather from the entire rigor of the law, they hear themselves called with fatherly gentleness by God, they will cheerfully and with great eagerness answer, and follow his leading. To sum up: Those bound by the yoke of the law are like servants assigned certain tasks for each day by their masters. These servants think they have accomplished nothing and dare not appear before their masters unless they have fulfilled the exact measure of their tasks. But sons, who are more generously and candidly treated by their fathers, do not hesitate to offer them incomplete and half-done and even defective works, trusting that their obedience and readiness of mind will be accepted by their fathers, even though they have not quite achieved what their fathers intended. Such children ought we to be, firmly trusting that our services will be approved by our most merciful Father, however small, rude, and imperfect these may be. . . . And we need this assurance in no slight degree, for without it we attempt everything in vain.[78]

"Because of justification," adds Ames, "the defilement of good works does not prevent their being accepted and rewarded by God."[79]

Not only does such a view properly ground works in faith; it also frees believers to love and serve their neighbors apart from the motive of gaining or fear of losing divine favor. It liberates us for a world-embracing activism as we are deeply conscious that although our love and service contribute nothing to God and his evaluation of our persons, they are, however feebly, half-heartedly, and imperfectly performed, means through which God cares for creation.

The evangelical doctrine of justification honors the law of God since it upholds rather than weakens, subverts, or circumvents the law. *The verdict of justification does not contradict but corresponds to the law's searching judgment: the righteousness required is in fact given in the gospel.* All other accounts must naturally view justification as in some sense a relaxation of the absolute demands of the law, some sort of balancing act between love and justice, grace and holiness, mercy and righteousness. The evangelical doctrine recognizes God as both just and the justifier of the ungodly. The law is upheld; only its condemnation, which holds us in bondage to fear, is abolished.

Far from providing an account of salvation as imputation without sanctification and ethics, the Scots Confession (1560) declares, "It is blasphemy to say that Christ abides in the hearts of those in whom there is no spirit of sanctification." "For as soon as the Spirit of the Lord Jesus, whom God's chosen children receive by true faith, takes possession of the heart of anyone, so soon does he regenerate and renew him, so that he begins to hate what before he loved, and to love what he hated before. Thence comes that continual battle which is between the flesh and the Spirit in God's children"[80] The Second Helvetic Confession reiterates the unanimous consensus of the Reformation concerning the nature of the faith that justifies:

78. Calvin, *Institutes* 3.19.5.
79. Ames, *The Marrow of Theology*, 171.
80. The Scots Confession, chap. 13, in *The Book of Confessions* (PC[USA], 1991).

> The same apostle calls faith efficacious and active through love (Gal 5:6). It also quiets the conscience and opens a free access to God, so that we may draw near to him with confidence and may obtain from him what is useful and necessary. The same [faith] keeps us in the service we owe to God and our neighbor, strengthens our patience in adversity, fashions and makes a true confession, and in a word, brings forth good fruit of all kinds, and good works.

Such good works are done not for any desire for personal gain or merit, but merely "to show gratitude to God and for the profit of the neighbor."[81]

Therefore, sanctification is not a human project supplementing the divine project of justification, nor a process of negotiating the causal relations between free will and infused grace, but the impact of God's justifying Word on every aspect of human life. The Westminster Confession states, "They who are effectually called and regenerated, having a new heart and a new spirit created in them, are further sanctified, really and personally, through the virtue of Christ's death and resurrection, by his Word and Spirit dwelling in them."[82] All of this is "in Christ," not in ourselves.[83] Instead of a double source (synergism), redemption is concerned with a double grace: justification and inner renewal. In Lesslie Newbigin's words,

> The idea of a righteousness of one's own is the quintessence of sin. Against this, therefore, against every trace of a holiness or righteousness which does not depend simply upon God's mercy to the sinner, we have to set our faces as relentlessly as Paul did. But equally with Paul we have to recognise that if any man be in Christ there is a new creation, not a fiction but a real supernatural new birth, the life of the risen Christ in the soul.[84]

Not content with "the life of the risen Christ in the soul," the triune God has yet another act of the drama awaiting us: the life of the risen Christ transforming us, and all of creation, from the inside out in consummated grace. It is to that topic that we now turn, as we explore the furthest reaches of the Word's justifying verdict.

81. The Second Helvetic Confession, chap. 16, in *The Book of Confessions* (PC[USA], 1991).
82. The Westminster Confession of Faith, chap. 15, in *The Book of Confessions* (PC[USA], 1991).
83. For a fine elaboration of this point, see again Webster, *Holiness*, 81.
84. Lesslie Newbigin, *The Household of Faith* (London: SCM Press, 1953), 128–29.

Chapter Twelve

The Weight of Glory
Justification and Theōsis

"Those whom he justified he also glorified." (Rom. 8:30)

In various challenges to Reformation positions, not only has mystical union with Christ marginalized justification, but also *a certain account* of participation (divinization or *theōsis*) has come increasingly to dominate the understanding of that union.

Why this topic, justification and divinization? First, it is the last indicative that Paul mentions in his *ordo* in Romans 8:30, which I am following as a general rubric for these chapters in part 2. Second, it represents a test case for the claim that a forensic ontology can sustain the entire *ordo*, even those aspects that are more than forensic. Even the last link in the chain—glorification—has a forensic core. If a covenantal ontology can prove sufficient without appeal to a medieval one, then surely this locus is a test case—particularly as I am attempting to locate potential areas of convergence between Eastern Orthodox and Reformed soteriologies. Third, this chapter highlights a theme that does not appear to me to be as prominent as it once was in Reformed faith and practice.

WHAT IS *THEŌSIS*?

"For Orthodoxy our salvation and redemption mean our deification," writes Bishop Kallistos Ware.[1] S. L. Epifanovic, perhaps the greatest authority on the thought of Maximus the Confessor, observed, "The chief idea of St. Maximus, as of all of Eastern theology, [was] the idea of deification."[2] Although divinization/ deification are well-attested in patristic sources, the doctrine of *theōsis* per se usually refers to its specific Byzantine formulation by Gregory Palamas. Since it is not only presumptuous but also impossible to treat the Orthodox doctrine of *theōsis* in any depth in this space, I will only indicate the main lines of thought.

Essence and Energies

Encountered already in a previous chapter, the essence-energies distinction emphasizes the Creator-creature distinction. While Western theology typically recognizes only a distinction between the divine essence and the created effect of the divine cause, Eastern theology views God's energies as neither. God's energies are radiations of divine glory, but are no more the divine essence than rays are the sun itself. God's uncreated glory emanates, but the essence does not. Without this distinction, the frequent analogy of sun-and-rays could easily empty into pantheism, which was in fact a constant threat for Western mysticism. At the same time, while creation itself is the result of God's energies, the latter themselves are, we might say, God-in-Action; in fact, they are often referred to also as God's works, power, life, glory, and grace. They are not God's essence, but a certain quality of God's self-revelation and saving love.

According to the East, then, union with God is not mere intellectual contemplation of God's hidden essence, as it often is in Western mysticism.

> This light (φῶς) or effulgence (ἔλλαμψις) can be defined as the visible quality of the divinity, of the energies or grace in which God makes Himself known. It is not a reality of the intellectual order, as the illumination of the intellect, taken in its allegorical and abstract sense, sometimes is. Nor is it a reality of the sensible order. This light is a light which fills at the same time both intellect and senses, revealing itself to the whole man, and not only to one of his faculties.[3]

So in one sense, the Eastern view is more restricted than dominant Western views, since there is no access to God's hidden essence. Yet in another sense it is more comprehensive, since the whole person is *imago Dei* and is therefore the subject of divinizing energies.

1. Timothy (Kallistos) Ware, *The Orthodox Church*, rev. new ed. (New York: Penguin Books, 1997), 231.

2. Cited by Jaroslav Pelikan, *The Christian Tradition: A History of the Development of Doctrine*, vol 2, *The Spirit of Eastern Christendom (600–1700)* (Chicago: University of Chicago Press, 1974), 125.

3. Vladimir Lossky, *The Mystical Theology of the Eastern Church* (Crestwood, NY: St. Vladimir's Seminary Press, 1976), 221.

Reflecting this emerging distinction, Athanasius affirmed, "[God] is outside all things according to his essence, but he is in all things through his acts of power."[4] Similarly, Basil writes, "We know the essence through the energy. No one has ever seen the essence of God, but we believe in the essence because we experience the energy."[5] Ware explains:

> If we knew the divine essence, it would follow that we knew God in the same way as he knows himself; and this we cannot ever do, since he is Creator and we are created. But, while God's inner essence is forever beyond our comprehension, his energies, grace, life and power fill the whole universe, and are directly accessible to us. . . . Thus the essence-energies distinction is a way of stating simultaneously that the *whole* God is inaccessible and that the *whole* God in his outgoing love has rendered himself accessible to man.

So there is deification without pantheism, union without fusion.[6] It was especially in the Byzantine development of Gregory Palamas that the essence-energies distinction was fully developed and became a major interpretive category. According to Maximus the Confessor, "We do not know God in his essence. We know him rather from the grandeur of his creation and from his providential care for all creatures. For by this means, as if using a mirror, we attain insight into his infinite goodness, wisdom and power."[7]

As Robert Jenson explains, the Eastern theologians realized that qualifications were needed. "A definition of Anastasius of Sinai, often quoted in Eastern theology, provides the one: 'Deification is elevation to a higher plane, not an enlargement or transformation of nature.'"[8] On the other hand, "Because we become God, we do not cease to be creatures; we will be those creatures who are indissolubly one with the creature God the Son is. This leads us to the second qualification."

> Athanasius's aphorism, "He became man in order that we might become God," while indeed true just as it stands, can be misleading out of its context. Irenaeus can supply the needed precision: the God who becomes what we are is the God-man; what he becomes is what we actually are, "fallen and passible man, condemned to death"; and we become what he is, humans so united with God as to "receive and bear God." An asymmetry observable in Irenaeus's doctrine points to the third needed qualification: the God-man becomes one of us, but the redeemed do not become additional God-humans. Rather they become participants in the one God-man, members of the *totus Christus*; they are God-bearers communally and not otherwise.[9]

4. Athanasius, *On the Incarnation* 17, trans. R. W. Thomson, *Athanasius: Contra gentes and De incarnatione* (Oxford: Clarendon Press, 1971), 174; quoted by Timothy (Kallistos) Ware, *The Orthodox Way* (Crestwood, NY: St. Vladimir's Seminary Press, 1979), 22.

5. Basil, in *Doctrina Patrum de incarnatione verbi*, ed. Franz Kiekamp, 2nd ed. (Münster: Aschendorff, 1981), 88–89.

6. Ibid., 23.

7. Maximus, *On Love* 1.96, in *The Philokalia*, trans. G. E. H. Palmer, Philip Sherrard, and Kallistos Ware, vol. 2 (London: Faber & Faber, 1981), 64; cited by Ware, *The Orthodox Way*, 25.

8. Robert Jenson, *Systematic Theology*, 2 vols. (New York: Oxford University Press, 1997–99), 2:341, quoting Anastasius of Sinai, *The Guide* 2 (PG 89:36).

9. Jenson, *Systematic Theology*, 2:341.

Transfiguration and Resurrection

To be deified is to be transfigured, so that the rays of God's energies (again, not the divine essence) permeate (rather than obliterate) the creature. The Old Testament theophanies, the transfiguration of Jesus, and the experience of Paul on the Damascus road represent such events.[10]

> St Gregory Nazianzen takes up the same images, especially that of Moses. "I was running," he says, "to lay hold on God, and thus I went up into the mount, and drew aside the curtain of the cloud, and entered away from matter and from material things, and as far as I could I withdrew within myself. And then when I looked up, I scarce saw the back parts of God; although I was sheltered by the Rock, the Word that was made flesh for us. And when I looked a little closer, I saw, not the first and unmingled nature, known to itself—to the Trinity, I mean; not that which abideth within the first veil, and is hidden by the Cherubim; but only that nature, which at last even reaches us. And that, so far as I can learn, is the majesty, or as holy David calls it, the glory, which is manifested amongst creatures.[11]

In the transfiguration, Christ himself underwent no change, but during that time the apostles were able to see the glory (energies) that was always present yet previously hidden from their view. In this light, they saw light. "The apostles were taken out of history and given a glimpse of eternal realities."[12]

Alongside the unfortunate allegorical ascent (including the flight from matter) exhibited by Gregory's autobiographical account, there is also an eschatological and matter-affirming dimension. "Our ultimate destiny," says Lossky, "is not merely an intellectual contemplation of God; if it were, the resurrection of the dead would be unnecessary. The blessed will see God face to face, in the fullness of their created being."[13] St. Symeon said that there are two judgments: a judgment in this life that leads to salvation (despair leading to repentance and forgiveness), where the depths of our sin are made known only to us, and a future judgment to condemnation, where sin is made public.[14] Lossky explains:

> Those who in this life undergo such a judgment [to salvation] will have nothing to fear from another tribunal. But for those who will not, in this life, enter into the light, that they may be accused and judged, for those who hate the light, the second coming of Christ will disclose the light which at present remains hidden, and will make manifest everything which has been concealed.[15]

The second coming will be a manifestation of sin "'outside grace,' as St. Maximus has it."[16]

10. Ibid., 223.
11. Ibid., 36.
12. Ibid.
13. Ibid., 224.
14. Ibid., 233–34.
15. Ibid., 234.
16. Ibid.

What man ought to have attained by raising himself up to God, God achieved by descending to man. . . . Nicholas Cabasilas, a Byzantine theologian of the fourteenth century, said on this subject: "The Lord allowed men, separated from God by the triple barrier of nature, sin and death, to be fully possessed of Him and to be directly united to Him by the fact that he has set aside each barrier in turn: that of nature by His incarnation, of sin by His death, and of death by His resurrection."[17]

Recent Appeals to *Theōsis*

Interpreting the Eastern tradition in the light of his own more Augustinian-Thomistic (and I would add, somewhat Hegelian) framework, Jenson expresses the divinizing union as follows:

> Were I, within the eschatologically perfected *totus Christus*, to say "I am God," the first person singular would remove me from the union, so that the sentence would be false. It would after all be the "old man" talking, the person not yet one with Christ and so still implicated in the communities of domination. But Christ has no old man; and if we can imagine him within the triune-human community saying "I am God," it would be a simple and humble observation of fact.[18]

Although they appeal to *theōsis* and the East, many (like Jenson) side with the West when it comes to the crucial essence-energies distinction. In fact, Jenson quotes Thomas: "The vision by which we will then see God in his essence, is the same as the vision by which God sees himself."[19] The extent to which this approximates Meister Eckhart's "The eye with which God sees me is the eye with which I see God" is an interesting question, and to my mind it justifies the Orthodox suspicion that Western accounts can easily drift toward pantheism even in the hands of eminent advocates of the Creator-creature distinction. Jenson notes that Gregory Palamas "emphatically and directly denied" the Western move: "Even the redeemed cannot see God 'according to his—hyperessential—essence [*hyperousian ousian*], but only according to his deifying energy.' For being seen is a relation, but 'God's *ousia* has no relations' and 'transcends everything in God that can be shared.'" "We have already regretted Palamas's doctrine at this point," Jenson adds, judging that it is still "too uncritically implicated in Pseudo-Dionysius's barely Christianized Neoplatonism."[20] "In Thomas's metaphysics, the divine essence is simply 'what [God] is,' *quid sit*, and he knows no *hyperousia* beyond this."[21]

Engaging Jenson's criticism of this distinction as "barely Christianized Neo-platonism" would take us too far afield. However, at least one should say that

17. Ibid., 136.
18. Ibid.
19. Thomas Aquinas, *ST* 1.2.1; Suppl.92.1; cited by Jenson, *Systematic Theology*, 1:227–28.
20. Jenson, *Systematic Theology*, 2:342.
21. Ibid., 345.

however accurate a description of Dionysian theology generally this is, the East's move, at least on this point, reflects a *more* Christianized Neoplatonism. While on the surface it may seem like the Plotinian "One" beyond being, the essence-energies distinction itself simply guards the Creator-creature difference. If one is serious about the doctrine of analogy, it would seem to be the only appropriate move, since God *is* beyond being (*hyperousia*) in the sense that divine existence is qualitatively and not just quantitatively different from that of creatures. Despite its emphasis on affinity in divinization, the Eastern view at this point is not as susceptible as the Western view to allowing the absorption of the creature into the Creator and plurality into unity. The doctrines of creation ex nihilo and the Trinity become more legible, I suggest, in the Eastern account. Further, precisely because creatures participate in the energies rather than in the essence of God, there is no need to talk about kenotic theories that imply a more emanationist scheme of diminishing "being" as one descends the ontological ladder.

REFORMED THEOLOGY AND *THEŌSIS*

Theōsis or divinization does not occupy a locus in Reformed theology, much less serve as a central dogma of its soteriology. In fact, in at least some of its representative expressions, the doctrine seems to Reformed ears susceptible to becoming a theology of glory. In my critique of Christian Platonism and Neoplatonism thus far, I have repeated the Reformed emphasis on the redemption *of* rather than *from* creation. While difference is infinitely established in the Creator-creature distinction, opposition results only from ethical fault—transgression of the covenant, and humanity can only attain the consummation now by being united to Christ, the New Adam, who has successfully completed the trial as our covenant head.

Whatever convergences we may find therefore between Reformed treatments of glorification and notions of deification will exclude any suggestion of transcending our humanity as such. The total person is the subject of glorification; there is no elevation of a privileged aspect of humanity (viz., the soul) above its own created nature. Not surprisingly, then, Ireneaus occupies a leading role as a patristic source, although other ancient Greek theologians also occupy a privileged place in Calvin's reading, especially John Chrysostom and Cyril of Alexandria.[22]

Further, as J. Todd Billings cautions, a certain account of divinization (the Byzantine version of *theōsis* articulated by Palamas) is often read back into the earlier tradition as the definitive Eastern position. Whatever convergences might obtain between this position and Reformed theology, Billings wisely suggests that they should be related to the concept of *divinization* more broadly rather than to

22. See Irena Backus, "Calvin and the Greek Fathers," in *Continuity and Change: The Harvest of Later Medieval and Reformation History*, ed. Robert J. Bast and Andrew C. Gow (Leiden: Brill, 2000), 253–76; cf. Johannes Van Oort, "John Calvin and the Church Fathers," in *The Reception of the Church Fathers in the West: From the Carolingians to the Maurists*, ed. Irena Backus (Leiden: Brill, 1997).

the doctrine of *theōsis* with its distinct Palamite refinements.[23] Exploring these connections should be of great importance for greater mutual enrichment of both traditions.[24]

In evaluating potential lines of convergence, I will group my summary under the most crucial components of the *theōsis* doctrine: (1) union with Christ as involving "divinization," (2) the essence-energies distinction, (3) a closely related emphasis on the economy of the divine persons rather than on the hidden essence of deity, (4) the beatific vision as eschatologically oriented to the resurrection and consummation, and (5) the event of Jesus' transfiguration. Of course, even if we are able to discern convergences on these points, significant differences would remain over justification and synergism. However, my focus in this section is limited to these points.

Union and Divinization

Although, as I have already stated, union with Christ was a cherished and even integrating motif for Calvin and Reformed theology, those who would make Calvin a patron of union with Christ *over against* justification must simply ignore the reformer's explicit statements to the contrary. At the same time, Calvin can speak just as freely of gifts that we have in Christ other than justification. He can even say, "Let us mark that the end of the gospel is to render us eventually conformable to God, and, if we may so speak, to deify us." Nevertheless, he immediately adds the following qualification:

> But the word nature is *not here essence but quality.* The Manicheans formerly dreamt that we are a part of God, and that after having run the race of life we shall at length revert to our original. There are also at this day fanatics who imagine that we thus pass over into the nature of God, so that his swallows up our nature. Thus they explain what Paul says, that God will be all in all (1 Cor 15.28) and in the same sense they take this passage. But such a delirium as this never entered the minds of the holy Apostles; they only intended to say that when divested of all the vices of the flesh, we shall be *partakers of divine and blessed immortality and glory,* so as to be as it were *one with God as far as our capacities will allow.* This doctrine was not altogether unknown to Plato, who everywhere defines the chief good of man to be an entire conformity to God; but as he was involved in the mists of errors, he afterwards glided off to his own inventions. But we, disregarding empty

23. J. Todd Billings, "United to God through Christ: Assessing Calvin on the Question of Deification," *Harvard Theological Journal* 98, no. 3 (2005): 315–34. While pointing out potential parallels, Billings carefully distinguishes Calvin's references to "deification" (which are sparse to begin with) from the distinctively Palamite notion of "*theōsis.*"

24. Thomas F. Torrance has fruitfully explored this relationship in the Orthodox-Reformed discussions, especially (on the Reformed side). However, J. Todd Billings is, in my view, a more reliable guide for interpreting Calvin's relationship to the topic of divinization. See especially his *Calvin, Participation, and the Gift: The Activity of Believers in Union with Christ* (New York and Oxford: Oxford University Press, 2007).

> speculations, ought to be satisfied with this one thing—that the *image of God in holiness and righteousness is restored* to us for this end, that we may at length be partakers of eternal life and glory *as far as it will be necessary for our complete felicity*. (emphasis added)[25]

This is a gloss on 2 Peter 1:4, the only biblical passage that speaks directly of our sharing in the divine nature. Nevertheless, while cautioning us against "empty speculations," Calvin here seems to affirm a sharing in the energy ("quality") rather than in the essence of God and even includes under this many of the attributes that the East has identified (divine immortality and glory through the restoration of the image of God in holiness and righteousness).

Essence and Energies

John of Damascus expresses the goal of salvation: "becoming deified, in the way of participating in the divine *glory* and not in that of a change into the divine *being*" (emphasis added).[26] The Palamite distinction between essence and energies further distances the classic position of Orthodoxy from Western scholasticism and mysticism, including some recent attempts to make Luther and Calvin more *theōsis*-friendly. As I have indicated, Calvin and the Reformed tradition were actually more congenial to Eastern accounts of divinization than some of the recent (mainly Protestant) proposals that claim this heritage.

Focusing on the economy of grace as it is revealed in Scripture, rather than on the essence as an object of speculation, Calvin stipulated, "The essence of God is rather to be adored than inquired into."[27] In fact, Calvin adds, "They are mad who seek to discover what God is."[28] This does not mean that we cannot describe God's attributes as they are revealed in the works of creation, providence, and redemption—interpreted through the spectacles of Scripture. However, God provides this revelation in an accommodated form through an analogical discourse that yields a "who" rather than a "what."[29] For both Orthodox and Reformed interpretation, the following statement from Paul is key: "Ever since the creation of the world [God's] eternal power and divine nature, invisible though they are, have been understood and seen through the things he has made" (Rom. 1:20). Yet even the knowledge of God discovered in Scripture (which Calvin certainly identifies with God's own divinity) does not communicate the

25. John Calvin, *Commentaries on the Catholic Epistles*, trans. and ed. John Owen (repr., Grand Rapids: Baker, 1996), 371, on 2 Pet. 1:4.
26. John of Damascus, *An Exact Exposition of the Orthodox Faith*, in *A Select Library of Nicene and Post-Nicene Fathers of the Christian Church*, 2nd series, vol. 9, trans. S. D. F. Salmond (Grand Rapids: Eerdmans, 1973), 31.
27. Ibid., 1.2.2.
28. John Calvin, *Commentary on Paul's Epistle to the Romans* (Edinburgh: Calvin Translation Society, 1844; repr., Grand Rapids: Baker Books, 1993), on Rom. 1:19.
29. See my discussion in Michael S. Horton, *Lord and Servant: A Covenant Christology* (Louisville, KY: Westminster John Knox, 2005), esp. 9–11.

divine essence as it is in itself. "Thereupon his powers are mentioned, by which he is shown to us *not as he is in himself*, but *as he is toward us*: so that this recognition of him consists more in living experience than in vain and high-flown speculation" (emphasis added).[30]

Far from distorting Calvin in the direction of rationalism, Reformed scholasticism insisted that, in the words of Turretin, "theology treats God not like metaphysics as a being or as he can be known from the light of nature, but as the Creator and Redeemer made known by revelation."[31] Rather than being motivated by nominalism, these Reformed scholastics were actually reacting to the univocity of being as introduced by Franciscus Suárez among others.[32] In particular, they stressed the Thomistic analogy of being over against the univocal understanding of Suárez.[33] However, they went further than Thomas by emphasizing that we can know God not by probing his essence (the hidden majesty that would destroy us), but only according to his works (the revealed economy of grace that redeems us). This is why the covenant becomes the critical site where God's being is revealed for our benefit.

Emphasis on the "Personal Properties" of the Divine Persons of the Trinity

Although sometimes differences here are exaggerated, the tendency of Western Trinitarian theology has been to focus on the one divine essence, and it usually treats the persons as relations, while Eastern theology begins with the persons. According to the East, it is not the divine essence that gives rise to the persons, but the person of the Father who yields an eternally begotten Son and an eternally proceeding Spirit. Calvin's concentration on the "personal properties" of each member of the Trinity more than on the divine essence reflects, in both direct and indirect ways, a more Eastern (Cappadocian) frame of thought. Consequently, the persons are not simply relations. In fact, Calvin directly appeals to the Cappadocians, particularly Gregory of Nazianzus. "And that passage in Gregory of Nazianzus vastly delights me: 'I cannot think on the one without quickly being encircled by the splendor of the three; nor can I discern the three without being straightaway carried back to the one.' Let us not, then, be led to imagine a trinity of persons which includes an idea of separation, and does not at once lead us back to that unity."[34]

---

30. Calvin, *Institutes* 1.10.2.

31. Francis Turretin, *Institutes of Elenctic Theology*, ed. J. T. Dennison Jr., trans. G. M. Giger, 3 vols. (Phillipsburg, NJ: P&R Publishing, 1992–97), 1:16–17.

32. Richard Muller, *Post-Reformation Reformed Dogmatics*, vol. 3, *The Divine Essence and Attributes* (Grand Rapids: Baker Academic 2003), 109

33. Ibid., 113.

34. Calvin, *Institutes* 1.13.17. The influence of Hilary of Poitiers seems to have been critical as a medieval conduit of Cappadocian thought to the West, and Calvin cites him frequently.

For both Eastern and Western theologies, soteriology (as other loci) is teth-ered to the doctrine of the Trinity and vice versa.[35] This is especially so, I would argue, in Eastern and Reformed theologies, where the focus is on the identity of the three persons in their economic operations rather than on the inner essence. Thus, theology must always be on guard against both subordinationism and modalism, Calvin insisted.[36] Each person is active in every divine operation *ad extra*, but in distinct ways appropriate to the person. If we are guided by Scrip-ture rather than by "high-flown speculations," we will discover this pattern: "To the Father is attributed the effective principle of what is done, and the fountain and wellspring of all things; to the Son, wisdom, counsel, and the ordered arrangement of what is done; but to the Spirit is assigned the power and efficacy of the action."[37] This emphasis on the personal attributes does not lead to trithe-ism, says Calvin. "For in each hypostasis the whole divine nature is understood, with this qualification—that to each belongs his own peculiar quality. The Father is wholly in the Son, the Son wholly in the Father, even as he himself declares: 'I am in the Father, and the Father in me' (Jn. 14:10)."[38]

Calvin can use realistic language to speak of the believer's incorporation into the very life of the Trinity, without (as is often done in contemporary theologies) simply identifying this communion with the unique perichoresis of the divine persons. Peter van Mastricht is representative of the Reformed scholastics when he adds that in their union with Christ "there is a certain shadowing forth" of the unity of the divine persons in the Trinity.[39] That qualification, "a certain shad-owing forth," preserves the Creator-creature distinction, maintaining an analog-ical rather than univocal connection. To repeat a line from Calvin cited above, "We shall be partakers of divine and blessed immortality and glory, so as to be as it were one with God *as far as our capacities will allow*." At no point does the reformer countenance a communication of the divine essence.

Although in other respects he was rather traditionally Western in his Trini-tarian theology (viz., the *Filioque*), some of the sharpest criticisms of his other-wise honored source, Augustine, concern the bishop of Hippo's more speculative attempts to think about the essence of God along the lines of psychological analo-gies that tended to reduce the persons to mere relations. Covenant theology, as we have seen, particularly with its intratrinitarian *pactum salutis* as the eternal ground of all of God's covenantal purposes in history, deepens Calvin's empha-sis. We name God as Father, Son, and Spirit because these are the divine persons who meet us in the historical economy as it is revealed in Scripture. We only

35. For recent consensus on the Trinity and Christology between mainline Reformed and Ortho-dox bodies, see *Growth in Agreement II: Reports and Agreed Statements of Ecumenical Conversations on a World Level, 1982–1998*, ed. Jeffrey Gros, Harding Meyer, and William G. Rusch (Geneva: World Council of Churches; Grand Rapids: Eerdmans, 2000), 275–90.

36. Calvin, *Institutes* 1.13.5–16.

37. Ibid., 1.13.18.

38. Ibid., 1.13.19.

39. Quoted by Heinrich Heppe, *Reformed Dogmatics*, rev. and ed. E. Bizer, trans. G. T. Thom-son (London: G. Allen & Unwin, 1950; repr., London: Wakeman Trust, 2002), 512.

encounter the one essence of God by way of the distinct persons who meet us in revelation.

The Beatific Vision as Resurrection/Consummation

Crucial to Calvin's understanding of redemption broadly considered is union with Christ, who is none other than God. Calvin affirms, as does the first answer of the Westminster Shorter Catechism (echoing Calvin's Geneva Catechism), that the chief end of human existence is the glorification and enjoyment of God. Although revised in some significant ways, the mystical piety of Augustine, the Cappadocians, Hilary, and Bernard is freely appropriated in an ad hoc manner. Calvin writes:

> The ancient philosophers anxiously discussed the sovereign good and even contended among themselves over it. Yet none but Plato recognized man's highest good as union with God, and he could not even dimly sense its nature. And no wonder, for he had learned nothing of the sacred bond of that union. Even on this earthly pilgrimage we know the sole and perfect happiness; but this happiness kindles in our hearts more and more each day to desire it, until the full fruition of it shall satisfy us. *Accordingly, I said that they alone receive the fruit of Christ's benefits who raise their minds to the resurrection.* (emphasis added)[40]

In that last sentence we notice the raising of the mind, not in Plato's contemplative ascent beyond material things (as emphasized in both Eastern and Western mysticism), but in consideration of Jesus' bodily resurrection, in which we share. That "beatific vision" extolled by the ancient philosophers is "not even dimly sensed" apart from Christ and the resurrection. Why the resurrection particularly? The reason will become clearer as we elaborate his treatment.

However, before we arrive at his connection between vision (divinization-glorification) and the resurrection, we should recognize that restoration of the *imago* is also crucial in Calvin's understanding of the Spirit's work of making us participate in Christ and all of his benefits. In fact, as Butin recalls, "Calvin's most complete definition of the *imago Dei* in the *Institutes* is based on the assumption that 'the true nature of the image of God is to be derived from what scripture says of its renewal through Christ.'"[41] This is true, by the way, not only for Calvin but also for the whole tradition: rather than ground the *imago Dei* in a general anthropology, the Reformed scholastics worked backward from the New Testament passages concerning the renewed image in Christ.[42]

The Son is God's image, Calvin writes, not only according to his deity but according to his humanity—the true image of the Adamic representative.[43] In

40. Calvin, *Institutes* 3.25.2.
41. Philip Walker Butin, *Revelation, Redemption, and Response: Calvin's Trinitarian Understanding of the Divine-Human Relationship* (New York: Oxford University Press, 1995), 68.
42. I offer further citations and development of this in *Lord and Servant*, chap. 4.
43. John Calvin, *Commentary on the Gospel according to John*, trans. William Pringle (1847; repr., Grand Rapids: Baker, 1996), on 17:21.

278   Covenant and Salvation

fact, the whole purpose of the gospel is to restore this image.[44] This correlation of divinization with restoration of the *imago* reflects an important convergence with patristic teaching. However—and this is a critical point that reflects a more Eastern than Western emphasis—human participation in this image is mediated by the Son in the Spirit; it is not an immediate participation in God's deity.

> In refuting Servetus' idea that "some portion of immeasurable divinity had flowed into man," Calvin had emphasized instead that the Holy Spirit is the proper agent of the restoration of the divine image. . . . He inferred from II Corinthians 3:18 that a human being "is made to conform to God, not by an inflowing of substance, but by the grace and power of the Spirit." . . . Eschatological categories ultimately shape the way in which Calvin understands the progressive and gradual nature of this trinitarian restoration . . . : "we now begin to be reformed to the image of God by His Spirit so that the complete renewal of ourselves and the whole world may follow in its own time."[45]

It should also be added that the dispute with Osiander was also formative for the reformer's emphasis on pneumatological mediation. Instead of fusing the believer's essence with Christ's (and therefore God's), Calvin recognized the Spirit as the bond of union.

To be sure, justification and inner renewal are completely distinct. "Yet you could not grasp this [imputed righteousness] without at the same time grasping sanctification also," Calvin insists. "For he 'is given unto us for righteousness, wisdom, sanctification, and redemption' [1 Cor. 1:30]."[46] Butin notes:

> The question that governs Book III is that of "how we receive those benefits which the Father bestowed on his only-begotten Son—not for Christ's own private use, but that he might enrich the poor and needy." Calvin's answer, which follows in III.1.1, consists in the recognition that, "to communicate to us what he has received from the Father, he must become ours, and dwell within us." . . . There is an explicit continuity here with Calvin's assignment of "efficacy" to the Spirit under the "distinction of properties" that he had affirmed in 1559 *Institutes* I.13.18.[47]

So far, then, we may see that for Calvin (and the Reformed tradition generally), the notion of participation in God—with its ancillary concepts of the *visio Dei* and divinization—is eschatologically oriented, with vertical descents of the Son and the Spirit moving redemptive history forward to the consummation. Fully Trinitarian (with some Eastern accents), and grounded in a christocentric concept of the *imago Dei*, this view does not hesitate to affirm that believers participate in God's glory. However, Calvin cannot take his eyes off the economy. Even his appropriation of medieval spirituality was carefully conditioned by these emphases, making him more sympathetic to Irenaeus and Bernard than to Dionysian mysticism.

44. John Calvin, *The Second Epistle of Paul the Apostle to the Corinthians . . .* , ed. D. W. Torrance and T. F. Torrance (Grand Rapids: Eerdmans; Carlisle: Paternoster, 1996), on 2 Cor. 3:18.
45. Ibid., 69, quoting Calvin's *Harmonia ex tribus evangelistis composita*, on Luke 17:20.
46. Calvin, *Institutes* 3.16.1.
47. Butin, *Revelation, Redemption, and Response*, 80.

Because of this emphasis on the economy of grace, Calvin and the wider tradition emphasized the future resurrection of the dead as the place where the consummation occurs. The cosmic, eschatological, and redemptive-historical event of the Parousia—not the allegorical, contemplative, striving ascent of the lone soul—characterizes the Reformed expectation of the beatific vision.

Reformed theology comes closest to the classic category of divinization when it takes up the topic of *glorification* as both final vindication and restoration of the image. Yet even here, Reformed theology insists on looking forward by looking back at justification. There is no final vindication or justification that is anything other than the verdict that has already been rendered in this present age. Thus, William Ames can say that redemption in general and glorification in particular refer to "a real deliverance from the evils of punishment, *which is actually nothing but the carrying out of the sentence of justification.* For in justification we are pronounced just and awarded the judgment of life. In glorification the life that results from the pronouncement and award is given to us: We have it in actual possession" (emphasis added).[48] In glorification of the saints, the effective Word that pronounces the ungodly just finally reaches to the last vestiges of sin and death. *It is not a different Word that renews and glorifies, but the same Word in its different operations and effects.* At last, salvation will have been worked out for us and within us, from the inside out, until the new age has fully transformed every part of creation (as in Rom. 8:18–25).

The closest these Reformed writers come to a participation in God's essence is in their direct discussion of the beatific vision, which they always restrict to the glorified saints in heaven (*theologia beatorum* or *theologia visio*). Yet here too they back away from any essential union. It is God's life, glory, and righteousness (in Eastern parlance, energies) that are communicated to believers, in restoration of the *imago Dei*. Echoing the East's emphasis on the whole person as the subject of this vision, Turretin criticizes Thomists and Scotists for forcing a choice between the intellect and the will as the seat of human agency, with its corollary choice between vision and love, respectively.[49] "Sight, joy, and love" are the essential features of the eternal state, yet at no point are uncreated and created essences fused, any more than rays become the sun itself. Nevertheless, it is not a created glory that causes the blessed to shine forever, but glory that "effloresces" (energizes) from God, says Turretin.

> For from these effloresces that ineffable glory with which the blessed will shine forever on account of their fruition of the supreme good. . . . Sight contemplates God as the supreme good; love is carried out towards him, and is most closely united with him; and joy enjoys and acquiesces in him. Sight perfects the intellect, love the will, joy the conscience. Sight answers to faith,

48. William Ames, *The Marrow of Theology*, trans. John D. Eusden (Boston: Pilgrim, 1968; repr., Durham, NC: Labyrinth, 1983), 172.

49. Turretin, *Institutes of Elenctic Theology*, 3:209: "Both are at fault in this—they divide things that ought to be joined together and hold that happiness is placed separately, either in vision or in love, since it consists conjointly in the vision and the love of God. . . . This the Scripture teaches, describing it now by 'sight' (1 Cor. 13:12; 2 Cor. 5:7; 1 Jn. 3:2), then by 'love' and perfect holiness (1 Jn. 4:16; 1 Cor. 13:13)."

which is the substance of things hoped for and the evidence of things not seen. . . . Love consummated, by which we will be united with God, will answer to love begun, which sanctifies the heart. Joy answers to hope, which accompanies the fruition of the thing hoped for. Vision begets love. God cannot be seen without being loved; love draws joy after it because he cannot be possessed without filling with joy.[50]

Interpreting 1 Corinthians 13:12, Turretin surmises that while the beatific vision involves a clearer, intuitive apprehension of God, "the distinction between the Creator and the creature is preserved, so that only a similarity, not an equality is denoted."[51]

On this point, of course, Thomas would have said as much, with his doctrine of analogy. Affirming analogy, the Reformed nevertheless went further than Aquinas by denying access to the divine essence on either an ontic or epistemic level. "Finally," writes Turretin concerning the beatific vision, "neither the whole essence can thus be seen (because there is no proportion between the faculty and the object, between the finite and the infinite); nor a part (because it would thus be made divisible and mortal)."[52] Still, our eyes as well as the rest of our bodies will remain corporeal. God is no less infinite from created intellect than from created senses. It is the Creator-creature distinction, not the intellectual-corporeal distinction, that renders direct access to God's essence impossible.[53] In a direct nod to the East, Turretin adds:

> God cannot be seen by the creature with an adequate and comprehensive vision, but only with an inadequate and apprehensive [vision] because the finite is not capacious of the infinite. In this sense John of Damascus truly said, "The deity is incomprehensible" (*akatalēpton to theion*). And if anywhere the saints are said to be apprehenders, this is not to be understood in relation to vision as if they could apprehend God, but in relation to the course and the goal. For the race having been finished, they are said to have apprehended (i.e., to have reached the goal, Phil. 3:13, 14).[54]

Notice again the eschatological orientation. Rather than an upward, contemplative ascent, the direction is turned toward the future: finishing the race, reaching the promised goal. Yet reaching that goal remains for us now a matter of hope. God can be spiritually seen in this life "by the light of grace and by the specular knowledge of faith; in the other life, however, by an intuitive and far more perfect beatific vision and by the light of glory." Since Scripture does not tell us whether we will behold God's essence, we have no right to speculate.

> Still that seems to us the more probable opinion which asserts that the essence of God cannot be immediately attained by the saints so as to be seen

50. Ibid., 609.
51. Ibid., 610.
52. Ibid.
53. Ibid., 611.
54. Ibid., quoting John of Damascus, *The Orthodox Faith*, 3 (1.1).

just as it is, on account of the infinite disproportion and distance between the finite and the infinite. Nor is what is said of the sight of face to face an objection, because it denotes only a clearer mode of the divine knowledge in comparison with the knowledge of faith (as we have already remarked).[55]

Turretin reflects the balance of the Reformed scholastics generally in affirming a genuine participation in God that is nevertheless distinct from a participation in God's essence. His view can be sharply contrasted with that of Aquinas when the latter writes, "When . . . a created intellect sees God in his essence, the divine essence becomes the intelligible form of that intellect."[56] Such expressions render questionable not only the epistemological distinction between archetypal and ectypal knowledge, but also the ontological distinction between created and creaturely being.

Yet even in the present, as a foretaste of the future, God personally indwells believers by the Spirit, who also joins us to the Father and the Son. All the saints possess not only the gifts but also the Giver. This does not violate the axiom that uniquely for God essence and existence are identical, since the question is not about God's essence "in itself," but about God's communication of life, salvation, and glory (i.e., his energies) to creatures. Turretin cites an intriguing verse from Psalm 17: "As for me, I shall behold your face in righteousness; when I awake I shall be satisfied, beholding your likeness" (v. 15).

> From [love] will afterwards flow a perfect likeness of the saints to God, the fulfillment of their desires and of their perfect happiness, to which tends, and in which is consummated, the covenant of God. There is nothing else than a certain effusion and emanation (*aporroē*) of the deity upon the souls of the saints, communicating to them the image of all his perfections, *as much as they can belong unto a creature.* (emphasis added)[57]

Notice again the assumption of an essence-energies distinction: what is shared with the creature is "the image of all his perfections," not his essence itself. Thus, redemption does not make humans something more than human, nor does it simply restore them to the original status of being innocent image-bearers; rather, it transforms them into the state of glorified image-bearers that was never attained by the first covenant head (Adam). The eschatological emphasis of Irenaeus, with the consummation as something beyond a mere return to an original state, is also a crucial working assumption of covenant theology.

The difference between this age and the age to come is not that God communicates himself only in the latter, but that only then will God "be all in all":

> God will be seen without end, loved without cloying, praised without weariness. "And he will be all in all" (1 Cor. 15:28) inasmuch as he will pour

---

55. Ibid.
56. Thomas Aquinas, *ST* i.12.5.
57. Turretin, *Institutes of Elenctic Theology*, 3:612.

immediately upon the saints his light, love, holiness, joy, glory, life and a fullness of all blessings and will dwell in them forever (Rev. 21:3). Here God in grace communicates himself to his people mediately by the word and sacraments and imparts his gifts not fully, but in part. But then he will communicate himself immediately to the saints, nor only in part but fully and wholly (*holos*). He will be "all things" as to the universality of good things which can be required for absolute happiness and "in all" as to the universality of the subjects because he will bestow all these blessings undividedly upon all the blessed. Here belongs what is said in Rev. 21:22, 23: "I saw no temple in the city: for the Lord God Almighty and the Lamb are the temple of it. And the city had no need of the sun, neither of the moon, to shine in it: for the glory of God did lighten it, and the Lamb is the light thereof.[58]

To be sure, although Thomas rejected the essence-energies distinction, he strongly affirmed analogy over univocity. Whether this is sufficient to guard the Creator-creature distinction remains in question, however. As we have seen, Turretin, summarizing the Reformed consensus, refused to consider God merely as "deity" (*in abstracto*)—a view he attributes to Thomas—but rather as the triune God who has "covenanted in Christ" (*in concreto*). Theology cannot be subsumed under metaphysics. Otherwise, the knowledge of God would be "deadly," since it could only reveal God's majesty (law) rather than God's mercy (gospel). Apart from Christ, the word "God" can only instill fear, given not only the Creator-creature distinction, but also the covenant-breaker's encounter with the infinitely holy God.

We begin to see a somewhat different rationale for the denial of access to God's hidden essence among the Reformed, with Luther's influence clearly discerned. It is not simply because of God's incomprehensibility and transcendence but because God is for sinners "a consuming fire" apart from Christ (Heb. 12:29), that we are to keep our feet on the ground and find God only where he has found us. Those who attempt to ascend the ladder of speculation, mystical experience, or merit will only find the devil rather than God, because "the devil disguises himself as an angel of light."[59] "So we stand in a profound predicament," in the words of Wolfgang Musculus, "with the most mighty and unsearchable Majesty of God on the one side, and the necessity of our salvation on the other."[60]

Nevertheless, if forced to choose between Thomas and the Eastern view, at least on this point, the broad consensus was in line with the latter: God according to his essence can never be known, in this life or the next. "For since 'God dwells in inaccessible light' (1 Tim. 6:16)," Calvin reasons, "Christ must become our intermediary."[61] Even in the kingdom of glory, Christ remains the mediator and covenant head of the church, Turretin argues.[62]

58. Ibid.
59. Walther von Loewenich, *Luther's Theology of the Cross*, trans. Herbert J. A. Bouman (Minneapolis: Augsburg, 1976), 42–49.
60. Quoted in Richard Muller, *Post-Reformation Reformed Dogmatics*, vol. 1, *Prolegomena to Theology* (Grand Rapids: Baker, 1987), 179.
61. Calvin, *Institutes* 3.2.1.
62. Turretin, *Institutes of Elenctic Theology*, 2:490–94.

In summary, Lutheran and Reformed theologies restricted the beatific vision to the consummation and distinguished even this from any *visio oculi*, "a vision of the eye, except with reference to the perception of the glorified Christ."[63] In contrast to the self's ascending, the emphasis of this version of the beatific vision falls on the Shepherd's gathering of scattered sheep in a communion of love that has been the Triune's purpose from eternity. It envisions a whole creation not only restored but also consummated. There is a movement from cross to glory, from the promise heard with the ear to the vision beheld with the eye, from justification to sanctification to consummation in glorification and the renewal of the whole creation. Commenting on Ephesians 1:10, Calvin writes:

> As for this word "gather," St. Paul meant to show us thereby how we are all of us in a state of dreadful dissipation, till such time as our Lord Jesus Christ restores us. And this has reference not only to us, but also to all other creatures. In brief, it is as though he had said that the whole order of nature is as good as defaced, and all things decayed and disordered by the sin of Adam till we are restored in the person of our Lord Jesus Christ.[64]

Even the angels are included, since all possibility for falling from their created integrity is excluded by this restoration as well.

> And here you see also why in the ladder that was shown to Jacob, it is said that God stood upon the top of it and touched both heaven and earth, and that the angels went up and down on it [Gen. 28:12]. Now our Lord Jesus Christ is the true living and eternal God who touches both heaven and earth, because in his person he has joined his own divine essence and human nature together. Thus, therefore, you see that heaven is open so that the angels begin to acquaint themselves with us, and even to become our servants, as is said in the Epistle to the Hebrews [1:14], because the care of our souls is committed to them and (as is said in the thirty-fourth Psalm) they encamp about us and watch, and are our guardians [v. 7]. You see then how we are united again to the angels of paradise by our Lord Jesus Christ.[65]

Jesus and his Parousia, not the believer and his or her ascent, is "Jacob's ladder" from heaven to earth.

Transfiguration and Resurrection

We have seen that Calvin and Reformed theology have regarded Christ's resurrection as the most illuminating category for understanding the union or participation in God that the ancient philosophers missed. As Lossky's narrative above

---

63. Richard Muller, *Dictionary of Latin and Greek Theological Terms Drawn Principally from Protestant Scholastic Theology* (Grand Rapids: Baker, 1985), 325.

64. John Calvin, *Sermons on the Epistle to the Ephesians*, trans. Arthur Golding, rev. ed. (Edinburgh: Banner of Truth Trust, 1973), 63.

65. Ibid., 64.

indicates, the *visio dei* (or deification) is a more eschatological concept in Eastern thought than one finds it typically in Western versions. However, to bring the Reformed tradition into conversation with the Orthodox doctrine of *theōsis*, it might be useful to refer to Calvin's interpretation of the transfiguration before we examine the role that the resurrection plays in his wider account of participation.

Exhibiting his rigorously *sensus literalis* hermeneutic, Calvin eschews any allegorization of this event. The three disciples (Peter, James, and John) are there as legal witnesses ("at the mouth of two or three witnesses," Deut. 17:6).[66] The setting is legal: a courtroom drama with a judge (the Father's voice), the heavenly witness of the Spirit (the cloud), and the earthly witnesses (Moses and Elijah as well as the disciples), with Jesus on trial. Yet it is also mystical. Calvin relates the transfiguration to the Old Testament theophanies displaying God's rays (energies) rather than the divine essence: "Thus in ancient times God appeared to the holy fathers, not as He was in Himself, but so far as they could endure the rays of His infinite brightness; for John declares that not until *they are like him will they see him as he is* (1 John iii.2)."[67]

Moses and Elijah were selected from all of the Old Testament witnesses "to demonstrate that Christ alone is the end of the Law and of the Prophets."[68] They talked about Christ's impending death, which remains the focus even as they are bathed in radiant glory, the foretaste of the resurrection.[69] After the episode, Peter was still thinking in terms of tabernacles, longing for that which is merely temporal and already fading, when they had just experienced a foretaste of heaven itself. Yet, Calvin wonders, what would have become of our salvation if this had been the climax of the covenant?[70] Again, the accent is on the redemptive-historical economy rather than on allegorical ascent. The *conversation* between Jesus, Moses, and Elijah as well as the divine *voice* from heaven highlight the significance of the Word even in the midst of an overwhelming vision of glory, since we enter the cloud by faith, not by sight.[71]

The Son is raised above the servants in the Father's utterance, "This is my beloved Son. Hear him."[72] "He is the *Sun of righteousness*, whose arrival brought the full light of day."[73] The judicially approved Son tenderly touches the frightened disciples, so "that his majesty, which otherwise would swallow up all flesh, might no longer fill them with terror. Nor is it only by his words that he comforts, but by *touching* also that he encourages them [Matt. 17:7]."[74] We honor Moses, Elijah, and other saints by ascribing all glory to Christ alone, as they did.

66. John Calvin, *Commentary on a Harmony of the Evangelists*, trans. William Pringle, vol. 1 (1845; repr., Grand Rapids: Baker, 1996), 309.
67. Ibid., 310.
68. Ibid., 311.
69. Ibid.
70. Ibid., 312.
71. Ibid., 313–14.
72. Ibid., 314.
73. Ibid., 315.
74. Ibid., 316.

> In the disciples themselves we may see the origin of the mistake; for so long as they were terrified by the majesty of God, their minds wandered in search of men, but when Christ gently raised them up, they saw him alone. If we are made to experience that consolation by which Christ relieves us of our fears, all those foolish affections, which distract us on every hand, will vanish away.[75]

Where the ascent of mind transforms Jesus-history into the soul's vision of God, the relationship between the general resurrection and glorification is left unclear.[76]

Reformed systems retained the topic of *theologia unionis* (theology of union): that is, the face-to-face knowledge of God that belongs not to a few special pilgrims on the way but to all of the glorified saints. One discerns in Calvin a strong Irenaean emphasis that is at once forensic and ontological. "Christ aggregated to his body," says the reformer, "that which was alienated from the hope of life: the world which was lost and history itself."[77] It is not the essence of the historical person of Christ, either his deity or humanity, that is communicated to us, but his energies: life, glory, righteousness, power, light—and the communion that he has with the Father and the Spirit. Similarly, Turretin writes that this glory will be bestowed "both as to the soul as to the body," to be "enjoyed by the whole person in communion with God forever, which on this account Paul calls 'a far more exceeding and eternal weight of glory' (2 Cor 4:17) under which the mind is so overwhelmed that it is better expressed by silence and wonder than by eloquence."[78] Scripture expresses it in metaphors of divine condescension. "Thus both on account of our weakness and on account of the sublimity of the things themselves, God borrows our words."[79] It is described as light, a nuptial feast, treasures of richest gems, an estate, a garden full of fruit-bearing trees, a land flowing with milk and honey, a royal priesthood and a kingdom, an eternal Sabbath free of oppression.[80]

We are not delivered from our body, but "'delivered from the bondage of corruption and from vanity' (Rom. 8:21)."[81] Christ's transfiguration was a foretaste of this "weight of glory," and his resurrection its beginning.[82] Although God alone possesses immortality (1 Tim. 6:16), "the saints are immortal by grace from the beatific vision of God."[83] There is no contrast drawn between an ostensibly immortal soul and a mortal body: both are mortal, but are raised in immortality by grace. "Now as dishonor denotes the meanness of human nature liable to various defects,

75. Ibid.
76. For fuller development of this theme, see Douglas Farrow, *Ascension and Ecclesia* (Edinburgh: T&T Clark, 1998), from which I will draw a great deal of inspiration for the opening chapter of the next volume.
77. John Calvin, *CO* 27 (CR 55): 219.
78. Turretin, *Institutes of Elenctic Theology*, 3:612.
79. Ibid., 614.
80. Ibid., 614–15.
81. Ibid., 618.
82. Ibid.
83. Ibid.

so this glory will consist of a splendor and beauty of the body by which they will shine and glitter like the stars and the sun, hardly capable of being looked at by mortal eyes." Foreshadowed by Moses' face (Exod. 34:29) and even more so in Christ's transfiguration (Matt. 17:2), "that splendor will flow both from the blessed vision of God, whom we shall see face to face, and from the glorious view of Christ exalted in his kingdom; and *it will be nothing else than the irradiation of God's glory, from which the bodies will be made to shine.*"[84] They will be agile bodies: "vigorous, firm and strong, able to perform their duties rightly."[85] As to spirituality, "this spiritual does not refer to the very substance of the soul, as if it [the spiritual body] was to be changed into a spirit, for thus it could no longer be called a body, but a spirit." Their bodies will be "spiritual"—that is, "purged from all impurity and defilement," but not "spirit."[86] Here the Irenean emphasis prevails over the Athanasian: just as Jesus' humanity was not swallowed by his deity, the consummation will not render us as something more than human but as perfectly human.

Language will even continue to characterize the society of the age to come, since "God is to be worshipped by the whole person, no less with the body than with the soul as he has commanded should be done now. . . . If the body no less than the soul was created and redeemed by God and is to be glorified by the same, what is more just than that this body glorified by him should glorify him both in works and in word?" Turretin also cites "the vocal language" of the doxologies in the Apocalypse and the conversation in the transfiguration.[87] With a common tongue, glorified and glorifying "in body and soul, we may in unison sing an eternal Hallelujah to him."[88]

This emphasis on the participation of the body in the new age is characteristic of these Reformed writers. Similarly, the seventeenth-century divine Thomas Watson first quotes the answer to question 38 of the Westminster Shorter Catechism: "At the resurrection, believers being raised up in glory, shall be openly acknowledged and acquitted in the day of judgment, and made perfectly blessed in the full enjoyment of God to all eternity." He then interprets, "Some hold that we shall be clothed with a new body; but then it were improper to call it a resurrection, it would be rather a creation. 'Though worms destroy this body, yet in my flesh shall I see God.' Job xix 26. Not in another flesh, but my flesh. 'This corruptible must put on incorruption.' I Cor xv 53."[89] This bodily resurrection is required by the fact that believers are mystically united to Christ's flesh, which has been raised. Further, Watson says:

> If the body did not rise again, a believer would not be completely happy; for, though the soul can subsist without the body, yet it has *appetitus unio-*

84. Ibid., 619.
85. Ibid., 620 (emphasis added).
86. Ibid.
87. Ibid., 635.
88. Ibid., 637.
89. Thomas Watson, *A Body of Divinity Contained in Sermons upon the Westminster Assembly's Catechism* (repr., Edinburgh: Banner of Truth Trust, 1986), 305–6.

nis; "a desire of reunion" with the body; and it is not fully happy till it be clothed with the body. Therefore, undoubtedly, the body shall rise again. If the soul should go to heaven, and not the body, then a believer would be only half saved.[90]

Anticipating the resurrection, then, Watson opines:

> What a welcome will the soul give to the body! Oh, blessed body! When I prayed, thou didst attend my prayers with hands lifted up, and knees bowed down; thou wert willing to suffer with me, and now thou shalt reign with me; thou wert sown in dishonour, but now art raised in glory. Oh, my dear body! I will enter into thee again, and be eternally married to thee.[91]

In fact, he goes so far as to conclude, "The dust of a believer is part of Christ's mystic body."[92]

In sum, wherever the Reformed typically addressed glorification and the beatific vision, it was ordinarily in connection with the resurrection of the body. Although the soul departs the body at death, there can be no glorification of the soul apart from its reunion with the body at the end of the age.[93] Not the mere intellectual vision of God (which can supposedly in some measure be attained at least by some saints now), but especially the bodily presence of the whole church with its glorified head in the everlasting presence of the triune God on the last day—that is the emphasis that one finds in Reformed theology under consideration of this topic.

Finally, if *glorification* has been given a noble place in the Reformed *ordo*, then the category of divinization itself, qualified by the essence-energies distinction, and distinguished from (though grounded in) justification, does not seem so alien. In fact, if divinization is understood as transfiguration and transformation, as proponents suggest,[94] then this theme is no more inimical to Reformed theology than its traditional affirmation of the beatific vision in a similarly qualified sense. The question would still remain, of course, as to whether justification is the basis of the union that reaches its climax in glorification/divinization or vice versa, and whether this consummating grace perfects rather than elevates or transcends nature.

Although the Reformed scholastics revised the beatific vision, pushing it in a more eschatological direction within the covenantal economy, the theme itself seems to have been eclipsed in more recent Reformed reflection. In terms of both

---

90. Ibid., 306.
91. Ibid., 308.
92. Ibid., 309.
93. See the quotations in Heppe, *Reformed Dogmatics*, 695–712.
94. Pelikan, Mannermaa observes, "understand *theōsis* as 'transformation,'" and since Dietrich Ritschl explores Athanasius's treatment of the topic in terms of the metaphor of light, Mannermaa judges that "it would have been more consistent of Pelikan to use the word 'transfiguration' for divinization." Tuomo Mannermaa, *Christ Present in Faith: Luther's View of Justification*, ed. Kirsi Stjerna (Minneapolis: Fortress, 2005), 3.

formal dogmatics and preaching (and therefore in the lives of Christians), the consensus so far summarized might strike many today as somewhat alien to the Reformed tradition. As we see in Barth, even where he has given renewed attention to the cross and the resurrection of Christ as completed events in the past, their connection with the "not-yet" of Christ's Parousia and the resurrection-glorification of the dead in Christ is less obvious. Consequently, the eschatological relationship of the head and members, the vine and its branches, the firstfruits and the full harvest—these recede in the experience of believers and the church.[95]

Not surprisingly, Pelikan and Jenson have pointed to Jonathan Edwards as a proponent of divinization, and Milbank also finds the Christian Platonism of "America's Theologian" congenial to the RO project. Within the Reformed tradition, however, Edwards has always been a controversial figure. Charles Hodge not only criticized him for tinkering with justification, but also for developing an ontological scheme that "in its consequences is essentially pantheistic."[96] As Michael J. McClymond has pointed out, there are striking similarities between Palamas and Edwards. Both emphasize divinization (although Edwards does not use the term itself, synonyms are abundant) and understand it in terms of an emanation of divine energies: a divine light that communicates God's nature and grace.[97] Edwards actually goes so far as to argue:

> God looks on the communication of himself, and the emanation of infinite glory and good that are in himself to belong to the fullness and completeness of himself, as though he were not in his most complete and glorious state without it. Thus the church of Christ (toward whom and in whom are the emanations of his glory and communications of his fullness) is called the fullness of Christ: as though he were not in his complete state without her; as Adam was in a defective state without Eve.[98]

95. This is not unique to Barth, however. More generally, with some notable exceptions, soteriology has sometimes been underdetermined by eschatology when the former is restricted to the accomplishment in the past and application of redemption in the present.

96. Michael J. McClymond, "Salvation as Divinization: Jonathan Edwards, Gregory Palamas, and the Theological Uses of Neoplatonism," in *Jonathan Edwards: Philosophical Theologian*, ed. Paul Helm and Oliver D. Crisp (Aldershot, UK: Ashgate, 2003), 139, quoting Charles Hodge, *Systematic Theology*, 3 vols (New York: Charles Scribner's Sons, 1872–73), 2:219.

97. The overlap between Palamas and Edwards is the thesis of McClymond's intriguing essay "Salvation as Divinization." Although Edwards does not seem to have read Gregory of Nyssa or other earlier advocates of divinization, McClymond points out his familiarity with the Cambridge Platonists. Unlike this circle, however, Edwards's thinking, like that of Palamas, is more affirming of matter (including the body's participation in divinization) and of God's genuine accessibility than is true of the "One" of Plotinus.

98. Ibid., 152, quoting Jonathan Edwards, *The End of Creation*, in *Ethical Writings*, ed. Paul Ramsey, vol 8 of *The Works of Jonathan Edwards* (New Haven: Yale University Press, 1989), 439–40. My own position is somewhere between Hodge and Edwards. Edwards's own system does seem essentially idealist and, by his own modification of justification, illustrates how easily mystical participation can swallow forensic imputation in a soteriology of infused habits. Not faith in Christ, but the *habitus* or disposition (love) in the soul justifies (citing Miscellany 27b, from *Miscellanies*, in *The Works of Jonathan Edwards*, vol. 13, ed. Thomas A. Schafer (New Haven: Yale University Press, 1994). At the same time, like Palamas, Edwards also modifies Neoplatonism in a more matter-affirming and relational direction. It is not surprising that Robert Jenson and John Milbank hold Edwards in high regard.

While sympathizing with Hodge's general appraisal of Edwards's thought, I also think that more modern Reformed and Presbyterian theologians (especially American) have been too suspicious at times of the mystical side of union with Christ.

Edwards surely went as far as anyone in the Reformed tradition ever has toward a Platonic and idealist metaphysics, even to the point of reducing all of reality to dispositions or habits. However, the statement that I have just cited does not seem to require his broader ontological assumptions. We have already seen some evidence of an older Reformed notion of divinization that is more oriented to the essence-energies distinction of the East.

While the Reformers and their scholastic heirs could hold the legal-forensic and mystical-organic aspects of the *ordo* together in a complementary system, Edwards and Hodge reflect some tendency to emphasize one at the expense of the other. If justification and mystical union can be simultaneously distinguished and held together in an inseparable unity, this becomes another false dilemma. Having offered lines of possible convergence between divinization and traditional Reformed treatments of glorification, I will offer my own suggestions for further development.

DIVINIZATION AND THE BEATIFIC VISION AS RESURRECTION AND SABBATH

In my view, renewed attention to eschatology, not only as a final locus but also as a lens through which we see the whole system, points up the unity of these dimensions. Whether by assimilating the forensic to the mystical, organic, and transformative aspects of salvation or vice versa, justification—even where it is carefully guarded as a forensic verdict—ceases to be relevant to sanctification and glorification, and then moralism gains ascendancy with respect to "the Christian life" and the future hope. With an eschatological emphasis, however, we not only are able to recognize the relation between forensic and transformative aspects of salvation, but also the individual and cosmic horizons as well. To indicate what this sort of development might yield, I will offer my own elaboration of this connection between divinization and glorification.

"Earthly Man"/"Heavenly Man"

As the firstfruits, the resurrection-justification of Jesus and his triumphal entry into the heavenly sanctuary (glorification) both ground and anticipate our justification in the present, which will be empirically verified in our own resurrection to life everlasting. Thus, the "heavenly man" (Jesus) is the eschatological person who was raised from the dead and ascended to heaven to reign at the Father's right hand.

The comparison of "the man of dust" (*anthrōpos ek gēs choikos*) and the "man of heaven" (*anthrōpos ex ouranou*) in 1 Corinthians 15 has nothing to do with the gnostic redeemer myth, but instead is thoroughly eschatological. Nor is there a contrast here between Adam as a mere human being and Christ as divine. As in Romans 1:3–4, Christ's "sonship" and glory are referred not simply to his eternal deity, but in these contexts also to his Adamic role. Had Adam, in imitation of the Creator, fulfilled the "six days" of labor successfully as our covenant head, he—and all of us in Adam—would have entered triumphantly into the "seventh day" of everlasting Sabbath. In other words, glorification (at once individual and cosmic, spiritual and bodily) would immediately have followed as the judicial verdict of the last day.

The fall, however, interrupted this protological goal, so Adam—and all of us in solidarity—remained "the man of earth," only now not only capable of mortality, but in actual fact sentenced to decay and death. There is no life in this covenant head, but only a poisoned stream. The second Adam, however, crossed over from death to life, from this age to the age to come, fulfilling the "six days" of probation in order to enter the "seventh-day" rest with liberated hosts in his train.[99] "Man of heaven" here is therefore the resurrected-vindicated, and therefore glorified, representative of his covenant people. Not only because he is the Son of God by eternal right, but also because he is the eschatological image-Son by his completion of his commission, does his resurrection achieve a public-representative rather than simply personal character.

Jesus' resurrection was not only the divine imprimatur on the judicial work of the cross, but was also itself a forensic act in its own right: he "was declared to be the Son of God with power according to the Spirit of holiness by resurrection from the dead" (Rom. 1:4). As Vos points out, "The reference is not to two coexisting sides in the constitution of the Saviour, but to two successive stages in His life. . . . By the twofold κατά the mode of each state of existence is contrasted, by the twofold ἐκ, the origin of each. Thus the existence κατὰ σάρκα originated 'from the seed of David,' the existence κατὰ πνεῦμα originated 'out of the resurrection from the dead.'"[100] While Jesus is the Son from all of eternity, his resurrection gives rise to "a new status of sonship" that is distinct from his essential deity.[101] John Murray comments:

> The title "Son" has reference to Christ as the only-begotten (cf. [Rom. 8] vss. 3, 32) and therefore the unique and eternal Sonship is contemplated. The conformity cannot, of course, have in view conformity to him in that relation or capacity; the conformity embraces the transformation of the body of our humiliation to the likeness of the body of Christ's glory (Phil. 3:21) and must therefore be conceived of as conformity to the image of the incarnate Son as glorified by his exaltation.[102]

99. I develop this theme more fully in chaps. 4 and 5 of *Lord and Servant*.

100. Geerhardus Vos, "Paul's Eschatological Concept of the Spirit," in *Redemptive History and Biblical Interpretation: The Shorter Writings of Geerhardus Vos*, ed. Richard B. Gaffin Jr. (Phillipsburg, NJ: P&R Publishing, 1980), 104.

101. Ibid.

102. John Murray, *The Epistle to the Romans* (Grand Rapids: Eerdmans, 1965), 319.

An eschatological reality, this is the type of "sonship" that can only be conferred upon the members by the forensic achievement of its head. Paul never thinks of Christ's resurrection as a merely personal event for Jesus, but as the advent of a new epoch with cosmic significance. His two-age contrast, one dominated by the flesh and the other by the Spirit, dominates this eschatological horizon. Hence, as Vos points out, Paul does not in Romans 1:3–4 first mention Christ's eternal deity, which one would expect if the reference was to his existence before the incarnation, but to his being descended from David according to the flesh.[103]

So it is not the case that the Spirit is waiting in the wings as the Son fulfills his mission, so that he can then work exclusively within individual believers. Paul of course speaks often about this aspect of the Spirit's work: calling believers, giving them faith, uniting them to Christ, sanctifying them, assuring them, interceding for them, and so forth. That is not the point here, however. The work of the Spirit is seen here as being just as comprehensive in its cosmic and eschatological scope as that of the Son, and from this wider horizon everything else that accrues to individual believers is surveyed.

> At this point we once more verify that our Lord's doctrine of the resurrection rests on a broader basis than that of individual soteriology. The raising of the dead forms part of a process of cosmic proportions which draws within its range the entire physical universe and therefore extends to the wicked as well as the righteous. Even in the case of the wicked the resurrection of the body and the recompense in the body are necessary to the completeness of the theodicy which forms the essence of the final coming of the kingdom.[104]

Vos also notes that Paul's conception of the "spiritual body" was undoubtedly impressed upon him by the Damascus road encounter with the glorified Christ. "And on general grounds as well as on the basis of the account of the transfiguration we must believe that our Lord was fully cognizant of the glory that was awaiting Him."[105]

The Spirit gives birth to the new age called into being by the Father in the Son. It is the Glory-Spirit by whom humanity was created as an image of the archetypal image-Son, who declares to the entire cosmos that those whom he now clothes with bodily glory are heavenly (glorified) rather than merely earthly (created and fallen) beings. *In other words, the day of judgment is the day of resurrection: they are one and the same event.*[106] The judgment that would have been

---

103. Vos, "Paul's Eschatological Concept of the Spirit," 106.

104. Geerhardus Vos, "Our Lord's Doctrine of the Resurrection," in *Redemptive History and Biblical Interpretation*, 322.

105. Ibid., 323.

106. Recently, John Fesko has presented a persuasive exegetical case for identifying the last judgment with the resurrection of the dead. Though still in manuscript form as I write, the title is *The Doctrine of Justification: A Contemporary Restatement of the Classic Reformed Doctrine* (Phillipsburg, NJ: P&R Publishing, forthcoming). I am grateful to him for sharpening my thoughts on this matter.

pronounced upon humanity in Adam after successful completion of the trial is pronounced upon Christ and all of those in union with him.

Nor is this only found in the Pauline corpus. Although even among the Pharisees there were various expectations concerning the nature of the resurrection and its relation to the last judgment, Jesus authorizes the expectation of rewards not at some event subsequent to the resurrection, but "at the resurrection of the righteous" (Luke 14:14; cf. 20:35). Those in their graves "will hear his voice and will come out—those who have done good, to the resurrection of life, and those who have done evil, to the resurrection of condemnation" (John 5:28–29).[107]

Similar to Reformed exegesis, N. T. Wright and others have pointed up the judicial aspect of the resurrection as the last judgment. However, he sees this as justification itself rather than its end result, namely, glorification: "Resurrection is therefore, as in much contemporary Jewish thought, the ultimate 'justification': those whom God raises from death, as in [Rom.] 8.11, are thereby declared to be his covenant people."[108] He correctly identifies the resurrection with the judicial atmosphere of the last judgment, yet fails to recognize that justification is the "already" verdict that corresponds to the "not-yet" verdict of glorification. There is no future aspect to justification itself. In justification, the believer has already heard the verdict of the last judgment. Glorification is the final realization not of our justification itself but of its effects.

Furthermore, this future event both *discloses* the true identity of the covenant people as an act of the cosmic revelation of the justified children of God (ecclesiology) and *actually transforms* the whole justified person into a condition of immortality and perfect holiness (soteriology). The great assize awaiting the world at the end of the age is therefore not with respect to justification but to glorification. All who have been justified as well as inwardly renewed are being conformed to Christ's image, but their cosmic vindication *as* the justified people of God will be revealed in the resurrection of the dead. "And just as it is appointed for mortals to die once, and after that the judgment, so Christ, having been offered once to bear the sins of many, will appear a second time, not to deal with sin, but to save those who are eagerly waiting for him" (Heb. 9:27–28). Through faith in Christ, the *verdict* of the last judgment itself has already been rendered in our favor, but as our meager growth in holiness and the unabated decay of our bodies attests, the full *consequences* of this verdict await a decisive future completion. We receive our justification through believing what we have heard; we receive our glorification by seeing the one we have heard face to face.

To the very last, therefore, the forensic Word of justification reverberates throughout the entire *ordo*. "The resurrection of the dead in general, therefore,

107. Only if this refers to justification is it susceptible to being interpreted as resurrection on the basis of works. However, such passages (as well as the Olivet discourse) merely identify the just(ified) as those who have been renewed and thus have begun even in this age to produce the fruit of the Spirit.

108. N. T. Wright, *Climax of the Covenant: Christ and the Law in Pauline Theology* (Edinburgh: T&T Clark, 1991), 203.

is primarily a judicial act of God," Bavinck notes.[109] The "inner nature," on the basis of justification and through the organic union with Christ, is being invisibly renewed through faith day by day according to the glorious image of the exalted Son even while the "outer nature" is visibly wasting away (2 Cor. 4:16–5:5). On the last day, however, the whole person—and the whole church—will be radiant with the light that fills the whole earth with the glory of God, and this new humanity will be joined by the whole creation as it is led by the Servant-Lord of the covenant into the day whose sun never sets. In this view, both justification and glorification are judicial verdicts resulting in transformative effects. Justification is the rendering of that verdict in the present, on the basis of which the inner renewal begins, while the resurrection of the body is the judicial investiture and enthronement of the children of God with their Son-King in glory, completing both the inward and outward renewal of all things. "Thus it is written, 'The first man, Adam, became a living being'; the last Adam became a life-giving Spirit" (1 Cor. 15:45).

If this is so, then the highest union that believers will ever attain with God is a gift of the resurrection on the last day, when they are raised to immortality. This *is* the last judgment, the final separation: a resurrection to death for unbelievers and a resurrection to life for those who are in Christ, clothed outwardly and inwardly with his beauty. That which has been possessed in faith will at last yield to public vision, with no more discrepancy between a perfect justification and an imperfectly realized sanctification or inward renewal and outward decay.

This argument, which we find especially in 2 Corinthians 4:16–18, is elaborated in terms of the metaphor of clothing, simultaneously a judicial and royal image signifying both the imputation of Christ's righteousness and the impartation of Christ's resurrection-immortality (5:1–5). "For in this tent we groan, longing to be clothed with our heavenly dwelling—if indeed, when we have taken it off we will not be found naked" (vv. 2–3). While the very distinction between inner and outer will be regarded as a Platonizing dualism by proponents of anthropological monism (i.e., physicalism), the divergence from Platonism is obvious.

No self-respecting Platonist would puzzle over the problem of being "found naked" by taking leave of the decaying body, since the flight of the soul from its fleshly prison-house *is* salvation. Yet in Paul's thinking, for the soul to be found naked is tantamount to condemnation. There is a judicial aspect to disembodied existence: it is a sign of sin and death, not of justification and immortality. If the outward renewal does not occur, then the judicial verdict has failed. It is no wonder, then, that we find the souls of the martyrs crying out from the heavenly throne, "Sovereign Lord, holy and true, how long will it be before you judge?" (Rev. 6:10). By faith, those who have already been inwardly renewed await with confidence this clothing of the "earthly tent" with immortality. "For while we are still in this tent, we groan under our burden, because we wish *not to be unclothed*

---

109. Herman Bavinck, *The Last Things*, ed. John Bolt, trans. John Vriend (Grand Rapids: Baker, 1996), 133. I am grateful to John Fesko for pointing out this quote in an as-yet unpublished essay.

but to be *further clothed*, so that what is *mortal* may be swallowed up by *life*. He who has prepared us for this very thing is God, who has given us the Spirit as a guarantee" (vv. 4–5, emphasis added). Not disembodiment versus embodiment, but this body in its mortality versus its immortality—that is the contrast we find here.

It is now the hour to "strip off the old self" and to "put on Christ" (cf. Col. 3:9–10; cf. Rom. 13:14; Gal. 3:27). Like the clothing of the priests (Exod. 40:14), which is already interpreted in terms of forgiveness and justification in the prophets (Isa. 59:6, 17; Jer. 4:30; Ezek. 16:10; and esp. Zech. 3) and in the Gospels (Matt. 22:1–14; Luke 24:4), Christ is the garment that allows believers to appear in God's presence (Eph. 6:13–17). Everything that God has done in, with, and for Christ, he has done and will do in, with, and for us. The forensic yields transformative consequences rather than the other way around, although the cosmic-eschatological is the wider frame of reference for both:

> Do not lie to one another, seeing that you have stripped off the old self with its practices and have clothed yourselves with the new self, which is being renewed in knowledge according to the image of its creator. In that renewal there is no longer Greek and Jew, circumcised and uncircumcised, barbarian, Scythian, slave and free; but Christ is all and in all! As God's chosen ones, holy and beloved, clothe yourselves with compassion, kindness, humility, meekness, and patience. (Col. 3:9–12)

Again, such calls to clothe ourselves with Christ are not exhortations to mere imitation, but to incorporation. Saved by grace alone through that faith which itself is a gift of grace, the beginning of that conformity to Christ's likeness is already under way. "For we are what he has made us, created in Christ Jesus for good works, which God prepared beforehand to be our way of life" (Eph. 2:10). In the last act of the redemptive drama, the truth, goodness, and beauty that define the consummated *imago* will be finally displayed before all of the powers and principalities, with Christ as the glorified head of his regally clothed body. The church exists because of the love, honor, glory, and majesty that the Father has wished to lavish on his Son in the Spirit. In the process of Christ's coronation, all who are united to him are graced with the same dignity.

This connection between the judicial aspect (the last judgment) and the transformative (the last resurrection) is explicitly drawn in the passage above (2 Cor. 5): "For all of us must appear before the judgment seat of Christ, so that each may receive recompense for what has been done in the body, whether good or evil" (v. 10). The judicial emphasis appears once more, with explicit appeal to the conscience, justification, and the forgiveness of sins through "the ministry of reconciliation" in the verses that follow (vv. 11–21). The link between justification in the present and glorification-resurrection in the future, of course, is the Spirit, who is the pledge or down payment on this final reality. By possessing the Spirit in the present, believers are assured of their final clothing (investiture) in glorification and resurrection, since it has already appeared in their justification and rebirth.

Adoption: Investiture as the Royal Image-Bearer of the Great King

Adoption especially highlights this connection between the "already" of justification and the "not yet" of the resurrection-judgment. This adoption is in one sense a present possession, through justification and union with Christ by the indwelling Spirit: it was this aspect of adoption that I addressed in the previous chapter. However, it is also consummated when the whole person is clothed with glory, power, holiness, and immortality—hence, at the final resurrection as a cosmic judicial manifestation of the already-rendered judicial verdict (Rom. 8:23). "'Adoption,'" Vos writes, "is by parentage a forensic concept; yet it fulfills itself in the bodily transforming change of the resurrection. It has not been implausibly held that this forensic aspect of the resurrection as a declarative, vindicatory, justifying act, forms a very old, if not perhaps the oldest, element in Paul's doctrine on the subject."[110] This is especially plausible in light of the fact that Paul locates the power of death in the covenantal curse of the law in 1 Corinthians 15:54–57.

When Paul writes, "I consider that the sufferings of this present time are not worth comparing with the glory about to be revealed to us" (Rom. 8:18), he is not offering a pie-in-the-sky platitude. Still less is he offering that all-too-common consolation of the survival of the soul after death, even though he affirms an intermediate state (2 Cor. 5:8). Paul's soteriology is far richer, as becomes clearer in the following verses of Romans 8: "The creation itself will be set free from its bondage to decay and will obtain the freedom of the glory of the children of God" (v. 21). The labor pains of the present moment are actually part of the renewal that will be consummated with "the redemption of our bodies" (v. 23). Only then will the forensically charged Word have penetrated every ontological nook and cranny.

While the legal aspect of our adoption has been finalized, and we have been incorporated into the life of the family, there are still benefits of the inheritance held in trust for us. This is because the goal of adoption is nothing less than what Paul expresses in Romans 8:29: "For those whom he foreknew he also predestined to be conformed to the image of his Son, in order that he might be the firstborn within a large family" (cf. Eph. 1:5).

It is not too extravagant to designate this with the noble title of "divinization." Not only are adopted heirs the beneficiaries of divine love; their adoption also is itself caught up in the love of the Father and the Spirit for the Son. With respect to Romans 8:29, this completes a thought begun in verse 14. Conformity to

---

110. Geerhardus Vos, *The Pauline Eschatology* (Princeton, NJ: Princeton University Press, 1930; repr., Phillipsburg, NJ: P&R Publishing, 1994), 152.

Christ's image is judicial, moral, and spiritual at present; at the resurrection, not only will this inner renovation become instantaneously complete; it also will finally involve the full restoration of the whole person as the beautiful image of Christ. "For the creation waits with eager longing for the revealing of the children of God" (Rom. 8:19). As he shared with us in our flesh, so our flesh will share in his exaltation (Heb. 2:10–18). This became a characteristically Irenaean motif and informs both the Eastern doctrine of divinization and the Reformed doctrine of glorification.

Even greater than the glorification of the believer is the glory that accrues to Christ as the head of the family. Paradoxically, the Father has made the cosmic revelation of the preeminence of his Son dependent on our adoption as coheirs who reflect the image of the "Only-begotten." Christ's relation to his image-bearers can be understood both in reference to his status as the eternal Son (since he was the archetypal *eikōn tou theou* even in creation) and in his office as the second Adam. As to the first, Ridderbos observes, "What was lost in the first Adam is regained in the second *in a much more glorious way*," since the second Adam is the Son of God both as human and as divine.[111]

"Firstborn" refers not only to Christ's preeminent status in this family, but also to the eschatological relationship between his exalted state (glorification) and our own. He is already that which we will certainly be: this, and not an essential fusion of personalities, is what a covenantal sense of *totus Christus* at least affirms.

Therefore, our election, justification, sanctification, and glorification are means to the greater end of bringing glory to Christ.

> He is the head of the body, the church; he is the beginning, the firstborn from the dead, so that he might come to have first place in everything. For in him all the fullness of God was pleased to dwell, and through him God was pleased to reconcile to himself all things, whether on earth or in heaven, by making peace through the blood of his cross. (Col. 1:18–20)

No wonder, then, that we can "consider that the sufferings of this present time are not worth comparing with the glory about to be revealed to us" (Rom. 8:18). The last judgment is a settled affair for those who are in Christ, for whom there "is therefore now no condemnation" (8:1), while even now "the wrath of God abides on" those who do not believe in Christ (John 3:18–21, 36 NKJV). There is, therefore, an already–not yet aspect to this total restoration, but not to justification and rebirth. The latter are the "already," which correspond to the "not yet" of bodily resurrection and glorification.

In this way, the believer's hope is directed not to a timeless allegory of the soul's ascent, but once again to the economy of grace—in this case, to the Parousia. To reign with Christ in the future, however, we must suffer with Christ in the pres-

---

111. Herman Ridderbos, *Paul: An Outline of His Theology*, trans. John R. De Witt (Grand Rapids: Eerdmans, 1975), 85.

ent. Our union with Christ is an exodus *through* the cross to a glory that is as yet dimly perceived.

Transfiguration and Resurrection-Glory

It is with good reason that the transfiguration event figures so prominently in Orthodoxy, since there we find right in the middle of Christ's ministry the prolepsis of the glory that awaited him and still awaits us. The account in Matthew 17:1–21 follows in broad outline the details of Moses' mediation in Exodus 24. In the first half of Exodus 24, Moses, Aaron and his sons, and seventy elders are called up the mountain, but only Moses is allowed to "come near," and after this Moses returns to the people below with the words of the law. After they swear, "All that the LORD has spoken we will do," Moses sprinkled the blood on the people to ratify their oath (vv. 1–8). In the second half (vv. 9–18), Moses and his lieutenants go up the cloud-covered mountain again. "The glory of the LORD settled on Mount Sinai, and the cloud covered it for six days; on the seventh day he called to Moses out of the cloud." Moses entered the radiant cloud and was on the mountain for forty days and forty nights. "Six days" is always suggestive of the work-week trial, with the seventh day being held out as the Sabbath rest, in imitation of God's own pattern of creation-work and entering his glory.

In Matthew's Gospel Jesus and three disciples ascend the mountain of transfiguration "after six days." The cloud that descended on the mountain (Exod. 34:29–35; cf. 2 Cor. 3:7–18), filled the tabernacle (Exod. 40:34), and led Israel (40:36–38) is no less than a theophany of the Spirit of Glory in person, the judicial witness from heaven par excellence. Arriving at the summit, Jesus "was transfigured [*metamorphoō*] before them, and his face shone like the sun, and his clothes became dazzling white" (v. 2). While Moses' face *reflected* the light, Jesus *is* the light. Suddenly, Moses and Elijah appear, conversing with Jesus, while Peter, ever ready in his eschatological impatience to make preparations for the inauguration day, offers to set up tabernacles to house Jesus and his distinguished guests. "While he was still speaking," however, "suddenly a bright cloud overshadowed them, and from the cloud a voice said, 'This is my Son, the Beloved; with him I am well pleased; listen to him!'" (v. 5). Peter wants to do something, while the voice's point was to simply share in the joy of something that God was bringing about. Yet interrupted by the Father's voice and enveloped in the Spirit, Peter and the other two witnesses are as terrified as the people were at the voice that shook Sinai (v. 6). With these words, the solemn imprimatur pronounced at Jesus' baptism is now repeated: Jesus is now the mediator greater than Moses and the prophet greater than Elijah, to whom the law and the prophets have witnessed. Thus, after Jesus gently consoles his frightened disciples, we read, "When they looked up, they saw no one except Jesus" (v. 8).

As we learn from the debriefing between Jesus and his disciples in the aftermath of this event, neither Moses' nor Jesus' transfiguration is intended to be a symbol or allegory of a timeless ascent of mind. Rather, they are eschatological sign-events. No one can repeat or imitate either Moses' ascent of Mount Sinai or Jesus' transfiguration, much less his ascension in the flesh. These are unrepeatable, unique redemptive-historical events on the basis of which we are assured of our own resurrection. The event could not even be prolonged by Peter's zealous labors. Rather, as Jesus explains in answer to their confusion over the meaning of this strange episode, the "teachers of the law" are still looking for Elijah, yet Messiah has already come (vv. 10–12 NIV). Jesus responds by identifying John the Baptist with the Elijah figure of Malachi 3:1 and 4:5, and predicts that he too will suffer for his true and faithful witness at their hands as John did (vv. 12–13). There is a final parallel between these two transfigurations. Just as Moses returned to find Israel breaking the law, Jesus descends to find his disciples faithless in the exercise of the ministry he has given them to heal and triumph over the demons in his name (17:14–20).

Moses was the paradigmatic prophet of the covenant, but one was already promised who would be "a prophet like Moses" (Deut. 18:15–22), which, after Pentecost, Peter identified with Jesus (Acts 3:22–26). As M. G. Kline notes,

> The apostle had grasped the significance of the event of Jesus' transfiguration, recognizing it as a counterpart to Moses' experience under the overshadowing Glory-cloud at Sinai. In the command of the voice from heaven, "Hear him," Peter perceived the ultimate application of the Deuteronomic requirement that Israel obey God's prophet (Deut. 18:18). That was God's own identification of Jesus as *the* prophet like unto Moses.[112]

He is further linked to the Isaianic Servant of the Lord, "raised up by the elective call of God (42:1, 6; 49:1) and Spirit-endowed (42:1; 61:1); he is cognizant of the divine counsel (50:4f.) and made an effective 'mouth' for the Lord (49:2; 50:4; 61:1f.); and he is mediator of the redemptive covenant in fulfillment of covenantal promises of deliverance and kingdom inheritance through righteous judgment (42:1ff., 6ff.; 49:5ff.; 53:4ff.; 61:1ff.)."[113] As the theophanic "angel of the LORD," all along "Jesus was that archetypal prophet behind the human prophet paradigm."[114]

Second Corinthians 3 and 4 then carry forward the image: as Moses was transformed by God's glory, so also we are being transformed from glory to glory by beholding God in the face of Christ. Unlike Moses' transformed visage, however, this glory is permanent and incapable of being diminished. While Moses' face was transformed, the *doxa* of the resurrection will transform our entire corruptible flesh into incorruptibility. "To speak more literally," writes Vos, "it is the Gospel by which this mysterious process is mediated, whence the Apostle calls it in iv. 4 'the gospel of the glory of Christ.'"[115] In fact, this glory is explicitly linked to the

112. Meredith G. Kline, *Images of the Spirit* (Grand Rapids: Baker, 1980; repr., South Hamilton, MA: M. G. Kline, 1986), 81–82.
113. Ibid., 82.
114. Ibid., 83.
115. Vos, *The Pauline Eschatology*, 202.

resurrection on the last day (4:14), even though at present the apostle's deadly perils are described in terms of "always bearing about in the body the dying [*nekrōsis*] of Jesus [4:10 KJV]."[116] Thus, the glory now is beheld dimly as "in a mirror," but on the last day, "face to face" (1 Cor. 13:12). The unrepeatable event of which the transfiguration of Jesus was a prolepsis is none other than the resurrection.

Like Peter, James, and John, we are witnesses (hence, the connection in the Old Testament between the glory-image, the Spirit, and the prophetic office), and the form in which this future glory now comes to us is hidden in the apparent simplicity, weakness, and foolishness of the gospel. While we cannot ascend the hill of the Lord, he has descended to us and "raised us up . . . in the heavenly places in Christ Jesus, so that in the ages to come he might show the immeasurable riches of his grace in kindness toward us in Christ Jesus" (Eph. 2:6–7). And he will raise us bodily as well. While we cannot build tabernacles to house the Spirit of Glory, something much greater has now appeared: believers themselves, individually and corporately, as the temple. As the glory of Moses' ministry has faded, the morning of Christ's glorious ministry has dawned. "For if there was glory in the ministry of condemnation, much more does the ministry of justification abound in glory!" (2 Cor. 3:9). In fact, it is this ministry of justification that grounds our confidence that more than justification lies ahead, even as we are even now "being transformed into the same image from one degree of glory to another; for this comes from the Lord, the Spirit" (v. 18).

By focusing on the economy of grace, the redemptive-historical events of Christ's descent-ascent-return in the flesh, as well as the descent of the Spirit to raise us with Christ—all these orient the beatific vision toward a corporate and corporeal future rather than to a timeless individual and intellectual encounter with the "naked God." For Jew and Gentile alike, only in Christ is Moses' veil removed (2 Cor. 3:7–4:6). From such passages Reformation theology has maintained that the divinization or participation of human beings in the glory of God is never something to be attained by human ascent, but is a divine Word (energy) that has been spoken into our hearts and will be definitively pronounced over our bodies. It is not something that we have to go and get, but something that comes to us through the Word of Christ (Rom. 10:6–17). It is that light, always mediated through the incarnate Son, which has already dawned, that will be reflected in its effulgence in the consummation. We have *been justified*; we have *been given* new birth and have *been seated* with Christ; even now we are "*being transformed* into the same image [as Christ] from one degree of glory to another" (2 Cor. 3:18, emphasis added). Although they give rise to human action, these are all passive verbs.

The Golden Chain

I am suggesting that we view each item in the Pauline *ordo* as constituting one train, running on the same track, with justification as the engine that pulls adoption, new

116. Ibid., 203.

birth, sanctification, and glorification in tow. In the person of Christ as the "engine," the train has arrived at its destination. "Those whom he justified he also glorified" (Rom. 8:30). This means that we never leave the forensic domain even when we are addressing other topics in the *ordo* besides justification proper. Although there is more to the new birth, sanctification, and glorification than the forensic, all of it is forensically charged. Grace is never a supernatural substance infused into the soul, but the favor of God that justifies and the gift of God that renews (both *favor* and *donum*, as Luther expressed it). In addition to this grace that is equally shared by every believer, God gives varying graces (charisms) for the upbuilding of the church (Eph. 4), but even these are energies or actions—most notably, speech-acts—of God rather than a communication of divine essence. Instead of saying that our judicial acceptance is rooted in justification while our sanctification is grounded in an infused *habitus* of grace, the New Testament repeatedly returns to the forensic domain even in treating the new birth and sanctification.

Yet beyond this, even the resurrection of the dead is interpreted as the consequence of a judicial verdict. Christ was raised *because death no longer has a legal claim on him* (Rom. 6:9). Therefore, "the life that he [now] lives, he lives to God" (v. 10 NKJV). Precisely the same is true of all those who are in Christ, says Paul. In other words, he is not thinking in terms of two sources of Christ's resurrection life: one derived from his judicial vindication and another from his resurrection from the dead. Rather, the latter is simply the final, outward, and fully visible consequence of the former. This means that "the life that he now lives . . . to God" is the result of his justification. His resurrection was the public unveiling in the cosmic courtroom of the forensic verdict: the last judgment begun with respect to our covenantal head, and announced to us now, even on this side of our own resurrection glory. Righteousness is "imputed to us who believe in him who raised up Jesus our Lord from the dead. He was delivered up for our sins and was raised for our justification" (4:24–25, au. trans.). That is why Paul can refer even to glorification in his *ordo* (8:30) in the aorist: it is an already-certain event because it is already true of its head and is therefore in principle already assured for the rest of his body.

Consistent with the broader covenantal assumptions of death as an effective power at work precisely because it is the judicial sanction for covenant-breaking, Paul says that "the sting of death is sin, and the power of sin is the law" (1 Cor. 15:56). While exercising mysterious forces well beyond the judicial sphere, into every nook and cranny of creaturely reality, death is fundamentally recognized by Paul as "the wages of sin" (Rom. 6:23). Death came to everyone in Adam because of sin (Rom. 5). On the other hand, the second Adam was raised from the dead because there was no legal claim that death could secure on the basis of the law. Christ's victory over the powers is predicated on the cancellation of the legal debt (Col. 2:12–15). Christ *for* us is the basis of Christ *in* us, and this is the "mystery, which is Christ in you, the hope of glory" (1:27).

The same Spirit who made the Word fruitful in creation and pronounced his approval, who led his people safely through the Red Sea, whose presence in pillar and cloud provided a clear judicial witness to their status, who raised Jesus from the dead and made him participate fully in the age to come as our representative head—this same testifying Spirit is now a present possession of believers as they await the last installment of the inheritance. As in every other aspect of redemption, the Spirit's work within the heirs of the new creation is both judicial and transformative. To be "in the Spirit" is to be vindicated as God's elect, his adopted children. The possession of the Spirit as a "down payment" (2 Cor. 1:22; 5:5; Eph. 1:14) on glorification and as the source of definitive and progressive sanctification in the present are both grounded judicially in the Word that has been spoken for us in Christ's obedience and to us in the proclamation of the gospel. That which has been accomplished outside of us, once and for all, is (and always remains) the basis for all of that remarkable work that is done within us by the Spirit.

Glorification, then, is the consummation of our union with Christ, writes Elizabethan divine William Perkins:

> In this union not our soul alone is united with Christ's soul, or our flesh with his flesh, but the whole person of every faithful person is verily conjoined with the whole person of our saviour Christ, God and man. The manner of this union is this. [A believer] first of all and immediately is united to the flesh or human nature of Christ and afterward by reason of the humanity to the Word itself, or divine nature. For salvation and life dependeth on the fullness of the Godhead which is in Christ, yet it is not communicated unto us but in the flesh and by the flesh of Christ.

It is a "spiritual union" because it is the Holy Spirit who effects it, but it is a union of the whole believer with the whole Christ.[117] As "head of the faithful," Christ "is to be considered as a public man sustaining the person of all the elect."[118] Therefore, "glorification is the perfect transforming of the saints into the image of the Son of God."[119]

To be united to God in Christ is to be *where* Christ is (in the everlasting Sabbath) and *what* Christ is (glorified, beyond the reach of sin and death). As goes the King, so go the people; as goes the head, so go the members. This is what Reformed theology understands by glorification—and why it is so closely tied to justification in the past, sanctification in the present, and the resurrection in the future.

If the tendency in Roman Catholic and Orthodox theologies is to confuse justification and sanctification, the tendency in Protestant theologies is sometimes to treat these two events more like two trains running on parallel tracks. In the latter case, justification is seen as the answer to one soteriological problem (viz.,

117. William Perkins, *The Golden Chaine*, in *The Work of William Perkins*, ed. Ian Breward, Courtenay Library of Reformation Classics 3 (Appleford, Abingdon, UK: Sutton Courtenay, 1970), 226–27.
118. Ibid., 227.
119. Ibid., 246.

guilt), and inner renewal (regeneration and sanctification) is seen as the answer to a different one (viz., corruption). I have already indicated why I think this problem is motivated by a schizophrenic tendency to allow a thoroughgoing forensicism with respect to justification while presupposing a different ontology as the basis for other elements in the *ordo*.

A FINAL COMPARISON AND CONTRAST

As Douglas Farrow reminds us, Irenaeus saw the so-called deification of believers as their true *humanization*, another inbreathing of the Spirit to make a new creation, alive in Christ; later writers like Athanasius would say that "God became man [so] that man might become God."[120] God did not become human so that humans might become God, or even supernatural, but so that humans who had fallen into sin and death could be redeemed, reconciled, justified, renewed, and glorified as the humanity that we were created to become. In my view the category of divinizing energies is superior to habitual and infused grace, as long as it is construed in this Irenaean direction. When we treat God's energies (neither God's essence nor created effect) as the source of a real communion with Christ and his benefits, a door is open to a notion of deification that finally humanizes us according to the Son as the original blueprint.

If we draw the East's concept of "energies" into a more communicative ambit, we can identify these divine "workings" with the Word of God, understood here as God's creative speech distinct from the eternally generated hypostatic Word, who forms its archetype. This communicative "working" is neither an emanation of divine essence nor merely a creaturely effect. Categories of essence and cause do not provide a rich-enough ontology for describing this divine agency. God's Word, for example, "goes forth" from God's mouth, yet it is also not merely a creaturely product of divine power, but *God's* Word. Similarly, Christ communicates his person as well as his work to us through the sacraments, yet without any essential change in the creaturely elements, as in the Thomistic doctrine of transubstantiation. The same ontology that yields the eucharistic doctrine of transubstantiation feeds a theory of divinization that eliminates mediating "workings" (energies) in favor of a fusion of essences and an infusion of a gracious substance. We need a rich-enough lexicon to be able to talk about God's works both as a noun (products or effects) *and* as a gerund (God's "actings").

To speak of knowing God only by his working and not in his essence means not only that we recognize God by *what he has made* (though that is certainly true), but by his *making*—his actual course of action as revealed to us. God not only acts *upon* the world, as a solitary agent, but the Father also speaks creation into existence in the Son and brings about its intended effect through the Spirit. God's speech *does* things. More than merely a creaturely result of divine action,

120. Farrow, *Ascension and Ecclesia*, 61.

such speech *is* divine action. Words not only *refer*, we also *do* things with words, and so does God. The East's concept of energies gives us a useful category for God's effective speech as something between univocity and equivocity—in other words, analogy. The signs (words and sacraments) are not the divine essence, and yet they are not simply creaturely symbols or witness, but "go forth" like rays from the sun to bring about a change in creaturely conditions.

Although the analogy of sun-and-rays has enjoyed a notable legacy in both Eastern and Western theology, a more active and vocal conception of God's energies fits better with the ways in which Scripture itself describes God's manner of working. Long before J. L. Austin, Scripture had understood creation as the result of divine utterance: "By the word of the LORD the heavens were made, and all their host by the breath of his mouth" (Ps. 33:6). Of course, none of us denies this, but is it as hermeneutically significant in our theologies as it appears to be in Scripture? God's acts of creation, providence, incarnation, and redemption do not radiate silently, but "sound forth" as a "living and active" word (Heb. 4:12) that does not "return to [God] without having accomplished the mission for which it was sent" (Isa. 55:11, au. trans.; cf. 9:8; 40:8; 45:23; 51:16; Jer. 20:9; Ezek. 12:28; Mic. 2:7; Matt. 24:35; Luke 24:19; John 1:14; 6:63; 14:24; 17:7; Col. 3:16; 1 Thess. 1:5; Heb. 1:3; 4:12; James 1:21; 1 Pet. 1:23; 2 Pet. 3:5; Rev. 19:13). It is difficult to think of rays being sent on missions and returning with success. Light is also a biblical analogy for God's work, of course, and Orthodoxy often eschews Neoplatonic abstractions (as well as its theory of emanation) by identifying this illuminating source with the Holy Spirit.[121] Nevertheless, "light" in Scripture typically refers to the *witness* of creation to the work of its Creator. In this way the visual metaphor of light is in the service of a theology of the Word rather than vice versa.

As I argue in the next volume, the metaphorics of light have dominated theology, reflecting a more Greek bias toward vision rather than the Hebrew orientation to hearing the word. From the church fathers onward, the treatment of the Son as Word of God increasingly moved toward visual metaphors (light, image, etc.). These are complementary metaphors, but the sonic character of "Word" has been downplayed. Walter Ong, S.J., has helpfully pointed out, "An oral-aural theology of revelation through the Word of God would entail an oral-aural theology of the Trinity, which could explicate the 'intersubjectivity' of the three Persons in terms of communication conceived of as focused (analogously) in a world of sound rather than in a world of space and light. Such a theology is still so underdeveloped as to be virtually nonexistent." Instead, we have a Trinitarian theology of "'relations' (a concept visually based: *referre, relatus,* to carry back, carried back)."[122]

---

121. Of course, Orthodoxy also affirms ex nihilo creation, so there are other points at which emanationism is not allowed any foothold.

122. Walter J. Ong, *The Presence of the Word: Some Prolegomena for Cultural and Religious History* (New Haven: Yale University Press, 1967; repr., Minneapolis: University of Minnesota Press, 1981), 180.

"The communication of the Persons with one another is typically treated in terms of *circumincessio*, a 'walking around in' (one another)."[123] Yet once again we see that covenant theology, with its formulation of an intratrinitarian *pactum salutis*, already suggests a more richly verbal, communicative perichoresis. Developing the essence-energies distinction in a more oral/aural way highlights the centrality of the economy of grace with its promise-fulfillment pattern rather than the essentially private quest of the beatific vision.

The connection between divinization and the resurrection of the body offers another valuable convergence. In the marvelous expression of Maximus, "At the day of Resurrection the glory of the Holy Spirit comes out from within, decking and covering the bodies of the saints—the glory which they had before, but hidden within their souls. What a person has now, the same then comes forth the externally in the body."[124]

Like the East (though more similar to Irenaeus and the Cappadocians than to Maximus), Reformed soteriology sees pneumatology as the crucial link that is often missing in Western preoccupation with participation in the divine essence. In the New Finnish interpretation of Luther, Christ is not only truly present and offered in the signs, but also, "the essence of the representation is the essence of what is being represented."[125] This seems to be the corollary not of an Eastern doctrine of *theōsis*, but a Western refusal to distinguish essence and energies, with transubstantiation as the most obvious example of this ontology. Grace, accordingly, is not God's liberation of nature to serve its created ends, but the essential elevation of nature to be something other than itself.

Along with comparisons, obvious contrasts remain. First of all, while Lossky as well as Timothy (Kalistos) Ware and other Orthodox writers demonstrate the seminal differences between Orthodoxy and Platonism/Neoplatonism, the tradition itself seems to yield ambiguous testimony. There are the remarkable passages about the incarnation affirming and redeeming matter. Yet there are abundant examples also of a quite different emphasis on the ascent from matter to mind, which funded asceticism and monasticism. According to Maximus, for example, "deifying" is equivalent to "nonmaterial," and sexual propagation itself was a result of the fall. "For this reason the Logos of God became man, to set man free from this passion and to restore him to the condition for which he had been created."[126] "Through 'practical philosophy' or the active life of the Christian," Pelikan explains, "some believers rose from the flesh of Christ to his soul; through contemplation others were enabled to go on from the soul of Christ to the 'mind'

123. Ibid., 181.
124. Maximus the Confessor, *Homilies of Macarius* 5.9; quoted by Ware in *The Orthodox Church*, 233.
125. Mannermaa, *Christ Present in Faith*, 83.
126. Pelikan, *The Spirit of Eastern Christendom (600–1700)*, 11, citing Maximus the Confessor, *Ambigua* 42 (PG 91:1348–49).

of Christ; and through mystical union some few were able to move further still, from the mind of Christ to his very Godhead."[127]

Lossky attributes Platonizing tendencies in both the East and the West to Origen. "With Origen, Hellenism creeps into the church."[128] Although Lossky insists that the essence-energies distinction preserves Orthodoxy from such distortions, he too speaks of a gnosis that involves striving, from glory to glory.[129] Yet, whatever can be said in favor of the place of striving in the Christian life, 2 Corinthians 3:18 does not mention our striving, but our *being* transformed into the same image from one degree of glory to another; *for this comes from the Lord, the Spirit*" (emphasis added). Beholding God means beholding Christ, and beholding Christ means hearing his gospel and receiving it through baptism and the Supper, the triumphant indicative that gives power to divine imperatives. It is through the working of God through Word and sacrament, received by faith, that the Spirit clothes us with Christ inwardly in this age and outwardly adorns us with righteousness, beauty, glory, and immortality in the age to come.

Furthermore, the Word and Spirit are the common property of all Christians, promiscuously distributing Christ and his benefits while also endowing each believer with his or her unique charism. However, in both Eastern and Western mystical traditions, the beatific vision at least in this life is the prize of a special class. In this gnosis, which is awareness of God's light, "this light fills the human person, who has attained union with God."[130] "Few, even of the great saints, reach this state in their earthly life."[131] "It is the beginning of the parousia in holy souls; the first-fruits of the final revelation, when God will appear to all in His inaccessible light."[132] While the eschatological and economic emphasis generated by the essence-energies distinction remains in the background, the foreground is nevertheless a union in the present that is achieved not by the justification of the ungodly through faith alone, but by a synergistic effort that yields too much glory now for too few of the saints. "If someone asks 'How can I become god?'" says Ware, "the answer is simple: go to church, receive the sacraments regularly, pray to God 'in spirit and in truth,' read the Gospels, follow the commandments. The last of these items—'follow the commandments'—must never be forgotten. Orthodoxy, no less than western Christianity, firmly rejects the kind of mysticism that seeks to dispense with moral rules."[133] Although I would affirm the last statement, Ware's answer to the question that is equivalent to the query "How can I be saved?" seems to be essentially law rather than gospel, however much grace is affirmed and extolled.

127. Ibid., 12.
128. Lossky, *The Mystical Theology of the Eastern Church*, 32.
129. Ibid., 228–29.
130. Ibid., 229.
131. Ibid., 230.
132. Ibid., 233.
133. Ware, *The Orthodox Church*, 236.

For all of its improvements over Western ontologies, both East and West emphasize grace as an elevating of creatures beyond their essential capacities. We have already encountered Anastasius of Sinai's oft-quoted definition: "Deification is elevation to a higher plane."[134] Despite its stated motive (viz., affirming nature qua nature), for all of the reasons I have indicated in chapters 9 and 10, this tends to make salvation a matter of being saved *from* nature after all.

Although Radical Orthodoxy and the Helsinki school appeal to the East for their emphasis on ontological participation, at the point of their greatest vulnerability, they are actually more Western in orientation. Neither Mannermaa nor Jenson, much less Milbank, shies away from the claim that believers participate in the essence of divinity. Jenson, in fact, explicitly and carefully argues the case for Thomas with respect to "the vision of God in his essence."[135] Earlier he wrote, "At this juncture we have chosen—without prejudice—to make the Western move."[136] Just as I have suggested a more word-oriented interpretation of energies, Jenson adjusts Thomas's concentration on knowing-as-seeing with "hearing," so that in the consummation, "the hearing of the redeemed will be itself a seeing."[137] Nevertheless, at this point I maintain that the situation of the new Finnish school within a Western ontology renders its account of participation more problematic than the Eastern doctrine itself.

My most fundamental criticism of the Finnish version of justification-as-*theōsis*, however, is that instead of treating justification as a purely forensic Word that opens up a new transformed and transforming reality, it repeats the fatal mistake of Osiander. This is particularly evident in Jenson's insistence (following Mannermaa) that "when the Father judges the believer and says that he or she is righteous, the Father is simply acting as a just judge who finds the facts—about the only moral subject that actually exists in the case, Christ in the believer and the believer in Christ. Justification is thus 'a mode of deification.'"[138] Eschewing distinctions between essence and energies, Jenson and Mannermaa collapse justification into union, specifically, divinization: "Justification as an act of the Spirit is the *achieving* of righteousness" (emphasis original).[139] With the additional appeal to the *totus Christus*, Jenson can say that "God himself is my living Ego, indeed the omnipotent agent of my righteous personhood."[140] This represents a uniquely modern (specifically, Idealist) version of Western mysticism.

It is by situating our soteriology within a forensic ontology of the Word spoken by the Father in the Son by the Spirit—at once individual and cosmic in its result—that we recognize the effective and cosmic renewal in the bargain. If we reverse this relation, even the transformative renewal is left suspended in midair.

---

134. Jenson, *Systematic Theology*, 2:341, quoting Anastasius of Sinai, *The Guide* 2 (PG 89.36).
135. *De articulis fidei et ecclesiae sacramentis*, 257a–b; cited by Jenson, *Systematic Theology*, 2:341.
136. Ibid., 1:224.
137. Ibid., 2:345.
138. Ibid., 2:296.
139. Ibid., 2:301.
140. Ibid., 2:299.

To put it more succinctly, what happens *for* us is the basis for what happens *to* us and *in* us—and to reverse that order is to eventually surrender soteriology to ecclesiology or ethics without remainder. A community "living the gospel" is not good news, especially when we know ourselves—and the community of which we are a part, all too well. Jesus came to save the church because the church too is part of the problem. Only Jesus Christ is the solution. With the disciples on the Mount of Transfiguration, all we see is Jesus.

Evil, death, and cosmic powers no longer have any ultimate claim on us, not because they never really did but because Christ has conquered them in his body, by taking away any legal basis for their jurisdiction over us. Because of this, we can say with the apostle, "I have been crucified with Christ; it is no longer I who live, but Christ lives in me; and the life that I now live in the flesh I live by faith in the Son of God, who loved me and gave himself for me. Therefore, I do not set aside the grace of God; for if righteousness comes through the law, then Christ died for nothing" (Gal. 2:20–21 NKJV alt.).

Conclusion

The goal of this volume has been to define justification and participation in the light of the interpretive framework of this four-volume project, and to relate these themes specifically to the loci commonly treated under the *ordo salutis*. While covenant and eschatology, in an analogical mode and with the metaphor of drama, have been the overarching themes of this project generally, their purchase is especially realized in consideration of election, justification, sanctification, and glorification. After all, these are the benefits that are actually conferred in the covenant of grace.

Which covenant theology? In part 1, I concentrated on the definition of the covenant of grace and its distinction from law-covenants, particularly in relation to recent exegetical challenges presented by the New Perspective(s) on Paul. Only this distinction between different types of covenants, well-attested by biblical scholarship, can keep us from the reductionism and false choices that are demanded both by the NPP and by more systematic-theological challenges to traditional Reformation teaching on justification. Furthermore, with the covenant of grace as the wider matrix for justification, rather than treating justification as a central dogma from which everything else is deduced, we avoid the false choices between the forensic and the effective, the *ordo salutis* and the *historia salutis*, the legal and the relational, soteriology and ecclesiology.

Which account of participation? Part 2 related this interpretation of covenant theology to the theme of participation as union with Christ, once more, with the aim of deconstructing false choices. Interacting with alternative paradigms of participation, especially that of John Milbank, I articulated a covenantal (and therefore Trinitarian) account of participation that affirms both affinity and difference: "meeting a stranger," rather than "overcoming estrangement." Moving through the *ordo*, I suggested some ways in which Reformed theology might be still more deeply shaped by its covenantal ontology, beyond infusionist and causal paradigms. Once again, seeing the covenant and union with Christ as the wider matrix for treating justification and sanctification, I defended a complementary rather than antagonistic relationship between these two aspects of salvation, with the forensic character of divine speech-acts as the source of effective transformation. Finally, I applied these conclusions to classical and more recent formulations of *theōsis* or divinization. In the final volume, I will explore the inextricable connection between union and communion: soteriology and ecclesiology. With the ascension, Pentecost, and Parousia as the eschatological coordinates, I will return to some of these themes in consideration of a covenantal account of the kingdom of God, the nature of the church, and its mission, with special attention given to the ministry of the church through Word and sacrament and the new economy that this creates in this time between the times.

Moving, as the Heidelberg Catechism does, from guilt to grace to gratitude, this volume leaves us at the place where at last the covenant servant, a new humanity participating in its new Adam, is not only fully accepted and reconciled to its covenant Lord, but can take its proper place in leading the procession of creation into the Sabbath consummation for an unending antiphonal liturgy and eucharistic receiving-and-giving. We conclude this volume with the covenant servant finally issuing the faithful "amen" to God's promise and command. At last, amid the sound of fleeing footsteps, God has heard and even now is hearing the effects of his word with ever-greater and ever-widening intensity in the answer, "Here I am. Let it be done to me according to your word."

Index of Subjects and Names